THE DUAL STATE

INTERNATIONAL AND COMPARATIVE CRIMINAL JUSTICE

Series Editors:

Mark Findlay, *Institute of Criminology, University of Sydney, Australia*
Ralph Henham, *Nottingham Law School, Nottingham Trent University, UK*

This series explores the new and rapidly developing field of international and comparative criminal justice and engages with its most important emerging themes and debates. It focuses on three interrelated aspects of scholarship which go to the root of understanding the nature and significance of international criminal justice in the broader context of globalization and global governance. These include: the theoretical and methodological problems posed by the development of international and comparative criminal justice; comparative contextual analysis; the reciprocal relationship between comparative and international criminal justice and contributions which endeavor to build understandings of global justice on foundations of comparative contextual analysis.

Other titles in the series:

Policing in Hong Kong
Kam C. Wong
ISBN 978 1 4094 1060 7

Criminal Law Reform and Transitional Justice
Human Rights Perspectives for Sudan
Edited by Lutz Oette
ISBN 978 1 4094 3100 8

Codification, Macaulay and the Indian Penal Code
The Legacies and Modern Challenges of Criminal Law Reform
Edited by Wing-Cheong Chan, Barry Wright and Stanley Yeo
ISBN 978 1 4094 2442 0

Exploring the Boundaries of International Criminal Justice
Edited by Ralph Henham and Mark Findlay
ISBN 978 0 7546 4979 3

The International Criminal Court and National Courts
A Contentious Relationship
Nidal Nabil Jurdi
ISBN 978 1 4094 0916 8

The Dual State

Parapolitics, Carl Schmitt and the National Security Complex

Edited by

ERIC WILSON
Monash University, Australia

Routledge
Taylor & Francis Group
LONDON AND NEW YORK

First published 2012 by Ashgate Publishing

2 Park Square, Milton Park, Abingdon, Oxon OX14 4RN
711 Third Avenue, New York, NY 10017, USA

Routledge is an imprint of the Taylor & Francis Group, an informa business

First issued in paperback 2016

British Library Cataloguing in Publication Data
The dual state : parapolitics, Carl Schmitt and the
national security complex. -- (International and
comparative criminal justice)
1. Schmitt, Carl, 1888-1985--Political and social views.
2. State, The. 3. National security. 4. Domestic
intelligence. 5. Critical criminology. 6. United States--
Politics and government--2001-2009.
I. Series II. Wilson, Eric Michael, 1961-
327.1'01-dc23

Library of Congress Cataloging-in-Publication Data
Wilson, Eric Michael, 1961-
The dual state : parapolitics, Carl Schmitt and the national security complex / by Eric Wilson.
p. cm.
Includes bibliographical references and index.
ISBN 978-1-4094-3107-7 (hardback) -- 1. Schmitt, Carl, 1888-1985--Political and social views. 2. Schmitt, Carl, 1888-1985--Influence. 3. State, The--History--20th century. 4. State, The--History--21st century. 5. Political science--History--20th century. 6. Political science--History--21st century. 7. World politics--1989- I. Title.

JC263.S34W55 2013
320.1--dc23

2012014884

ISBN 978-1-4094-3107-7 (hbk)
ISBN 978-1-138-27384-9 (pbk)

This book is dedicated to my Father, Don Gale Wilson, who gave to me that most precious of gifts—the love of reading.

Contents

Notes on Contributors

Nafeez Mosaddeq Ahmed is an international security analyst specializing in the historical sociology and political ecology of mass violence. He is Executive Director at the Institute for Policy Research & Development in London, and has taught international relations, contemporary history, empire and globalization at the University of Sussex and Brunel University. His work has been used by the 9/11 Commission, the U.S. Army Air University's "Causes of War" collection (2007); the UK Ministry of Defence's Joint Services Command & Staff College *Research Guide on Counter-Terrorism and the GWOT* (2008); Chatham House's Middle East Programme; the International Labor Organization's (ILO) World Commission on the Social Dimension of Globalization (2003); the *Oxford Handbook of Genocide Studies* (2010), among others. He testified in U.S. Congress about his research on Western intelligence policies toward al-Qaeda in 2005, and has advised a range of agencies, including the Royal Military Academy Sandhurst; the UK Parliamentary Select Committee for Communities & Local Government in its Inquiry into the Government's "Preventing Violent Extremism" (PVE) program; and the Metropolitan Police on delivery of the Government's Channel Project. His latest book is *A User's Guide to the Crisis of Civilization: and How to Save It* (London: Pluto/Macmillan, 2010).

Len Bracken is an author and journalist living in Washington, DC. He is the author of three novels and three nonfiction books, including the biography *Guy Debord—Revolutionary* and works involving theories of terrorism and civil war. As a legal journalist he covers international trade policy issues concerning legislation, negotiations, regulations and court decisions.

Enrico Carisch is a Partner in Compliance and Capacity International, L.L.C, a consulting firm that advises international organizations, states, the private sector and civil society on multilateral sanctions implementation and compliance. He served as a member of Security Council-mandated panels and groups of sanctions monitors, to gather information on violations of UN sanctions in Somalia, Liberia and the Democratic Republic of the Congo. Most recently he coordinated the UN Panel of Experts on the Sudan. He has worked as a financial and natural resources expert, advised European and Central African governments as well as to the International Conference on the Great Lakes in capacity-enhancement projects for secure and legal exploitation of natural resources in the region. Prior to his service to the international community, Carisch worked for over 25 years as an investigative journalist for print media and television.

Mark Findlay holds the Chair in Criminal Justice at the Law School, University of Sydney, and a Chair in Law at the Law School, Singapore Management University. Professor Findlay is the Deputy Director of the Institute of Criminology, University of Sydney, and the leader of the Worldwide Universities Network on International and Comparative Criminal Justice (ICCJ Net). His current research interests focus on international and comparative criminal justice, and on regulating global crises. Wider cross-interdisciplinary dimensions of his work cut across globalization, global governance and cultures in transition.

Daniele Ganser (b.1972) is a Swiss historian who specializes in international relations and international history from 1945 to today. His research interests are peace research, geo-strategy, secret warfare, resource wars, globalization and human rights. He is the Director of the Swiss Institute for Peace and Energy Research (SIPER) in Basel. He studied history and international relations at Basel University in Switzerland, Amsterdam University (UVA) in the Netherlands and at the London School of Economics and Political Science (LSE) in England and received his PhD in modern history from Basel University in 2001. He was a Senior Researcher at the Center for Security Studies at the Swiss Federal Institute of Technology (ETH) in Zurich. His most recent book on NATO's secret armies and terrorism in Western Europe (Frank Cass, 2005) was translated into 10 languages.

David N. Gibbs is Professor of History at the University of Arizona. His most recent book is *First Do No Harm: Humanitarian Intervention and the Destruction of Yugoslavia* (Nashville: Vanderbilt University Press, 2009).

Jeff Kinkle (b.1979) is a writer, translator and researcher based in New York City. He received his PhD from the Centre for Cultural Studies at Goldsmiths, University of London in 2010. Together with social theorist and philosopher Alberto Toscano, he is currently finishing the manuscript for a book about aesthetics and global capitalism to be published by Zer0 Books. He is a member of the *SITE Magazine* editorial board and co-founder of the artist group Sakerna with Emanuel Almborg.

David MacGregor, Professor of Sociology, King's University College at the University of Western Ontario, London Ontario, is the author of three books and many articles on Hegel and Marx, including *The Communist Ideal in Hegel and Marx* (Toronto, 1984), *Hegel, Marx and the English State* (Boulder, 1992) and *Hegel and Marx after the Fall of Communism* (Aberystwyth, 1998). He has contributed articles on automobility, the sociology of aging and modern terrorism, including "The Deep Politics of September 11: Political Economy of Concrete Evil" (*Research in Political Economy*, 2002); September 11 as "Machiavellian State Terror" (*Research in Political Economy*, 2006) and "Community and Community Development: The Strange History of My Father and Why It Matters" (*Deliberations on Community Development*, New York, 2012).

Stig A. Nohrstedt (b.1946) is professor of media and communication studies in the School of Humanities at Örebro University and guest professor in journalism at the Linneaus University (Sweden). He has a PhD in political science from Uppsala University and a Docent title (assistant professor) in journalism and mass communication at Göteborg University. His primary research interests include war and conflict journalism, journalistic ethics and roles, risk and crisis communication as well as media and structural discrimination. His most recent book is *Communicating Risks – Towards the Threat Society?* (Nordicom, 2011).

Rune Ottosen (b.1950) is professor in journalism at Oslo and Akershus University College of Applied Sciences He holds a position as professor of journalism at the University of Nordland. He has written extensively on press history and media coverage of war and conflicts. He is co-editor with Stig A. Nohrstedt of several books, the latest *Global War – Local Views: Media Images of the Iraq War*. In 2008 Ottosen published *VG, Saddam og vi. Et kritisk blikk på nyhetsdekning av kriger og konflikter*. In 2010 he was one of the editors and co-authors of the four-volume Norwegian Press History, *Norsk Presses historie (1767–2010)*.

Guido Giacomo Preparata, born in Boston, Massachusetts, and raised in the United States, France and Italy, completed his PhD in Political Economy and Economic History at the University of Southern California in 1998. Formerly an Associate Professor of Political Economy at the University of Washington and Fulbright Scholar to the Middle East, he is presently a lecturer in Criminology at Kwantlen Polythechnic University in Vancouver, Canada.

William Rasch is Professor of Germanic Studies at Indiana University, United States. He is the author of books on the work of Niklas Luhmann and Carl Schmitt, has edited a volume of essays by Luhmann, co-edited volumes on Luhmann and postmodernism, postwar German cinema, and the World War II bombing campaigns, and has also co-edited or edited numerous special issues of various journals dealing with Luhmann or Schmitt. His essays have dealt with social and political theory as well as topics in German culture and literature.

Tom Reifer is an Associate Professor of Sociology, and an Affiliated Faculty in the Ethnic Studies Department, and Women & Gender Studies Program at the University of San Diego, where he formerly sat on the Advisory Board of the Joan B. Kroc Institute for Peace & Justice. Previously Reifer served as the Associate Director of the Institute for Research on World-Systems, and the Program on Global Studies, at the University of California Riverside; and a Senior Research Associate at Focus on the Global South, based in Asia. Dr. Reifer is an Associate Fellow of the Amsterdam based Transnational Institute, a worldwide fellowship of committed scholar-activists. Dr. Reifer publishes widely on issues of U.S. foreign policy, torture, human rights, inequalities of race, class, gender and nation, environmental racism, global warming, Tupac's hip-hop theory of criminal (in)justice, social movements, labor, and global peace and justice issues, including in the *Cambridge Dictionary of Sociology*, *New Left Review*, the *Austrian Journal of Development Studies*, the *Journal of World-Systems Research*, the *International Encyclopedia of the Social Sciences*, the *Wiley-Blackwell Encyclopedia of Globalization* and the *Routledge Handbook of World-Systems Analysis*. His current book project is *Lawyers, Guns & Money: Wall Street & the American Century*.

Ola Tunander is a Research Professor at the Peace Research Institute, Oslo (PRIO), Norway. In 1989, he was awarded a PhD for a dissertation on geopolitics and U.S. maritime strategy and was appointed Senior Researcher at PRIO, where he headed its Foreign and Security Policy Program for several years. In 2000, he was appointed Research Professor. He has lectured worldwide, contributed to projects of ministries of foreign affairs and defence and initiated Nordic-Russian dialogues (The Barents Euro-Arctic Region) and Nordic-China dialogues. He has contributed to journals such as the *Review of International Studies*, *Geopolitics*, *Security Dialogue* and *Cooperation & Conflict* and been a peer-reviewer for the Harvard-based *International Security*, *European Journal of International Relations* and the London-based *Millennium*. He is the author and editor of 12 books on history, geopolitics, political philosophy and military strategy—including *Cold Water Politics: The US Maritime Strategy and Geopolitics of the Northern Front* (1989), *The Barents Region: Cooperation in Arctic Europe* (1994), *Geopolitics in Post-Wall Europe: Security, Territory and Identity* (1997), *European Security Identities* (2000) and *The Secret War against Sweden – US and British Submarine Deception in the 1980s* (2004).

Eric Wilson is senior lecturer of public law at Monash University, Melbourne, Australia. He received a Doctorate in History from Cambridge University in 1991 and a Doctorate of Juridical Science from the University of Melbourne in 2005. His publications include *The Savage Republic: De Indis of Hugo Grotius, Republicanism, and Dutch Hegemony in the Early Modern World System (c.1600–1619)* (Martinus Nijhoff, 2008). He is currently editing a series of volumes on critical criminology devoted to the relationships among covert government agency, organized crime and extra-judicial forms of governance; the first volume in the series, *Government of the Shadows: Parapolitics and Criminal Sovereignty*, was published by Pluto Press in 2009. His research interests are critical criminology, the history and philosophy of international law, the comparative law of Southeast Asia, cultural studies and critical jurisprudence.

Acknowledgments

I would like to thank the Faculty of Law, Monash University, for providing me with a research and publication grant for the completion of this book. I would also like to thank my editorial assistant, Ms. Sanah W. Banihali, who labored above and beyond the call of duty in the preparation of the text.

Eric Wilson,
Faculty of Law,
Monash University,
Clayton Campus,
Melbourne

No one is illegal.
But we are all criminals ...
I must find a new language, one that avoids empty words like justice and crime and punishment and problems and solutions.

Charles Bowden[1]

---

1 Bowden, C. 2010. *Dreamland: The Way Out of Juarez*. Austin University of Texas Press. 26 and 12.

Chapter 1
The Concept of the Parapolitical

Eric Wilson

> The impulse to secrecy and to learn the secret is the first tendency of any power, whatever form of government or method of administration it serves. No ruler can escape this impulse, which becomes greater and more intense the stronger and more effective power becomes.
>
> Carl Schmitt

If Carl Schmitt (1888–1985) did not exist, it would have been necessary for the parapolitical scholar to have invented him. For both Schmitt and the analyst of covert phenomena, the outstanding political problem is the disassociation between the legality and the legitimacy of the contemporary (neo-)liberal state—within liberalism, "legitimacy and legality cannot be the same; indeed, they stand in contradiction to each other."[1] The structural, and largely unacknowledged (or "repressed") reason for this is the lurking presence of the dual state: the bifurcation of the ostensibly monistic liberal state into a parallel phenomenon of public/judicial/rational and private/extra-judicial/irrational, the myriad relationships between the two sets governed by a strictly binary operational logic. Schmitt, when read closely—which is to say when read "against himself"—may be understood as providing what is, in effect, the constitutional blueprint for the dual state. For the parapolitical scholar, therefore, Schmitt is "good to think."

What is Parapolitics?

> Real power begins where secrecy begins. (Hannah Arendt)

The seminal figure in parapolitical studies is Peter Dale Scott, who strives to formulate a new terminology, or even a poetics, with which to convey new understandings of hitherto un-describable political phenomena.

> Parapolitics: 1. A system or practice of politics in which accountability is consciously diminished. 2. Generally, covert politics, the conduct of public affairs not by rational debate and responsible decision-making but by

1 Strong, T. B. 2007. Foreword: Dimensions of the New Debate around Carl Schmitt, in Schmitt, C. *The Concept of the Political*, trans. George Schwab. Chicago: University of Chicago Press. xv.

> indirection, collusion, and deceit. Cf. *conspiracy*. 3. The political exploitation of irresponsible agencies or parastructures, such as intelligence agencies.[2]

> The Dual State. A *State* in which one can distinguish between a *public state* and a top-down *deep state*. The deep state emerges in a false-flag violence, is organized by the military and intelligence apparatus and involves their link to organized crime. Most states exhibit this duality, but to varying degrees. In America the duality of the state has become more and more acute since World War II.[3]

Scott's language has been strongly influenced by that of the Swedish national security scholar Ola Tunander, who was the first to coin the term "security state." Again, the vital issue is that extra-judicial convergence of the public body with covert agency which can only be described as parapolitical.

> After September 11, the U.S. "democratic state" (characterised by openness, legal procedures and free elections) is forcefully … subsumed under a "security state" (characterised by secrecy and military hierarchy). Much of the public life is "securitized" and the President and his close advisors are focused on the War on Terror, not on civilian matters. "I am a war President. I make decisions … with war on my mind." President Bush said.[4]

As progressive scholars the irrationality of parapolitics is what interests us the most; for Scott, the essence of the parapolitical is an "*intervening layer of irrationality under our political culture's rational surface*."[5] The submerged, or repressed, nature of covert agency is not only an ontological problem but an epistemological one as well; it is precisely because of its irrational nature that the

2 Scott, P. D. 2008. *The War Conspiracy: JFK, 9/11, and the Politics of War*. New York: Mary Ferrell Foundation Press. 238.

3 Scott, P. D. 2008. 238. In turn, the "dual state" equates with a "deep political system," which Scott defines as "one which habitually resorts to decision-making and enforcement procedures outside as well as inside those publicly sanctioned by law and society. In popular terms, collusive secrecy and law-breaking are part of how the deep political system works." Scott, P. D. 1993. *Deep Politics and the Death of JFK*. Berkeley: University of California Press. xi–xii.

4 Ola Tunander cited in Scott, P. D. 2007. *The Road to 9/11: Wealth, Empire, and the Future of America*. Berkeley: University of California Press. 244. For both the "deep state" and the "security state," see Tunander, O. 2009. Democratic State vs. Deep State: Approaching the Dual State of the West, in *Government of the Shadows: Parapolitics and Criminal Sovereignty*, edited by E. Wilson. London: Pluto Press, 56–72. Reflecting upon the U.S. invasion of Iraq in 2003, Scott comments that "Since the mid-1970s the deep state has increasingly taken refuge in the *powers* conferred upon the CIA and Pentagon, as opposed to the bureaucracies of those institutions." Scott, P. D. 2008. 17.

5 Scott, P. D. 1993. 6–7.

parapolitical evades cognitive recognition, with all of the attendant ideological implications. According to Tunander:

> Liberal political science has been turned into an ideology of the "deep state" because undisputable evidence for the [national security] "deep state" is brushed away as pure fantasy or conspiracy[6] ... Thus, the problem with liberalism in political science and legal theory is not its ambition to defend the public sphere, political freedoms and human rights, but rather its claim that these freedoms and rights define the Western political system.[7]

I have made a similar point elsewhere:

> Just as politics as a field ("political science") studies the overt politics of the public state, so parapolitics, as a field, studies the relationships between the public state and the political processes and arrangements outside and beyond conventional politics. However, conventional, or liberal, political science assumes the normalcy of the state, both in its constitutional and normative dimensions, as a given and studies political phenomenon from the perspective of the state. Parapolitics, in contrast, constitutes a radically nominalist critique of conventional political studies. Parapolitics uses the varying levels of interaction between conventional states and quasi-statist entities as the basis for formulating an analytical perspective that privileges neither the state nor its alternatives as legitimate international actors. Although of no determinative political bias, parapolitics does foster a basic scepticism regarding the coherence of orthodox liberal understandings of the state.[8]

The relevance of Schmitt to parapolitics is obvious: he offers a comprehensive anti-liberal notion of statist modernity as "*modern bourgeois politics*"; "Schmitt is concerned with demonstrating the impossibility of understanding the legal order in *exclusively rationalist terms*, that is, as a self-sufficient, complete legal system of legal norms after the fashion of legal positivism."[9] Not for nothing has Schmitt been called the Martin Heidegger of political theory.[10] Broadly following Heidegger,[11] Schmitt argues that neither the liberal state, nor its corollary "the Law," can successfully achieve a form of self-grounding that is commensurate

---

6 Ola Tunander cited in Wilson, E. 2009. Deconstructing the Shadows, in *Government of the Shadows: Parapolitics and Criminal Sovereignty*, edited by E. Wilson. London: Pluto Press. 13–55 at 29.

7 Tunander, O. 2009. 68. See Wilson, E. 2009 on this same point.

8 Wilson, E. 2009. 30.

9 Wolin, R. 1992. Carl Schmitt the Conservative Revolutionary: Habitus and the Aesthetics of Horror. *Political Theory*, 20/3, 424–47 at 431.

10 Strong, T. B. 2007. ix–xxxi.

11 See below.

with their own professed first principles; "Law cannot itself form a completely rational and lawful system; the analysis of the state must make reference to those agencies which have the capacity to decide on the state of exception[12] and not merely a formal plenitude of power."[13] According to Paul Hirst:

> Governmental agencies concerned by and large with matters of social and economic organization operate through managerial imperatives and are subject to at least some minimal legal regulation and political control. But they do not exhaust the state. Schmitt is valuable because he stresses that all legal orders have an "outside" and that definite agencies within the state have the option (if not the formal constitutional right) to act extra-legally.[14]

Crucial to Schmitt's work is the notion that liberalism culminates in a self-serving strategy of de-politicization, or "neutralization," in which the liberal state both induces and polices a kind of collective false consciousness concerning the "true" nature of the political.

> The systematic theory of liberalism concerns almost solely the internal struggle against the power of the State. For the purpose of protecting individual freedom and private property, liberalism provides a series of methods for hindering and controlling the State's and government's power.[15]

It is liberalism's reduction of politics to both rationality and discourse that effects this colossal act of self-induced amnesia. 19th-century liberal democracy is "rendered impotent by a rule-bound legalism, a rationalistic concept of political debate, and the desire that individual citizens enjoy a legally-guaranteed 'private' sphere protected from the state," constituting the single greatest crime against the true political nature of Man: "The political is none of those things. Its essence is struggle."[16] Insofar as liberalism "wishes to substitute procedure for the struggle" it "will tend to undermine the possibility of the political."[17] For Schmitt, the only way out of this interminable crisis of the False, which is in equal parts political and existential, is to induce the wholesale collapse of the public and

---

12 In the alternative, "the extreme state": that is, the moment in real time that the formal recognition and naming of The Enemy actually takes place, which is the auto-determination by the Sovereign that the conditions of "the normal state" no longer prevail. See below.

13 Hirst, P. 1987. Carl Schmitt's Decisionism. *Telos*, 72, 15–26 at 21.

14 Hirst, P. 1987. 25.

15 Schmitt, C. 1996. *The Concept of the Political*, trans. George Schwab. Chicago: University of Chicago Press. 70.

16 Hirst, P. 1987. 16.

17 Strong, T. B. 2007. xv.

private realms and to transpose in its entirety the classical Realist conception of international politics to the domestic realm of the state.

Nomos and Originary Violence

> The concept of the State presupposes the concept of the political. (Carl Schmitt)

> For the State as an essentially political entity belongs the jus belli, i.e., the real possibility of deciding in a concrete situation upon the enemy and the ability to fight him with the power emanating from the entity. (Carl Schmitt)

Given the centrality of Heidegger to Schmitt's own thought,[18] it would be worthwhile to frame the jurist's critique of the liberal state in terms of the political ontology of the philosopher.[19] For Heidegger, the inherently political nature of the relationship between the political being of the state and political reason (*ratio*):

> [S]prings from the essence of truth as correctness in the sense of the self-adjusting guarantee of the security of domination. The "taking as true" of *ratio*, of *reor*, becomes a far-reaching and anticipatory security. *Ratio* becomes counting, calculating, calculus. *Ratio* is self-adjustment to what is correct.[20]

In Heidegger's view, political "truth" that equates with correctness is both delimited by a homogeneous discursive space and subjugated to the political will to domination; "The essence of truth as *veritas* [i.e. correctness] is *without space* and without ground,"[21] signifying the un-reality of the heterogeneous, or the "different"; "The result is the *presence* of truth as self-evidence, or the presence of thought to itself in the manner of self-identity" within an exclusively homogenous discursive space.[22] *Veritas* is the ground of Western jurisprudence's conflation of Law with Reason, establishing an undifferentiated chain of signifiers delimiting the parameters of "orthodox" or "common" legal speech. Homogeneity guarantees that whatever is not identical with *ratio* cannot constitute a portion of reality and,

18 For Schmitt's "complex and over-determined relationship to Heidegger," see Derrida, J. 2005. *The Politics of Friendship*, trans. George Collins. London: Verso. 84–5.

19 See Wilson, E. 2009. The Republic of Heterogeneity: *De Indis* of Hugo Grotius, Deconstruction and the Political Ontology of the Dutch State. *The Journal of the Philosophy of International Law*, 3, 57–76.

20 Heidegger, M. 1992. *Parmenides*, trans. Andre Schuwer and R. Rojcewicz. Bloomington: Indiana University Press. 50.

21 Heidegger, M. 1992. 50.

22 Bell, J. A. 2006. *Philosophy at the Edge of Chaos: Gilles Deleuze and the Philosophy of Difference*. Toronto: University of Toronto Press. 28. "There is no space, no distance, between our true thoughts concerning a state of affairs in the world and that state of affairs: the two coincide." Bell, J. A. 2006.

by political implication, cannot constitute an actual attribute of the "true" state. Consequently, "the idea of sovereignty, which clearly implies but one absolute power laying in the social order, with all relationships, all individuals ... ultimately subject to it, has been the characteristic approach to the political community."[23]

Nationalism is secular mythology.[24] The onto-political division that originated with Plato serves as the historical originary of the modern nationalistic myth of the homogeneous nation-state. With Hegel, "the transformation of veritas into certitudo is completed. This completion of the Roman essence of truth is the proper and hidden historical meaning of the nineteenth century."[25] It is also, however, very much the "historical meaning" of the "long sixteenth century" (1492–1648), the critical incubating period for early modern international law; the Dutch Republic of the early 17th century had emerged as a self-grounding juro-political space, delimited by three undifferentiated signs sovereignty (*potestas*), freedom (*libertas*) and right (*ius*).[26] Although Heidegger situates the historical victory of political monism in the post-Napoleonic period, it is clear that onto-political homogeneity—or what is also known as the indivisibility of sovereignty[27]—had achieved an irreversible ascendancy by the time of Jean Bodin (1529/30–1596), as Jens Bartelson has established:

> Since Bodin, indivisibility has been integral to the concept of sovereignty itself. In international political theory, this means that whenever sovereignty is used in a theoretical context to confer unity upon the state as an acting subject, all that it conveys is that this entity is an individual by virtue of its indivisibility [i.e. its homogeneous space], which is tautological indeed. What follows from this search for the locus of sovereignty in international political theory, however necessary to its empirical testability is thus nothing more than a logical sideshow; the essential step towards unity is already taken whenever sovereignty figures in the definition of political order. Whether thought to be upheld by an individual or a collective, or embedded in the State as a whole, sovereignty entails self-presence and self-sufficiency; that which is sovereign is immediately given to itself, conscious of itself, and thus acting for itself. That is, as it figures in international political theory, sovereignty is not an attribute of something whose

---

23 Nisbet, R. 1974. *The Social Philosophers: Community and Conflict in Western Thought*. London: Heinemann. 386.

24 Anderson, B. 1991. *Imagined Communities*. London: Verso.

25 Heidegger, M. 1992. 58.

26 See Wilson, E. 2008. *The Savage Republic: De Indis of Hugo Grotius, Republicanism, and Dutch Hegemony in the Early Modern World-System (c.1600–1619)*. Leiden: Martinus Nijhoff.

27 Wilson, E. 2008.

> existence is prior to or independent of sovereignty; rather, it is the concept of sovereignty itself which supplies this indivisibility and unity.[28]

Hegel notwithstanding, it was the early modern nation-state that acted as the discursive space of the identity of unity with political power (*potestas*). The presence of unity/monism equates with the absence of pluralism, which is the multiplication, or proliferation, of political identities and entities. According to Robert Nisbet:

> It has been the fate of pluralism in Western thought to take a rather poor second place to philosophies which make their point of departure the premise of, not the diversity and plurality of things, but, rather, some underlying unity and symmetry, needing only to be uncovered by pure reason to be then deemed the "real", the "true", and the "lasting."[29]

Yet the Platonic denial of difference contains within itself the very grounds of its actual reversal. The apparent falsity of the originary myth, the inversion of Bartelson's "empirical testability," is affirmed by the historical continuation of difference(s). As contemporary anti-Hegelian thought insists, the nation-state "is not best and fully understood as a teleological unity, directed exclusively at attending some single end or as having a single function"[30]—a profoundly parapolitical insight. In other words, the persistence of difference is itself the space of contestation of the Platonic myth; this is the central assumption of Heidegger's anti-Hegelian project. For Heidegger, "serious"—that is, metaphysical—thought within the post-Hegelian state demands a return to the early Hellenic concept of *alethia* (the "un-concealed"[31]) that pre-dated *veritas*,[32] which is both the awareness and the actively making aware of the governing presence of ontology (Being) in all forms of thought and speech, "the uncommon within the common"; "For us, the matter of thinking is the Same, and this is Being—but Being with respect to its difference from beings."[33] Until this moment, what has been lacking in Western *logos* is the primacy of heterogeneity, the "essential space of *alethia*, the unconcealedness of things … a space completely covered over by debris

28 Bartelson, J. 1995. *A Genealogy of Sovereignty*. Cambridge: Cambridge University Press. 28. See Wilson, E. 2008. 189–93.

29 Nisbet, R. 1974. 386. Nisbet's language repeats the tenor of Platonic myth.

30 Geuss, R. 2001. *History and Illusion in Politics*. Cambridge: Cambridge University Press. 61.

31 That is, a non-correspondence notion of "truth."

32 Bell's commentary on this is excellent. "Truth as *alethia*, as the unstable Being and clearing which allows for the presencing of thinking and being, is stabilised and replaced by the Roman view of truth as *veritas*, as correctness." Bell, J. A. 2006. 26.

33 Heidegger, M. 1969. *Identity and Difference*, trans. J. Stambaugh. New York: Harper & Row Publishers. 47 and 50.

and forgotten."[34] Ironically, the fatal flaw of the Heideggerian project lies within this very move toward the un-concealing of heterogeneity: whenever Heidegger attempts to convey a positive definition of Being, as opposed to the mere invocation of it, he reduces it to a self-identical and (re-)unifying "ideal of simplicity, purity and self-containment."[35] To think about Being as such is to repeat, on another level, the original sin of Platonism: the fetishizing of the (self-)identical. The true substitution of homogeneity with heterogeneity demands a radical and unconditional *rapprochement* with difference(s)/being(s): *the proof of the absence of the homogeneous is the sign of the presence of a potentially radical and discursively de-stabilizing heterogeneity*. The implications of this critique of Heidegger's political ontology for Schmitt's relationship to parapolitics will be made clear in what follows.

It is not the least part of Schmitt's rhetorical genius that he takes Heidegger's exceptionally rarefied concepts and invests them with a mytho-poetic vitality: *ratio* and *veritas* are transformed into bloody, but heroic, acts of appropriation and domination, signified through the erection of a series of impenetrable walls, both physical and metaphorical, that belie the originary violence that lies at the very foundation of the state, including its degenerate 19th-century liberal descendant.[36] The central text of Schmitt's later career, *The Nomos of the Earth* (1950), undertakes a neo-Heideggerian exercise in constitutional foundationalism: both the political "being" of the state (political ontology) and the heuristic apparatus of law are grounded on the terrestrial, or telluric, reality of the polity. "In mythical language, the *earth* became known as the mother of law. This signifies a threefold root of law and justice":[37] the planet ("Gaia"),[38] the land, and, most interestingly, boundaries, or walls.

> Soil that is cleared and worked by human hands manifests firm lines, whereby definite divisions become apparent. Through the demarcation of fields, pastures, and forests, these lines are engraved and embedded … the solid ground of the

34 Heidegger, M. 1992. 50.

35 Bell, J. A. 2006. 150. Being "is the unifying One, in the sense of what is everywhere primal and thus most universal; and at the same time it is the unifying One in the sense of the All-Highest (Zeus)." Heidegger, M. 1992. 69. "Truth"—that which is un-concealed—is difference, the being(s) within Being. However, within the Heideggerian schema, beings are ultimately revealed as embedded within the primordial and universal One.

36 For what follows, see Wilson, E. 2011. Magnum Latrocinium and Private Avengers: Carl Schmitt and Hugo Grotius on Piracy. *Leidschrift: Historisch Tijdschrift*, 26/3, 75–97.

37 Schmitt, C. 2003. *The Nomos of the Earth in the International Law of the Jus Publicum Europaeum*, trans. G. L. Ulmen. New York: Telos Press Publishing. 42.

38 "First, the fertile earth contains within herself, within the womb of fecundity, an inner measure, because human toil and trouble, human planting and cultivation of the fruitful earth is rewarded justly by her with growth and harvest. Every farmer knows the inner measure of this justice." Schmitt, C. 2003. 42.

> earth is delineated by fences, enclosures, boundaries, walls, houses, and other constructs. Then, the orders and orientations of human social life become apparent. Then, obviously, families, clans, tribes, estates, forms of ownership and human proximity, also forms of power and domination, become visible.[39]

I argue that it is precisely this uncommon emphasis upon the impermeability of borders, both legal and political, that distinguishes Schmitt from the rest of the pantheon of international lawyers. Whereas most international jurists are, by definition, "globalist" to some degree, Schmitt authors a model of international public order premised upon a radically homogenous notion of the state that: (i) eternally exists in a condition of potential enmity with all other states; and (ii) unconditionally withholds recognition of the legal identity of any actor or entity that does not strictly conform to his model of the state. According to Schmitt:

> In this way, the earth is bound to law in three ways. She contains law within herself, as a reward for labor; she manifests law upon herself, as fixed boundaries; and she sustains law above herself, as a public sign of order. Law is bound to the earth and related to the earth. This what the poet means when he speaks of the infinitely just earth: *justissima tellus*.[40]

This eccentric re-presentation of the telluric as judicial foundation makes more sense when we situate it within the context of Schmitt's overarching project: the identification of European legal order (the *ius publicum Europaeum*) with the demarcation, or "bracketing," of war and inter-state violence.

> The essence of European international law was the bracketing of war. The essence of such wars was a regulated contest of forces gauged by witnesses in a bracketed space. Such wars are the opposite of disorder. They represent the highest form of order within the scope of human power. They are the only protection against a circle of increasing reprisals, i.e., against nihilistic hatreds and reactions whose meaningless goal lies in mutual destruction. The removal and avoidance of wars of destruction is possible only when a form for the gauging of forces is found. This is possible only when the opponent is recognized as an enemy on equal grounds—as a *justus hostis*. This is the given foundation for a bracketing of war.[41]

Two rhetorical maneuvers are central to this strategy. Firstly, modern European law must be thoroughly secularized, making it the exclusive possession of "profane" states that are governed by an exclusively positivist legal rationality.

---

39 Schmitt, C. 2003. 42.
40 Schmitt, C. 2003. 42.
41 Schmitt, C. 2003. 187.

> The justice of war no longer is based on conformity with the content of theological, moral, or juridical norms, but rather on the institutional and structural quality of political forms. States pursued war against each other on one and the same level, and each side viewed the other not as traitors and criminals, but as *justi hostes*. In other words, the right of war was based exclusively on the quality of the belligerent agents of *jus belli*, and this quality was based on the fact that equal sovereigns pursued war against each other.[42]

Secondly, both the political and legal relationships between states must governed by a strict reciprocity; now that the domain of international legal personality is exhausted by the secular state, the neutrality and the objectivity of the law of war can be secured through the exclusionary identification of the "violent" party with the statist form.

> The sovereign territorial state initiated war "in form"—not through norms, but through the fact that it bracketed war on the basis of mutual territoriality, and made war on European soil into a relation between specific, spatially concrete, and organized orders, i.e., into a military action of state-organized armies against similarly-organized armies on the opposing side.[43]

This explains Schmitt's obsession with the telluric: the reduction of the state to terrestrial "walls" secures onto-political and judicial certainty by precluding the existence of both non-state political actors and legal personalities.

> The binding character of a comprehensive spatial order immediately is recognizable if the spatial order is conceived of as a *balance*[44] … Only armed struggle between state sovereigns was war in the sense of international law, and only this type of struggle fulfilled the requirements of the concept of *justus hostis*. Everything else was criminal prosecution and suppression of robbers, rebels, and pirates … To the essence of *hostis* belongs the *aequalitas*. Robbers, pirates, and rebels are not enemies, not *justi hostes*, but objects to be rendered harmless and prosecuted as criminals.[45]

---

42 Schmitt, C. 2003. 143.

43 Schmitt, C. 2003. 157–8. It is widely agreed that Schmitt's political ontology, like Heidegger's, has its intellectual roots in German Catholicism. "The juridic formulas of the omnipotence of the state are, in fact, only superficial secularizations of theological formulas of the omnipotence of God." Schmitt, C. 1996. 42. For an excellent discussion of Schmitt's political philosophy as grounded upon faith, see Meier, H. 1995. *Carl Schmitt and Leo Strauss: The Hidden Dialogue*, trans. J. Harvey Lomax. Chicago: University of Chicago Press.

44 Schmitt, C. 2003. 188.

45 Schmitt, C. 2003. 153.

And this, in turn, explains the title of the text: *nomos* is the wall that signifies not only the establishment of boundaries (both material and epistemological) but the onto-political foundation of the polity itself.[46]

> *Nomos* is the *measure* by which the land in a particular order is divided and situated; it is also the form of the political, social, and religious order determined by this process. Here, measure, order, and form constitute a spatially concrete unity. The *nomos* by which a tribe, a retinue, or a people becomes settled, i.e., by which it becomes historically situated and turns part of the earth's surface into a force-field of a particular order, becomes visible in the appropriation of land and in the founding of a city or a colony.[47]

According to Schmitt, "the term land-appropriation is better than land-division, because land-appropriation, both externally and internally, points clearly to the constitution of a radical title."[48] The originary act of the appropriation of radical title is foundational in two ways: it secures the homogeneity, both political and ontological, of the resulting polity and it guarantees the epistemic regime of the juridical order.

> Thus, in some form, the constitutive process of a land-appropriation is found at the beginning of the history of every settled people, every commonwealth, every empire. This is true as well for the beginning of every historical epoch. Not only logically, but also historically, land-appropriation precedes the order that follows from it. It constitutes the original spatial order, the source of all further concrete order and all further law. It is the reproductive root in the normative order of history. All further property relations—communal or individual, public or private property, and all forms of possession and use in society and in international law—are derived from this radical title. All subsequent law and everything promulgated and enacted thereafter as decrees and commands are *nourished*, to use Heraclitus' word, by this source.[49]

The importance of the telluric for the coherence of *ius publicum Europaeum*, therefore, cannot be over-estimated. It is the primary appropriation and secondary division/demarcation that infuses the *nomos* that validates both the objective legal identities of the actors within the order and the epistemic unity of the juridical system governing their actions—the "bracketing" of war.

---

46 "In particular, *nomos* can be described as a wall, because, like a wall, it, too, is based on sacred orientations. The *nomos* can grow and multiply like land and property: all human *nomoi* are 'nourished' by a single divine *nomos*." Schmitt, C. 2003. 70–71.

47 Schmitt, C. 2003. 70.

48 Schmitt, C. 2003. 81.

49 Schmitt, C. 2003. 48.

> This fundamental process of land-appropriation preceded the distinction between public and private law, public authority and private property, *imperium* and *dominium*. Land-appropriation thus is the archetype of a constitutive legal process externally (*vis-à-vis* other peoples) and internally (for the ordering of land and property within a country). It creates the most radical title, in the full and comprehensive sense of the term *radical title*.[50]

Thus, Schmitt is able to conclude that land-appropriation "precedes the distinction between private and public law; in general, it creates the conditions for this distinction. To this extent, from a legal perspective, one might say that land-appropriation has a categorical character."[51] But it is precisely this strict demarcation between public/private and legal/criminal that proves the most discursively unstable part of Schmitt's constitutional theory.

The Originary Decision: The Friend–Foe Dichotomy

> For to the enemy concept belongs the ever present possibility of combat. (Carl Schmitt)

The foundational nature of originary violence ("land appropriation") along with the radical indivisibility of the state (*nomos*), are the two necessary corollaries to Schmitt's signature concept: *the state of exception*. "A definition of the political can be obtained only by discovering and defining the specifically political categories[52] … The specific political distinction to which political actions and motives can be reduced is that between friend and enemy."[53] This neo-Heideggerian re-conceptualization of the onto-political (and existential) basis of the state as the practical exercise of executive power[54] effectively reduces sovereignty to *decisionism*; "What always matters is the possibility of the extreme case taking place, the real war, and the decision whether this situation has or has not arrived."[55] Political *existenz* as space coupled with force moves war to the center of life, yielding a radically dualistic *weltanschaung*: "War as the most extreme political means discloses the possibility which underlines every political idea, namely, the distinction of friend and foe."[56] The German word *Feind* encapsulates two categories that are formally distinct in English: *enemy*, in the sense of a rival or

50 Schmitt, C. 2003. 46–7.

51 Schmitt, C. 2003. 46.

52 Schmitt, C. 1996. 25.

53 Schmitt, C. 1996. 26.

54 "The political is the arena of authority rather than general law and requires decisions which are singular, absolute, and final." Strong, T. B. 2007. xiv.

55 Schmitt, C. 1996. 35.

56 Schmitt, C. 1996. 35.

an opponent (*inimicus*), who is ordinarily the object of a "private" conflict, and *foe*, the combatant or "absolute enemy" (*hostis*), with whom the entire community engages in "public" combat, or war, properly so-called; "An enemy exists only when, at least potentially, one fighting collectivity of people confronts a similar collectivity."[57]

Of the greatest interest here is how Schmitt quite artfully blends two different sets of considerations into a single ontological postulate: (i) the political with the existential, and (ii) the private with the public. "The definition of the political suggested here neither favors war nor militarism, neither imperialism nor pacifism";[58] what is essential, rather, is the demarcation of political space into a duality that is both the sign and the signifier of an authentic form of political commitment that is identical with "truth."

> Just as the term enemy, the word combat, too, is to be understood in its original existential sense … The friend, enemy, and combat concepts receive their real meaning precisely because they refer to the real possibility of physical killing. War follows from enmity. War is the existential negation of the enemy. It is the most extreme consequence of enmity. It does not have to be common, normal, something ideal, or desirable. But it must nevertheless remain a real possibility for so long as the concept of the enemy remains valid.[59]

And it is the etymological imprecision of the word *Feind* itself is what allows Schmitt to postulate an almost subliminal movement, or iteration, between public/*hostis* and private/*inimicus*: "War is neither the aim nor the purpose nor even the very content of politics. But as an ever present possibility it is the leading presupposition which determines in a characteristic way human action and thinking and thereby creates a specifically political behavior."[60] Combat, therefore, which is identical to the moment of the decision—the "naming" of the Enemy/Other[61]—is, to a perfectly inverse degree, *not* identical with war. Rather, war is both politically and existentially the most extreme form of combat—an apotheosis—the latter serving as the onto-political *grund* of the former, encapsulating both public and private systems of meaning; "War, the readiness of combatants to die, the physical killing of human beings who belong on the side of the enemy—all this has no normative meaning, but an existential meaning only, particularly in a real combat situation with a real enemy."[62] Schmitt's theory of combat-as-politics

57 Schmitt, C. 1996. 28.

58 Schmitt, C. 1996. 33.

59 Schmitt, C. 1996. 33.

60 Schmitt, C. 1996. 34.

61 The enemy is "the other, the stranger; and it is sufficient for his nature that he is, in a specially intense way, existentially something different and alien, so that in the extreme conflicts with him are possible." Schmitt, C. 1996. 27.

62 Schmitt, C. 1996. 48–9.

is not mere existentialism ("justice does not belong to the concept of war"[63]), but *radical* existentialism; by "radical" I mean that both the truth and the value of the object (existent) in question is determined by an unconditional and irreducible "giveness" that appears to the existentially "inauthentic" Self as an irruption by an alien Other.

> There exists no rational purpose, no norm no matter how true, no program no matter how exemplary, no social ideal no matter how beautiful, no legitimacy nor legality which could justify men in killing each other for this reason. If such physical destruction of human life is not motivated by an existential threat to ones way of life, then it cannot be justified. Just as little can war be justified by ethical and juristic norms. If there really are enemies in the existential sense as meant here, then it is justified, but only politically, to repel and fight them physically.[64]

And it is this iterability between war and combat, mediated through the act of recognition of the enemy, that is the logical outcome of a decisionism that subverts the foundational liberal principle of the public/private distinction: the politico-existential effect of the primal decision is projected simultaneously into external and internal space.

> Political thought and political instinct prove themselves thematically and practically in the ability to distinguish friend and enemy. The high points of politics are simultaneously the moments in which the enemy is, in concrete clarity, recognized as the enemy[65] … But also vice versa: everywhere in political history, in foreign as well as in domestic politics, the incapacity or the unwillingness to make this distinction is a symptom of the political end.[66]

Most unnerving for the orthodox liberal is Schmitt's radical—but wholly logical—conclusion that the sovereign as the executor of the decision is not itself reducible to (or exhausted by) law but acts as the sign of an inchoate extra-judicial "space" of primordial order that is the true guarantor of "law."[67] The state, as a supposedly

---

63 Schmitt, C. 1996. 49.

64 Schmitt, C. 1996. 49. The deep irony, and therefore the unsettling effect, that this passage has on the liberal-bourgeois reader is that the first sentence reads like a conventional argument in favor of pacificism: *nothing* is worth the taking of human life. The "alien" nature of Schmitt's thought is evidenced by the manner in which he re-deploys orthodox anti-war rhetoric in his justification of a more "truthful" form of violence that is identical with a "higher" form of politics.

65 Schmitt, C. 1996. 67.

66 Schmitt, C. 1996. 68.

67 "The political consists not in war or armed conflict as such, but precisely in the relation of enmity: not competition but confrontation. It is bound by no law: it is prior to law." Hirst, P. 1987. 17.

"legal personality," is not exhausted, or even explicable, in terms of the law; in order for it to exist as a lawful entity, it must necessarily invoke the presence of the extra-legal.

> The State as the decisive political entity possesses an enormous power: the possibility of waging war and thereby publicly disposing of the lives of men. The *jus belli* contains such a disposition. It implies a double possibility: the right to demand from its own members the readiness to die and unhesitatingly to kill enemies. The endeavor of a normal state consists above all in assuring total peace within the state and its territory. To create tranquility, security, and order, and thereby establish the normal situation is the prerequisite for legal norms to be valid. Every norm presupposes a normal situation, and no norm can be valid in an entirely abnormal situation.[68]

It is at this juncture that the first of several "dangerous supplements" announce their presence within the Schmittian sub-text. By reducing sovereignty to decision—which is the logical corollary of the Friend/Self-Enemy/Other dichotomy—and by postulating combat (potentially a private act) as the originary ground for war (an exclusively public enterprise), then Schmitt inadvertently admits to the possibility of the sovereign as a *non-state actor*: "War has its own strategic, tactical, and other rules and points of view, but they all presuppose that the political decision has already been made as to who the enemy is."[69] The identity, or "truth," of the sovereign will stand revealed through the deconstruction of this political decision.

The *Alethia* of Parapolitics: Liberalism and Originary Violence

> All essential concepts are not normative but existential. (Carl Schmitt)

> At each moment of its existence, the police remind the State of the violence, the banality, and the darkness of its beginnings. (Tiqqun)[70]

As Tracy B. Strong has perceptively observed, "Liberals are horrified at Schmitt because he offends against one of the deepest premises of liberalism: politics is necessary but it should not become too serious."[71] As Schmitt forcibly reminds us, to see liberalism "as an historical event means that one understands it as the inheritor and bearer not only of rights and freedoms but also of structures of

68 Schmitt, C. 1996. 46.

69 Schmitt, C. 1996. 34.

70 Tiqqun. 2010. *Introduction to Civil War*, trans. Alexander R. Galloway and Jason E. Smith. Los Angeles: Semiotexte, 105.

71 Strong, T. B. 2007. xxvi.

power and domination, of colonial and class exploitations, of the hatred of, rather than the opposition to, the Other."[72] In my opinion, the true value of Schmitt's juro-political philosophy lies within his radical juxtaposition of liberalism with its own Enemy: political violence and its ideological corollary, "extremism." What "primarily interests Schmitt … is to complete the critique of liberalism,"[73] a goal achieved through his existential critique of liberalism's "bad faith" concerning the onto-political foundation of the primal decision: "Distinguishing the adversary as political and oneself as non-political (i.e., scientific, objective, neutral, etc.) is in actuality a typical and unusually intensive way of pursuing politics."[74] In Schmitt's view, one which accords well with both Tunander and Scott, it is the "liberal state" itself that is the embodiment of a higher form of immorality.

In existential terms, the question is whether liberal society can "really leave behind what it was."[75] For Schmitt, the essence of "the definition of the bourgeois" is "aspiring to life without political risk."[76] Yet, with our awareness of the lurking presence of the decision, we know that the "peaceful, legalistic, liberal bourgeoisie is sitting on a volcano and ignoring the facts. Their world depends on a relative stabilization of conflicts within the state and on the state's ability to keep at bay other potentially hostile states."[77] He writes that the "problematic or unproblematic conception of man is decisive for the presupposition of every further political consideration, the answer to the question whether man is a dangerous being or not, a risky or a harmless creature."[78] Hence, liberalism:

> [H]as produced a doctrine of the separation and balance of power, i.e., a system of checks and controls of state and government. This cannot be characterized as either a theory of state or a basic political principle. What remains is the remarkable and, for many, certainly disquieting diagnosis that all genuine political theories presuppose man to be evil, i.e., by no means an unproblematic but a dangerous and dynamic being.[79]

And, according to Schmitt's sometime correspondent Leo Strauss:

---

72 Strong, T. B. 2007. xix.

73 Meier, H. 1995. 11.

74 Schmitt, C. 1996. 21 fn. 2.

75 Pippin, R. B. 2010. *Hollywood Westerns and American Myth: The Importance of Howard Hawks and John Ford for Political Philosophy*. New Haven: Yale University Press. 24.

76 Schmitt, C. 1996. 51 fn. 22.

77 Hirst, P. 1987. 17.

78 Schmitt, C. 1996. 58.

79 Schmitt, C. 1996. 61. "A part of the theories and postulates which presuppose man to be good is liberal." Schmitt, C. 1996. 60.

> In order to remove the smokescreen over reality that liberalism produces, the political must be made apparent as such and simply undeniable. The political must first be brought out of concealment into which liberalism has cast it, so that the question of the State can be seriously put.[80]

The critique of liberalism, therefore, is we should have come to expect, not merely a political one but an existential one: enduring the trauma of Heidegger's *alethia*.

According to Jacques Derrida, "what is at stake" in the act of commitment that is "the decision" as to the identity of the Enemy is "indeed a phenomenalization as revelation, manifestation, unveiling."[81]

> This undecidable decision[82] bestows the force of unveiling. This deciding signification which unveils the kernel of things … accrues to the decision. The unveiling of things, of the heart of things in the coming asunder of decision, is perhaps accomplished not in the act of war which bears death, but surely in the assundering possibility, of a killing, in this possibility *qua* real and present possibility. The latter can uncover the heart of things only in undressing the other, in uncovering the possibility of what Schmitt called … "physical killing."[83]

As Derrida rightly intuits, Schmitt acts as the surveyor of a crisis of an existential and not merely a political "crisis of meaning"; "The political unit is always, as long as it is present at all, the authoritative unit, total and sovereign. It is 'total' first because every matter can be potentially political and therefore can be affected by the political decision; and second because man is totally and existentially grasped in political participation."[84] Schmitt's concern with political meaning as existential dilemma unmistakably marks him as a "Germanic thinker."[85] According to Strauss, Schmitt "affirms the political because he sees in the threatened status of the political a threat to the seriousness of human life. The affirmation of the political is ultimately nothing other than the affirmation of the moral."[86] When it is said that "the political is a basic characteristic of human life," argues Strauss,

---

80 Strauss, L. Notes on Carl Schmitt in Schmitt, C. 1996. 100.

81 Derrida, J. 2005. 131.

82 "Undecidable" in that the "truth" of the Enemy exists nowhere outside of the commitment to the friend–foe distinction that is itself "the decision."

83 Derrida, J. 2005. 128.

84 Schmitt in Meier, H. 1995. 16.

85 "Since the end of the nineteenth century, longing for the realization of man's humanity has fueled many of the most influential trends in German social criticism—so much so that there are few surer signs that a social critic has been educated in the German/continental philosophic tradition than complaints about dehumanization or demands that or autonomy be embodied in our institutions." Yack, B. 1992. *The Longing for Total Revolution: Philosophic Sources of Social Discontent from Rousseau to Marx and Nietzsche*. Berkeley: University of California Press. 365.

86 Strauss, L. 2007. 117.

"in other words that man ceases to be man if he ceases to be political, this statement also, and precisely, means that man ceases to be human when he ceases to be political."[87] For Schmitt, the "distinction of friend and enemy denotes the utmost degree of intensity of a union or separation, of an association or disassociation";[88] as a result, "The greater the intensity the closer to the Truth we come."[89]

Precisely because the bourgeois is the antithesis of the heroic[90] liberalism and its resultant political rationality can neither compel *nor explain* instances of *sacrifice*, either of self or of other.[91] From this follows the "immorality" of liberalism that under "no circumstances can anyone demand that any member of an economically determined society, whose order in the economic domain is based upon rational procedures, sacrifice his life in the interest of rational operations."[92] Yet, it is political violence and its attendant irrationality, in the way in which both Scott and Tunander define it, that constitutes the essence of clandestine agency; the sheer proliferation of parapolitical phenomena itself belies the coherence of liberalism's auto-poetic narrative. Schmitt's neo-Heideggerian critique is wholly congenial to parapolitical scholarship which, like existentialism, seeks to "de-construct" (or, in the original Derridean sense "destroy") the orthodox sense and understanding of the (liberal) political self. This heady, and discursively unstable, onto-political admixture of the originary, the decision and authenticity, however, is precisely what allows me to undertake a two-prong deconstruction of Schmitt's own self-limiting concept of the political. The profound irony here is that it is Schmitt's own radically singular critique of the liberal state that facilitates the parapolitical appropriation of his oeuvre.

---

87 Strauss, L. 2007. 110. See Meier, H. 1995. 56–8 for the exchange between Schmitt and Strauss over the grounding of conflict/violence in human nature.

88 Schmitt, C. 1996. 26.

89 On the basis of this existential preoccupation, Wolin is able to situate Schmitt within the vitalist critique of rationalism, a defining feature of German revolutionary conservatism; "one of the patented conceptual oppositions proper to the conservative revolutionary habitus was that between the 'hero' (or 'soldier') and the 'bourgeois'. Whereas the hero thrives on risk, danger, and uncertainty, the life of the bourgeois is devoted to petty calculations of utility and security." Wolin, R. 1992. 427 and 431.

90 "The bourgeois is an individual who does not want to leave the a-political riskless private sphere. He rests in the possession of his private property, and under the justification of his possessive individualism he acts as an individual against the totality. He is a man who finds his compensation for his political nullity in the fruits of freedom and enrichment and above all in the total security of its use. Consequently he wants to be spared bravery and exempted from the danger of a violent death." Schmitt, C. 1996. 62–3.

91 "The central task in the founding of a modern political order was to find a way to denigrate, contain, and de-emphasize the chief pre-modern mark of distinction, glory, with all the militaristic and violent and dangerous dimensions of the task, in favor of a more scientific view of the primacy of the fear of death and the desire for peace." Albert O. Hirschmann cited in Pippin, R. B. 2010. 25.

92 Schmitt, C. 1996. 48.

The First Reversal: Decisionism and Sovereignty

> Sovereign is he who decides the exception. Only this definition can do justice to a borderline concept. (Carl Schmitt)

It is through his essentializing reduction of sovereignty to decisionism that Schmitt inadvertently subverts the longed-for totalizing unity of *nomos*. The truth of politics is violence (combat), which, through its own dynamic, escalates and multiplies itself over time through the proliferation of actors and entities, yielding a radical pluralizing the domain of legal personality. As Slavoj Zizek has opined, decisionism as the foundational principle of "the rule of law ultimately hinges on an abyssal act of violence (violent imposition) which is grounded in itself; that is, every positive order to which this act refers, to legitimize itself, is self-referentially posited by this act itself."[93]

> According to Schmitt, it is not possible to pass directly from a pure normative order to the actuality of social life—the necessary mediator between the two is an act of Will, a decision, grounded only in itself, which *imposes* a certain order or legal hermeneutics (reading of abstract rules). Any normative order, taken in itself, remains stuck in abstract formalism, that is to say, it cannot bridge the gap that separates it from actual life. However—this is the core of Schmitt's argumentation [*sic*]—the decision which bridges this gap is not a decision for some concrete order, but primarily the decision for the formal principle of order as such.[94]

If we take Schmitt and his word—that the "political is the most intense and extreme antagonism, and every concrete antagonism becomes that much more political the closer it approaches the most extreme point, that of the friend-enemy grouping"[95]—then we have opened the doors to a potentially endless reversal of political and existential meanings: any particular "combat situation" can serve as the ground of the emergence of a new sovereignty. If it is true that "Sovereign is he who decides on the exception," then it is equally true that "He who decides the exception is the sovereign."

One of the most self-subverting elements of Schmitt's political ontology is the extreme precariousness governing the relationship between the quasi-theological essentialism of the *nomos* and the radical nominalism of the friend–enemy distinction.

---

93 Zizek, S. 1999. Carl Schmitt in the Age of Post-Politics, in *The Challenge of Carl Schmitt*, edited by C. Mouffe. London: Verso. 18–37 at 18.

94 Zizek, S. 1999. 18.

95 Schmitt, C. 1996. 29.

> Only the actual participants can correctly recognize, understand, and judge the concrete situation and settle the extreme case of conflict. Each participant is in a position to judge whether the adversary intends to negate his opponent's way of life and therefore must be repulsed or fought in order to preserve one's own form of existence … Thereby the inherently objective nature and autonomy of the political becomes evident by virtue of its being able to treat, distinguish, and comprehend the friend-enemy antithesis independently of other antitheses.[96]

As Zizek has accurately observed:

> Schmitt's notion of the exception is necessarily ambiguous: it stands simultaneously for the inversion of the Real (of the pure contingency ["the concrete situation"] which perturbs the universe of symbolic *automaton*) *and* for the gesture of the Sovereign who (violently, without foundation in the symbolic norm) imposes a symbolic normative order … the Master-Signifier.[97]

Zizek's turn to the language of deconstruction is most welcome here: the successful performance of the act of recognition of the enemy is the decision that signifies the presence of sovereignty (and, therefore, of "true" politics). Conversely, the constitutive act of recognition, or de-notation, is simultaneously the announcement/perception of the friend, a non-identical "self" with whom one does not exist in a state of combat. The Enemy/Other stands revealed not as a given fact (objective) but as a contingent construction (subjective) of "the-will-of-the-decider." The act (or, temporally, the precise *moment*) of "the decision" is the invocation of the presence of the Enemy/Other which is, itself, the signification of the absence of the Friend/Self. Enmity (the Friend/Self-Enemy/Other distinction) serves as the basis of true politics only because it enables the circulation of the master-sign of sovereignty, the ability to effect the command over "life and death." The Sovereign not only decides, or commands, within the duration of the state of emergency, but also decides whether the state of emergency (which is identical to the naming of the enemy) has even been reached in the first instance. So conceived the decision is radically contingent, not self-grounding, as the ontological monism of *nomos* would seem to require.

> First, all political concepts, images, and terms have a polemical meaning. They are focused on a specific conflict and are bound to a concrete situation; the result (which manifests itself in a war or a revolution) is a friend-enemy grouping and they turn into empty and ghost-like abstractions when this situation disappears.[98]

96 Schmitt, C. 1996. 27. Emphasis added.

97 Zizek, S. 1999. 19.

98 Schmitt, C. 1996. 30.

Intriguingly, Schmitt gives periodic indications that he seems aware of the radically contingent nature of sovereignty, which would render the decision more fully compatible with the repressed tradition of pluralism; the "concept of the political yields pluralistic consequences, but not in the sense that, *within one and the same political entity*, instead of decisive friend-and-enemy groupings, a pluralism could take its place without destroying the entity and the political itself."[99] If Schmitt yields to the fragmentation of *nomos* then he must renounce his political ontology in toto; his solution, therefore, is to re-formulate the empirical instances of pluralism as errors—or "enemy mis-identification."

> For as long as a people exists in the political sphere, this people must, even if only in the most extreme case—and whether this point has been reached has to be decided by it—determine by itself the distinction of friend and enemy … The justification of war does not reside in its being fought for ideas or norms of justice, but in its being fought against a real enemy. All confusions of this category of friend and enemy can be explained as results of blendings of some sort of abstractions or norms.[100]

The employment of the term *blendings* here is most interesting, suggesting as it does some sort of accidental spillage, or leakage, between normally sealed and separate containers. Once Schmitt clearly nominates the collectively deciding (but infinitely divisible) "people" as the sovereign, he is compelled to open up the originary act to an empirical historical investigation: if the decision exists nowhere outside of the concrete, then the question must now be what is the particular set of events governing the process of naming the enemy in any specific situation? The parapolitical scholar would strive to replace Schmitt's a priori reasoning ("the sovereign is he who decides") to a rigorously a posteriori approach: who (or what) has succeeded in deciding the given situation before us?

The Second Reversal: The Dual State and Criminal Sovereignty

> In the life, as in the theory, of the law, the incorporation of the negation is anything but a "primacy" of what is negated. A trial as legal action only becomes thinkable at all when a law is negated. Punishment and criminal law posit at their beginning not a deed but a criminal misdeed. Does such a positing perhaps reflect a "positive" attitude toward criminal misdeeds and toward a "primacy" of crime? (Carl Schmitt)

One of the most signature characteristics of Schmitt as a thinker is his steadfast refusal to undergo "the deconstructive turn" even at the expense of imperilling

99 Schmitt, C. 1996. 45. Emphasis added.

100 Schmitt, C. 1996. 49–50.

the fundamental coherence of his thought. This has been beautifully conveyed by Derrida in his seminal writings on Schmitt.

> Hence a first possibility of semantic slippage and inversion: the friend (*amicus*) can be an enemy (*hostis*); I can be hostile towards my friend, I can be hostile towards him publicly; and conversely I can, in privacy, love my enemy. From this, everything would follow, in orderly, regular fashion, from the distinction between private and public. Another way of saying that at every point where the border is threatened, fragile, porous, contestable (we thus designate so many possibilities that "our time" is accentuating and accelerating in countless ways) the Schmittian discourse collapses. It is against the threat of this union that his discourse takes form. It defends itself, walls itself up, reconstructs itself endlessly from what is to come; it struggles against the future with a prophetic and pathetic energy.[101]

Schmitt's political ontology both logically and rhetorically compels him to negate the autonomy of civil society, sacrificing it to the preservation of the radical monism of *nomos*; the pluralistic beings of civil society are discursively embedded within the primordial and universal One—the state. Through the decision, the state monopolizes the domain of the political, but is not itself reducible to it; rather, the universal or "total" state thoroughly inter-penetrates all dimensions of civil society.

> In reality there exists no political society or association, but only one political entity—one political community. The ever present possibility of a friend-and-enemy grouping suffices to forge a decisive entity which transcends the mere societal-associational groupings. The political entity is something specifically different, and vis-a-vis other associations, something decisive[102] ... By virtue of this power [the decision] over the physical life of men, the political community transcends all other associations or societies. Within this community, however, sub-ordinate groupings of a secondary political nature could exist with their transferred rights, even with a limited *jus vitae ac necis* over members of smaller groups.[103]

Nonetheless, in a largely unremarked passage in his seminal text *The Concept of the Political*, we find the following assertion that is replete with deconstructive significance.

> What always matters is only the possibility of conflict ... Should the counter-forces be strong enough to hinder a war desired by the State that was contrary to

101 Derrida, J. 2005. 88.
102 Schmitt, C. 1996. 45.
103 Schmitt, C. 1996. 47–8.

> their interests or principles, but not sufficiently capable of themselves of deciding about war, then a unified political entity would no longer exist. However one may look at it, in the orientation toward the possible extreme case of an actual battle against a real enemy, the political entity is essential, and it is the decisive entity for the friend-or-enemy grouping, and in this (and not any kind of absolutist) sense, it is sovereign. Otherwise the political entity is nonexistent.[104]

To the parapolitical scholar, two questions immediately spring to mind: (i) what is there within Schmitt's own schema that prevents these "counter-forces" from constituting a "sovereign" entity within their own right, and (ii) could these "counter-forces" be defined so as to include clandestine entities?

In his rather late work *The Politics of Friendship* (1994) Derrida posits the possibility of a new form of political crime that, by its very nature, supersedes, and ultimately suspends, all orthodox conceptions of the "natural" relationship between legality and criminality, state and transgression. The *grund* of such a post-juridical aberration is nothing other than that originary violence of *nomos* that has been so well mapped out by Schmitt himself.

> [A] political crime of which it is no longer known—this is the creation of borders—and if it is to be defined *in the order of borders* (for instance, when there is assassination, torture, or terrorism in a given state for political reasons) or if it is a crime *against the political itself*, when in one way or another it puts to death that without which a political crime could no longer be defined or distinguished from other sorts of crimes, when appeal to political reason or to some critique of political reason would no longer be possible.[105]

The parapolitical term for this hitherto nameless entity is *criminal sovereignty* and has been explored most thoroughly by Robert Cribb:

> Parapolitics, then, is the study of criminal sovereignty, of criminals behaving as sovereigns and sovereigns behaving as criminals in a systematic way. It was not just a topic but an analytical conclusion. On the one hand, it goes significantly beyond the proposition that relations between security and intelligence organisations, international criminal networks and quasi-states are occasional and incidental, the work of "rogue elements" and the like. On the other hand, it falls significantly short of grand conspiracy theory: it does not suggest that the world of visible, "normal" politics is an illusion or that it is entirely subordinated to "deep" politics. Rather, it proposes that the tripartite relationship between security and intelligence organisations, international criminal networks and quasi-states is systematic, extensive and influential. The task of parapolitics as a

104 Schmitt, C. 1996. 39. Emphasis added.

105 Derrida, J. 2005. 83.

> discipline is to identify the dynamics of that relationship and to delimit precisely the influence that it has, or does not have, on public politics.[106]

Understood this way, I can hypothesize that criminal sovereignty would possess four necessary attributes: duality (the iterable relationship between "law" and "crime"); governance (the collapse of the distinction between "public state" and "civil society," resulting in an open-ended "privatization" of the state); nomadicism (a chaotic proliferation of supra-statist, statist and sub-statist entities, all of an indeterminate legal nature, that regularly transverse established juro-political boundaries[107]); and the irrational (the invisible co-option of the "public interest" by the "private actor").

All of which, of course, is anathema to Schmitt. As we should expect, Schmitt vigorously upholds the demarcation between politics and crime; more importantly, he insists that war, the *telos* of politics, can only be properly waged by lawful combatants (*justus hostis*). The judicial anomaly of the unlawful combatant—or "partisan" in Schmitt's terminology—threatens the unity of legal discourse; the irregular combatant "confounds the unity and order of the rationalist scheme" (*ius publicum Europaeum*).[108] "Law is the unity of order and orientation, and the problem of the partisan is the problem of relations between regular and irregular struggle";[109] accordingly, it is "political recognition that the irregular fighter needs in order not to be considered in the un-political sense of a thief or a pirate, which here means: not to sink into the criminal realm."[110] The one thing that must never be conceded within this schema is the iterability between the partisan—understood by Schmitt as the "irregular combatant" of the Developing World—and the criminal, for to do so would imperil the entirety of Schmitt's political ontology.

> The intense political [public] character of the partisan must be kept in mind, because he must be distinguished from the ordinary thief and violent criminal, whose motives are directed towards private enrichment. This conceptual criterion of the *political* character [of the partisan] has the *un-political* character of his evil deeds, which are focused on private robbery and theft. The pirate has,

106 Cribb, R. 2009. Introduction: Parapolitics, Shadow Governance and Criminal Sovereignty, in *Government of the Shadows: Parapolitics and Criminal Sovereignty*, edited by E. Wilson. London: Pluto Press. 1–9 at 8.

107 Here, I am employing "nomadicism" in the sense of "the nomadic" as developed by Deleuze, G. and Guattari, F. 1988. *A Thousand Plateaus: Capitalism and Schizophrenia*, trans. Brian Massumi. London: The Athlone Press. 351–423. The nomadic denotes not only a free moving material agent or agency, but also the ontological indeterminacy of the nomadic force, the equivalent of the "un-decidable" in deconstruction.

108 Schmitt, C. 2005. *Political Theology: Four Chapters on the Concept of Sovereignty*, trans. George Schwab. Chicago: University of Chicago. 14.

109 Schmitt, C. 2007. *Theory of the Partisan: Intermediate Commentary on the Concept of the Political*, trans. G. L. Ulmen. New York: Telos Press Publishing. 69.

110 Schmitt, C. 2007. 75.

> as the jurists say, *animus furandi* [evil intent]. The partisan fights at front, and precisely the political character of his acts restores the original meaning of the word *partisan*. The word derives from *party*, and refers to the tie to a fighting, belligerent, or politically active party or group. These ties to a party become especially strong in revolutionary times.[111]

If the boundaries between public and private, polity and property, are shown to be luminal or porous, however, then both the intelligibility (epistemic) and the legitimacy (normative) of the state dissolve: the true source of sovereignty can be crime. And once again it is Schmitt himself who sows the seeds for his own "deconstruction."

Schmitt's etymological pun (partisan = party = politics) is of the greatest importance, precisely because it serves as the site of reversal that the actor/entity of indeterminate judicial status requires in order to acquire political identity through combat—which, as we have already seen, cannot be discursively restricted to the level of inter-state conflict. Precisely because irregular forces are political they are, even if only potentially, sovereign. But, most subversive by far, the irregular force—the one that "confounds the unity and order of the rationalist scheme"—is thoroughly nomadic, migrating not only across boundaries but equally throughout the entirety of *nomos*. It is the violent truth of the partisan—the onto-political "unknown"—that forces Schmitt to contemplate the hitherto unthinkable: civil war and insurrection are moments of decision.

> The equation politics = party politics is possible whenever antagonisms among domestic political parties succeed in weakening the all-embracing political unit, the State. The intensification of internal antagonisms has the effect of weakening the common identity vis-à-vis another State. If domestic conflicts among political parties have become the sole political difference, the most extreme degree of political tension is thereby reached, i.e., the domestic, not the foreign friend-and-enemy groupings are decisive for armed conflict. The ever present possibility of conflict must always be kept in mind. If one wants to speak of politics in the context of the primary of internal politics, then this conflict no longer refers to war between organized nations but to civil war … War is armed combat between organized political entities; civil war is armed combat within an organized unit.[112]

The "intensification of internal antagonisms" signifies a shift toward combat and the political properly so called. It is decisionism itself, the "concept of the intensity of the political [that] allows Schmitt to encompass war and revolution. Now the enemy can easily be conceived as the relative, the brother, the equal."[113]

---

111 Schmitt, C. 2007. 14–15.

112 Schmitt, C. 1996. 32.

113 Meier, H. 1995. 23.

Far from perpetrating a humanitarian outrage, therefore, the state that wages war against its own people is merely exhibiting its Schmittian pedigree—"As long as the State is a political entity [the] requirement for internal peace compels it in critical situations to decide also upon the domestic enemy."[114] And it is the waging of war against "people" in all of its myriad forms, both domestic and foreign, that is the unique preserve of clandestine agency, generically designated the National Security State Complex.[115]

According to Schmitt, within the people's capacity to recognize and name the Enemy "resides the essence of its political existence. When it no longer possesses the capacity or the will to make this distinction, it ceases to exist politically. If it permits this distinction to be made by another, then it is no longer a free people, and is absorbed into another political system."[116] But it is equally true that the parapolitical apparatuses of the state exist precisely in order to covertly manipulate the processes of recognition and de-notation. It follows, therefore, that the ubiquity of the clandestine is itself the primary sign of the lurking presence of an extra-legal form of sovereignty. Hirst has stated this plainly:

> The nuclear-security apparatus reserves to itself considerable powers of control over economic resources, special police measures, etc., and has a capacity for secret policy-making whose limits are difficult to determine. If we take Schmitt's claim seriously that "sovereign is he who decides on the exception" seriously, then most of our formal constitutional doctrines are junk.[117]

"Junk" indeed, although "simulacrum" might be a more accurate term. Seen through parapolitical lenses, Schmitt's onto-politics is revealed to contain a "double movement" at its heart, a perpetual migration between two sets of parallel antinomies: (i) one between the public (political) and the private (covert) forms of the decision; and (ii) other between the outside/inside (*nomos*) and the enemy/friend distinctions. And it is precisely within this eternally unstable double movement that the covert power of the parapolitical resides. The Report of the 9/11 Commission released in 2004 has stated this with remarkable clarity:

> In the post 9/11 world *threats are defined by the fault lines within societies, than by the territorial boundaries between them.* From terrorism to global disease or environmental degradation the challenges have become trans-national rather than inter-national. That is the defining quality of world politics in the [21st century] … In this sense, 9/11 has taught us that that terrorism against American interests "over there" should be regarded just as we regard terrorism against

114 Schmitt, C. 1996. 46.
115 See Chapter 2, this volume.
116 Schmitt, C. 1996. 49.
117 Hirst, P. 1987. 26.

> American interests "over here." *In this same sense, the American homeland is the planet.*[118]

We all know that the originary event of the open-ended (space) and infinitely durable (time) "War on Terror" consisted of nothing more than a sum total of a series of decisions made by clandestine agencies concerning the identity and the presence of the Enemy. In this way, the Second Gulf War constituted a "double" decision: the private and covert one (WMDs) and the public and democratic one (Operation Iraqi Freedom). Yet, the public decision was not the "real" one: it was the simulacrum produced by the anterior (and more primary) covert manipulation of the collective processes of recognition and de-notation. To the extent that international relations and foreign policy are subordinated to the paradigm of "securitization" and the technocratic computations of anticipatory self-defense, true politics becomes the exclusive domain of parapolitical entities who are continuously deciding the emergency within an eternal (and historically suspended) present. With the onto-political reduction of the people to an "un-real" simulacrum, the existentially defining moment of decision escapes "democratic political control"; as Hirst reminds us, "operational decision-making" has become so restricted to such "a small circle of persons that it does not become a simple matter of the 'morally exacting' decision. In that sense we do have a very clear 'sovereign' and a perpetual prospect of the state of exception."[119]

Amor fati.

Conclusion: The Truth of Parapolitics

> Politics is destiny. (Carl Schmitt)

Or should I say: parapolitics is destiny.

Schmitt is the (para-)constitutional architect of the dual state by way of a political ontology of both presence and absence. By presence, he successfully completes the neo-Heideggerian project of uncovering the originary violence of the "junk" democratic/public state, revealing it as the simulacrum of a foundational decisionism. Two of the central components of the parapolitical world-view—the unstable iterability of legal personality and the radical multiplicity of clandestine entities—receive formal philosophical expression through Schmitt's postulation of sovereignty as the juridical correlative of the existential friend–foe distinction. More than any other political theorist of the 20th century, Schmitt has framed most clearly the violence of sovereignty as the dangerous supplement to liberalism.

118 Coker, C. 2009. *War in the Age of Risk.* Cambridge: Polity Press. 76–7. Emphases added.

119 Hirst, P. 1987. 25.

Within Schmitt's (para-)constitutional schema, any entity—private trading companies in the Congo,[120] Swedish and Italian "stay behinds,"[121] The Royal Canadian Mounted Police,[122] even international non-governmental regulatory agencies[123]—is capable of receiving formal (and informal) recognition of sovereignty through the political ontology of decisionism. The unconditionally *existential* nature of politics-as-combat, one that thoroughly supersedes the more formal norms of the ethical or the legal, effectively places the "irregular force" of the parapolitical sovereign outside of the orthodox discursive realms of both law and crime: "criminal sovereignty" is now revealed as a *post-judicial* ontology.

Conversely, by absence Schmitt reveals that if the state is a true plurality, then liberalism can never exhaust the truth (*veritas*) or being (*ratio*) of the post-judicial order. The realm of parapolitical phenomena exists within the fissures of the "deconstructed" Schmittian state (of exception), which is itself identical with the dual state: the absolute splintering of the monsistic "decisive" state is consummated through the unending proliferation of covert decision-making sovereigns. The *grund* of the dual state is *duality* itself; a liminal space of uncertain and un-definable agencies, entities and powers.

The concept of the dual state, then, denotes the irreducible liminality of juridical identity, and, therefore, of onto-political Being (*Sein*). The dual state is not primarily a series of parallel clandestine structures (although it certainly is that), but rather an eternally uncertain and perilous migration across borders, boundaries and walls.

120 See Chapter 6, this volume.

121 See Chapters 8 and 10, this volume.

122 See Chapter 9, this volume.

123 See Chapter 7, this volume.

Chapter 2
State–Corporate Globalization and the Rise and Demise of the New Deal World Order

Tom Reifer

The fall of the Soviet empire and breakup of the USSR raised hopes for a peace dividend that would inaugurate a new era of peace, prosperity and social reconstruction. Instead, recurrent wars in the Persian Gulf and the larger Middle East, along with related conflicts, continue to ensure Cold War levels of U.S. military spending and overseas power projection. The need for better analysis of the socioeconomic and political functions of militarism was brought out tragically by the September 11 terrorist attacks and Anglo-American embrace of a so-called war on terrorism and against what was dubbed an "Axis of Evil." For today, instead of realizing a peace dividend, we are instead seeing resurgence of the National Security State Corporate Complex (NSSCC), denoting the changing and contradictory fusion of U.S. private corporate power and public state bureaucracy.

Yet while National Security ideology and practice is universally traced to World War II and the Cold War, new archival discoveries dramatically reveal its origins in the birth and vast expansion of the U.S. state–corporate nexus during a similar wave of militarized globalization in the late 19th and early 20th centuries.[1] This chapter draws on these new findings to analyse the evolution of this U.S. state–corporate nexus, underscoring its critical role in the rise and demise of the New Deal world order and the reconfiguration of U.S. hegemony and contemporary globalization on increasingly narrow, militarized and financially unstable social foundations.

The original concept of the NSSCC has numerous advantages over alternative formulations, notably President Eisenhower's focus on the nexus between state

1 National Security League. 1916a, *Officers, Committee, and Branches.* National Security League New York. National Security League. 1916b. *Proceedings of the National Security Congress*. Washington, DC. January 20–22, 1916, National Security League National Headquarters, New York; National Security League, January 25–27, 1917, *Proceedings of the Congress of Constructive Patriotism*, Washington, DC. National Security League National Headquarters. New York. This chapter represents a preview of a longer work in progress entitled *Lawyers, Guns and Money: Wall Street and the American Century*.

military power and private firms in the military–industrial complex, an observation that goes back as far back as the work of Aristophanes, as Max Weber pointed out long ago. For the rise of the NSSCC was part of a long process of structural transformation and race, class and gender formation in the Anglo-American warfare-welfare states, intimately related to waves of globalization and global militarization.[2] The utility of the concept of the NSSCC is that it highlights the entwined origins and evolution of the National Security State, the militarized state–corporate nexus and the related development of the U.S. governing class, including the role of corporate lawyers, investment bankers and allied industrialists who have been its primary stewards.[3] The geopolitical economy presented here thus integrates the entwined geopolitical–military and economic realms into a single theoretical framework.

The rise of the NSSCC was the latest organizational revolution in the strategies and structures of state-making, war-making and capital accumulation that have been central to each hegemonic cycle and related stages of global accumulation.[4] The adumbration of this structure of militarized state–corporate capitalism in the late 19th and early 20th centuries provided the model for U.S. hegemony on the enlarged social foundations of the New Deal "warfare-welfare state" and related world order.[5] Yet the contradictions of this New Deal world order undermined its material foundations, hastening its liquidation via regressively financed neoliberal militarization.[6]

During World War II and the early years of the Cold War, U.S. military spending—based on progressive taxation of corporations and the wealthy, with limitations on pecuniary accumulation—provided for the rise of the New Deal world order based on reform at home and support for socioeconomic reconstruction

2 Robert, D. 1991. *Imperial Brotherhood: Gender and the Making of Cold War Foreign Policy*. Amherst: University of Massachusetts Press; Rosenthal, M. 1984. *The Character Factory: Baden-Powell's Boy Scouts and the Imperatives of Empire*. New York: Pantheon.

3 Bird, K. 1992. *The Chairman: John J. McCloy/The Making of the American Establishment*. New York: Simon & Schuster.

4 Arrighi, G. 1994. [2010]. *The Long Twentieth Century: Money, Power and the Origins of Our Times*. New York: Verso. 14; Reifer, T. 2002. Globalization and the National Security State Corporate Complex (NSSCC) in the Long Twentieth Century, in *The Modern/Colonial Capitalist World-System in the 20th Century*, edited by G. Ramon and M. Rodriguez, M. Westport: Greenwood Press. 3–20; Reifer, T. 2009. Capital's Cartographer: Giovanni Arrighi: 1937–2009. *New Left Review*, 60, 119–30. Available at: www.newleftreview.org/?view=2814 (accessed July 6, 2012).

5 O'Connor, J. 1973. *The Fiscal Crisis of the State*. New York: St. Martin's Press; Bensel, F. R. 1984. *Sectionalism and American Political Development: 1880–1980*. Madison: University of Wisconsin Press. 116; Brinkley, A. 1995. *The End of Reform*. New York: Vintage Books.

6 Borrowing money at high interest rates from the wealthy awash in tax cuts was regressive as it resulted in a higher burden of taxation being borne by middle and lower income groups than the rich.

abroad.[7] Yet this U.S. global military spending altered the geopolitical economy, leading to the phoenix-like resurgence of the global capital markets that provided the surplus capital for the United States' increasingly regressively financed remilitarization.[8] Thus, rather than expanding the New Deal world order through taxation on corporate profits and the rich, as during the early phase of the Cold War, new rounds of neoliberal militarization, increasingly deficit-financed through U.S. state borrowing on the global capital markets, helped usher in its global demise.[9]

The contradictions of the New Deal world order thus led to the abandonment of its hallmark—the relative subordination of private to public finance—via regressively financed militarization, which now exerts pressures on social welfare programs across the globe. Neoliberal militarization, in turn, continues to play an important part in the growth of the global capital markets, transnational corporations and U.S.-dominated supranational institutions such as the IMF and World Bank that are among the most conspicuous features of neoliberal globalization.[10] Just as "States competed for mobile capital, which dictated to them the conditions under which it would assist them to power" in the early modern capitalist world, so too is massive U.S. borrowing on the global capital markets increasing the power of bondholders and other wielders of mobile capital over all states.[11]

As in the past, the obverse side of this period of heightened inter-state and inter-firm competition for mobile capital characteristic of waves of globalization and global militarization was the reciprocal stimulus of militarized industry and high finance. Wall Street investment bankers and corporate lawyers handling their legal work were instrumental here, both in supplying the capital necessary for U.S.-deficit financed militarization and in the corporate restructuring of military industry through mergers that increased dependency on high levels of U.S. military expenditures and overseas arms sales.[12] These developments speeded up

7 See Van der Pijl, K. 1984. *The Making of An Atlantic Ruling Class*. London: Verso.

8 See Steinherr, A. 2000. *Derivatives, the Wild Beast of Finance*. New Jersey: John Wiley and Sons. Capital markets are where capital funds, namely debt and equity, are traded, including those in private placements and organized market exchanges, Downes, J. and Goodman, J. E. eds. 1998. *Dictionary of Finance and Investment Terms*. Barron's Financial Guides. Barron's Educational Series. 82.

9 Davis, M. 1986. *Prisoners of the American Dream*. New York: Verso; Davis. Mike. 2002 *Dead Cities*. New York: New Press. Chapter 13.

10 Arrighi, G. 2010; Helleiner, E. 1994. *States and the Reemergence of Global Finance: From Bretton Woods to the 1990s.* Ithaca: Cornell University Press; Broad, R. 1988. *Unequal Alliance*. Berkeley: University of California Press.

11 Weber, M. 1961. *General Economic History*. New York: Collier Books. 249. Canterbery, E. R. 2000. *Wall Street Capitalism: The Theory of the Bondholding Class*. Singapore: World Scientific Publications; Gowan, P. 1999. *The Global Gamble*. New York: Verso. Steinherr, A. 2000.

12 Markusen, A. 1998. The Post-Cold War Persistence of Defence Specialized Firms, in *The Defence Industry in the Post-Cold War Era*, edited by G. I. Susman and S. O'Keefe. Amsterdam: Pergamon. 121–46.

the liquidation of the New Deal world order, while reinforcing the militarization of U.S. foreign policy and power of corporate firms, state agencies and social constituencies at the heart of the NSSCC.

Lawyers, Guns and Money and the Origins of the American Century

In dramatic contrast to previous empires, U.S. hegemonic classes, most especially corporate lawyers and investment bankers, expanded transnational institutions such as multinational corporations, supranational (albeit U.S.-dominated) systems of law and governance, and U.S.-led global military alliances such as the IMF, World Bank, WTO and NATO.[13] C. Wright Mills underscored this centrality of corporate lawyers and investment bankers long ago.[14] In light of Mills' emphasis, not surprisingly, Saskia Sassen, a leading theorist of contemporary globalization, has highlighted the leading role of Anglo-American investment bankers and corporate law firms in the "new set of intermediary strategic agents" in today's global economy.[15] Here, Sassen points to the rise of a new Anglo-American "legal regime" governing "cross-border economic transactions" as well as the "peculiar passion for legality (and lawyers)" driving globalization.[16] The power of investment bankers and corporate lawyers handling their legal work derives from their intermediary role in overlapping processes of war-making, state-making and capital accumulation, as well as the unique role of law and lawyers in the United States. These groups raise funds on the money and capital markets for states and firms, along with engaging in more pure forms of financial speculation.[17]

By the late 19th century, internationally oriented U.S. corporate lawyers "exercised a more profound influence on the formulation of US foreign policy

13 Reifer, T. 2009–2010. Lawyers, Guns and Money: Wall Street Lawyers, Investment Bankers and Global Financial Crises, late 19th to 21st Century. *Nexus: Chapman University Journal of Law and Public Policy*, Special Issue on the 80th Anniversary of the Great Crash of 1929: Law, Markets and the Role of the State, 15, 119–33. Available at: www.tni.org/paper/lawyers-guns-and-money-wall-street-lawyers-investment-bankers-and-global-financial-crises (accessed July 6, 2012).

14 Wright, Mills. C. 1956. *The Power Elite*. New York: Oxford University Press. 288.

15 Saskia, S. 1999. Embedding the Global in the National: Implications for the Role of the State, in *States and Sovereignty in the Global Economy*, edited by D. A. Smith, D. J. Solinger and S. C. Topik. New York: Routledge. 159–60; Saskia, S. 1996. *Losing Control? Sovereignty in an Age of Globalization*. New York: Columbia University Press. 12–21.

16 Saskia, S. 1999. 159–63; Saskia, S. 1996. 5.

17 Quigley, C. 1966. *Tragedy and Hope*. New York: Macmillan Co. 61. Money markets, in contrast to capital markets, are markets for short-term debt instruments, i.e., short-term Treasury bills as opposed to long-term government bonds and so forth (paraphrasing Downes, J. and Goodman, J. E. 1998. 258).

than they had as a group at any time since the founding of the Republic."[18] The ascendancy of corporate lawyers, investment bankers and allied industrialists, was part of the rise of a new bloc of business, government organizations and social classes that have been an integral part of hegemonic transitions. As the growth of capitalist organizations and related legal transformations facilitated increased capital concentration and inequality, Anglo-American elites turned to militarized overseas expansion to deflect rising class conflict at home and to provide outlets for rising surplus capital and productive capacity abroad.[19]

During this period, politico-military conflict was fueled with resources provided by capitalist firms, who used the intensified inter-state competition as engines for their own self-expansion.[20] This was exemplified on the plane of high finance at the turn of the century, as the House of Morgan's incorporation of leading members of the English Establishment helped ensure Britain's turn to the firm to finance hundreds of millions in bond floatation needed for its war of South African conquest.[21] This was the beginning of the transatlantic migration of financial power from London to New York and the ascendancy of the House of Morgan within London-based haute finance.[22]

Moreover, Britain's Boer War helped in turn seal the Anglo-American alliance of World War I and the House's role as the central intermediary in financing and supplying the allies during the conflict, the second major act in this ongoing transfer of world money and power from England to the United States.[23] Yet what is virtually unknown is that the Boer War gave birth to a war preparedness movement in the UK, its white dominions and the U.S. that played a decisive role in U.S. entry into World War I and the making of the modern U.S. Establishment. More importantly, U.S. entry into the war gave further stimulus to the model of state–corporate capitalism that became the basis for the consolidation of NSSCC during World War II and the Cold War, initially on the enlarged social foundations of the New Deal warfare-welfare state and world order.

After the Boer War, a new generation of imperial enthusiasts began a military preparedness movement in England to ready the country for a coming conflagration with Germany. Many of the key leaders of this movement were the followers of Cecil Rhodes, including one-time South African Proconsul and head

18 Boyle, F. A. 1999. *Foundations of World Order*. Durham, NC: Duke University Press. 18.

19 Perrow, C. 2002. *Organizing America: Wealth, Power, and the Origins of Corporate Capitalism*. Princeton: Princeton University Press; Hobson, J. A. 1938. *Imperialism: A Study*. London: George Allen & Unwin; Hobson, J. A. 1928. *The Evolution of Modern Capitalism: A Study of Machine Production*. London. George Allen & Unwin. Chapter 10.

20 Arrighi, G. 2010.

21 Kynaston, D. 1995. *The City of London, Volume II: Golden Years, 1890–1914*. London: Chatto & Windus. 190; Burk, K. 1989. *Morgan Grenfell 1838–1988*. New York: Oxford University Press. 57–9.

22 Kynaston, D. 1995. 270–271. Burk, K. 1989. 111–25.

23 Kynaston, D. 1995; Burk, K. 1989. 125–34.

of the Rhodes Trust Alfred Milner, a leading figure of the British Establishment, who along with his acolytes played a key role in forming the racist Union of South Africa in 1910 and the adumbration of apartheid.[24] The key preparedness organization in England was the National Service League (1903), whose original executive committee included London House of Morgan partner, and close friend and associate of Alfred Milner, Clinton Dawkins. Milner and his acolytes later organized the Round Table group and related influential Establishment think tanks, the Institute for International Affairs, in Britain and the dominions, working closely with their U.S. counterparts in the Council on Foreign Relations (CFR) and U.S. Round Table Dining Club.[25]

The leading war preparedness organization in the United States, modeled after its English counterpart, was the National Security League (NSL), headed by Theodore Roosevelt's former Ambassador to England from 1899 to 1905, Joseph Choate.[26] Choate, like his counterpart, colleague and friend Lord Roberts, were the respective Presidents of the Anglo-American friendship groups, the Pilgrims Society of England and of the United States, formed in 1902 and 1903 respectively.[27] A leading corporate lawyer, Choate had argued the case in the Supreme Court striking down the income tax on behalf of wealthy U.S. families and firms in the late 19th century. Choate went on to serve as an Executive Committee member of the Carnegie Endowment, and to represent the Rockefellers in their anti-trust cases and the House of Morgan in the Money Trust Congressional investigations of 1912–1913. The Money Trust investigations are important here as they document

24 Magubane, B. M. 1994. *The Round Table Movement: Its Influence on the Historiography of Imperialism*. South Africa: Printing and Publishing House; Magubane, B. M. 1996. *The Making of a Racist State: British Imperialism and the Union of South Africa 1875–1910*. Trenton: Africa World Press; Marlowe, J. 1976. *Milner, Apostle of Empire*. London: Hamish Hamilton; Bosco, A. and May, A. 1997. *The Round Table, The Empire/Commonwealth and British Foreign Policy*. London: Lothian Foundation Press.

25 Round Table Dining Club. 1958. *The Roster of the Round Table Dining Club*. Privately Printed; Quigley, C. 1966; Quigley, C. 1981. *The Anglo-American Establishment: From Rhodes to Cliveden*. New York: Books in Focus. There is not the time or the space to go into the secret aims of British foreign policy during this period. See however the important works of Wilson, K. M. 1985. *The Policy of the Entente: Essays on the Determinants of British Foreign Policy, 1904–1914*. Cambridge: Cambridge University Press and Narizny, K. 2007. *The Political Economy of Grand Strategy*. Ithaca: Cornell University Press, both of which have to be understood in terms of the theory of logrolled coalitions and myths of empire analysed by scholars from Eckart Kehr to Jack Snyder. This can be fruitfully compared with the latest restatement of the more traditional view in Steiner, Z. S. and Neilson, K. 2003. *Britain and the Origins of the First World War*. Second Edition. London: Palgrave Macmillan.

26 Chambers II, J. W. 1987. *To Raise an Army*. New York: Free Press.

27 Baker, A. P. 2002. *The Pilgrims of Great Britain: A Centennial History*. London: Profile Books; Baker, A. P. 2003. *The Pilgrims of the United States: A Centennial History*. London: Profile Books.

the politico-economic power the House of Morgan later brought to bear in funding and organizing the U.S. war preparedness movement.[28]

Resources from the Rhodes Trust, Money Trust and Carnegie Trust helped bankroll the Anglo-American war preparedness movement which, reinforcing the host of structural geopolitical-economic interests between the UK and United States, paved the way for the wartime alliance of the two states. At the heart of the Anglo-American war preparedness movement, in both the UK and the United States, not to mention other white settler states, such as Australia, Canada and New Zealand, were each countries' respective albeit interconnected Round Table groups.[29] Here, as one historian has written of the House of Morgan during this period, was the "Anglo-American alliance in microcosm."[30] With the help of leaders of the House of Morgan who were actively funding and participating in the Anglo-American war preparedness movement, such as Robert Bacon and Henry Davison, the firm secured its role as the central intermediary in financing and supplying the allies. Bacon was a one-time J. P. Morgan partner and one of the directors of the House of Morgan's U.S. Steel, the world's first billion dollar corporation. Davison was one of the largest funders of the National Security League, and Bacon its President. Many of the leading participants, financiers and beneficiaries of the war preparedness movement were men and firms identified in the Money Trust investigations of 1912–1913.[31] The preparedness activities of these power elites during World War I and World War II were run to a significant extent out of the

---

28 De Long, J. B. 1992. Money Trust, in *The New Palgrave Dictionary of Money and Finance*, edited by P. Newman, M. Milgate and J. Eatwell. London: Macmillan. 192; Hobson, J. A. 1938. The inquiries revealed that prior to World War I, corporate securities floatation of $10 million or more invariably passed through J.P. Morgan or related investment banking firms such as Kuhn Loeb, First National Bank, National City Bank and Lee, Higginson and Company, giving them immense politico-economic power. De Long, J. B. 1992. 808–10. As de Long notes, "The partners and directors of these institutions were directors, voting trustees, or major stockholders of corporations with a total capitalization—debt plus equity—including subsidiaries, of nearly $30 billion." Brandeis, L. D. 1914. *Other People's Money, and How the Bankers Use It*. New York: Frederick A. Stokes. "In perspective, this sum bore the same relation to the size of the U.S. economy then that $7.5 trillion bears today; it amounted to one and a half years' national product and 40 percent of the country's produced capital." Goldsmith, R. 1954. *The Balance Sheet of the United States*. Princeton: Princeton University Press.

29 See Marlowe, J. 1976. See United States Congress. *National Security League*. Volume I–II. 1918. 1919. Round Table Dining Club. 1958.

30 Chernow, R. 1990. *The House of Morgan*. New York: Simon & Schuster. 98.

31 United States Congress. *National Security League*. Volume I–II. 1918. 1919. Chernow, R. 1990. 190 and 128–30. Earlier, Davison played a major role in founding the Federal Reserve in 1913, a process crucial in both the class formation of the U.S. ruling class and rise of U.S. hegemony. Livingston, J. 1986. *Origins of the Federal Reserve System: Money, Class and Corporate Capitalism, 1890–1913*. Ithaca: Cornell University Press; Lawrence, J. B. 1997. *The International Origins of the Federal Reserve System*. Ithaca: Cornell University Press.

Harvard, Yale and Bankers Clubs, as well as the law and investment banking firms of New York City.[32]

One of the most important NSL leaders was Elihu Root, Secretary of War and State under President McKinley and President Theodore Roosevelt, President of the Carnegie Endowment and the creator and Honorary President of the CFR. Root, along with Choate, who he succeeded after the latter's death as Honorary President of the NSL, were both members of the influential Round Table Dining Club in the United States, whose origins go back to the late 19th century, and which included a *Who's Who* of the American Establishment, including Leonard Wood, the key figure in the Plattsburgh military preparedness movement. Wood was inspired in this by his meeting with Lord Roberts, British Commander General in the Boer War, who subsequently headed the National Service League in England, until he was succeeded by the leading figure in the British Round Table movement, Alfred Milner. The U.S. Round Table Dining Club also included prominent members of the House of Morgan, such as Thomas Lamont and John W. Davis, the latter the House of Morgan's long time general counsel and President of the Council on Foreign Relations from 1921 to 1955.

Root worked closely with his former corporate law partner Henry Stimson in the war preparedness effort. Root and Stimson were widely considered two of the founding fathers of the modern American Establishment.[33] Stimson was particularly important here, for he served as either Secretary of War or State to Presidents Taft, Hoover, FDR and Harry Truman. Stimson's influence on his protégés, notably Robert Lovett, Harvey and McGeorge Bundy and John Jay McCloy—a number of whom went onto serve at the highest levels in many of the most powerful institutions of the NSSCC during the American Century—was profound.[34]

Participants in the NSL, the volunteer military training movement and the Yale Naval Aviation unit financed by Morgan partners, included towering figures of the American Century such as "Wild Bill Donovan," founder of the Wall Street filled OSS and CIA; future Stimson aides Robert Lovett, who became Truman's Defence Secretary, John J. McCloy—once nicknamed Chairman of the U.S. Establishment—and Harvey Bundy, father of William and McGeorge, prominent Cold War statesmen and key architects of the Vietnam War.[35]

---

32 Clifford, J. G. and Spencer, Jr., S. R. 1986. *The First Peacetime Draft*. Lawrence: University Press of Kansas; Wood, L. 1909–1918. *Diaries*. Washington, DC: Library of Congress Archives.

33 Isaacson, W. and Thomas, E. 1986. *The Wise Men: Six Friends and the World They Made*. New York: Simon & Schuster. Bird, K. 1992.

34 Bird, K. 1992. Isaacson, W. and Thomas, E. 1986.

35 National Security League. 1916b. *Proceedings of the National Security Congress*. Washington, DC, January 20–22, 1916, National Security League National Headquarters, New York; National Security League, *Proceedings of the Congress of Constructive*

> These men helped establish a distinguished network connecting Wall Street, Washington, worthy foundations, and proper clubs. "The New York financial and legal community," former JFK aide Arthur Schlesinger, Jr. wrote in 1965, "was the heart of the American Establishment. Its household deities were Henry L. Stimson and Elihu Root; its present leaders, Robert A. Lovett and John J. McCloy; its front organizations, the Rockefeller, Ford and Carnegie foundations and the Council on Foreign Relations."[36]

And one could add the U.S. Round Table Dining Club and the NSL, as the war preparedness movement was headed by many of the same men, notably Wall Street corporate lawyers, investment bankers and allied industrialists who presided over the corporate revolution of U.S. capitalism, facilitating the repression of workers at home and expansion of state–corporate power abroad.[37] This was a formative period in the making of American militarized state–corporate capitalism and the U.S. Establishment. In the U.S. war preparedness movement and related state–corporate war collectivism, "Public and private policy became irremediably intertwined."[38] So, when United States entered the war, its first act was to grant the allies a billion dollars in credit, thereby shoring up transatlantic finance, trade and geopolitical alliances.[39] U.S. entry into the war brought corporate dollar-a-year men into the state to run the wartime economy, presaging arrangements in World War II. This fusion of private corporate power and public state bureaucracy became the model for the NSSCC, reconstituted on changing social foundations during the rise and demise of the New Deal world order.[40]

Patriotism, Washington, DC, January 25–27, 1917, National Security League National Headquarters, New York; Bird, K. 1992; Isaacson, W. and Thomas, E. 1986.

36 Isaacson, W. and Thomas, E. 1986. 28–9 and 47–8. See also Bird, K. 1992.

37 National Security League. *Proceedings of the National Security Congress.* Washington. DC. January 20–22, 1916. National Security League National Headquarters. New York. 1916b, National Security League. *Proceedings of the Congress of Constructive Patriotism*. Washington. D.C. January 25–27, 1917, National Security League National Headquarters. New York. 1917.

38 McNeill, W. H. 1982. *The Pursuit of Power: Technology, Armed Force, and Society since A.D. 1000.* Chicago: University of Chicago Press. 292–3 and 327.

39 Chernow, R. 1990. 201.

40 "Corporate dollar-a-year men" refers to the fact that corporate officials joined the wartime state while continuing to be paid by their private firms, and only nominally paid by the government, a dollar a year; hence the term dollar a year. This also bears similarities to England's gentry, which at Max Weber noted, took over local government in the interest of their own social power. This then was a quite distinctive aspect of Anglo-American and U.S. entwined processes of class and state formation. McNeill, W. H. 1982. 346.

In the Shadow of Versailles: Anglo-American Capital, the Axis Powers and Rise of the New Deal World Order

After the war, Anglo-American funneling of billions in liquidity into the militarized material expansions of the future Axis powers then moving inexorably to the right, Italy, Japan and Germany, was of world-historical significance. Important too was the related industrial investment, cartel agreements and diplomatic support for the new Germany from influential networks, including members of All Souls, the Round Table, Chatham House, the CFR, and the City–Bank of England–Treasury nexus.[41] These developments laid the foundations for the world arms race in the wake of the Great Depression that ultimately helped stimulate a new militarized material expansion of the world economy. America's geo-economic interests in the future Axis powers here presaged their postwar restoration that was so instrumental in the origins and evolution of the Cold War.[42]

During the 1920s the White Anglo-Saxon Protestant (WASP) Establishment grouped around Wall Street, notably the House of Morgan, dominated the capital markets, infrastructural investments and heavy industry. Yet, ironically, the rapid growth of the working class and material production stimulated by inter-

---

41 Hersh, B. 1992. *The Old Boys: The American Elite and the Origins of the CIA*. New York: Charles Scribner's Sons. See Chernow, R. 1990. 277–8, 337–45; Newton, S. 1991. The "Anglo-German Connection" and the Political Economy of Appeasement. *Diplomacy and Statecraft*, 2/3, 178–207; Newton, D. 1997. *British Policy and the Weimar Republic 1918–1919*. Oxford: Clarendon; Bosco, A. and May, A. 1997. Fears of Bolshevism at home and abroad, including concerns that a war would shift power to the left in England and lead to the dismantling of its empire abroad, as well as related material interests in Anglo-German cooperation, led to widespread English elite support for Germany (Newton, S. 1991). Furthermore, a number of the leading policymakers who played critical roles in imposing the harsh Versailles Treaty on Germany that greatly weakened Weimar democracy and paved the way for the rise of Nazism, notably influential members of the British Round Table, became key supporters of cooperation with Nazi Germany and the policy of so-called appeasement—or more accurately collaboration with the Nazis (Newton, D. 1997. 426); see Newton, S. 1991. Bosco, A. and May, A. 1997 and Newton, D. 1997 makes the salient point that many of England's policymakers "refused" "'Appeasement', from a position of dominance, that would have strengthened the founders of the Weimar Republic ... but 'appeasement', from a position of weakness, designed to buy time and deflect the threat of Nazism onto others, was granted to the Nazi destroyers of that same republic." Newton, D. 1997. 426. See Green, S. J. D. and Peregrine H. 2011. *All Souls and the Wider World: Statesmen, Scholars, and Adventurers, c. 1850–1950*. Oxford: Oxford University Press. Thanks to Peregrine Horden for sending me a complimentary review copy of this book. See also Chapter 1, All Souls, the British Empire, and World Power 1897–1918 in Louis, W. R. 1992. *In the Name of God, Go! Leo Amery and the British Empire in the Age of Churchill*. New York: W.W. Norton and Company and Chapter 5, The Milner Group, Rhodes, and Oxford, 1901–1925, in Quigley, C. 1981.

42 Simpson, C. 1995. *The Splendid Blond Beast: Money, Law, and Genocide in the Twentieth Century*. Monroe: Common Courage; Hersh, B. 1992; Van der Pijl, K. 1984.

state militarization from the late 19th century on facilitated the steady rise of industrial capital within the overall profit distribution process. In the context of mass working class protest, economic crisis and transformation, the second-generation ethnic immigrants that formed the bulk of the CIO, elite ethnic groups and newly independent capital groups that had escaped Morgan control, broke the stranglehold of the old WASP Establishment on the commanding heights of the corporate economy.[43]

These conditions led to the passage of much of the historic legislation creating basic U.S. social provisions, albeit through an unequal system of civil, social and political citizenship stratified by race, gender, class and nation.[44] A host of New Deal reforms during this period dismantled investment banking control over the capital markets, unleashing technologically advanced U.S. industrially based multinationals and their commercial banks. In addition, the second New Deal paved the way for the military "tax-led" industrialization of the Sunbelt, which became the promised region for the New Right, one dependent on high-levels of military spending and the overseas projection of U.S. military influence for its continued profits and power.[45]

Wartime remilitarization facilitated the rise of internally generated corporate funds. With the help of government, industry thus became self-financing, for a time displacing the powerful influence of financiers. During this wartime period, the NSSCC, whose origins stretched back to the entwined expansion of the U.S. naval and steel industry at the turn of the century, was thus reborn on broader social foundations.[46] Here, the ascendance of the NSSCC governing class that came with the re-entry of corporate lawyers and investment bankers of the Wall Street Stimsonian Establishment into the wartime state—now increasingly serving the needs of industrial capital—led to both the New Deal's wartime transformation and partial liquidation as well as its globalization during the early years of the Cold War. Important in this was the creation of the regime of fixed exchange rates that helped produce a climate of global expansion conducive to the socioeconomic objectives of the New Deal world order.[47]

---

43 Van der Pijl, K. 1984; Davis, M. 1986.

44 Jenkins, J. C. and Brents, B. G. 1989. Social Protest, Hegemonic Competition and Social Reform: A Political Struggle Interpretation of the Origins of the American Welfare State. *American Sociological Review*, 54, 891–909; Gordon, L. 1994. Welfare Reform: A History Lesson. *Dissent*, 323–8; Brown, M. 1999. *Race, Money and the American Welfare State*. Ithaca: Cornell University Press.

45 See Part II, in Davis, M. 1986; Davis, M. 1990. *City of Quartz*. New York: Verso. 120 and 386–93.

46 Brinkley, A. 1995. See Krause, P. 1992. *The Battle for Homestead 1880–1892*. Pittsburgh: University of Pittsburgh Press. See Misa, T. 1995. *A Nation of Steel*. Baltimore: The Johns Hopkins Press.

47 See Arrighi, G. 1994. 295–6.

Militarization, Neoliberal Globalization and the Demise of the New Deal World Order

Many structures of the NSSCC—the National Security Council, the CIA, the Joint Chiefs of Staff and an independent Air Force—were formally consolidated in 1947 with the passage of the National Security Act, often supported by the Stimsonian alumni of the World War I preparedness movement and protégés, who then often later headed many of its most prominent institutions, including some of the most prominent members of the U.S. Round Table Dining Club (1958, 1968). These included Allen Dulles, John Jay McCloy, General (and later President) Dwight Eisenhower, and James Conant, long time President of Harvard University, co-director of the Manhattan Project, and founder and head of the original Committee on the Present Danger.[48] As in World War I, the entry of corporate dollar-a-year men into the U.S. state assured corporate power within agencies overseeing foreign affairs, the military and macroeconomic policy.[49] Yet the full emergence of the U.S. warfare-welfare state and NSSCC only came with the rise in military spending from roughly $10 to $50 billion, setting off the Korean War boom.

This fulfilled the policy of NSC 68, drafted in the spring of 1950 by corporate lawyer, Secretary of State Dean Acheson and aide, Paul Nitze, a Dillon Read investment banker heading the State Department's Policy Planning Staff.[50] NSC 68 provided for the militarized material expansion of the world economy and enmeshment of allies into U.S. global military alliances as "semi-sovereign states," limiting nationalism through a global U.S. informal empire containing enemies and allies. Changes that might close markets, curtail U.S. access to resources, break up the world economy, or stimulate aggression by depriving the Eurasian core of hinterlands, were minimized through U.S. overseas military alliances and a global program of counterrevolutionary violence to ensure an Open Door for corporate capital.[51] At the same time, in the interest of reviving Japan as the industrial workshop of East Asia, reintegrating the region into the world economy while building up counterweights in the global balance of power against the USSR and China, the U.S. tolerated radical restrictions on U.S. foreign direct investment there.[52]

Equally important, U.S. planners used the economic stimulus provided by such military spending to successfully redirect U.S. labor away from its efforts to expand universalistic social programs and organize the South through

48 Grose, P. 1994. *Gentleman Spy: The Life of Allen Dulles*. Boston: Houghton Mifflin Company; Grose, P. 1996. *Continuing the Inquiry: The Council on Foreign Relations from 1921 to 1996*. New York: Council on Foreign Relations.

49 Davis, M. 1986. 165.

50 Borden, W. S. 1984. *The Pacific Alliance*. Madison: University of Wisconsin Press.

51 Borden, W. S. 1984; Davis, M. 1986.

52 Cumings, B. 1998. The Korean Crisis and the End of "Late" Development. *New Left Review*, 231, 43–72. Borden, W. S., 1984.

Operation Dixie as part of its plans for postwar social democracy. Workers were incorporated instead as junior partners in the overseas expansion of U.S. state–corporate power, with military spending providing for private welfare states tied to the firm.[53] Universalistic social programs were sacrificed to garner support for Cold War policies from right-wing Asia-first Republicans and Southern Democrats, the Congressional hold of the latter a legacy of slavery, the defeat of black reconstruction, the exclusion of Southern blacks from the New Deal and labor's alliance with the Southern-dominated Democratic Party.[54]

Wartime mobilization in World War II and the Cold War did much to halt the progressive transformation of race, class and gender relations essential to the reform thrust of the New Deal. Unionization by bureaucratic fiat in World War II and the Cold War—via injections of military spending—took a lethal toll, becoming a substitute for mass organizing in solidarity with women and persons of color who increasingly formed the bulk of the U.S. working class. Such developments reinforced racial, gender segregation and related forms of craft exclusivism among organized labor and the working class.[55] The purging of up to a million members of the CIO's left-led unions was a heavy blow here to the struggle for racial/gender equality and working class mobilization for social reform. For despite the racism of the white working class and all the CIO's failures in organizing in solidarity with persons of color and female workers, notable progress had been achieved in these areas, especially by the CIO's left unions.[56] Given the relationship between employment and public and private social provisions, the curtailing of the CIO and labor reform further reinforced the stratification of the warfare-welfare state and U.S. as a whole by race, gender, class and nation.

This bifurcated structure of the U.S. ruling class, largely divided between its Sunbelt and North-eastern segments, consolidated a "trifurcated" New Deal warfare-welfare state and related unequal system of social and political citizenship.[57] Instead of universalistic programs, veteran's benefits, the watershed GI Bill of Rights, low interest loans and unemployment benefits initially went primarily to white male citizen-soldiers. Social Security entitlements went for shop-floor citizens, also initially largely white males, who benefited from militarily subsidized private welfare states tied to firms. Second-class means tested benefits,

---

53 See Davis, M. 1986.

54 Davis, M. 1986. Du Bois, W. E. B. 1969. *Black Reconstruction in America*. New York: Atheneum.

55 Davis, M. 1986.

56 Davis, M. 1986.

57 See Campbell, A. D. 1997. *The Invisible Welfare State: Class Struggles, the American Legion and the Development of Veteran's Benefits in the Twentieth Century United States*. Dissertation. UCLA. Ann Arbor. 107; Gordon, L. 1994. 323–8; Gordon, L. 1998. *Pitied But Not Entitled: Single Mothers and the History of Welfare*. Cambridge, MA: Harvard University Press.

stigmatized as welfare, went disproportionately to women, persons of color and the poor.[58] This unequal system of social and political citizenship in the U.S. warfare-welfare state provided for the incorporation of organized labor and veterans as junior partners in U.S. hegemony, helped ensure labor's hostility to the civil rights, student, anti-war and feminist movements. This in turn facilitated the rise of the New Right and right turn of the Eastern Establishment.[59]

In these ways, the stratification of the New Deal warfare-welfare state by race, gender and class facilitated the decline of U.S. unionism. The movement of capital to the United States and global South, along with the resentment against and scapegoating of "welfare" recipients, helped paved the way for the break-up of the New Deal coalition, the rise of the New Right and the demise of the New Deal world order.[60] Here, the creation of militarily subsidized private welfare states tied to firms, rather than universalistic social provisions, created huge incentives and means for employers to send capital to the United States and global South, so as to undermine unions at home once profits came under pressure. U.S. foreign policy, by destroying unions and nationalist governments in much of the Third World, thus helped create the conditions for such overseas capital flight.[61]

Southern domination of Congress and its committees due to disenfranchisement of blacks and the seniority system also played a major part in this rightward shift by ensuring that federal military spending was disproportionately transferred to the Sunbelt. This promised region of the New Right—the "land of sunshine and the Open Shop"—is now the most militarily dependent in the country.[62] The region continues to provide a "geographical 'safe-house' for capital," having providing an exit from unions and the New Deal at home even before the massive expansion of capital abroad.[63]

In addition to these developments, over time, the militarized material expansion of the world economy eventually ushered in growing amounts of money capital that could not be profitably invested in trade and production. As full employment and global economic competition increased, profitable opportunities for expanding trade and production correspondingly decreased.[64] The New Deal coalition and

58 Campbell, A. D. 1997.

59 Brown, M. 1999. Davis, M. 1986. Ellsberg, D. April 3, 1990. Unions, Conversion, Social Democracy: A Line of Advance for the Post-Cold War US? Unpublished paper.

60 Gordon, L. 1994. 323–8. Gordon, L. 1998. Davis, M. 1986.

61 Broad, R. 1988. Ellsberg, D. April 3, 1990.

62 Davis, M. 1990. 106–20. Kane, M. *Research Report: Defence Spending in the Northeast-Midwest: Fiscal 2000*. September 2001. Northeast-Midwest Institute; Trubowitz, P. 1998. *Defining the National Interest: Conflict and Change in American Foreign Policy*. Chicago: University of Chicago Press; Luker, Jr., B. 1997. The Public Sector and Sunbelt Development. *Challenge*, 58–82; Wiley, P. and Gottlieb, R. 1982. *Empires in the Sun: The Rise of the New American West*. Tucson: University of Arizona Press.

63 Moody, K. 1988. *An Injury to All: The Decline of American Unionism*. London: Verso. 39. Du Bois, W. E. B. 1969; Davis, M. 1986. 194–5; Markusen, A. 1998. 131.

64 Arrighi, G. 1994. 300–324.

related world order thus became increasingly unsustainable in the context of the guns and butter policy pursued by U.S. officials during the Vietnam War. The 1968 balance of payments crisis, triggered by speculative attacks against the dollar and the related fixed exchange rates regime, exemplified the growing contradictions of the New Deal world order and between the power pursuits of the U.S. state and the profit imperatives of U.S. multinational corporations.[65]

U.S. firms were increasingly keeping dollars abroad to escape taxation and restrictions on foreign direct investment seen as essential by state managers to meet the huge fiscal burdens of the U.S. warfare-welfare state. Yet this merely increased incentives for overseas borrowing and the non-repatriation of dollars to the United States.[66] The result was the vast growth of the Eurocurrency markets facilitated by U.S. money-centered banks, multinational firms and the City–Bank of England–Treasury nexus.[67] Over time, this led to the U.S. abandonment of the gold-dollar standard and the move to flexible exchange rates.[68]

The end of the regime of fixed exchange rates shifted the burden of foreign exchange risks from public authorities to private firms, compelling transnational corporations to further globalize their operations and states to liberalize their capital controls. This was needed to hedge against fluctuations in currency values by diversifying the geographical location of firms and the portfolio holdings of currencies by states.[69] Government borrowing further increased the volume of world liquidity, exacerbating global stagnation and world inflation, while undermining state control over world monetary policy.[70] Demand for liquidity by states needed to cope with the heightened mobility and volatility of capital flows, exchange and interest rate fluctuations, as well as speculative attacks against their currencies, thus increased exponentially, to the great benefit of Wall Street from the 1980s to the 2000s.[71]

President Richard M. Nixon's grand design had been to lessen the contradictions of U.S. hegemony by adopting an offshore naval-air strategy while supporting

---

65 Arrighi, G. 1994. 300–324. Helleiner, E. 1994.

66 Burk, K. ed. 1992. Witness Seminar on the Origins and Early Development of the Eurobond Market. *Contemporary European History*, 1/1, 65–87; Strange, S. 1986. *Casino Capitalism*. Oxford: Basil Blackwell. 5–20.

67 Burn, G. 1999. The State, the City and the Euromarkets. *Review of International Political Economy*, 6/2, 225–61; Ingham, G. 1994. States and Markets in the Production of World Money: Sterling and the Dollar, in *Money, Power and Space*, edited by S. Corbridge, R. Martin and N. Thrift. New York: Basil Blackwell. 29–48.

68 Helleiner, E. 1994; Burk, K. 1992; Strange, S. 1986. 5–22; Gowan, P. 1999; Schurmann, F. 1987. *The Foreign Politics of Richard Nixon: The Grand Design*. Berkeley: University of California Press.

69 Eatwell, J. and Taylor, L. 2000. *Global Finance at Risk*. New York: New Press. Chapter 1; Strange, S. 1986. 8–20; Arrighi, G. 1994. 310–11; Gowan, P. 1999.

70 Strange, S. 1986. 8–20; Arrighi, G. 1994. 306–24.

71 Gowan, P. 1999. Reifer, T. 2009–2010. 119–33.

increased oil prices and the exchange of petrodollar payments for U.S. protection.[72] As Europe and Japan were heavily dependent on dollar-denominated oil, hundreds of billions of dollars were recycled back—via U.S. Middle Eastern client states—into U.S. Treasury securities, military-industrial, financial and energy-related construction firms, notably those based in the Sunbelt, such as Bechtel and Halliburton's Kellog, Brown and Root.[73] This exchange of petrodollar payments for protection made the Middle East ever more central in the U.S. informal empire, assuring flows of liquidity into the NSSCC and continued denomination of oil in dollars necessary for U.S. privileges of seigniorage, the right to mint the coin of the realm.[74]

Yet the embrace of floating exchange rates along with the vast increase in the price of oil and the related recycling of petrodollars into large scale purchases of U.S. exports, notably from arms related firms, all contributed to the further globalization, financialization and militarization of the world system. These developments thus increased the power of the core firms, state agencies and social constituencies at the heart of the NSSCC.[75] Over time, these contradictions of the New Deal coalition and world order contributed to the global stagflation that helped to usher in the rise of the broad based Anglo-American New Right and the era of Thatcherism and Reaganism.[76]

Today, the turn of the century Anglo-American axis of money capital based on New York and the City of London has been reconstructed. The hallmark of the New Deal world order, the relative subordination of private to public finance, has been jettisoned in favor of structural adjustment loans and volatile forms of speculative capital such as hedge funds that played such an important role in the East Asian financial crisis.[77] The United States had earlier tolerated restrictions on

72 Schurmann, F. 1987; Hulbert, M. 1982. *Interlock*. New York: Richardson and Snyder; Bill, J. A. 1988. *The Eagle and the Lion: The Tragedy of American-Iranian Relations*. New Haven: Yale University Press; Spiro, D. E. 1999. *The Hidden Hand of American Hegemony: Petrodollar Recycling and International Markets*. Ithaca: Cornell University Press.

73 Schurmann, F. 1987; Wiley, P. and Gottlieb, R. 1982; Pratt, J. A. and Castaneda, C. 1999. *Builders: Herman and George R. Brown*. Austin: Texas A and M University Press.

74 Spiro, D. E. 1999.

75 Strange, S. 1986. 5–14. Bichler, S. and Nitzan, J. 1995. Bringing Capital Accumulation Back In: The Weapondollar-Petrodollar Coalition-Military Contractors, Oil Companies and Middle East "Energy Conflicts." *Review of International Political Economy*, II–III, 446–515; Bichler, S. and Nitzan, J. 1996. Putting the State Back In its Place: US Foreign Policy and Differential Capital Accumulation in Middle East "Energy Conflicts." *Review of International Political Economy*, 3/4, 608–61; Davis, M. 1986.

76 Davis, M. 1986; Helleiner, E. 1994; Boies, J. 1994. *Buying for Armageddon*. New Brunswick: Rutgers University Press.

77 Gowan, P. 1999; De Brouwer, G. 2001. *Hedge Funds in Emerging Markets*. Cambridge: Cambridge University Press. On the devastating impact of neoliberal structural adjustment programs and/or speculative capital flows forcing states to cut social

its foreign capital penetration of East Asia. With the fall of the USSR, the United States moved forcefully to open up the regions markets to U.S. investment and speculative capital flows, thus helping to pave the way for the Asian economic crisis.[78] Moreover, the expansionary fiscal policies for "development" promoted in the Third World during the early Cold War years as a whole was relegated to a thing of the past.[79]

The U.S. boom cycles of the 1980s, 1990s and 2000s had a historical precedent. Just as the old exclusive WASP Establishment reaped the fruits of the inflated capital values of a bygone era in the 1920s, so too has the rise of a broad based New Right aimed to valorize the accumulated gains of corporate capital and the broad propertied strata from the 1980s right up to the present. This new hegemonic social bloc—which included the more privileged segments of the white ethnic working classes and middle strata, arrayed against workers of color, labor and the poor—was initially solidified through President Ronald Reagan's military Keynesianism and the then unparalleled opportunities for financial accumulation that its regressive financing allowed, and more recently with the stock market and housing bubbles, right up until the 2008 global financial crisis and Great Recession.[80]

Whereas earlier Republicans traditionally had been fiscally conservative, tilting toward the high-tech sectors of the Air Force and Navy, Democrats had historically embraced expansionary fiscal policies. Reagan gave elites from the corporate, state sector and upper-middle strata the best of both worlds, by funding military spending in the most regressive way possible, taxing the poor, working class and middle strata rather than corporations and the rich.[81] And as states and firms competed "for mobile capital," its wielders, notably investment bankers and corporate lawyers handling their legal work, once again "dictated to them the conditions under which" they "would assist them to power."[82]

At roughly the same time the leveraged buyout movement orchestrated by investment bankers and corporate lawyers got underway on Wall Street, Reagan initiated a "leveraged buyout of the country" via regressively financed militarization, notably through U.S. government issuance and rollover of some $13.5 trillion in marketable securities from 1981 to 1990.[83] America's deficit-financed militarization here simultaneously consolidated the power of the NSSCC and the larger Wall Street–Federal Reserve–Treasury–Bretton Woods nexus of

---

expenditures and sell off national firms to transnational capital, see Ellsberg, D. April 3, 1990; Broad, R. 1988; Gowan, P. 1999.

78 Cumings, B. 1998; Bhagwati, J. 2000. *The Wind of the Hundred Days: How Washington Mismanaged Globalization*. Cambridge, MA: MIT Press; Gowan, P. 1999.

79 Broad, R. 1988; Arrighi, G. 1994. Chapter 4.

80 Davis, M. 1986. 302, 157–255; Reifer, T. 2009–2010.

81 Davis, M. 1986.

82 Weber, M. 1961. 249; Markusen, A. 1998. 121–46.

83 Smith, Roy C. 1993. *Comeback: The Restoration of American Banking Power in the New World Economy*. Boston: Harvard Business School. 19 and 87.

which it is a part. This structure has alternately provided for the subordination of money capital to productive expansion, the vast growth of money capital and policies of "stock market Keynesianism" combined with supply-side economics, or the end of expansionary fiscal policies.[84] Funding for the NSSCC would now come at the cost of New Deal social programs and policies. Sales of U.S. public debt provided a means for raising money for the state by selling it to private investors. U.S. borrowing at high rates gave a huge shot in the arm to the global capital markets, so crucial in the Wall Street boom and recurrent speculative bubbles, from the stock market boom to subprime mortgages.[85] The obverse side of this was the devastation of the highly indebted global South, including U.S. urban areas increasingly populated by persons of color, immigrants and the poor, and the growing polarization of wealth and income at home and abroad, which led the Occupy Wall Street movement and its rapid spread across the globe.[86]

The accumulation of excess liquidity on the money market with the rise of institutional investors combined with the threats to the commercial banking industry and U.S. military–industrial and monetary supremacy in the 1970s and 1980s thus became translated into an increasingly assertive U.S. foreign policy in both the politico-military and economic spheres. The fall of U.S. client states Iran and Kuwait, along with the Soviet invasion of Afghanistan also generated support for an increasingly aggressive foreign policy to counter heightened threats to U.S. control over Middle Eastern oil. Power elites aimed to restore U.S. profits and power, upholding the dollar's value and the profitable exchange of Middle Eastern petrodollar payments for protection so important for the state–corporate nexus.[87] Former representatives of oil, finance, arms, military-engineering and

84 Jagdish Bhagwati (2000), drawing on the work of C. Wright Mills on the power elite and President Eisenhower's notion of the military-industrial complex, first coined the term Wall Street–Treasury complex, noting the role of the liberalization of capital controls in financial crises, as in Asia. Here, the term is enlarged to include the role of the Federal Reserve, the IMF and World Bank, while underscoring their relationship with the U.S. military–corporate complex as a whole. Ellsberg, D. April 3, 1990; Gowan, P. 1999.

85 Gowan, P. 1999; Canterbery, E. R. 2000.

86 Davis, M. 1986; Davis, M. 1990; Davis, M. 2002. Chapter 13.

87 Hulbert, M. 1982; Bill, J. A. 1988; Boies, J. 1994. On the role of power elites and corporate lawyers in lobbying the U.S. government to allow the Shah into the country, which helped to trigger the takeover of the U.S. embassy and hostages that played such a huge role in Reagan's election victory, as well as the subsequent freezing and recovery of Iranian assets, see Bill, J. A. 1988; Hulbert, M. 1982; Bird, K. 1992. Chapter 28. The purchase of major shares of U.S. banks, Chase Manhattan (now JPMorgan Chase) and Citicorp (now Citigroup)—then on the verge of collapse—by Gulf investors after the war, was undertaken with the help of the Carlyle group (see Abelson, A. April 13, 1998. How Greenspan Fathered Citigroup: Big Deal. *Barron's*. LXXVIII/15, 3–4; Briody, D. 2003. *The Iron Triangle: Inside the Secret World of the Carlyle Group*. New Jersey: John Wiley and Sons; Steinherr, A. 2000). Carlyle is now one of the world's largest private equity/leveraged buyout firms and the 11th largest military contractor in the United States.

related firms were well represented in the Reagan and Bush administrations, as they were in President George W. Bush's. These corporations were extensively tied via interlocking directorates and institutional shareholdings, with U.S. banks holding an average of 18.01 percent stock in six of the major aerospace producers, four times more than their average Fortune 500 holdings.[88]

By the time Iraq invaded Kuwait, the United States had spent trillions of borrowed dollars on the military that helped bring about the Soviet empire's collapse without an actual war. Deprived of a much-needed enemy, President Bush decided to put these enormous military capabilities to use in war. In embracing the warrior-statesmen ethic, President Bush was following in the footsteps of his hero, World War I war preparedness leader Henry Stimson. In fact, Bush had followed Stimson into the same exclusive prep school—which as C. Wright Mills noted, determined entrance into the exclusive private clubs and societies of Ivy League universities and hence the country—as did his son President George W. Bush, Jr.[89] Father and son were both tapped for Skull and Bones, the Yale secret society of which Stimson was a senior member, long a training group for the U.S. ruling class. Similarly enough, after the terrorist attack against the United States in 2001, President Bush, strongly backed by his British ally Prime Minister Tony Blair, soon declared this the "first war of the 21st century," noting that 2002 would be "a war year," as would all the years into the foreseeable future. The making of Anglo-American militarism in the war preparedness movements of the turn of the century is thus now being reaffirmed at the dawn of the 21st century, most recently with the Anglo-American invasions of Afghanistan, Iraq, and the more recent NATO bombings of Libya.

The synthesis of violence, profits and power through the U.S. state–corporate nexus here is illustrative of the role of finance, oil and military-related industry in U.S.-led globalization, militarization and ruling class formation, as the following anecdote reveals. In June 1991, a parade, Operation Welcome Home, was held in New York City to salute veterans of the Gulf victory. Up in the top Wall Street law firm of Skadden, Arps, Slate, Meagher and Flom, there is an advertisement from Merrill Lynch celebrating the parade, autographed for the firms' senior partner, Joseph Flom, co-chair of the event, by victorious Gulf War General, Norman

---

The firm is filled with a *Who's Who* of the U.S. power elite, from former President George Bush to former Treasury Secretary and Secretary of State, James Baker of Baker and Botts, the Texas corporate law firm that is a leader in the field of global oil and energy.

88 See Bichler, S. and Nitzan, J. 1996 and Bichler, S. and Nitzan, J. 1995 for an analysis of the changing attitudes of segments of the U.S. state–corporate community toward militarization. See also Hulbert, M. 1982. 89–92. U.S. Senate, Committee on Governmental Affairs. *Structure of Corporate Concentration: Institutional Shareholdings and Interlocking Directorates Among Major U.S. Corporations* 96th Congress, 2nd Session. Volumes I and II.

89 Wright Mills, C. 1956. 61–70.

Schwarzkopf.[90] Skadden was Wall Street's premier global law firm, pioneering the legal side of the 1980s leveraged buyout merger and acquisitions boom.[91]

The financial side of the hostile merger wave was led by the firm that grew like a phoenix out of ashes of the Drexel–Morgan alliance of the late 1800s that had financed mergers, and naval producers like Carnegie Steel. This firm, Drexel, Burnham, Lambert, played a key role in stimulating the merger wave and financial expansion by "enhancing the liquidity of the market" with high risk high yield junk bonds.[92] While there were roughly 1,500 mergers and acquisitions on Wall Street at a value of some $33 billion in 1980, by 1988 this climbed to some 3,500 at a value of $227 billion, while from 1980 to 1988, 26,000 took place, with a value of $1 trillion.[93]

Skadden became "the richest law firm in the world" and a leading representative of corporate America.[94] Skadden's role in the celebration of U.S. violence, profits and power were in keeping with the visions of President Bush and Henry Stimson. This is no surprise, as Skadden's origins traced back to the law firm of Elihu Root, Jr., a prominent member of the U.S. Round Table Dining Club and son of one of the founding fathers of the U.S. Establishment, Elihu Root, and his law partner Grenville Clark, two of the main leaders of the World War I–II war preparedness movements.[95] Skadden's two original founding partners had been members of the Root and Clark firm—now Dewey, Ballantine—and Skadden got its original corporate clients from there.[96] These continuities in networks of power reflect the unique development of the U.S. ruling class and the structural imperatives of the NSSCC they constructed to secure U.S. state–corporate hegemony.

---

90 Caplan, L. 1993. *Skadden: Power, Money and the Rise of a Legal Empire*. New York: Farrar, Straus and Giroux. 3–5. Reagan's Treasury Secretary and Chief of Staff Don Regan formerly headed Merrill Lynch, which led the rise of the mutual funds industry and owned the global investment firm of White Weld, one of the original funders of the World War I preparedness movement (*New York Times*. April 7, 1916. *New York Times*. April 16, 1916, various articles). White Weld assisted the Saudi Arabian Monetary Agency in managing its $100 billion portfolio and inflow of some $450 million petrodollars a day under David Mulford, who went onto become the Treasury's Assistant Secretary and Undersecretary of International Affairs in the Reagan and Bush administrations. Bichler, S. and Nitzan, J. 1996; Bichler, S. and Nitzan, J. 1995; Spiro, David E. 1999. Chapter 5.

91 Caplan, L. 1993. 327.

92 Stewart, J. B. 1991. *Den of Thieves*. New York: Simon & Schuster. 46.

93 Zey, M. 1993. *Banking on Fraud*. Berlin: Aldine de Gruyter. 142.

94 Caplan, L. 1993. 327.

95 Clifford, J. G. and Spencer, Jr. S. R. 1986.

96 Caplan, L. 1993. 15.

Conclusion

This chapter has traced the origins and changing combination of private corporate power and public state bureaucracy in the NSSCC as part of waves of globalization, militarization and race, class and gender formation in the rise and demise of the New Deal world order. The analysis reveals the reconstitution of U.S. global hegemony on an increasingly narrow social basis. U.S. structural path dependence on regressively financed neoliberal militarization and globalization leaves U.S. elites with the hopeless task of trying to contain global violence while legitimizing their own use of force globally. Rather than spending money on a global New Deal, the United States is gearing up to spend anywhere from a half a trillion to a trillion dollars annually toward rising military budgets and further militarization, exacerbating global polarization and worldwide militarization. America's increasing use of violence in the service of U.S.-led state–corporate globalization, both to fund high technology firms at home, while providing outlets for surplus capital and to protect increased commercial investment abroad seems much more likely to usher in increasing conflict and instability in the global system rather than a new phase of robust hegemony. Nevertheless, such a path is one that gives a new lease of life to the military–corporate complex at the core of U.S. hegemony and the dynamics of contemporary state–corporate globalization.

Chapter 3

Capitalism, Covert Action and State Terrorism: Toward a Political Economy of the Dual State

Nafeez Mosaddeq Ahmed

Introduction

In the name of fighting the post-9/11 "War on Terror" Western states have with increasing impunity bent, stretched and broken the rule of law on the pretext of defending national security: the illegal invasion and occupation of Iraq; the politicization and fabrication of intelligence on WMD; the routine use of torture in Iraqi prisons; the violation with impunity of the Geneva Conventions and other laws of war in Iraq, Afghanistan and northwest Pakistan; the arbitrary labeling of ordinary citizens as "terror suspects" without evidence, their kidnapping and human trafficking in the form of extraordinary rendition, their indefinite detention in inhumane conditions; Guantanamo Bay; military commissions run by military officers outside the jurisdiction of domestic and international law; the regular input of false information gleaned from torture into the production of "intelligence" to justify new counter-terror and surveillance operations; and so on.[1]

The persistence and proliferation of these crimes is prima facie evidence of an increasing criminalization of Western state practices, consistent with mounting empirical and historical evidence that state military and intelligence practices intersect *systematically* and *institutionally* with a wide variety of extra-legal non-state actors, such as transnational corporations and lobbies, private mercenaries, terrorist networks, organized criminal syndicates, drugs and arms trafficking groups, and so on.[2] Although analysis of the criminalization of the state remains a marginal endeavor within political science and IR, the seminal work of

---

1 For an excellent survey of the totality of these practices see especially Todd, P., Bloch, J. and Fitzgerald, P. 2009. *Spies, Lies and the War on Terror*. London: Zed.

2 Wilson, E. ed. 2009. *Government of the Shadows: Parapolitics and Criminal Sovereignty*. London: Pluto Press; Napoleoni, L. 2009. *Rogue Economics: Capitalism's New Reality*. New York: Seven Stories Press; Homes, L. ed. 2010. *Terrorism, Organized Crime and Corruption: Networks and Linkages*. Camberley: Edward Elgar.

Canadian political scientist Peter Dale Scott stands out for its focus on framing this phenomenon within a more systematic framework. This chapter explores the implications of Scott's concept of "*deep politics*" for understanding covert action and state-sponsored terrorism, through the lens of Carl Schmitt's theories of the sovereign, as well as the Copenhagen and Paris schools of Security Studies. These different but converging theories of state securitization will be critically reformulated against the insights of a political Marxist approach to understanding the evolution of modern state-sovereignty in the context of capitalist social-property relations. This leads to an exploration of the shifting parameters of political violence under capitalism, and the need under capitalist crisis to resort to novel forms of covert action. This illustrates how capitalism's eminent compatibility with *deep* political and economic activities, and its co-optation of criminal economic networks, has through the postwar period increasingly elevated the power of a U.S.-dominated transnational capitalist class. Two major cases of international terrorism—Cold War communism and post-Cold War Islamist extremism—become explicable within this framework.

Deep Politics, the Dual State and the State of Exception

Peter Dale Scott coined the term *deep politics* to designate the study of criminal practices linked to the state. He defined a *deep political* system or process as one in which institutional and non-institutional bodies, criminal syndicates, politicians, judges, media, corporations and leading government employees, resort to "decision-making and enforcement procedures outside as well as inside those sanctioned by law and society. What makes these supplementary procedures 'deep' is the fact that they are covert or suppressed, outside public awareness as well as outside sanctioned political processes."[3] *Deep political analysis* is therefore concerned with revealing the tendency of the state to enter into criminal activity outside of the state's own rule of law. From the viewpoint of conventional political science, law enforcement and the criminal underworld are opposed to each other, the former struggling to gain control of the latter. But as Scott observes:

> A deep political analysis notes that in practice these efforts at control lead to the use of criminal informants; and this practice, continued over a long period of time, turns informants into double agents with status within the police as well as the mob. The protection of informants and their crimes encourages favours, payoffs, and eventually systemic corruption. The phenomenon of "organized crime" arises: entire criminal structures that come to be tolerated by the police because of their usefulness in informing on lesser criminals.[4]

---

3 Scott, P. D. 1996. *Deep Politics and the Death of JFK*. California: University of California Press. 8.

4 Scott, P. D. 1996.

This can lead to a form of state–crime symbiosis, blurring the defining parameters of which side controls the other, and underscoring the emergence of an invisible *deep* dimension to state activities tying it to organized crime. More recent research on the *deep state* has largely drawn on various forms of securitization theory. Ola Tunander refers to "the godfather" of Realism, Hans Morgenthau, who in a 1955 study of the U.S. State Department, discussed the existence of a U.S. "*dual state*" encompassing a visible "regular state hierarchy" acting according to the rule of law and a clandestine "security hierarchy" monitoring the former. This "security" aspect of the state is able to "exert an effective veto over the decisions" of the regular state hierarchy, when deemed necessary to limit the range of democratic politics due to unprecedented emergencies. This hints at a novel but under-theorized conception of the modern liberal state as a complex dialectical structure composed of a public democratic face which could however be routinely subverted by an unaccountable security structure. Morgenthau's empirical assessment of the "dual" structure of the U.S. state was inspired by Carl Schmitt's theorization of the "sovereign."[5]

Schmitt's thought is notable due to its evolution in the context of the rise and consolidation of National Socialism in Germany. His concept of the "sovereign" was developed to justify executive government by emergency decree, as enacted in Article 48 of the Weimar Republic. For Schmitt, true sovereignty could only emerge in the context of emergencies, social crises and political disorder. Such emergencies, engendering constitutional crises, necessitate the resort to extra-legal interventions on the grounds of the state's imperative for survival. In other words, real sovereignty can only be found in the capacity to enact the *state of exception*, beyond any pre-existing legal framework.[6] Schmitt's reverence for the state of emergency was linked to his perspective of the inherently problematic nature of liberal democracy, which by its fractious, pluralistic and heterogeneous nature, requires sovereign control. "Democracy requires therefore first homogeneity and second – if the need arises – elimination or eradication of heterogeneity," he wrote, referring to Turkey's "radical expulsion of the Greeks" and Australia's restriction on the immigration of "unwanted entrants." He adds: "A democracy demonstrates its political power by knowing how to refuse or keep at bay something foreign and unequal that threatens homogeneity." As a functioning democracy thus requires the virtually unanimous consensus of all its members to sustain the viability of the social contract, it can only be maintained through perpetually demonstrating the "friend-enemy distinction"—the core of Schmitt's understanding of politics highlighting

5 Tunander, O. 2009. Democratic State vs. Deep State: Approaching the Dual State of the West, in *Government of the Shadows: Parapolitics and Criminal Sovereignty*, edited by E. Wilson. London: Pluto Press. 56–72.

6 Schmitt, C. 2005. *Political Theology: Four Chapters on the Concept of Sovereignty*. Chicago: University of Chicago Press. 5.

the danger of internal and external enemies, fear of which homogenizes the body politic under the sovereign.[7]

This authoritarian trend reappears in Schmitt's attempt to excavate the origins of true legal power through his exploration of the "concrete-order" in terms of the *nomos*, representing "the full immediacy of a legal power … an act of legitimacy, whereby the legality of a mere law is first made meaningful." Here, the defining constitutive moment upon which any legal-territorial order is premised is simply a decisive act of violence to capture, control and occupy land. Thus, the settler-colonial appropriation and distribution of land manifests the "political and social order" through which the *nomos* becomes "spatially visible."[8] Schmitt thus erected a conceptual architecture in which "mass democracy" was stabilized in the context of permanent imperial warfare abroad co-extensive with emergency rule at home, implicating the multiplication of internal and external enemies to sustain a homogenous body politic. Yet the problem that prevails throughout Schmitt's work is its being posited in a sociological and theoretical vacuum. As Benno Teschke argues: "Since Schmitt's method – be it decisionism, the friend–foe distinction, or concrete-order-thinking – is bereft of any sociology of power, decisionism lacks the analytics to identify what constellation or balance of socio-political forces can activate, in what kind of situation, the politics of the exception and fear."[9] Indeed, Schmitt established much of his conceptual apparatus to legitimize the German executive's extension of emergency powers, culminating in his embrace of Nazism.[10]

The Copenhagen school of Security Studies departs normatively from Schmitt's scheme with a critical appraisal of the danger posed by the concept of security to society. Ole Wæver's seminal concept of *securitization* referred to a "speech act"—an act of labeling—whereby political authorities identify an *existential threat* to the state which, because of its extreme nature, justifies moving beyond conventional security measures within the public rule of law, thus permitting the execution of extra-legal emergence powers that are henceforth "above politics."[11] Thus, Buzan et al. argued that "the priority and the urgency of an existential threat" permits the state to resort to consistent "violations of rules that would otherwise have to be obeyed." Securitization thus legitimizes the state

7 Schmitt, C. 1985. *The Crisis of Parliamentary Democracy*. Cambridge, MA: MIT Press. 9. See Chapter 1, this volume.

8 Schmitt, C. 2003. *The Nomos of the Earth in the International Law of the Jus Publicum Europaeum*, trans. G. L. Ulmen. New York: Telos Press. 70–73.

9 Teschke, B. January/February 2011. Decisions and Indecisions: Political and Intellectual Receptions of Carl Schmitt. *New Left Review*, 67, 80.

10 Teschke, B. January/February 2011. 72–9.

11 Wæver, O. 1995. Securitisation and Desecuritisation, in *On Security*, edited by R. D. Lipschutz. New York: Columbia University Press. Buzan, B. Wæver, O. and Wilde, J. de. 1998. *Security: A New Framework for Analysis*. Boulder: Lynne Reiner. 23.

of exception and the suspension of democracy.[12] Whereas Schmitt was inspired by the Hobbesian assertion of the concrete existence of human amity/enmity and the eternal possibility of war, the Copenhagen school privileges the role of language and ideas in constructing social reality. Thus, the mere identification of a security issue does not necessarily correspond to an objective threat, but represents the interests of power. This also means that the state of exception cannot simply be unilaterally decreed by the sovereign, but that the act of speech must conform to a normative grammar of security by a position of authority speaking to an audience that understands and is convinced by this act. Yet, while Schmitt glorifies the state of exception as necessary for survival in the heterogeneous brute uncertainties of international politics, Wæver et al. de-mystify and deconstruct the securitization speech act as ultimately a counter-democratic maneuver to manufacture consent in the removal of an issue from the realm of public law, debate and choice.[13]

Yet once again, the specific socio-political relations that lead to securitization are under-theorized. As Matt McDonald points out, the "potential for security to be constructed over time through a range of incremental processes and representations is not addressed, and the question of why particular representations resonate with relevant constituencies is under-theorized."[14] He notes that questions like "Why are some political communities more likely to view certain actors and dynamics as threatening? What role do narratives of history, culture and identity have in underpinning or legitimating particular forms of securitization?" are obscured.[15] Yet answers to such questions must go beyond a form of discourse-reductionism focusing exclusively on "narratives of history, cultural and identity," to explore the *political economy* with which these narratives are co-extensive. As Doug Stokes points out:

> While the WoT ["War on Terror"] is undoubtedly a discursive complex whereby modes of representation about terrorism, non-Western populations and the construction of stark boundaries (you are either with us or with the terrorists) operate to exclude and include, it is also intimately bound up with political and economic processes … Specifically, the wars launched in the name of counter-terrorism are not purely driven by certain hegemonic discourses, but are also part of the West's economic interests in oil, strategic interests in military bases in the Middle East and the desire to maintain American hegemony into the twenty-

12 Buzan et al. 1998. 25.

13 Ejdus, F. April–June 2009. Dangerous Liaisons: Securitization Theory and Schmittian Legacy. *Western Balkans Security Observer*, 4/13, 9–16.

14 McDonald, M. 2008. Securitisation and the Construction of Security. *European Journal of International Relations*, 14/4, 564.

15 McDonald, M. 2008. 573.

> first century by controlling one of the crucial resource-rich regions for global capitalism.[16]

In other words, the hegemonic construction of exclusionary discourses is always inherently politically-constituted, and therefore by the same token, politically-embedded and politically-transformative. Rather than securitization merely justifying the suspension of law to pave the way for *exceptional* measures outside the political, contemporary security constructions of "Islam" and "Muslims" show that it can also lead to a form of governmentality that permanently transforms the way in which populations are politically managed and reproduced.[17] The Paris school of Security Studies thus points out that securitization is equally about risk management, actively conducted by security professionals working across multiple social bureaucracies in the army, intelligence services, police forces, border controls, defence companies, insurance firms, and so on. Their activities construct "regimes of truth" which draw on "numerical data and statistics, technologies of biometrics and sociological profiles of potential dangerous behaviour" to "determine what exactly constitutes security" and whose expertise empowers them to advise state-leaders.[18] Securitization therefore "works through everyday technologies, through the effects of power that are continuous rather than exceptional, through political struggles, and especially through institutional competition within the professional security field in which the most trivial interests are at stake."[19]

The Paris school thus highlights that the state-level "speech act" privileged by the Copenhagen school cannot simply appear *ex nihilo* as a discursive rupture that innovates a completely new "regime of truth," but must emerge from prior "normal" political processes therefore amplifying pre-existing exclusionary "regimes of truth" in new directions. Yet while identifying the role of "interests," "institutional competition" and the status of the "professional security field," the Paris school offers no exploration of the concrete political and economic structures by which these are constituted, and how they thus interact with and relate to the operation of state power. By what socio-political relations is the expertise of security professionals privileged and sanctioned by the state? What historically-

---

16 Stokes, D. 2009. Ideas and Avocados: Ontologising Critical Terrorism Studies. *International Relations*, 23/1, 88.

17 Cesari, J. April 2009. The Securitisation of Islam in Europe. *Challenge: Liberty and Security Research Paper* 15. Available at: www.euro-islam.info/ei/wp-content/uploads/pdfs/the_securitisation_of_islam_in_europe.pdf (accessed March 12, 2011). Mavelli, Luca. 2008. Appropriation and Redemption in Contemporary Western Discourses on Islam in Europe. *St Antony's International Review*, 3/2, 74–93.

18 Bigo, D. 2008. Globalized (In)security: The Field and the Ban-opticon, in *Terror, Insecurity and Liberty: Illiberal Practices of Liberal Regimes after 9/11*, edited by D. Bigo and A. Tsoukala. London: Routledge. 12.

19 Bigo, D. 2002. Security and Immigration: Toward a Critique of the Governmentality of Unease. *Alternatives*, 27/1, 73.

specific social conditions prompt the construction of exclusionary "regimes of truth" through processes of everyday political institutional struggles, as well as through extraordinary acts of state-level decisionism enforcing exceptional measures?

Furthermore, the sharp theoretical distinction between the Copenhagen and Paris schools collapses in the face of historical and empirical reality. Anti-Western terrorist attacks such as 9/11 prompt state-level emergency responses which, justified by the perception of unprecedented threat, lead to adoption of extraordinary military and police responses. Yet these responses do not merely suspend constitutional law in the face of emergency—they establish permanence precisely through exploiting the declared state of emergency to legitimize the *institutionalization of exceptional measures within the body politic*, thus purporting to permanently transform the constitutional order. Securitization, in other words, can lead to wholesale *militarization* of society. Yet what remains unanswered here is the very nature of the political processes that drive securitization, their institutional origin, and the socio-political relations by which they are constituted.

The Socio-Political Relations of Securitization

Securitization theory as such has little to say on this, except to assume that the genealogy of securitizing tendencies of the modern liberal state leads back to the secularization processes linked to the violence of the early 16th- and 17th-century wars of religion. These contained "an intellectual battle over the grounds for rational belief or assent in matters of faith," resolved through the Hobbesian removal of "destructive conflict engendered by irresolvable questions of religious truth from the political realm."[20] The resulting consolidation of absolutist state-sovereignty confining religion to the private sphere of morality thus seems to underpin the securitizing tensions between modern Western secular states and the political revival of Islamism.[21]

The elementary problem in this subliminal reversion to Realism is that this orthodox account of the secular constitution of state-sovereignty is in danger of chronologically conflating the entirety of the preceding several centuries as one long continuum of European secular tension with political Islamism.[22] While there

20 Williams, M. C. 2005. *The Realist Tradition and the Limits of International Relations*. Cambridge: Cambridge University Press. 34.

21 Sheikh, M. K. and Wæver, O. March 2005. Lines in Water and Sand: Comparative Secularism as Analytical Tool for Conflict Containment. Paper prepared for International Studies Association Convention. Hawaii. Available at: www.ipri.pt/eventos/pdf/Paper_Waever.pdf (accessed March 12, 2011).

22 See for example Roy, O. 2007. *Secularism Confronts Islam*. New York: Columbia University Press; Qureshi, E. and Sells, Michael A. eds. 2003. *The New Crusades: Constructing the Muslim Enemy*. New York: Columbia University Press.

may be some truth to this, it cannot alone explain the radical distinctiveness of the post-9/11 era—what constellation of social forces means that Islam is now being scrutinized in this way, as opposed to previously? Further missing is the recognition that the separation of public and private power that became integral to the modern notion of sovereignty could not have been possible in any case without the emergence of capitalist social-property relations, first in England, and later throughout Europe—a process which transformed the parameters of political violence from a means of feudal land-appropriation, to a public force for the protection of the legal framework and property rights enabling private economic enterprise.[23]

Indeed, the evolution of the modern state, national sovereignty, the secular separation between Church and state, and between public and private power, was co-extensive with the evolution of capitalism. Furthermore, the emergence of capitalism gave rise to a new era of periodic socioeconomic crisis and class struggle which enabled a hitherto unprecedented transformation in the parameters of political violence. Under English feudalism, political violence was entwined with economic production. Lords extracted tribute from their landed peasant subjects through application of military force. The expansion of tribute-extraction thus required the intensification of violence and the annexation of new territories. Absolutism centralized the locus of this military-economic power under the emerging bureaucratic hegemony of the monarchy. Yet the emergence of agrarian capitalism led to a permanent transformation in the relations between military, political and economic power. Eco-demographic crisis induced by the Black Death led lords to increase rents to sustain falling incomes in the wake of drastic population declines, igniting peasant resistance and the 1381 rebellion. Consequently, peasants secured land by copyhold, long-term leases. While peasant status and income increased during the 15th century, the lords' capacity to enforce the extraction of surplus diminished. They soliciting monarchical support for raising rents, charging large entry fines, and refusing renewal of leases, leading to increasing numbers of forcible peasant evictions during the 16th and 17th centuries. The unintended result was the formation of new classes, namely a landed capitalist aristocracy who owned the means of production, and a landless politically-free peasantry who no longer accessed the means of their own subsistence. Landlords leased out their lands to capitalist tenants who employed wage-labor to conduct commercial farming. This process escalated principally between the 1688 Revolution and 1713.[24]

The democratization of parliament was a key lever by which increasingly powerful capitalist land-owners undermined the hold of both Crown and Church

23 Rosenberg, J. 1994. *The Empire of Civil Society: A Critique of the Realist Theory of International Relations*. London: Verso.

24 Brenner, R. 1976. Agrarian Class Structure and Economic Development in Pre-industrial Europe. *Past and Present*, 70, 30–74; Brenner, R. 1982. The Agrarian Roots of European Capitalism. *Past and Present*, 97, 16–113.

on government. They pushed toward new legislation to create a private-property regime that would stipulate the rights of capitalist landlords and regulate the new-found freedoms of former peasants dispossessed from the land, now potential wage workers.[25] The effort to break the absolutist Church-backed authority of the Crown shifted the parliamentarian cause in 1641–1642 to "a struggle to revolutionise the city's constitution and to abolish episcopacy root and branch as the prelude to the introduction of a Presbyterian or Independent order in the church." This translated ultimately into de-sanctifying the political by separating the established Episcopal hierarchy entirely from the levers of political power.[26] The new, competitive dynamic eventually converted English society into the "workshop of the world," forcing its European rivals to catch up, leading unevenly and disparately to transformations of social relations across the Western hemisphere culminating in the emergence of an Anglo-centric "Lockean heartland" at the centre of the emerging capitalist global political economy.[27]

As a direct corollary of this process, the capitalist state and its capacity for violence no longer had an obligatory role in administering the process of production. Formal political equality was integral to the new capitalist relations of production, where "the direct extraction of a surplus is accomplished through 'non-political' relations," relegating it to the private sphere. State power henceforth assumed a new "centralised monopoly of jurisdiction" asserted through an "impersonal rule of law," designed to guarantee contracts between free private individuals, uphold private property rights and protect exchange relations by managing the means of violence to maintain order internally and externally.[28]

The function of political violence under capitalism is thus dramatically different from that under pre-capitalist social formations. Marx attempted to capture this in his concept of "primitive accumulation" to emphasize the continual dependence of the capitalist social relation from inception to expansion on political violence—particularly the manipulation of the political to engineer the rule of law in capitalist interests, and when this is insufficient the deployment of extra-legal political violence. It is here that we recognize that the *political economy of the state of exception is precisely a crisis of capitalism.*

Firstly, military power is mobilized to enforce the very process of enclosure by which former landed peasant classes were expelled from access to the means of subsistence, thus generating the basis of the capitalist social relation—the dispossession of labor from its own conditions, and the centralized private ownership of the means of production. Marx introduces primitive accumulation as

---

25 Brenner, R. 1993. *Merchants and Revolution: Commercial Change, Political Conflict and London's Overseas Traders 1550–1653.* Cambridge: Cambridge University Press.

26 Brenner, R. 1993. 693.

27 Van der Pijl, K. 1998. *Transnational Classes and International Relations.* London: Routledge.

28 Rosenberg, J. 1994. 124–6 and 130.

"the historical process which by divorcing workers from their means of production converts them into wage workers."[29]

Secondly, once this historical process of dispossession is consolidated, military power recedes from the sphere of social life through a centralized monopoly in the means of violence by which the state is able to uphold a regulatory framework of public order co-extensive with constitutional law, equality of citizenship, personal liberty, contract laws, property rights, and so on. This framework of order underpins the autonomy of the private sphere of economic production. "Once developed historically, capital itself creates the conditions of its existence (not as conditions for its arising, but as results of its being)."[30] Capital accumulation therefore relies primarily on "the silent compulsion of economic relations [which] sets the seal on the domination of the capitalist over the worker." When this silent compulsion is challenged, the private capitalist class exerts pressure on the state to innovate new laws by which to control and pacify labor: "The bourgeoisie at its rise, wants and uses the power of the state to 'regulate' wages, i.e. to force them within the limits suitable for surplus value making, to lengthen the working day and to keep the labourer himself in the normal degree of dependence. This is an essential element of the so-called primitive accumulation."[31] In the same vein, Marx notes that political and ideological means of mobilization are integral to these processes: "as soon as the workers learn the secret of why it happens that the more they work, the more alien wealth they produce … so soon does capital and its sycophant, political economy, cry out at the infringement of the 'eternal' and so to speak 'sacred' law of supply and demand."[32] Hence, capitalists seek to camouflage capitalism as part of the natural order, the way things have always been and must always be, and whose laws therefore cannot be violated.

Thirdly, capitalism remains inherently prone to social crises. Class struggle between labor and capital ensues whereby workers seek to resist capitalist strategies of reproduction and profit-maximization involving wage-minimization and investment in labor-saving technologies of production. Cyclical economic crises in the form of periodic over-production, over-accumulation, unemployment and/or under-consumption (and so on) intensify these struggles between labor and capital, during which the state exploits both its military-police powers as well as ideological propaganda to enforce and justify social control legislation to inhibit the scope of labor action. However, consistent *failure* of the normal functioning of capitalism under crisis requires exceptional measures. "Direct extra-economic force is still of course used," notes Marx, "but only in exceptional cases. In the

29 Marx, K. and Engels, F. 1975. *Selected Correspondence, 1846–1895*. Westport: Greenwood Press. 293.

30 Marx, K. *Grundrisse*. London: Penguin. 493.

31 Marx, K. 1976. *Capital: A Critique of Political Economy Vol. 1*. London: Penguin. 651. Emphasis added.

32 Marx, K. 1976. 793.

ordinary run of things, the worker can be left to the 'natural laws of production.'"[33] And similarly: "[A]s soon as ... adverse circumstances prevent the creation of an industrial reserve army, and with it the absolute dependence of the working class upon the capitalist class, capital ... rebels against the 'sacred' law of supply and demand, and tries to make up for its inadequacies by *forcible means*" [emphasis added].[34] Hence, juridical authority, ideological power and police action, backed by a monopoly in the means of violence, can be mobilized in exceptional crisis to forcibly suspend the law to interfere in the private realm of surplus extraction.

Fourthly, capitalists seek to expand profit-maximization by identifying new and cheap sources of labor, raw materials and technologies of production abroad, as well as by identifying new markets for sale of capitalist goods and services. Both, to be integrated into the orbit of capitalist heartlands, require application of military-political violence either to subordinate non-capitalist surplus to metropolitan circuits of capitalist accumulation, and/or to forcibly re-organize their domestic social relations to establish regulatory frameworks necessary to permit peripheral capitalist reproduction in service of the metropolis. Marx thus extends the concept of primitive accumulation to the international:

> The discovery of gold and silver in America, the extirpation, enslavement and entombment in mines of the aboriginal population, the beginning of the conquest and looting of the East Indies, the turning of Africa into a warren for the commercial hunting of black-skins, signalised the rosy dawn of the era of capitalist production. These idyllic proceedings are the chief moments of primitive accumulation... In England at the end of the 17th century, they arrive at a systematical combination, embracing the colonies, the national debt, the modern mode of taxation, and the protectionist system. These methods depend in part on brute force, e.g., the colonial system.[35]

The character of these imperial moments of primitive accumulation—colonization, slavery, inter-state war, debt, modern taxation and protectionism—were not predetermined by a prior capitalist logic, although their implementation was instrumental in increasing capitalist metropolis subordination of large areas of the non-capitalist world to metropolitan accumulation:

> The colonial system ripened, like a hot-house, trade and navigation. The "societies Monopolia" of Luther were powerful levers for concentration of capital. The colonies secured a market for the budding manufactures, and, through the monopoly of the market, an increased accumulation. The treasures

33 Marx, K. 1976. 899–900.
34 Marx, K. 1976. 794.
35 Marx, K. 1976. 918.

> captured outside Europe by undisguised looting, enslavement, and murder, floated back to the mother-country and were there turned into capital.[36]

Thus, Marx indicates that *criminal* means of direct force were deployed by the empire to increase accumulation. Capitalists are thus capable of drawing on state power to forcibly accommodate non-capitalist relations of exploitation to extract surplus for input into the circuits of metropolitan capital accumulation. He observes, for instance, that despite the rise of industrial capitalism in England, "Liverpool grew fat on the basis of the slave trade" because "this was its method of primitive accumulation."[37] He goes on to emphasize the direct connection between capital accumulation in the metropolis and primitive accumulation in the imperial periphery: "In fact the veiled slavery of the wage-labourers in Europe needed the unqualified slavery of the New World as its pedestal."[38]

The problem that capitalist states face in the application of such diverse forms of *criminal political violence*, is simply that within the rubric of the modern political sovereignty by which capitalist states are now constituted, and by which capitalism itself is enabled, the use of criminal political violence to navigate the dynamic tension between capital and labor *must be concealed*—precisely in the interests of sustaining capitalist exploitation. Marx suggests that the democratic state constitutes a site of struggle between labor and capital, wherein capitalists exert a variety of bureaucratic, political and economic levers to push the state to enact military, legal and economic policies in their own interests, with a view to limit the power of labor and maximize opportunities for capitalist surplus extraction, both at home and abroad.[39] Simultaneously, the influence of capitalist actors on the state and the associated deployment of criminal political violence must be concealed to maintain the illusion that state power functions in the interests of labor. In other words, while the consolidation and expansion of capitalism remains predicated on the systematic application of criminal political violence at home and abroad, to maintain the stability of the capitalist system requires that this violence be axiomatically concealed from public knowledge, and/or justified within the public framework of the rule of law, and/or legitimized through the extension or re-organization of that very framework.[40]

---

36 Marx, K. 1976. 918.

37 Marx, K. 1976. 924.

38 Marx, K. 1976. 919–20 and 925.

39 See especially Clarke, S. ed. 1991. *The State Debate*. London: Palgrave; Tsokalis, A. August 2010. Opening Up Open Marxist Theories of the State: A Historical Materialist Critique. *British Journal of Politics and International Relations*, 12/3, 387–407.

40 Carey, A. 1995. *Taking the Risk Out of Democracy: Corporate Propaganda versus Freedom and Liberty*. Sydney: University of New South Wales Press; Herman E. S. and McChesney, R. W. 1997. *The Global Media: The New Missionaries of Corporate Capitalism*. London: Continuum; Klaehn, J. ed. 2005. *Filtering News; Essays on Herman and Chomsky's Propaganda Model*. New York: Black Rose.

It is in this context that capitalism's inherent propensity toward *deep political* forms becomes clear, for capitalism operates and thrives ideal-typically in labor's belief in its own freedom. Unlike pre-capitalist social forms which relied openly and entirely on the use of violence to forcibly extract surplus from landed peasants, capitalism's continual dependence on violence to respond to periodic economic crises, forcibly open up new markets, subordinate new territories to capitalist imperatives, and integrate non-capitalist economies into the orbit of capitalist reproduction—as well as to suppress labor efforts toward self-organization to challenge such practices—cannot be admitted without endangering the entire edifice of the capitalist social relation of dispossession. It is thus within the nexus between the legal domain of public state power and the extra-legal domain of private capitalist enterprise that we see the emergence of a new *deep* apparatus by which private actors could leverage the state into instrumentalizing or facilitating the criminal political violence necessary to sustain and expand accumulation. Furthermore, capitalists may continuously deploy criminal political violence, but then they must also continuously conceal that violence from public awareness or rehabilitate its legitimacy by the construction of new narratives of crisis/threat which can justify the use of exceptional violence as a matter of survival—or even normalize the repeated use of exceptional violence until its institutionalization permits it to become part of the everyday practice of politics. The crisis-generating tendencies and self-stabilizing responses of capitalism, in other words, constitute the fundamental precondition for the *deep political* emergence of Schmitt's state of exception, or Morgenthau's "dual state"—securitization, in other words, is an eminently capitalist strategy of reproduction.

Capitalist Globalization and the Transnationalization of Deep Politics: The Internationalization of State Terrorism and the Cold War Strategy of Tension

It is for this reason that the emergence of the "deep state"—the covert extra-legal structure of the state bureaucracy—began to develop concertedly in the early twentieth century in the context of the transatlantic consolidation of competing but nevertheless interconnected capitalisms in the United States, Great Britain and Western Europe. Surveying this history, one finds that the direction of *deep politics* is inexplicable without understanding, firstly, the state's embeddedness in a globalizing capitalist political economy (that is, its existence as a site of struggle by which vested interlocking corporate interests were able to encourage *deep state* practices which could re-organize local, regional and global frameworks of order along lines that subordinate labor); second, that the rise of *deep politics* as a tool of statecraft historically coincided with the consolidation of local state-capitalisms; and third, that the globalization of capitalism increasingly entailed the internationalization of *deep politics* as a tool of transnational capital by which local statecraft could be manipulated. To this extent, capitalism not only facilitated the institutionalization of a new form of *deep politics* frequently involving forms of criminal political violence amounting to state terrorism; the globalization of capitalism enabled the emergence and expansion of a U.S.-dominated transnational *deep system* which transfigured, and continues to attempt to manipulate, the trajectories of local and regional politics. There is thus a correlation between capitalist globalization and the internationalization (and intensification) of deep state-sponsored criminal political violence.

In the early twentieth century, British imperial geo-strategists feared that Russia and Germany might come together to form an alliance that would dominate the Eurasian continent and thus block British access. As Sir Halford Mackinder succinctly expressed in his seminal 1904 paper, due to its unique concentration of population, resources and industrial might, Eurasia was a geographical and strategic pivot of world control: "Those who control eastern Europe dominate the Heartland: those who rule the Heartland dominate the World Island (that is, Eurasia): those who rule the World Island dominate the world"—an assessment that influenced British foreign policy up to around 1919.[41] Michael T. Klare reports that, in similar vein, U.S. defense planners feared the imminent prospect of mergers between German-controlled continental Europe and Russia, together with a Japanese-dominated China and Southeast Asia, into vast continental powers capable of dominating the Eurasian heartland, thereby reducing the United States to a marginal power. This fear galvanized American leaders during World War II, prompting Franklin D. Roosevelt to push for U.S. involvement in the war.[42]

In the United States, the Office of Strategic Services (OSS) established in June 1942 went on to dispatch hundreds of spies to penetrate both Berlin and Nazi-occupied Europe. OSS operatives collected intelligence, conducted psychological operations, and implemented acts of sabotage and demolition behind enemy lines to support resistance fighters. But their activities were hardly limited to Nazi Germany—rather they were broadly oriented to destabilize key U.S. and British rivals in Eurasia, namely the USSR, Japan and China, as well as Burma, Indochina and Turkey.[43] Based on an extensive analysis of declassified OSS documents, Paul Wolf shows that the OSS routinely organized "sabotage operations" and forms of "psychological terror" as part of a coherent global strategy of covert action:

---

41 Mackinder, H. J. 1996. The Geographical Pivot of History, in *Democratic Ideals and Reality*. Washington, DC. National Defence University Press. 175–94. Available at: www.ndu.edu/inss/books/Books%20-%201979%20and%20earlier/Democratic%20Ideals%20and%20Reality%20-%201942/DIR.pdf (accessed January 19, 2011).

42 Klare, Michael T. July 2003. The New Geopolitics. *Monthly Review*. Available at: www.monthlyreview.org/0703klare.htm (accessed January 19, 2011). Preparata, Guido G. 2005. *Conjuring Hitler: How Britain and America Made the Third Reich*. Ann Arbor: University of Michigan.

43 CIA Office of Public Affairs. 2008. *The Office of Strategic Services: America's First Intelligence Agency*. Washington, DC: Center for the Study of Intelligence. Available at: www.cia.gov/library/center-for-the-study-of-intelligence/csi-publications/books-and-monographs/oss/index.htm (accessed January 19, 2011).

> Morale Operations (MO) were intended to generate panic, intimidate, demoralize, and spread confusion and distrust among enemy civilians and military forces; and to stimulate feelings of resentment and rebellion among occupied populations … SI agents were tasked to collect information about the vulnerabilities of enemy groups, both civil and military, and about neutral populations, to be exploited by psychological warfare … The Foreign Nationalities Branch, headed by Dewitt Poole, engaged in political warfare abroad using anti-Axis and immigrant groups based in the United States.[44]

After World War II, the United States determined that it would maintain a permanent military presence in all of the rim-lands of Eurasia—that is, Western Europe, the Pacific Rim and the Middle East—and thereby continue to contain any emerging "heartland" power.[45] This simultaneously involved the postwar reconstruction of Europe and Japan, their integration into the U.S.-dominated world capitalist economy, and the opening up of Europe's colonial peripheries to U.S. capital penetration: for U.S. capital to flourish required the industrial development of its erstwhile capitalist allies, and this in turn entailed the formation of a nascent U.S.-led "transnational managerial class."[46] The United States thus spearheaded a process of North Atlantic transnational class formation, culminating after World War II in three major politico-economic offensives to achieve Atlantic integration, described by Kees van der Pijl:

> the Roosevelt offensive, in FDR's third term; the Marshall offensive, coincidental with the initial four years of the Marshall Plan; and the Kennedy offensive spanning the first half of the 1960s. As far as the global structure of imperialism was concerned, the offensives (alternating with periods of relative American defensiveness in international affairs) represented concerted efforts of the United States to break into the colonial empires or peripheral domains of the European powers while keeping the Soviet Union at bay. Atlantic unity, the American nuclear posture, and its militancy in the underdeveloped periphery itself, were all aimed to prevent socialist forces from interfering with the delicate process of transition from colonialism to neo-colonialism, and more particularly, to prevent the linkage of Soviet power and local insurgency. Paradoxically, Atlantic integration therefore represented a process of redistribution of spheres-of-influence at the expense of Western Europe, facilitated by American control of the international monetary system and its virtual monopoly, on the capitalist side, of the means of nuclear destruction. In this process of confrontation

44 Wolf, P. 2004–2005. *OSS – The Psychology of War 1941–1945*. Washington, DC: Office of Paul Wolf Attorney-at-Law. Available at: www.icdc.com/~paulwolf/oss/oss.htm (accessed January 19, 2011).

45 Klare, M. July 2003.

46 Cox, R. 1987. *Production, Power and World Order: Social Forces in the Making of History*. New York: Columbia University Press. 359.

> and redistribution, Atlantic unity was cemented by the support the American offensives could draw upon in Western Europe.[47]

The conceptual foundations for this emerging order had already been explored during the war in the Grand Area strategy drawn up by the War and Peace Studies Project, a series of working groups established by U.S. State Department planners in partnership with the Washington-based Council on Foreign Relations. The planners identified a minimum "world area" comprising the entire "Western Hemisphere, the former British Empire and the Far East," economic control over which they believed to be "essential for the security and economic prosperity of the United States and the Western Hemisphere." This control was premised on being able "to secure the limitation of any exercise of sovereignty by foreign nations that constitutes a threat" to this world area, which to be effective required "an integrated policy to achieve military and economic supremacy for the United States." On this basis, planners argued that the concept of U.S. "security interests" should be extended to include the domination of these regions considered "strategically necessary for world control." The documents thus already contained a rationale for the "securitisation" of events in certain imperial peripheries to justify imperial expansion.[48] Grand Area strategy, ultimately, aimed to permit the United States to re-organize societies according to principles that would facilitate U.S. capital penetration—hence, the promulgation of the "open door" principle in international trade and investment, whereby "American enterprises in other countries should be assured the right of access to raw materials and markets and to labour supply of the host country on the same terms as business enterprises operated therein by its citizens or by citizens of third countries."[49] Crucially, however, the planners recognized the necessity for the bulk of these policies to be pursued covertly—and highlighted the necessity of psychological operations to legitimize and beautify military expansionism:

> If war aims are stated, which seem to be concerned solely with Anglo-American imperialism, they will offer little to people in the rest of the world … Such aims would also strengthen the most reactionary elements in the United States and the British Empire. The interests of other peoples should be stressed, not only those of Europe, but also of Asia, Africa and Latin America. This would have a better propaganda effect.[50]

---

47 Van der Pijl, K. 1984. *The Making of an Atlantic Ruling Class*. London: Verso.

48 Shoup, L. H. and Minter, W. 1977. *Imperial Brain Trust: The Council on Foreign Relations and US Foreign Policy*. New York: Monthly Review Press.

49 Curtis, M. 1995. *The Ambiguities of Power: British Foreign Policy since 1945*. London: Zed. 17.

50 Shoup, L. H. 1975. Shaping the Postwar World. *Critical Sociology*, 5, 3.

Thus, the cadre of U.S. military, intelligence and financial leaders involved in the establishment of the OSS went on to use their associated *deep* networks to meet these imperial objectives in the postwar period. OSS leaders William Donovan and Allen Dulles lobbied for the creation of the Central Intelligence Agency (CIA) through the National Security Act of 1947, but simultaneously established private alternatives for covert operations that would operate outside government control, such as the World Commerce Corporation (WCC).[51] In the words of former CIA executive director A. B. Buzzy Krongard, "the whole OSS was really nothing but Wall Street bankers and lawyers."[52] A year later, the National Security Council established the Office of Policy Coordination (OPC), led by Dulles and Frank Wisner, a State Department official who wielded unprecedented power due to his position in New York law and financial circles. Scott's striking account of this process illustrates that from inception, the covert military-intelligence apparatus that was developed as part of state structures did not originate purely from inside the regular state hierarchy, but was the outcome of concerted lobbying efforts by a powerful network of an already emerging military-industrial-corporate complex, represented by only a select few U.S. government officials. The real source of agency, then, for the extension of covert military intelligence operations by the state, was not the civilian administration itself, but a wider interlocking network of transnational corporate arms, defense, energy and media interests representing U.S. capital, which in turn was increasingly internationalizing through evolving *deep* exchange relations with other state and non-state sources of capital.[53]

The Europe-wide network established through the OSS was retained by the CIA, and re-mobilized in the context of the Cold War on the order of British Prime Minister Winston Churchill, who in July 1940 called for the establishment of a secret army to "set Europe ablaze by assisting resistance movements and carrying out subversive operations in enemy held territory."[54] By October 4, 1945, the British Chiefs of Staff and the Special Operations branch of MI6 directed the creation of what Daniele Ganser describes as a "skeleton network" capable of expansion either in war or to service clandestine operations abroad: "Priority was given in carrying out these tasks to countries likely to be overrun in the earliest stages of any conflict with the Soviet Union, but not as yet under Soviet domination."[55] In the ensuing years, Sir Colin Mcvean Gubbins of the Special Operations branch of MI6 cooperated closely with Frank Wisner's OPC on White House orders, and

51 Scott, P. D. 2001. *American War Machine: Deep Politics, the CIA Global Drug Connection, and the Road to Afghanistan*. Boston: Rowman & Littlefield.

52 Loeb, V. and Schneider, G. March 17, 2001. Colourful Outsider is Named No. 3 at the CIA. *Washington Post*.

53 Scott, P. D. 2001.

54 Ganser, D. 2005. *NATO's Secret Armies: Operation Gladio and Terrorism in Western Europe*. London: Routledge. 40.

55 Ganser, D. 2005. 41.

in turn coordinated U.S. and UK Special Forces, to establish stay-behind secret armies across Western Europe.[56]

As is now well-documented, the program became a conduit for no less than state-sponsored terrorism. Among the most intriguing pieces of evidence that emerged on the NATO "stay-behind armies" is the classified U.S. Army Field Manual 30-31, authored by the Pentagon's Defense Intelligence Agency (DIA), to train thousands of stay-behind officers around the world. The document first surfaced in the 1987 parliamentary report of the Italian parliamentary investigation into the terrorist activities of P2, the CIA–MI6 sponsored Italian anti-communist network, and was confirmed as authentic by both former CIA deputy director Ray Cline, as well as P2 leader Licio Gelli.[57]

Along these lines, the "stay-behind" networks were responsible for waves of terrorist attacks throughout Western Europe, for instance in Italy, Spain, Germany, France, Turkey, Greece and elsewhere, that were officially blamed on communists linked to the Soviet Union. The "strategy of tension" became a matter of public record when revealed in parliament in August 1990 by Italian Prime Minister Giulio Andreotti, who confirmed he had been privy to an operation known as "Gladio" being run by a secret sub-section of Italian military-intelligence services, and which was responsible for domestic bombings blamed on Italian communists. The operations of NATO stay-behind networks were for the most part never the prerogative of the regular state hierarchy, nor even of the state's conventional security forces, although elements of these forces may have been infiltrated or recruited on behalf of the CIA–MI6 stay-behind network—leaving at most only one or two government officials actually aware of the existence of the program. Indeed, the primary objective of covert action was the manipulation not merely of public opinion in host countries, but of local state political and economic policies. Thus, FM 30-31 instructs:

> There may be times when *Host Country Governments* show passivity or indecision in the face of Communist subversion … U.S. army intelligence must have the means of launching special operations which will *convince Host Country Governments and public opinion of the reality of the insurgent danger.* To reach this aim U.S. army intelligence should seek to penetrate the insurgency by means of agents on special assignment, with the task of forming special action groups among the most radical elements of the insurgency … In case it has not been possible to successfully infiltrate such agents into the leadership

56 Ganser, D. 2005. 42.

57 *Commissione parlamentare d'inchiesta sulla loggia massonica P2*. 1987. Allegati alla Relazione Doc. XXIII. n. 2-quarter. 7. 1 Serie II. Vol. VII Tomo I. Roma. 287–98; O'Shaughnessy, H. July 7, 1992. Codename Gladio – has this Secret Network become a Front for Terrorism and the Far-right? *Observer*; Ganser, D. 2005. 235.

of the rebels it can be useful to instrumentalise extreme leftist organizations for one's own ends in order to achieve the above described targets.[58]

As a consequence of these practices, Western Europe was increasingly willing to integrate under U.S.-dominated security frameworks. The United States thus successfully established itself at the center of a dense web of "hub and spokes" security relationships, a bilateral architecture extending throughout the strategically pivotal theatres of Cold War confrontation. In Europe, NATO became a critical element of this pattern of U.S.-centric alliance structures.[59] In other words, the function of *deep state* covert action was precisely to "calibrate the level of violence" in such a way as to manipulate the socio-political orientation of host country governments and populations.[60] In the context of the Cold War, the "strategy of tension" ensured the political and economic integration of Western Europe under the global capitalist mantle of U.S. military and economic supremacy, thus meeting the mutual class interests of both U.S. and local capital.[61] Overall, within the capitalist metropolis, *deep political* violence functioned to extinguish potential inter-capitalist rivalries between the United States, Britain and Europe by triggering and (seemingly) substantiating an exclusionary anti-left securitization discourse that, in turn, justified integration into a U.S.-dominated economic and security architecture. The historical and empirical record suggests that security agency involvement in such "calibration" practices was achieved through both military-industrial-corporate dominance of the security industry co-optation of the state through lobbying efforts, institutional "revolving doors" and even espionage.[62]

This had a corollary strategy in the imperial periphery. As is revealed by the declassified British Foreign Office archives, neither U.S. nor British planners ever expected a Soviet invasion even during the height of the Cold War. Detailed threat assessments of Soviet and communist influence not only in Europe, but also in the Middle East, North Africa, the Far East, South Asia and Southeast Asia, concluded its "negligible" or marginal role compared to the "problem of nationalism."[63] A Foreign Office memorandum of 1950, for instance, emphasized the connection

58 Ganser, D. 2005. 234 and 297.

59 Mastunduno, M. 2003. Incomplete Hegemony: The United States and Security Order in Asia, in *Asian Security Order: Instrumental and Normative Features*, edited by M. Alagappa. Stanford: Stanford University Press. 141–70.

60 Tunander, O. 2009. Humanitarian Intervention and Calibration of Violence: Some Comments on the U.S. Dual Policy in Afghanistan. *Confidential Report to the Norwegian Ministry of Foreign Affairs*. Oslo: International Peace Research Institute.

61 Parenti, M. 1997. *Blackshirts and Reds: Rational Fascism and the Overthrow of Communism*. San Francisco: City Lights.

62 See Shorrock, T. 2008. *Spies for Hire: The Secret World of Intelligence Outsourcing*. New York: Simon & Schuster; Beder, S. 2006. *Suiting Themselves: How Corporations Drive the Global Agenda*. London: Earthscan.

63 Curtis, M. 1995.

between "communism" and Western economic insecurity: "it is obvious that when an area falls into Communist hands, its economic and trading value to the Western world becomes greatly reduced, while Western capital assets are liquidated with little or no compensation."[64] Thus, the securitization of communism was prompted by the requirements of Grand Area geo-strategy, formulated to engineer a political and economic order which would concord with the requirements of U.S.-dominated transatlantic capitalism. The program of state-sponsored terrorist activity that enveloped Western Europe under the "strategy of tension" lent credence to public political claims regarding the Soviet threat, which in turn justified policies of military expansionism in much of the periphery. Curtis reports:

> Policy in, for example, Malaya, Kenya, British Guiana and Iran was geared towards organizing Third World economies along guidelines in which British, and Western, interests would be paramount … Similarly, U.S. interventions overseas – in Vietnam, Nicaragua, the Dominican Republic, Cuba, Chile, et cetera – were designed to counter threats to the Western practice of assigning the Third World to mere client status to Western business interests. British and U.S. forces have acted as mercenary – and often extremely violent – mobs intended to restore "order" in their domains and to preserve the existing privileges of elites within their own societies.[65]

The vast bulk of the Cold War, then, was not really about fighting or deterring the Soviet Union, but on the contrary amounted to a vast transitional program of political economic rehabilitation of the imperial system to subvert de-colonization and impose global capitalist discipline against anti-imperialist resistance, whereby U.S. and British planners aimed explicitly "to protect and advance [their] economic and political interests in these changing circumstances."[66] Thus, D. K. Fieldhouse observes that the continuing economic dependence of former colonies on the capitalist metropolis was "the intended result of de-colonialism."[67]

The 80-plus military and intelligence operations conducted in the South in the postwar period[68] thus constituted a militarized extension of 16th-century English agrarian enclosure on a global scale—a vehicle of Anglo-American primitive accumulation by which political violence and state terrorism were deployed to

---

64 Memorandum for the Permanent Under-Secretary's Committee. April 27, 1950. *Documents on British Foreign Policy*. Ser. II. Vol. II. 162, in Curtis, M. 1995.

65 Curtis, M. 1995.

66 Gifford, P. and Roger L. W. eds. 1982. *The Transfer of Power in Africa: Decolonisation 1940–1960*. London: Yale University Press. 261.

67 Fieldhouse, D. K. 1986. *Black Africa 1945–80: Economic Decolonization and Arrested Development*. London: Allen & Unwin. 5.

68 Blum, W. 2003. *U.S. Military and CIA Interventions Since World War II*. London. Zed; McClintock, M. 1992. *Instruments of Statecraft: US Guerrilla Warfare, Counterinsurgency and Counterterrorism, 1940–1990*. New York: Pantheon.

forcibly open markets and establish national political-institutional architectures conducive to labor dispossession and Western capital penetration. Yet this program, integral to the success of capitalist expansion, has been concealed from domestic public understanding not only through liberal ideologies that naturalize globalization as an inevitable techno-economic process, but also through political propaganda premised on a process of securitization focusing on the construction of the Soviet Union as an imminent existential threat and concretized through the sponsorship of terrorist activities that could be blamed on left-wing movements. This *deep political securitization matrix* justified the adoption of draconian emergency powers, along with the institutionalization of anti-left policies, and the radicalization of foreign policy in strategic peripheries—a wholesale process of societal militarization.

The galvanizing factor for the initiation of this *securitization matrix* after World War II was precisely the *crisis of empire* facing Britain and Western Europe. While the war had left the United States in a hegemonic position, it had also weakened its postwar allies to such an extent that continued colonial domination in the wake of emerging mass revolts and uprisings was simply unsustainable. The crisis of empire necessitated and enabled a new approach to imperial power more acutely in tune with the capitalist socio-political formation of the U.S. hegemon—an imperialism "without empire" suitable for the rising post-colonial era. This *securitization matrix* of exclusionary narrative and deep political violence generated a decisionist posture of exception that pushed as its internationalist resolution forms of "democratization" and "liberalization" designed to forcibly quash national independence movements for non-capitalist development, and install the formal "sovereignty" required for institutional enforcement of contracts, the rule of law and respect for private property—thus securing the political space for sustained capital accumulation.[69] Critically, then, it is through this protracted violent process of primitive accumulation continuing through the 1970s, 1980s and 1990s that the United States, with conditional support principally from the UK and Western Europe, was able to forcibly establish across the former colonies the institutional conditions necessary to eventually facilitate the "deep integration" central to contemporary capitalist globalization, namely the internationalization of trade and financial flows, and the transnationalization of the production process.[70]

Toward the twilight of this period of the "golden age" of neoliberal globalization, one finds the consolidation of what Loretta Napoleoni calls "rogue economics," a criminal and financial underworld that although external to the

---

69 Joya, A. December 2005. Theorizing Post-Cold War US Imperial Strategies in the Middle East: Integrating the Region into the Capitalist World Market. *YCISS Working Paper No. 37*. York: York University. Available at: www.yorku.ca/yciss/publications/documents/WP37-Joya.pdf (accessed November 15, 2010). Colas, A. 2008. *Empire*. Cambridge: Polity Press.

70 Robinson, W. I. and Harris, J. 2000. Toward a Global Ruling Class? Globalization and the Transnational Capitalist Class. *Science and Society*, 64, 1.

conventional legal economy, remains entirely incubated by it. A prime example is the entrenchment and deepening of new forms of slavery to underpin metropolitan capital accumulation, such as the use of child slaves in Ivory Coast plantations to produce cocoa for transnational corporations like Nestle and Starbucks.[71] Another example is the Sony Corporation which reportedly used a contraband network in Asia as a part of its overall strategy in the region. Napoleoni shows that such instances are part of a larger pattern in which the instantiation of formal democracy, bringing with it market liberalization and deregulation, systematically enables the criminalization of the economy. In other words, the interdependencies between global capital markets and the international criminal economy have fundamentally blurred the distinction between legal and illegal finance, to the extent that the U.S.-dominated transnational capitalist class itself is now inherently entangled with criminal networks. Napoleoni illustrates this increasingly criminal character of transnational capital with some startling statistics. Rampant financial deregulation enforced by states under U.S. leadership allowed diverse armed and terrorist networks "to link up with each other and with organised crime" generating a total value of $1.5 trillion (higher than the GDP of the United Kingdom), consisting of illegal capital flights, profits from criminal enterprises, drug trading, smuggling, legal businesses, and so on. The bulk of this money "flows into Western economies, where it gets recycled in the U.S. and in Europe. It is a vital element of the cash flow of these economies." As the primary medium of exchange for this criminal economy is the U.S. dollar, its rate of growth "is roughly indicated by the yearly infusion of new U.S. dollars." In the year 2000 alone, as much as two-thirds of the U.S. money supply in circulation had been removed from the U.S. monetary system and taken abroad in criminal transactions in total "equivalent to $500 billion." The implication is that "the rate of monetary growth of the terror/illegal economy is higher than that of the U.S. economy." More intriguingly, she observes that as the U.S. dollar is the world reserve currency, the greater the stocks of dollars held abroad, the greater the "source of revenue for the U.S. Treasury through seignorage," as the U.S. can issue Treasury bills and "borrow against the total stock of dollars held in the world, not just on the stock held inside the US," amounting to a "considerable tax write-off." The economic power of the U.S. Treasury is thus significantly conditional on the economic immunity of criminal networks—thus, the globalization of capitalism has entailed the increasing criminalization of the U.S.-dominated transnational capitalist class.[72]

The upshot is that capitalists are capable of applying whatever means necessary and convenient to maximize profits, including means of violence or exchange

71 Napoleoni, L. 2008. *Rogue Economics: Capitalism's New Reality*. New York: Seven Stories Press.

72 Napoleoni, L. January 7, 2005. Money and Terrorism. Madrid: FRIDE. Available at: www.fride.org/publication/93/money-and-terrorism (accessed November 16, 2010). Also see Napoleoni, L. 2004. *Terror Inc.: Tracing the Money behind Global Terrorism*. London. Penguin.

relations unsanctioned by the formal political-legal architecture historically erected to sustain the very existence of capitalist social relations and accumulation. Yet more than ever, capitalism's structural dependence on legal public political forms necessitates the "deep" suppression of illicit practices through new clandestine mechanisms. Hence, the deployment of criminal political violence by an already increasingly criminalized military-industrial-corporate complex through the conduits of state security agencies no longer appears as an aberration from an ideal-typical rational politico-legal order, but rather can be understood as integral to the *deep political economy* of global capitalism.

Unconventional Warfare and Post-Cold War Collaboration with Islamist Terrorism

The *deep political securitization matrix* evident during the early period of the Cold War was also implicated in the eventual decision to foster Islamist mujahideen networks in Afghanistan linked to Osama bin Laden—though of course in distinctive geopolitical conditions. Once again, however, the impetus for U.S. involvement in Afghanistan was its status as a geographical entry-point into Eurasia, still viewed as a fundamental geopolitical pivot, control of which is a precondition of continued U.S. pre-eminence.[73]

The logistical, military and financial support for the Afghan networks was paralleled by similar programs of support to Islamist networks across the Middle East and Central Asia through local state conduits (like Saudi Arabia, Pakistan, Azerbaijan, Algeria, Turkey and so on). The objective was to foster political movements in the Muslim-majority world that would act as a counterweight to left-wing influence. The process was inextricably entwined with criminal practices, as the Islamist militant movements largely expanded with covert U.S. and Western support through investment firms, banks and shell companies, as well as drug-trafficking, weapons smuggling and money laundering. "Far from raising obstacles to the new configurations of global capitalism, Islamist ideology is becoming part of its new superstructures," observes Richard Labévière. "It provides … military-racketeering networks that merge very easily into the filaments of the networks of organized crime, the supreme stage of capitalism." The stability of the global economy cannot do without the input of up to trillions of dollars of "hot money" linked to Islamist militant networks, which makes up for "some $800 billion dollars [that] seems to have disappeared from the planet's accounts" between 1989 and 1997. "Osama bin Laden [was] the perfect embodiment of the 'privatization' of Islamist terrorism. He [enjoyed] a solid credit rating in the highest realms of

73 Brzezinski, Z. 1998. *The Grand Chessboard: American Primacy and its Geostrategic Imperatives*. New York: Basic Books.

international finance, where he [controlled] a patrimony of more than $3 billion."[74] The practical implications should not be underestimated, particularly given mounting evidence from U.S. intelligence sources of continuing relationships with the wider bin Laden family, and that family's entrenched financial relations with the U.S. military-industrial-corporate complex, such as the defence investment company Carlyle Group.[75]

Given the continuity of such financial relationships, it is perhaps not so surprising that the end of the Cold War did not signify the end of the West's *deep* geopolitical relationships with these networks. In September 1999, Graham Fuller, former Deputy Director of the CIA's National Council on Intelligence, alluded to the continuing covert use of Islamism to promote U.S. interests and counter Russian and Chinese geopolitical influence: "The policy of guiding the evolution of Islam and of helping them against our adversaries worked marvellously well in Afghanistan against the Red Army. The same doctrines can still be used to destabilize what remains of Russian power, and especially to counter the Chinese influence in Central Asia." Labévière points out that this normative remark in fact reveals actual U.S. policy, as "the convergence of strategic and economic interests between the American government and Sunni Islam is doing just fine."[76]

The implication is that despite the official end of the Cold War, militant Islamist networks were still seen as useful to destabilize key regions strategically close to Russian and Chinese influence, thus continuing the project of integrating these regions into the orbit of U.S.-dominated capitalist globalization. Notably, Fuller is also one of the individuals identified in the State Secrets Privilege Gallery of whistleblower and former FBI translator Sibel Edmonds—banned by the U.S. government from publicizing information on U.S. state collaboration with Islamist extremists (among other matters) released during her testimonials before the 9/11 Commission as well as the U.S. House and Senate.[77] In a recent interview, drawing on classified documents she translated, Edmonds says:

> I have information about things that our government has lied to us about. I know. For example, to say that since the fall of the Soviet Union we ceased all of our intimate relationship with Bin Laden and the Taliban – those things can

---

74 Labévière, R. 2000. *Dollars for Terror: The United States and Islam*. New York: Algora; Curtis, M. 2010. *Secret Affairs: Britain's Collusion with Radical Islam*. London: Vintage.

75 Until press revelations forced the bin Ladens to pull out, both they and the Bush family retained simultaneous investments in Carlyle, which was set to profit immensely from the U.S. militarization programs launched after 9/11. For references see Ahmed, N. M. 2005. *The War on Truth: 9/11, Disinformation and the Anatomy of Terrorism*. New York: Interlink; Unger, C. 2004. *House of Bush, House of Saud: The Hidden Relationship Between the World's Most Powerful Dynasties*. London: Gibson Square.

76 Labévière, R. 2000. 5–6.

77 Edmonds, S. *State Secret Privilege Gallery*. Available at: www.justacitizen.com/images/Gallery%20Draft2%20for%20Web.htm (accessed November 16, 2010).

> be proven as lies, very easily, based on the information they classified in my case, because we did carry very intimate relationship with these people, and it involves Central Asia, all the way up to September 11.[78]

Edmonds reveals that Turkey acted as a primary intermediary in the U.S.-led Central Asian operations, with assistance from Pakistan and Saudi Arabia, in order to sideline China and Russia by appealing to Central Asian aspirations for an Islamic and Turkic resurgence. Al-Qaeda and the Taliban were used as proxies in "a decade-long illegal, covert operation in Central Asia by a small group in the U.S. intent on furthering the oil industry and the Military Industrial Complex."[79] Citing intelligence and public record sources, Scott also documents the coincidence between U.S. military interventions and corporate/intelligence co-optation of al-Qaeda:

> What is slowly emerging from Al Qaeda activities in Central Asia in the 1990s is the extent to which they involved both American oil companies and the U.S. government. By now we know that the U.S.-protected movements of al Qaeda terrorists into regions like Afghanistan, Azerbaijan and Kosovo have served the interests of U.S. oil companies. In many cases they have also provided pretexts or opportunities for a U.S. military commitment and even troops to follow … thanks to al Qaeda, U.S. bases have sprung up close to oilfields and pipelines in Uzbekistan, Tajikistan, Georgia, and Kosovo.[80]

In other words, deep state covert action to mobilize al-Qaeda networks consistently served elements of the U.S. military-industrial-corporate complex. Thanks to Wikileaks, it is possible to recognize this sort of strategy as integral to the latest configuration of official U.S. unconventional warfare (UW) doctrine. Bearing uncanny resemblances to the Pentagon Field Manual leaked in relation to Operation Gladio half a century ago, a 2008 restricted U.S. Army Special Operations Field Manual, leaked three months after its publication, defined UW as: "Operations conducted by, with, or through irregular forces in support of a resistance movement, an insurgency, or conventional military operations."

78 Kane, M. July 31, 2009. Whistleblower: Bin Laden was US Proxy until 9/11. *Raw Story*. Available at: http://rawstory.com/08/news/2009/07/31/whistleblower-bin-laden-was-us-proxy-until-911 (accessed November 17, 2010).

79 Kane, M. July 31, 2009. Edmonds, S. and Giraldi, P. November 1, 2009. Who's Afraid of Sibel Edmonds. *American Conservative*. Available at: www.amconmag.com/pdfissue.html?Id=AmConservative-2009nov01andpage=06 (accessed November 17, 2010).

80 Scott, P. D. 2007. *The Road to 9/11: Wealth, Empire and the Future of America*. Berkeley: University of California Press. Chapter 8. Detailed historical and empirical case studies of these operations are provided in Ahmed, N. M. 2005; a shorter summary in Ahmed, N. M. 2006. Terrorism and Statecraft: Al-Qaeda and Western Covert Operations after the Cold War. *Research in Political Economy*, 23, 149–88.

Thus, the use of "irregular forces" is designed essentially to destabilize an existing government, either through support of U.S. military intervention or by fostering local rebellion. It then clarifies that for the most part, the "irregular forces" to be deployed should consist largely of criminal and terrorist networks:

> UW must be conducted by, with, or through surrogates; and such surrogates must be irregular forces … These forces may include, but are not limited to, specific paramilitary forces, contractors, individuals, businesses, foreign political organizations, *resistance or insurgent organizations*, expatriates, *transnational terrorism adversaries, disillusioned transnational terrorism members, black marketers, and other social or political "undesirables."*

Furthermore, the "strategic purpose" of UW, as with FM 30-31, is "to gain or maintain control or influence over the population":

> UW generally assumes that some portion of the indigenous population – sometimes a majority of that population – are either belligerents or in support of the UW operation. *UW is specifically focused on leveraging the unwillingness of some portion of the indigenous population to accept the status quo* or "whatever political outcome the belligerent governments impose, arbitrate, or negotiate." *A fundamental military objective in UW is the deliberate involvement and leveraging of civilian interference* in the unconventional warfare operational area (UWOA).

Thus, UW's overarching aim in the deployment of "irregular forces" is the political manipulation of host country public opinion. By this standard alone, UW unambiguously amounts to a form of state-sponsored terrorism. Further, the document points out that although UW is distinct from irregular warfare (IW), "UW is a component and method of prosecuting IW." Among the variety of "constituent activities" belonging to IW, the document lists the following: "*Insurgency*. COIN [counterinsurgency]. UW. *Terrorism*. CT [counterterrorism] … *PSYOP* [psychological operation] … *Transnational criminal activities, including narco-trafficking, illicit arms-dealing, and illegal financial transactions that support or sustain IW*."[81]

UW thus encompasses a whole host of activities—not only terrorism, crime, and insurgency but also the conventional military tools routinely implemented in response to them. This recent U.S. Special Operations document thus corroborates Tunander's conclusion that a core function of *deep political* activity is the "calibration of violence" largely through surrogate criminal and terrorist networks

81 U.S. Department of the Army Field Manual FM 3-05.130. September 30, 2008. *Army Special Operations Forces: Unconventional Warfare*. Washington, DC: Department of the Army. 1–7. Available at: www.wikileaks.org/leak/us-fm3-05-130.pdf [emphasis added] (accessed November 17, 2010).

to manipulate the temperature of conflict to influence the political choices of civilian populations in accordance with the requirements of (1) maintaining specific forms of capital accumulation (such as arms, defense and narco-trafficking), as well as (2) the very perpetuity of unilateral U.S.-domination of the global political economy by extinguishing inter-imperialist and geo-economic rivalries internal to the transnational capitalist class and their respective home countries.[82]

Up to and after 9/11, this trajectory of covert action in collaboration with Islamist militant groups has evolved in all the major strategic regions around Eurasia—North Africa, the Middle East, Central Asia, the Balkans, the Caucasus and the Asia-Pacific.[83] It still continues. In 2007, Seymour Hersh reported that as of around 2004, the Bush administration began covertly sponsoring al-Qaeda-affiliated groups across the Middle East and Central Asia to counter regional Shi'ite Iranian influence, funneling the money secretly through Saudi Arabia and Iraq without U.S. Congressional oversight: "We are simply in a situation where this president is … supporting groups indirectly that are involved with the same people that did 9/11, and we should be arresting these people rather than looking the other way."[84] Writing in *New Yorker* magazine, Hersh cited White House insiders and other U.S. government officials, confirming that this "redirection" has "brought the United States closer to an open confrontation with Iran and, in parts of the region, propelled it into a widening sectarian conflict between Shiite and Sunni Muslims." A by-product of these activities "has been the bolstering of Sunni extremist groups that espouse a militant vision of Islam and are hostile to America and sympathetic to Al Qaeda." The operations are kept secret "by leaving the execution or the funding to the Saudis, or by finding other ways to work around the normal congressional appropriations process."[85]

Of course, as former CIA official Robert Baer points out, controlling the Saudis is an impossible task.[86] Nevertheless, the policy was able to escalate throughout 2008 with bipartisan support. Early that year, George W. Bush signed a Presidential Finding informing U.S. Congress of his authorization of "a covert offensive against the Iranian regime … across a huge geographic area – from Lebanon to Afghanistan," to be financed by an additional $300 million.[87] Neither

82 Tunander, O. 2009. Humanitarian Intervention and Calibration of Violence. 39–43.

83 See especially Ahmed, N. M. 2005. Keenan, J. 2009. *The Dark Sahara: America's War on Terror in Africa*. London: Pluto Press; Scott, P. D. 2007.

84 CNN, Hersh: Bush Funnelling Money to al-Qaeda Related Groups. February 25, 2007. Available at: www.truthout.org/docs_2006/022607A.shtml [emphasis added] (accessed August 27, 2009).

85 Hersh, S. M. March 5, 2007. The Redirection. *New Yorker*. Available at: www.newyorker.com/reporting/2007/03/05/070305fa_fact_hersh (accessed August 27, 2009).

86 Baer, R. 2003. *Sleeping with the Devil: How Washington Sold Our Soul for Saudi Crude*. London: Crown.

87 Cockburn, A. May 2, 2008. Exclusive: Secret Bush "Finding" Widens Covert War on Iran. *Counterpunch*. Available at: www.counterpunch.org/andrew05022008.html (accessed August 27, 2009).

Republican nor Democrat Congressional representatives used this opportunity to challenge the offensive, and Obama's presidency has escalated the program, for starters retaining Bush's Defence Secretary, Robert Gates—the architect of Bush's Iran policy.[88] Through 2009–2010, Obama increased available funding for covert action against Iran in accordance with Special Operations UW doctrine. A new secret directive signed by General David Petraeus reportedly "authorises the sending of American Special Operations troops to both friendly and hostile nations in the Middle East, Central Asia and the Horn of Africa to gather intelligence and *build ties with local forces*" hostile to Shi'ite and Iranian influence. The directive also "permits reconnaissance that could *pave the way for possible military strikes in Iran*" and "appears to authorise specific operations in Iran" which can "*identify dissident groups that might be useful for a future military offensive*" [emphasis added].[89]

The *deep political securitization matrix* explored here allows the expansion of such covert action programs under Obama to be contextualized as a continuity of forms of primitive accumulation designed to discipline regimes resistant to integration into the U.S.-dominated global political economy, in this case Iran. Yet the continuity of the specific form of this covert action throughout the late Cold War and post-Cold War periods until today—as a collaborative (if selective) military-intelligence alliance with Islamist terrorist groups affiliated to al-Qaeda—suggests a deeper explanation. The geopolitical imperative of sidelining the influence of regional rivals such as Russia, China and Iran, coheres with the goal of integrating these regions (containing the world's most strategic conventional energy reserves) into the orbit of a U.S.-dominated unipolar order, in the interests of U.S.-dominated transnational capital. Simultaneously, the very Islamist militant networks covertly manipulated by elements of U.S. security agencies have continued to accelerate terrorist attacks against Western civilian targets. The very intensification of this anti-Western terrorist activity has enabled the increasing securitization of "Islam" and "Muslims" in such a way as to concretize and legitimize the U.S.-led "War on Terror." This has solidified international deference to U.S.-led security architectures particularly in Muslim-majority strategic regions in the Middle East, Central Asia, Northwest Africa (along with South Asia and Latin America), which happen to be home to the world's remaining energy reserves, and to key potential pipeline routes for the transport of energy to the United States, Russia, China and Europe.[90]

---

88 Synovitz, R. January 13, 2009. Reports Suggest Obama Faces Early Choice on Iran Covert Ops. *Radio Free Europe/Radio Liberty*. Available at: www.rferl.org/content/Reports_Suggest_Obama_Faces_Early_Choice_On_Iran_Covert_Ops/1369640.html (accessed May 3, 2011).

89 Mazzetti, M. May 24, 2010. U.S. is Said to Expand Secret Actions in Mideast. *New York Times*. Available at: www.nytimes.com/2010/05/25/world/25military.html?_r=1andsrc=meandref=world (accessed May 3, 2011).

90 Klare, M. T. 2005. *Blood and Oil: The Dangers and Consequences of America's Growing Dependency on Imported Petroleum*. New York: Henry Holt; Blank, S. 2007.

There is thus a direct link between the global permanent state of exception in the form of the "War on Terror," the intensifying securitization of "Islam" by state agencies and within civil society generally, and growing U.S. and Western elite perceptions of converging global ecological, energy and economic crises which threaten to undermine the political economic fabric of the postwar imperial system. Indeed, as defence planners have increasingly acknowledged the dangers posed by "new security challenges" such as climate change, water scarcity and energy depletion, their normative focus has remained fixed on how these crises could threaten continued capital accumulation while radicalizing the Muslim-majority countries where such crises could converge to generate state-failure—rather than on emancipatory solutions based on global political economic transformation.[91]

Conclusions

This analysis demonstrates that the postwar phenomenon of international terrorism has evolved largely through the co-optation of irregular non-state networks by *deep state* actors—specifically, the cases discussed here reveal a U.S. *deep state* subordinate to the interests of a military-industrial-corporate complex, mobilizing political violence to consolidate the transnational dominance of U.S. capital over its rivals, and to integrate them into a global U.S.-dominated unipolar security-economic architecture. However, the Schmittian conception of the "dual" or "deep state" deployed here is incoherent without recognizing the modern state's historical and socio-political constitution in the context of capitalist social-property relations, their inherent vulnerability to economic, financial and hence political crisis, and their structural re-configuration of the parameters of political violence to sustain the presupposing regulatory frameworks necessary for capital accumulation to exist.

Historically, capitalism's continued propensity for (and simultaneous disavowal of) political violence led to the development of new clandestine structures that could enact such violence in the name of "security" without public accountability. Moreover, the cases referred to above show that although the conduits of *deep politics* invariably include elements of state security agencies, the locus of agency does not reside inherently in the regular state hierarchy, but rather subsists in a heterogeneous network of interlocking military-industrial-corporate interests with strong institutional connections to elements of the state. This undercuts traditional Realist accounts of the unitary rational structure of the state, as well as Schmitt's totalitarian theorization of state power in terms of a unilateral, monist sovereign

U.S. Interests in Central Asia and the Challenges to Them. Ft. Belvoir: U.S. Army War College Strategic Studies Institute.

91 Recent U.S., British and EU defense planning documents to this effect are explored in Ahmed, N. M. 2010. *A User's Guide to the Crisis of Civilisation and How to Save It*. London: Pluto.

entity.[92] Instead, the modern liberal state appears not as the overriding driver of *deep political* action, but rather as a site of struggle between "dual" tensions amid labor and capital; the former originating from the popular will and affecting the public face of the civilian administration, and the latter emanating from the networked-power of lobbies co-extensive with the interests of increasingly criminalized U.S.-dominated transnational capital. Here, U.S.-led deployment of covert action emerges as a tool of the U.S. military-industrial-corporate complex in its struggle to "calibrate" levels of violence in such a way as to manipulate public opinion and state policy, and thereby dominate national constellations of transnational capital—with devastating consequences for national security.

Additionally, the trigger for the adoption of such exceptional measures is *elite perception of a crisis* which in some way is believed to fundamentally undermine the state's adherence to the political, economic and ideological practices most conducive to the interests of the emerging military-industrial-corporate complex. This of course had different implications in distinctive historically-specific geopolitical contexts. Thus, prior to and during World War II, elite crisis-perception was focused on the specter of rising dominion over Eurasia by rival powers, particularly Germany and secondarily the USSR, Japan and China. During the Cold War, the principal geopolitical obstacle to U.S. Eurasian hegemony remained the USSR, but the United States was also faced with the collapse of the British and European empires and their debilitation in the aftermath of the war. Local uprisings and contingencies continually generated new local crises eliciting diverse covert and overt U.S.-led responses. Finally, the post-9/11 trajectory of the "War on Terror" has become radicalized in the context of growing perceptions of an imminent decline in U.S. hegemony caused by multiple factors beyond immediate U.S. control—not merely the economic rise of rivals like China and India, but the recognition of the inherent structural fragilities of the global political economy due to ecological, energy and financial crises.

In these cases, the crisis-perceptions belonging to a U.S.-dominated transnational capitalist class preceded the intervention not simply of a U.S. *deep state*, but of a U.S.-dominated *deep system* which had already proliferated covert military, intelligence and financial relationships with a wide variety of other state actors and non-state networks. While these *deep political economic structures* might permit state security agencies to be routinely co-opted in the service of a complex and heterogeneous nexus of U.S.-dominated transnational capitalist class interests, this very co-optation requires for its legitimization new narratives of threat by which to construct these state activities as functioning in the national public interest. The *deep system* has thus driven the exclusionary securitization of specific social, political and religious groups, most prominently linked to the categories of "Islam" and "Muslim"; while simultaneously facilitating the activities of Islamist militant networks—with the combined result of legitimizing a permanent global state of exception in the form of the "War on Terror" and

92 See Chapter 1, this volume.

normalizing the exceptional through the institutionalization of new militarized social, political and cultural practices and values.

Practically, in the context of ongoing *deep* collaboration with Islamist extremists, this has left recent U.S. administrations in an impotent position—hopelessly firefighting against blowback from the clandestine activities of their own "security" agencies. This discussion thus has radical implications for our understanding of national security and terrorism, and thus for a truly critical terrorism studies. Not only is the distinction between state and non-state terrorism blurred, but orthodox categorizations of terrorism are naïve. On the contrary, the prevalence of terrorism emerged precisely in the context of the consolidation of the modern capitalist nation-state, and as a tool for its self-consolidation. This analysis has further shown that the continuing threat of international terrorism, particularly in its Islamist crystallizations, is directly linked to the criminalization of the global political economy as well as its over-dependence on hydrocarbon energies, along with associated U.S.-led military intelligence strategies developed to control them. From this perspective, the "War on Terror" is not merely an inherently self-defeating exercise that fuels the grievances behind terrorist recruitment, nor even simply a state-generated discursive securitization complex. Rather, it constitutes a matrix of exclusionary ideology and political violence generated as an exceptional U.S.-dominated transnational capitalist response to a looming ecological, energy and economic crisis of U.S. hegemony. Rolling back this *securitization matrix* will be no easy task, but it cannot even begin without greater interrogation of the political economy of the state of exception as equivalent to the *deep politics* of the capitalist economy.

Chapter 4
"America is Addicted to Oil": U.S. Secret Warfare and Dwindling Oil Reserves in the Context of Peak Oil and 9/11

Daniele Ganser

Global Oil Consumption and Population Growth

"America is addicted to oil," former U.S. President Gorge W. Bush declared in April 2006, and he was right.[1] Oil is the most important energy source today in the world. Oil covers 33 percent of the global energy demand and is more dominant than the other three non-renewable energy sources coal (25 percent) natural gas (23 percent) and nuclear energy (5 percent). I am convinced that the world must leave all non-renewable energies, enhance energy efficiency and shift to renewable energies including hydroelectricity, wind energy, sun energy, biofuels, biogas and geothermal energy. But the transformation of the global energy system will take time and faces a number of obstacles. In the meantime oil will remain dominant. The renewable energies are growing fast but still contribute only 14 percent to the global energy mix.[2]

It is rather difficult to understand how much oil we need every day, because the numbers are so huge. According to the BP Statistical Review of World Energy oil consumption stood at a recrod 87 million barrels (each about 159 liters) per day in 2010.[3] This equals 44 supertankers which the global economy needs every day. The world is very strongly addicted to oil. If the oil supply stopped overnight and the world was forced to live for a year without any oil at all the global economy as we know it would crash and go through a fundamental transformation. People who bet on non-renewable energies would lose a lot of money, while those who invest in renewable energies would become wealthy.

---

1 President Bush Jnr. April 25, 2006. *State of the Union Address*. The White House (accessed March 1, 2012).

2 On how fast the renewable energies grow compare*: REN21: Renewables 2011*. July 2011. Global Status Report. 115.

3 *BP Statistical Review*. June 2011. 46. Available at: bp.com/statisticalreview (accessed March 1, 2012).

Oil has been an integral part of the global energy mix for only 150 years. While I am writing this text I am 40 years old. Oil has always been around in my lifetime, it was always cheap and supply was abundant. I can hardly think of a world without oil. All readers of this text are younger than 150 years and have therefore always lived in the oil age like me and consume oil in one form or another. We are all in this together, and we have all become very used to the oil age. It has always been here throughout our lives. And therefore we used more and more of the oil without thinking about the consequences.

The world's oil consumption increases each year. The numbers are impressive: the age of crude oil began in 1850. At the outset, only relatively small amounts were extracted and consumed. The world's population was about seven times smaller than it is today. By the eve of World War I in 1914, consumption for the first time reached one million barrels per day. At the end of World War II, daily global consumption had climbed to six million barrels. Only after the end of World War II did the world experience its first real oil glut. Oil heating, cargo ships, automobiles, airplanes and plastic products started to become widespread and the thirst for oil increased. In 1962 when the Cuban Missile Crisis occurred, global daily consumption already had reached 22 million barrels. At the time of the Chernobyl nuclear disaster in 1986, global oil consumption stood at 61 million barrels per day. In 2010, as specified above, oil consumption had risen to a record 87 million barrels per day.

For the last 10 years I have studied the history of oil and taught history classes on the subject to my students at Basel University and Zurich University in my native Switzerland. It strikes me that during this time more and more credible oil experts have come forward to warn of dwindling oil supplies and a serious and long-lasting oil crisis in the near future, most likely before the year 2020.[4] Based on the data that I have seen I am convinced that these warnings are correct and must be taken very seriously. I believe that global oil production will reach a maximum called "peak oil" at less than 100 million barrels per day before the year 2020. Once peak oil is reached the oil crisis will start as supply will plateau and then decline. As far as the oil is concerned we are certainly living in revolutionary times because no generation before us has experienced global peak oil.

The relatively short oil age has seen a very strong population growth. In 2011 we reached the new record of seven billion people, never before in human history have we been so many on the blue planet. In the first year of the Common Era (C.E.) global population was around 300 million. It took more than 1,000 years to double this population to 600 million people as energy was scarce. In 1800 the world's population was one billion. Technological progress added coal, oil, gas and nuclear energy to the global energy mix. And in just 200 years, the global population has reached seven billion people; never before has the world population grown so quickly in such a short time. Today we add 80 million people

4 Compare: Campbell, C. 2011. *Peak Oil Personalities: What Happens when the Oil Starts to Run Out?* Skibbereen: Inspire Books.

(roughly the population of Germany) every year to the global population, and energy demand is therefore strong. It is remarkable that it took just 12 years for the population to increase from six to seven billion people.

U.S. Oil Consumption and the Ties of the Bush Administration to the Oil Industry

The United States is by far the biggest oil consumer of the world. According to the BP Statistical Review of World Energy U.S. oil consumption stood at 19 million barrels per day in 2010. This means that almost one out of four barrels which are available globally every day is being consumed by the United States, despite the fact that the United States has only 5 percent of the global population.

"We have about 50% of the world's wealth but only 6.3 of its population. This disparity is particularly great as between ourselves and the peoples of Asia," George F. Kennan, senior member of the U.S. Department of State, realized already in 1948 in a then top-secret and now declassified policy paper. Kennan argued that the United States can not promote human rights globally, but must focus on maintaining its privileges with the help of its military and defend this position of disparity.

> We should dispense with the aspiration to "be liked" or to be regarded as the repository of a high-minded international altruism … We should cease to talk about vague – and for the Far East – unreal objectives such as human rights, the raising of the living standards, and democratization. The day is not far off when we are going to have to deal in straight power concepts. The less we are hampered by idealistic slogans, the better.[5]

China is an oil-producing country. Until 1994 China was able to satisfy its oil thirst by pumping its domestic supply. Yet during the last two decades the oil consumption of China has increased strongly. China is no longer able to satisfy its oil demand with its own wells. With nine million barrels used per day China is the second largest consumer and competes with the United States over dwindling supplies. Japan ranks third with a consumption of more than four million barrels per day, India and Russia need around three million barrels every day, and Germany more than two million barrels. All these countries are important strategic players, and each would be devastated if its oil imports were cut off.[6]

5 Compare: McClintock, M. 1992. *Instruments of Statecraft: U.S. Guerrilla Warfare, Counterinsurgency, and Counter-Terrorism 1940–1990*. New York: Pantheon Books. 8.

6 BP Statistical Review. June 2011. 9.

The United States once used to be the world's biggest oil producer. Yet those days are gone; U.S. production reached a maximum in 1970 and then declined.[7] According to the BP Statistical Review of World Energy U.S. oil production now stands at 7.5 million barrels per day. This means that every day the United States must import more than 11 million barrels of oil or around six supertankers. This is an extremely difficult challenge as the largest oil reserves are in Muslim countries, some of which are hostile to the United States.

The White House, the Pentagon, the CIA and members of Congress are aware of the extremely strong U.S. dependence on oil imports. "And here we have a serious problem: America is addicted to oil, which is often imported from unstable parts of the world," President George W. Bush observed correctly in his State of the Union Adress in April 2006. The United States, the President argued, must "move beyond a petroleum-based economy, and make our dependence on Middle Eastern oil a thing of the past."[8]

Although the U.S. administration rarely admits it openly, it is willing to kill and fight wars in order to secure its oil supply. Furthermore, the evidence shows that the U.S. elite is willing to engage in criminal acts, including the presentation of lies to the United Nations Security Council, in order to justify wars of aggression to secure dwindling oil supplies. As the biggest oil reserves are in the Persian Gulf, including the countries Iraq, Iran, Kuwait and Saudi Arabia, this region has become of the greatest strategic importance to the United States.

Already in 1944 U.S. oil geologist Everette Lee DeGolyer, who inspected the Persian Gulf region on a secret mission on the orders of U.S. President Franklin Delano Roosevelt at the end of the World War II, was impressed how much oil there was in these Muslim nations. DeGolyer and his men found abundant supplies; "The oil in this region is the greatest single prize in all history," one of the astonished members of the secret mission told officials in the State Department.[9]

Ever since, the United States with its strong dependence on oil has tried to get access to the reserves in the Persian Gulf. John Bolton, former U.S. ambassador to the United Nations during the Bush administration and Senior Fellow with the Project for the New American Century (PNAC) on Fox News in 2011 described the Persian Gulf frankly as "the critical oil and natural gas producing region that we fought so many wars to try and protect our economy from the adverse impact of losing that supply or having it available at very high prices."[10]

When the Bush administration entered the White House in January 2001 it was acutely aware of the U.S. dependence on oil imports as many of its leading

---

7 Compare: Heinberg, R. 2003. *The Party's Over: Oil, War and the Fate of Industrial Societies*. Gabriola Island, BC: New Society Publishers.

8 President Bush Jnr. April 25, 2006. *State of the Union Address*. The White House.

9 Yergin, D. 1991. *The Prize: The Epic Quest for Oil, Money and Power*. New York: Free Press. 393.

10 *Interview on Fox News with John Bolton US Ambassador to the United Nations*. Aired on October 22, 2011.

representatives had close contacts to the oil industry and oil-producing countries. National Security Advisor Condoleezza Rice had served as one of the directors of the San Francisco-based multinational oil firm Chevron from 1991 to 2001. Chevron in 1995 had even named an oil tanker after her, but when she joined the Bush administration quietly renamed it *Altair Voyager*. Rice explained that Chevron had a policy of naming tankers after its directors, while the *San Francisco Chronicle* said the tanker was one of the "most visible reminders of the Bush administration's ties to big oil." Chuck Lewis of the Washington-based Center for Public Integrity stressed that the tanker's name showed "that there's never been an administration in power in this country that has been so close to a single industry – in this instance, the oil-and-gas industry."[11]

Vice-President Dick Cheney, the conservative hard-liner, was driectly linked both to an oil company as well to a war in an oil-producing country. From 1989 on Cheney had served as secretary of defense under Bush's father and had been actively involved in Operation Desert Strom and the war in Iraq and Kuwait in 1990 and 1991. Soon after leaving the Pentagon he became CEO of Halliburton, the large Texas-based energy and oil service firm, in 1995. He served until Bush Junior picked him to be his running mate for the election in the summer of 2000.

During his time as CEO of Halliburton Cheney had studied the peak oil problem and the coming oil crisis carefully. In 1999 he had given a remarkable speech on the subject to the Institute of Petroleum in London in which he had highlighted the problem with clarity: "Producing oil is obviously a self-depleting activity," Cheney said. "Every year, you've got to find and develop reserves equal to your output – just to stand still, just to stay even." This remains a huge challenge for oil companies. ExxonMobil has to secure "over a billion and a half barrels of new oil equivalent reserves every year just to replace existing production" Cheney explained. As older oil fields deplete the search for new reserves becomes more and more difficult, Cheney predicted correctly. "By some estimates, there will be an average of 2% annual growth in global oil demand over the years ahead along with, conservatively, a 3% natural decline in production from existing reserves. That means by 2010, we will need in the order of an additional 50 million barrels a day," Cheney explained in London and asked his stunned audience: "So, where is the oil going to come from?" Most people in the audience, including the President of the Institute of Petroleum, Chris Moorhouse, knew that only the Middle East had the capacity to fill the gap. And thus it was no surprise that Cheney—a few years before the attack on Iraq—concluded: "While many regions of the world offer great oil opportunities, the Middle East with two-thirds of the world's oil and

11 Marinucci, C. May 5, 2001. Chevron Redubs Ship named for Bush Aide. Condoleezza Rice Drew Too Much Attention. *San Francisco Chronicle*.

the lowest cost, is still where the prize ultimately lies, even though companies are anxious for greater access there, progress continues to be slow."[12]

Limited Oil Supply and the Problem of Peak Oil

Many people have not yet started to ponder the question how the oil age will end. Some are influenced by media headlines like "oil reserves last for 40 years," and then silently but wrongly conclude that this means that we will have no problems for 40 years and in the 41st year all oil will be gone. Yet that is not correct. Every successful oil well has a production profile that starts at zero, rises to a maximum level of output—the peak of production—and then declines again until it reaches the level where it becomes no longer economically justifiable for further production, whereupon it goes back to zero. Without exception, every production goes through this progression. Not only does every single successful oil well have a level of peak production. The same is true for every oil field, as well as each oil-producing region, every basin or country and cumulatively the entire world.

The term "peak oil" does not refer to the end of the age of crude oil, but rather to the maximum level that the world's crude oil supplies can achieve. Even in 2050, there will still be oil, but it will be less plentiful, and available only at much higher prices. The quicker a drilling site, field or basin is developed, and the quicker the production increases, the faster these sites will be exhausted, and the steeper will be the decline toward the end of production. At what point on the time axis, and at what volume of production, the peak is reached for a field or a country often becomes evident only retrospectively.

Great Britain can offer a concrete example. During the 1950s and 1960s, it produced absolutely no oil. Then came the discovery of reserves in the North Sea. Great Britain began producing oil offshore in 1970. At the beginning, production could be increased from year to year. In the mid-1980s, it reached an initial peak of 2.6 million barrels per day. Then the production unexpectedly dropped following a serious accident on the oil production platform Piper Alpha 170 kilometers off the coast, which led to loss of 167 lives. After the fire was put out, and following restoration of the site, Britain resumed production in the North Sea, which reached a peak production level of 2.8 million barrels in the year 2000. Because of a continual decline in pressure in the oil fields, there was a corresponding drop as well in the volume of oil produced. Since 2000, Great Britain's oil production has dropped by about 5 percent on an annual basis. Britain still produces oil but less from year to year.

At the same time British domestic oil consumption remains high and in 2006 stood at around 1.7 million barrels, while the declining fields provided just

---

12 Cheney, D. *IP Autumn Lunch*. Institute of Petroleum. London. Available at: http://web.archive.org/web/20000414054656/http://www.petroleum.co.uk/speeches.htm (accessed March 1, 2012).

1.6 million barrels. Since 2006 the British have been net oil importers. The government is frustrated that it exported oil while it was cheap and now has to import oil while it is expensive. The British still remain an important oil producer, but on the international oil market they are a buyer, not a seller. In 2012, Britain was producing only 1.3 barrels per day. In other words, over only 10 years, production has halved! It is expected that by the year 2050, Britain will cease producing oil. "This is not just a national problem – it is a global problem of supply and demand, not just in the short term, but the medium term and the long term" former British Prime Minister Gordon Brown correctly emphasized.[13]

Obviously Britain is only one of the world's 197 countries. Therefore most people completely ignore the fact that Britain reached peak oil and today suffers from a decline in production that turned the country into a net importer. Many hope that there are enough countries out there with huge oil reserves that can fill the gap so we can continue our oil consumption undisturbed as we did during the last 60 years. But we must realize that only 30 countries in the world out of 197 produce oil if we take 500,000 barrels of crude oil per day as a meaningful production threshold. In other words: not many countries produce oil; most, including my native Switzerland, produce no oil at all and are totally dependent on oil imports.

The 30 oil-producing countries which are of strategic relevance are well known. In Europe these are Great Britain, Norway and Russia; in the Middle East Saudi Arabia, Iraq, Iran, Kuwait, Qatar, Oman and the UAE; in Africa the countries are Nigeria, Libya, Egypt, Algeria and Angola; in the Americas the United States, Venezuela, Colombia, Mexico, Canada, Argentina, Brazil and Ecuador; in Asia China, Indonesia, Australia, Kazakhstan, Azerbaijan and Malaysia produce more than 500,000 barrels per day.

The stability of the global oil production depends on these 30 countries. This stability is now at risk because some of the world's 30 major oil-producing countries have reached peak oil and are now witnessing a significant drop in output. These countries include Great Britain, Norway, Mexico, Indonesia and the United States. Other countries, including Saudi Arabia, Iraq, Libya and Brazil, have not yet reached peak oil, and must compensate for the declines in production in other oil-producing nations and an increasing global demand.

As a result of peak oil, resource wars and political unrest, the world's oil supplies are in a critical phase. It must be stressed that this phase will hardly be one of short duration, like the oil crisis of 1973/1974 which lastet only a few weeks—but rather represents the beginning of a new energy age, one in which oil is scarce, fought over and expensive, while renewable energies, "clean technology" and "energy efficiency" are becoming more important with each passing year.

The crucial strategic question is: by how much can world oil production increase from its current level of 87 million barrels per day before reaching a global peak and going into decline? In its annual World Energy Outlook (WEO),

---

13 Porter, A. May 28, 2008. Gordon Brown: High Oil Prices will Remain. *Telegraph.*

the Paris-based International Energy Agency stated in 2004 that the global production of oil would increase until 2030 with no problem, and could be raised to a level of 121 million barrels. According to the IEA there was no peak oil in sight. In the 2005 WEO the IEA claimed that 120 million barrels per day would be produced in 2030. But the oil-producing industry, facing depleting oil fields, contested these optimistic forecasts. "Numbers like 120 million barrels per day will never be reached, never," declared Christophe de Margerie, CEO of French oil company Total.[14]

The IEA was forced to correct its optimistic prognosis. In 2006 it declared in the WEO that global oil production could rise to only 116 million barrels in 2030. Yet also this figure was too high. In the WEO of 2008, the level was further lowered, this time the IEA stated that the world would have to contend with a level of 105 million barrels per day in 2030. "I am sorry to say this, but we are headed toward really bad days," Fatih Birol conceeded, the main person responsible for the report and the chief economist of the IEA.[15]

When the IEA published its WEO in November 2009, and once again forecast a level of 105 million barrels for 2030, international media reacted with mistrust. "The number 120 was always nonsense," declared one IEA insider, who declined to be identified and was quoted in the British newspaper the *Guardian* a day before the publication of the report. "But even the current numbers are exaggerated, and the IEA knows this. Many people within the IEA believe it will not be possible to maintain production at 90 to 95 million barrels per day. But if the numbers are further lowered, some people fear panic could break out in financial markets."[16]

Based on the data to which I have access, I believe that the IEA's calculations for future oil production in all IEA reports over the past 10 years have been far too optimistic. It was in the WEO 2010, published in November 2010, that the IEA admitted for the first time that peak oil was a reality. The IEA explained that peak oil for conventional petroleum had been reached in 2006 at 70 million barrels per day. "The news are [*sic*] not very bright," Birol admitted. "We think that crude oil production has already peaked in 2006. The existing fields are declining sharply in the North Sea and in the United States … The time is running out."[17]

The publication of the WEO 2010 marked a historic turning point for oil, as it confirmed that production from conventional, and thus cheap, oil has reached a maximum level, will plateau for some years, and will then collapse. Although this situation is now a reality most people are not aware of it. Because unconventional oil from deep sea wells or derived from tar sands together with natural gas liquids will allow for some growth in global oil production according to the IEA.

14 Mortished, C. April 8, 2006. World Cannot Meet Oil Demand. *The Times*.

15 Walt, V. November 7, 2007. Oil Prices: It Gets Worse. *Time Magazine*.

16 Macalister, T. November 9, 2009. Key Oil Figures were Distorted by US Pressure, says Whistleblower. *Guardian*.

17 Fatih Birol interviewed by Dr. Jonica Newby. April 28, 2011. *Catalyst: The Oil Crunch*. Australian Broadcasting Corporation.

But unconventional oil is very expensive to produce and thus a heavy burden on the economy. The IEA therefore warned repeatedly of a coming energy crisis: "We are on the brink of a new energy order," Faith Birol declared in early 2008, shortly before the oil price rose to its all time high of 148 dollars. "Over the next few decades, our reserves of oil will start to run out and it is imperative that governments in both producing and consuming nations prepare now for that time. We should not cling to crude down to the last drop – we should leave oil before it leaves us."[18]

In the United States Republican Congressman Roscoe Bartlett warned regularly of peak oil and the dangers the country is about to face from oil shortages. On June 29, 2005, Bartlett met with President Bush at the White House for "an extensive discussion about peak oil— the end of cheap oil," as Bartlett summarized the meeting.[19] In public Bartlett stressed repeatedly that the peak oil challenge must be taken seriously. "Today, experts differ only on the timing of global peak oil," Bartlett said in 2006. "With world demand for oil increasing exponentially and no ready substitute of comparable energy density, the prospect of future and continuing declines in world oil production will inflict unprecedented pressures upon our people and national and international social, economic, and political institutions."[20]

We know that U.S. presidents including Bush and Clinton and Obama are well informed of the peak oil problem. Bill Clinton publicly spoke about the phenomenon after leaving office. "We may be at a point of peak oil production," Clinton declared in a speech at the London Business School in 2006. "The Indians and Chinese are in this huge fight now to see who can get the most oil" the former President observed and correctly predicted: "You may see $100 a barrel oil in the next two or three years."[21]

The Iraq War and the U.S. Struggle to Secure Dwindling Oil Supplies

Iraq has the third largest known oil reserves in the world, after Saudi Arabia and Iran. But following the Iran–Iraq War in the 1980s, the Kuwait War in 1990/1991 and the ensuing U.S. sanctions Iraq's oil facilities were starved of investment and in an advanced state of decay. Before the 2003 war Iraq exported only around 1.5 million barrels a day but U.S. energy experts suggested this could be increased

18 Birol, F. March 2, 2008. We Can't Cling to Crude: We should Leave Oil before it Leaves Us. *Independent.*

19 *The Peak Oil Crisis: Mid Year 2005.* July 13, 2005. Falls Church News.

20 *House Peak Oil Caucus Reaches Out to Sweden.* December 14, 2005. Environment News Service.

21 Clinton, B. March 28, 2006. *The Opportunity for Private Citizens to Effect Positive Change in an Increasingly Interdependent World.* Speech at the London Business School in: Clinton on Peak Oil and Global Warming. April 24, 2006. *Energy Bulletin.*

to six million barrels within five to 10 years if U.S. and other international oil companies were given access to the protected national Iraqi oil market.

Before the war, in December 2002, Fadel Gheit, a former ExxonMobil chemical engineer and then an investment specialist told 50 of the largest pension funds and financial investors in the United States that the expected war against Iraq was "all about oil" and that the global fight against terrorism was just "camouflage" to mask the real purpose. Based on the data that I have studied I fully agree with the assessment of Gheit. Fadel Gheit explained to the *Guardian* that:

> The Americans have nothing against the people of Iraq but our way of life is dependent on 20 million barrels a day and half of it has to be imported. We are like a patient on oil dialysis. It's a matter of life and death. The smart people [in Washington] all know this but its not generally advertised on the kind of shows that most people watch: MTV and soap operas.[22]

The Bush administration knew that securing the oil fields of Iraq would enable the United States to grab the oil for their own needs as well as to open up new reserves that could increase global production and thus help to ease the upward pressure on the oil price which made U.S. oil imports more and more expensive. "When there is a regime change in Iraq, you could add 3 million to 5 million barrels of production to world supply," President Bush's then-chief economic advisor, Lawrence Lindsey, suggested before the war in 2002. "The successful prosecution of the war would be good for the economy." Moreover, the United States could seize the Iraqi oil before China, India or the EU, all of whom depend heavily on oil imports.[23]

The Iraqis had little illusions that a war would be unleashed upon them because of the oil they possessed. "Our oil is the main reason America wants to attack Iraq," said Ali al-Rawi, head of the economics department at Baghdad University, before the United States attacked. "They want to control our oil and control price and production levels. They know the future oil resources for the world will continue to come from this area for many years."[24]

The United States did not attack Iraq alone but together with Great Britain. Like the United States the UK is facing a declining domestic oil production after having reached peak oil. Prime Minister Tony Blair stressed repeatedly in public that the Iraq War was not about the oil. Yet Michael Meacher, Environment Minister in the Blair government from 1997 to 2003, brazenly contradicted the Queen's First Minister. "The US and the UK are beginning to run out of secure hydrocarbon energy supplies," Meacher correctly stressed. "The so-called

22 Macalister, T. January 23, 2003. A Matter of Life, Death – and Oil. Weapons of Mass Destruction are cited as the Spur for Action. Perhaps the Real Motive is something just as Urgent? *Guardian*.

23 Salopek, P. July 29, 2006. A Tank of Gas, a World of Trouble. *Chicago Tribune*.

24 Macalister, T. January 23, 2003.

'war on terrorism' is being used largely as bogus cover for achieving wider US strategic geopolitical objectives," said Meacher after he was sacked by Blair in June 2003. "Nor has the UK been disinterested in this scramble for the remaining world supplies of hydrocarbons, and this may partly explain British participation in US military actions."[25]

The data which is available today proves that Meacher was right when he stressed that the Tony Blair government was interested in Iraq's oil. In October and November 2002, half a year before the invasion of Iraq, British government ministers met with representatives of the world's largest oil companies to discuss access to Iraqi oil. The relevant government documents, minutes of a series of meetings between representatives of BP and Shell with Baroness Elizabeth Symons, then the British Trade Minister, became public only in 2011, long after the outbreak of the war. But they clearly demonstrate that access to oil was crucial. "We see that oil was in fact one of the Government's most important strategic considerations," researcher Greg Muttitt found. Muttitt had obtained over 1,000 documents relating to oil and the Iraq War under the Freedom of Information Act. The British government "secretly colluded with oil companies to give them access to that huge prize," concludes Muttitt.[26]

Neither the U.S. nor the British government spoke of oil when addressing their own populations, let alone peak oil. Instead, the Bush administration and the government of Prime Minister Tony Blair argued that an attack on Iraq was necessary because the country was hiding dangerous weapons of mass destruction (WMD). "Intelligence gathered by this and other governments leaves no doubt that the Iraq regime continues to possess and conceal some of the most lethal weapons ever devised," President Bush claimed falsely on March 17, 2003, shortly before the attack on Iraq. "The danger is clear: using chemical, biological or, one day, nuclear weapons, obtained with the help of Iraq, the terrorists could fulfill their stated ambitions and kill thousands or hundreds of thousands of innocent people in our country, or any other."[27]

On February 5, 2003, one month before the war, U.S. Secretary of State Colin Powell had presented "evidence" of Iraq's alleged WMD to the United Nations Security Council. The UN members were not convinced and refused to pass a resolution that would have supported the U.S. war against Iraq. It later turned out that the doubts of the UN members were well founded. The WMD story was a lie. In 2005 Powell explained he felt "terrible" and apologized for having falsely presented an Iraqi weapons program that turned out not to exist. "I'm the one who presented it on behalf of the United States to the world … it will always be a part

25 Meacher, M. September 6, 2003. This War on Terrorism is Bogus. *Guardian*.

26 Muttitt, G. quoted in Bignell, P. April 19, 2011. Secret Memos Expose Link between Oil Firms and Invasion of Iraq. *Independent*. Compare also the book of Muttitt, G. 2011. *Fuel on Fire. Oil and Politics in Occupied Iraq*. London: Bodley Head.

27 President Says Saddam Hussein Must Leave Iraq Within 48 Hours. March 17, 2003. *The White House*, Office of the Press Secretary.

of my record." That is a "painful" and a permanent "blot" on my record, Powell said.[28]

On March 20, 2003 the United States started to bomb Iraq, and soon after U.S. forces based in Kuwait invaded the country. Iraq's President Saddam Hussein went into hiding. After he was found he was hanged in December 2006. Officially the Iraq War ended in December 2011 when most U.S. ground forces withdrew from the country. According to Brookings' Iraq index more than 150,000 Iraqis and 4,487 U.S. soldiers were killed.[29] The Congressional Research Service estimates the cost of the war at 800 billion dollars by the end of 2011, whilst the U.S. economist Joseph Stiglitz argued the costs were much higher and amounted to 3,000 billion dollars.[30]

Given the staggering costs in lives and money the question arises who wanted this war anyway? Already in 1998 the Project for a New American Century (PNAC) had urged in a letter to President Bill Clinton that "removing Saddam Hussein and his regime … now needs to become the aim of American foreign policy."[31] The neoconservative think tank PNAC headed by William Kristol was among those forces in the United States which pushed the Iraq War. PNAC members including Dick Cheney, Donald Rumsfeld and Paul Wolfowitz even participated in the war themselves after becoming members of the Bush administration.

Paul Wolfowitz, U.S. Deputy Defense Secretary and a strong advocate of military action against Afghanistan and Iraq, openly confirmed in an address to delegates at an Asian security summit in Singapore in June 2003 that the main reason for the U.S. attack on Iraq was the oil. Asked why a nuclear power such as North Korea was being treated differently from Iraq, where no weapons of mass destruction had been found, Wolfowitz said: "Let's look at it simply. The most important difference between North Korea and Iraq is that economically, we just had no choice in Iraq. The country swims on a sea of oil."[32]

Wolfowitz had previously described the story of the weapons of mass destruction (WMD) as a "bureaucratic" excuse for war. "For reasons that have a lot to do with the US government bureaucracy," Wolfowitz told *Vanity Fair*, "we settled on the one issue that everyone could agree on: weapons of mass

---

28 *Powell in Interview with Barbara Walters*, ABC News in Weisman, S. September 9, 2005. Powell Calls His U.N. Speech a Lasting Blot on His Record. *New York Times*.

29 *Brookings: IRAQ INDEX. Tracking Reconstruction and Security in Post-Saddam Iraq*. The Brookings Insitute Saban Centre for Middle East Study. Available at: www.brookings.edu/saban/iraq-index.aspx (accessed March 1, 2012).

30 Stiglitz, J. 2008. *The Three Trillion Dollar War: The True Cost of the Iraq Conflict*. New York: Norton and Company.

31 Hurst, S. 2009 *The United States and Iraq since 1979: Hegemony, Oil and War*. Edinburgh: Edinburgh University Press. 136.

32 Wright, G. June 4, 2003. Wolfowitz: Iraq War Was About Oil. *Guardian*.

destruction."[33] The WMD story was a lie to sell a war. It was told over and over again to the U.S. public, while the terms "peak oil" and "resource wars" barely surfaced in the U.S. media.

"The doctrine, that prevails in the United States and Britain, is that we have to believe the United States would have so-called liberated Iraq even if its main products were lettuce and pickles and the main energy resource of the world were in central Africa," MIT professor Noam Chomsky remarked.

But anyone with a functioning brain knows that that's not true—as all Iraqis do, for example. The United States invaded Iraq because its major resource is oil. And it gives the United States, to quote Zbigniew Brzezinski, "critical leverage" over its competitors, Europe and Japan ... that's the fundamental reason for invading Iraq, not anything else.[34]

We therefore find that both in the United States as well as in the UK there were high ranking observers who critisized the attack on Iraq. Also Alan Greenspan, Chairman of the Federal Reserve, for once agreed with Noam Chomsky and commented: "I am saddened that it is politically inconvenient to acknowledge what everyone knows. The Iraq war is largely about oil."[35]

The Terrorist Attacks of September 11 (9/11) and Dwindling Oil Supplies

States which want to go to war against the wishes of their citizens turn to propaganda as a tool of persuasion. Asked in a 2006 survey to explain their presence in Iraq, 85 percent of American soldiers said that the "main mission" was "to retaliate for Saddam's role" in the September 11 attacks. Another survey showed that about two-thirds of American civilians in the United States shared that misapprehension.[36]

Although it is generally difficult to convince citizens to go to war, particularly when their country has not been attacked, the data from the Iraq War clearly shows that large-scale social control is possible. The results of the above-mentioned surveys are frightening. They show that war propaganda works very well indeed. The majority of the U.S. soldiers in Iraq and the majority of the U.S. population believed the lies of the Bush administration. Not because the lies had been well founded, but because they had been repeated over and over again on TV.

This reminds me of Josef Goebbels, propaganda minister for Hitler's Nazi Party, who once explained: "If you tell a lie big enough and keep repeating it, people will eventually come to believe it." This is exactly what the Bush

33 Wright, G. June 4, 2003.

34 Hastings, M. January 4, 2006. Prof. Noam Chomsky interviewed by Michael Hastings. *Newsweek Magazine*.

35 Beaumont, P. September 16, 2007. Greenspan Admits Iraq was about Oil, as Deaths put at 1.2m. *Guardian*.

36 Amis, M. September 2, 2006. The Real Conspiracy behind 9/11. *The Times*.

administration did with the WMD lies before the attack on Iraq. Goebbels stressed, however, that every lie can be destroyed:

> The lie can be maintained only for such time as the State can shield the people from the political, economic and/or military consequences of the lie. It thus becomes vitally important for the State to use all of its powers to repress dissent, for the truth is the mortal enemy of the lie, and thus by extension, the truth is the greatest enemy of the State.[37]

This does not imply that there were no U.S. citizens who spoke out against the Iraq oil war; in fact there were thousands, many of whom protested publicly one month before the attack on February 15, 2003 in New York and other U.S. cities. Large anti-war demonstrations were also held in London, Paris and Rome. Among those who criticized the lies of the Bush administration was Michael Ruppert, an investigative journalist and former Los Angeles Police Department officer. "After the 9-11 attacks the US government lied to create a war for oil in Iraq telling us that Saddam Hussein had weapons of mass destruction, almost-ready atom bombs, poison gas and deadly germs," Ruppert asserted. "We were told that he helped execute the 9/11 attacks. It was all lies, and no one has held the US accountable."[38]

While I was teaching contemporary history at the history departement of Zuerich University and Basel University in Switzerland my students confronted me with the simple questions: if the Bush administration lied about the WMD, did they also lie about the terrorist attacks of September 11, 2001? Did they manipulate the attacks in order to get access to dwindling oil resources in the context of peak oil?

I found the question interesting, although I was of course aware that it was politically sensitive to discuss and research such a question. I know that many different views on what really happened on 9/11 circulate around the globe today, including fierce debates on who is right and who is wrong. Roughly speaking I see three different 9/11 theories that compete for the truth: SURPRISE, LIHOP and MIHOP.

The first 9/11 theory is the so-called SURPRISE. Offered by the Bush administration and the official 9/11 report it claims that Osama bin Laden conspired with Khalid Sheikh Mohammed, Mohamed Atta, and other men to attack the United States on 9/11. The SURPRISE theory argues that 9/11 was a Muslim conspiracy. It concedes that there were rumors about a looming attack, but insists that the U.S. intelligence community, including the NSA, CIA, FBI, DIA, and other intelligence services, along with the Pentagon, were unable to prevent

---

37 Josef Goebbels quoted in Martin, G. and Steuter, E. 2010. *Pop Culture Goes to War: Enlisting and Resisting Militarism in the War on Terror*. Plymouth: Lexington. 48.

38 Ruppert, M. C. August 16, 2006. *A Permanent Goodbye to the United States*. The Wilderness Publications. Available at: www.fromthewilderness.com/free/ww3/081606_burning_bridge.shtml (accessed March 1, 2012).

the conspiracy from being implemented. The second 9/11 theory on offer is the so-called LIHOP (Let It Happen On Purpose) theory. Like the surprise theory, it assumes that Osama bin Laden conspired with Khalid Sheikh Mohammed, Mohamed Atta, and other men to attack the United States on 9/11. In stark contrast to the SURPRISE theory, however, the LIHOP theory claims that persons within the U.S. government deliberately allowed the attacks to be carried out in order to be able to start a number of wars that had been planned in advance. The third 9/11 theory on offer is the so-called MIHOP (Make It Happen On Purpose) theory. It argues that "criminal persons" within the U.S. government, in the Pentagon and the intelligence community, carried out the attacks themselves in order to be able to start a number of wars that had been planned in advance.

It is important to stress that all of the theories about 9/11 are conspiracy theories. A conspiracy is a secret agreement between two or more persons to engage in a criminal act. Conspiracies are nothing unusual or new in the field of historical research. At least since the assassination of Julius Caesar in classical Rome more than 2,000 years ago, conspiracies have been an element of the political fight for influence and power. As 9/11 was a criminal act which was definitively not planned and carried out by one single person alone but by at least two or more persons who agreed on the plan before it was implemented, 9/11 must be classified as a conspiracy. Once we realize that none of the theories can be dismissed on the grounds that it is a "conspiracy theory," the real question then becomes: which conspiracy theory correctly describes the 9/11 conspiracy?

My students had to read the 571-page official account of the terrorist attacks: *The 9/11 Commission Report* (sometimes called the Kean-Zelikow Report) which was published in July 2004. The Kean-Zelikow Report supports the official narrative: that Bin Laden is responsible for 9/11, and the Bush administration, in gleeful accord, declared that the Kean-Zelikow Report is the correct version of history.

Yet other observers in the United States contradicted the state-sanctioned version. In the same year that the Kean-Zelikow Report was published Michael Ruppert presented a book on 9/11 called *Crossing the Rubicon* in which he linked 9/11 to peak oil. Employing a criminological focus, Ruppert carried out an in-depth investigation and argued that the Bush administration had not only lied about the WMD and the Iraq War, but also about 9/11. "It is my belief that sometime during the period between late 1998 and early 2000" the U.S. elites including Dick Cheney "became aware of the pending calamity of Peak Oil," Ruppert writes.[39] After securing control of the White House in the contested 2000 election Cheney with great urgency convened the National Energy Policy Development Group (NEPDG) in January 2001. The NEPDG looked at how much oil there was left in the different countries of the world. It concluded its work in late April 2001. Cheney and his oil experts in the NEPDG took a hard look at the numbers and

39 Ruppert, M. C. 2004. *Crossing the Rubicon: The Decline of the American Empire at the End of the Age of Oil*. Gabriola Island, BC: New Society Publishers. 572.

fought all the way to the Supreme Court to keep the NEPDG records secret from the American people.[40]

Ruppert believes that Cheney and many members of the NEPDG understood the reality of peak oil and decided to manipulate 9/11. "I believe that this was where the basic motive for 9/11 was fully articulated, understood, and accepted," Ruppert writes. "In May 2001 President Bush placed Dick Cheney in charge of all planning for a terror attack, effectively giving him complete control over FEMA, the military, everything."[41]

In the end, according to Ruppert, it was not Bin Laden as the SURPRISE theory claims but Cheney and his men who pulled the strings on 9/11 in order to shock the U.S. public, reduce civil liberties and start resource wars in the context of peak oil. "I have absolutely no doubt that on the day of September 11 Richard Cheney was in full and complete control," says Ruppert. "I believe it seemed to them the 'right' thing to do; after all, it was only a few thousand lives."[42]

Given the far-reaching claims that Ruppert made I expected a controversial public debate following the publication of his book to test his claims. Yet there was no debate, at least not in printed mainstream newspapers and not on mainstream television. However, on the Internet a growing group of people expressed their interest in peak oil and 9/11 and exchanged views and arguments.

In the 9/11 debate arguably the most controversial issue is the collapse of the 170-meter tall World Trade Center 7 (WTC7), the so-called "Third Tower." WTC7, a 47-story building, collapsed on 9/11 at 5:21 although unlike the Twin Towers WTC1 and WTC2 it had not been hit by a plane. According to my research there are only two explanations for how WTC7 came down: fire or controlled demolition. "Until now, the collapse of 7 World Trade has stood as one of the outstanding mysteries of the Sept. 11 attack," the *New York Times* observed in 2002, "since before then, no modern, steel-reinforced high-rise in the United States had ever collapsed in a fire."[43]

Historians awaited with much interest the official Kean-Zelikow report, for an explanation of the collapse of WTC7, yet were strongly disappointed when the official 9/11 report omitted WTC7 from its final report. "The Commission avoids another embarrassing problem – explaining how WTC7 could have collapsed, also at virtually free-fall speed – by simply not mentioning the collapse of this building," 9/11 researcher David Ray Griffin protested.[44]

On August 21, 2008 Shyam Sunder of the National Institute of Standards and Technology (NIST) presented an official governmental report on WTC7 in which

40 Ruppert, M. C. 2004. 674.

41 Ruppert, M. C. 2004. 574.

42 Ruppert, M. C. 2004. 574 and 591.

43 Glanz, March 2, 2002. Burning Diesel Is Cited in Fall Of 3rd Tower. *New York Times*.

44 Griffin, D. R. 2005. *The 9/11 Commission Report. Omissions and Distortions*. Northhampton: Olive Branch Press. 28.

he claimed that the building had collapsed due to fire. Richard Gage, a California architect and leader of a group called Architects and Engineers for 9/11 Truth, disagreed with the findings of the NIST: "There have been much hotter, longer lasting and larger fires in skyscrapers that have not fallen down."[45] Furthermore, Gage observed, WTC7 fell in perfect symmetry and at freefall from the very moment of its disintegration. Yet this, as Gage argued, was only possible if all steel columns of WTC7, more than 40 in all, were destroyed within one-tenth of a second. Fire, says Gage, cannot do this, only controlled demolition can.[46] Without any doubt, the 9/11 controversy will continue on the Internet and beyond and an agreement on what really happened on that day is not in sight.

Conclusion

Oil is the most important energy source today, but it is becoming scarce. As far as conventional oil is concerned peak oil was reached in 2006. Peak oil reminds the world that natural resources are limited. Personally I believe that we must leave oil before it leaves us and move toward renewable energies and energy efficiency. Terror and resource wars are not a sustainable answer to the peak oil problem.

Oil companies across the globe today invest heavily in non-conventional oil, including oil sands and deepwater oil. Following the explosion of the Deepwater Horizon oil platform in the Gulf of Mexico on April 22, 2010, U.S. President Obama recalled how difficult it is to leave oil: "For decades, we have known the days of cheap and easily accessible oil were numbered. For decades, we have talked and talked about the need to end America's century-long addiction to fossil fuels," Obama said. "And for decades, we have failed to act with the sense of urgency that this challenge requires. Time and again, the path forward has been blocked—not only by oil industry lobbyists, but also by a lack of political courage and candor."[47]

About a year later, in March 2011, the United States, together with France and the UK, started to bomb Libya. Muammar Gaddafi was removed from power and killed by rebels on October 20, 2011. In the context of peak oil the question arose once again whether the war in Libya had anything to do with access to oil reserves. France, the United States and UK insisted that Libya's oil had nothing to do with the war, they were only interesed in promoting democracy and human rights, they said.

---

45 Lipton, E. August 22, 2008. Report Says Fire, Not Explosion, Felled 7 W.T.C. *New York Times*.

46 Architects and Engineers for 9/11 Truth. 2011. 9/11 Explosive Evidence, Experts Speak Out. Available at: www.ae911truth.org (accessed March 1, 2012).

47 Cooper, H. June 15, 2010. Oval Office Speech: Obama Calls for New Focus on Energy Policy. *New York Times*. Compare also BP oil spill: Barack Obama's Speech in Full. *Telegraph*, June 16, 2010.

Chapter 5

Researching Parapolitics: Replication, Qualitative Research and Social Science Methodology

David N. Gibbs

When researching the topic of covert operations—one of the themes of this volume—we must of course use the same type of rigorous methodology we would use for any other social scientific topic. It is often claimed that replicability is one of the most important features for research. This chapter will explore the potential for research replication in social science and history. Though we will define replicability in greater detail later, the basic idea is simple: if an experiment is conducted properly, then another individual should be able to ask the same research question, re-gather data, undertake the experiment a second time—and come up with essentially the same result as the first experiment. In recent years, social scientists also have sought to establish a replication standard, to enhance the field's standing as an authentic science. Major figures in the profession[1] have called upon researchers to make their raw data available, to facilitate future replication studies; and for researchers to engage in publishable efforts, aimed at replicating the findings of others. Increasingly, social science journals are developing policies that facilitate replication.[2]

An obvious complication for advocates of replicability is the widespread use of qualitative techniques in research, which are based on narrative rather than statistical forms of exposition and analysis. However, Gary King and others imply that the replication standard should apply equally to qualitative research studies, just as in quantitatively oriented ones. As a general point, King insists that no fundamental distinction should be made between the techniques of qualitative and quantitative research. The widely influential *Designing Social Inquiry* begins by stating:

---

1 King, G. 1995. Replication, Replication. *PS: Political Science and Politics*, 28/3, 444–52.

2 Bueno de Mesquita, B; Gleditsch, N. P.; James, P.; King, G.; Metelits, C.; Ray, J. L.; Russett, B.; Strand, H.; Valeriano, B, 2003. ISP Symposium on Replication in International Studies Research. *International Studies Perspectives*, 4/1, 72–107. On the need for replication more generally, see also Firebaugh, G. 2007. Replication Data Sets and Favored Hypothesis Bias: Comment on Jeremy Freese and Gary King. *Sociological Methods and Research*, 36/2, 200–209.

> Our main goal is to connect the traditions of what are conventionally denoted "quantitative" and "qualitative" research … The two traditions appear quite different; indeed they sometimes seem to be at war. Our view is that these differences are mainly ones of style and specific technique. *The same underlying logic provides the framework for each research approach.* [Emphasis added][3]

Accordingly, no distinctions should be made regarding the need for replication. The specific proposal regarding the need for replicability elicited a long series of responses by various social scientists some of whom expressed skepticism at King's proposal. King's article and many of the responses focused on whether authors should be required to submit their original documentary sources to journals or publishers; most of the objections to King's article focused on the purported impracticality of his idea, that it would be excessively time consuming. Other, more fundamental issues raised by the discussion received only light scrutiny. In one reply to this discussion, Miriam Feldblum raised a series of objections and, most notably, she calls into question "the very conceptualization of research as replicable."[4] While we will not review the full content of the reply, Feldblum was right to note that the debate has so far focused on secondary issues, while it sidestepped the basic issue of whether replicability is an attainable goal.

This chapter will explore the possibility for research replication with regard to qualitative research studies. The basic argument is two-fold. Firstly, that, contrary to *Designing Social Inquiry*, qualitative research involves a distinct and separate logic of inquiry from quantitative studies, one that defies efforts at replication. Qualitative research emphasizes focused interpretation of data, requiring mental activity that is not consistently replicable, even in principle. However desirable the goal of replicability may be, it is one that cannot be applied to certain categories of analysis. Secondly, and more positively, it will be argued that the inability to replicate qualitative research does not by itself undermine the usefulness of qualitative methods.

Defining Replicability

Researchers in the natural sciences regularly replicate investigations to guard against idiosyncratic findings, tendentious research techniques, mistakes, or even fraud by the original investigator, and thereby ensure the reliability of the original finding.[5] Some qualifications are of course in order: practical considerations (such

---

3 King, G., Keohane, R. O. and Verba, S. 1994. *Designing Social Inquiry: Scientific Inference in Qualitative Research*. Princeton: Princeton University Press. 3.

4 Feldblum, M. 1996. The Study of Politics: What does Replicability Have to Do with It? *PS: Political Science and Politics*, 29/1, 7.

5 O'Hear, A. 1989. *Introduction to the Philosophy of Science*. Oxford: Clarendon Press. 61–2.

as limited time or funds) preclude replication of certain investigations. In research on some types of natural phenomena, such as the formation of supernovae or the evolution of extinct species, the underlying events themselves cannot possibly be replayed (except perhaps in a computer model, which is a very imperfect substitute for the real thing). And, as Thomas Kuhn[6] has famously argued, replicability and other investigational safeguards do not prevent such "irrational" factors as aesthetics or academic politics from influencing the direction of research.

With regard to the social sciences, Paul M. Sniderman has established three different levels at which replicability may occur:

> Level I: The researcher replicates previous research, by asking the same research question, using the same data, and using the same units of measure and estimation as the original researcher.
> Level II: The researcher asks the same research question and uses the same data. However, he/she uses different units of measure and estimation, to establish whether the original results can be replicated under a variety of conditions.
> Level III: The researcher once again asks the same research question. This time, however, entirely new data and new units of measure are used.

Levels I and II may be considered as largely technical exercises. Level III replication is by far the most useful from a research standpoint and, in the words of Sniderman, it constitutes "a necessary condition of scientific progress."[7]

Source Subjectivity

With this taxonomy of replication, let us now consider how well it applies to qualitative social scientific research. The difference between the natural and social sciences is most apparent when one looks at the types of source materials. A large percentage of sources in social science and history comprise documentary information, such as government materials, news accounts and memoirs, as well as secondary sources based on these. From these materials, the researcher endeavors to ferret out "the facts" that are useful for testing various theories. These types of narrative sources predominate in qualitative research. Ascertaining the facts from such sources is a highly subjective process. Uncertainties and inconsistencies in the factual record can create a serious, and potentially insurmountable, barrier to efforts at replicable research. All this points to a crucial difference between research in social science and in physics: the narrative sources of information

6 Kuhn, T. S. 1970. *The Structure of Scientific Revolutions*. Chicago: University of Chicago Press. 144–59.

7 Paraphrased from Sniderman, P. M. 1995. Evaluation Standards for a Slow Moving Science. *PS: Political Science and Politics*, 28/3, 464.

used in qualitative political research cannot be read with the same standards of objectivity or consistency as can the instrument panel on a cyclotron.

There is no clear-cut method, no algorithm that can help researchers discriminate among sources. The social scientist using qualitative sources faces the difficult task of determining which ones are correct and which are incorrect—a process unlikely to be replicated with any consistency. Consider such classic works as Barrington Moore's *Social Origins of Dictatorship and Democracy*; Theda Skocpol's *States and Social Revolutions*; Samuel Huntington's *Political Order in Changing Societies*; Immanuel Wallerstein's *The Modern World System*; Arno Mayer's *The Dynamics of Counter-Revolution in Europe*; or Rueschemeyer, Huber and Stephens' *Capitalist Development and Democracy*.[8] What each of the above studies has in common is that they reach general conclusions by extrapolating from several historical case studies of specific events pertaining to the selected research questions. For sources, each uses (primarily) a wide ranging survey of secondary literature, mostly by historians. The problem with this technique, as Ian Lustick remarks, is that the secondary studies are often in disagreement, and social scientists using historical studies tend to *select* particular works, often cited as especially "excellent" or "outstanding" in some way, to the exclusion of other studies that hold opposing points of view.[9] Lustick provides the specific example of Moore, who based his discussion on the development of English feudalism, and its relationship to the political development of England, on a specific study (that of R. H. Tawney) whose findings are controversial.[10]

The results are rendered essentially non-replicable, since one could have cited a different study on English feudalism and arrived at very different conclusions. This problem can of course be compensated for, at least to some extent, if authors of such studies were to justify their use of sources; Moore, for example, could have provided some justification as to why he chose to rely on a particular interpretation of feudalism and to reject others (and, indeed, at various points in his book, this was precisely his method). Such justifications undoubtedly make such studies more intellectually satisfying, but they fail to resolve the basic problem of replicability. Even if various authors were to provide justifications for their decisions to rely on certain sources and to slight others, their conclusions would

8 Moore, Jr., B. 1996. *Social Origins of Dictatorship and Democracy: Lord and Peasant in the Making of the Modern World*. Boston: Beacon Press; Skocpol, T. 1979. *States and Social Revolutions: A Comparative Analysis of France, Russia, and China*. Cambridge: Cambridge University Press; Huntington, S. 2006. *Political Order in Changing Societies*. New Haven: Yale University Press; Wallerstein, I. 1974. *The Modern World System*. New York: Academic Press. Mayer, A. J. 1971. *The Dynamics of Counter-Revolution in Europe, 1870–1956*. New York: Harper & Row. Rueschemeyer, D., Huber, E. and Stephens, J. D. 1992. *Capitalist Development and Democracy*. Cambridge: Polity Press.

9 Lustick, I. S. 1996. History, Historiography, and Political Science: Multiple Historical Records and the Problem of Selection Bias. *American Political Science Review*, 90/3, 605–18.

10 Lustick, I. S. 1996. 608–9.

probably remain controversial. Another scholar re-evaluating the controversy—in essence attempting to replicate the findings—could easily arrive at a different conclusion.

In general, comparative studies such as Moore's and the others cited above tend to base their overall conclusions on many hundreds of smaller conclusions, a significant portion of which are vital to sustaining the overall argument. Moore's judgment that a bourgeois revolution *did* in fact occur in England must itself rely on a series of secondary and tertiary judgments, rendered by Moore during the course of research, on how to interpret various bits of evidence regarding English historical development. If one considers the various data that were excluded from discussion—and given space constraints, all authors must exclude data—then the number of separate judgments might well run into the thousands.

With regard to Sniderman's hierarchy of replication, level II would not even apply, since this requires changing the standards of measurement and estimation; with Moore and most of the other works cited above there are no specified units of measure or estimation to allow such changes. Level I replication remains a hypothetical possibility: a second researcher could read the same source materials and seek to repeat the basic "experiment." For reasons noted above, it seems most unlikely to replicate the conclusions of the original authors. And if level I replicability is unlikely, then surely level III replicability—undertaking the research using different source materials—is virtually impossible.

In the field of history, where the idea of "historical science" never gained widespread acceptance, the non-replicable nature of research is well understood. Consider the observations of Bernadotte Schmidt, writing on controversies regarding the origins of World War I:

> [Sidney] Fay's *Origins of the World War* published in 1928, took a lenient view of Germany's responsibility, whereas my book *The Coming of the War, 1914* (1930), laid the chief burden on Germany. This has always troubled me. We had both taken advanced degrees at eminent universities … We used the same documents and read the same biographies and memoirs in preparing our respective books – and came up with quite different interpretations. It is sometimes asserted that we are both prejudiced because Fay studied in Germany and I in England, but surely there is more involved than that. Is there something wrong with our methods of historical study and training when two scholars draw such conflicting conclusions from the same evidence?[11]

One may consider the above case as a crude experiment regarding the potential for replicability in history, with a negative verdict. It is also interesting to note that in this case replication failed at level I, since the authors used basically the same sources of information. In the natural sciences, a failure to replicate an experiment

11 Schmidt, B. quoted in Allison, G. T. 1971. *Essence of Decision: Explaining the Cuban Missile Crisis*. Boston: Little. Brown. 14–15. The ellipses appears in the original.

at level I often reflects poorly on the capabilities of the researchers who performed the original experiment; in the above cases however, replication failed despite the fact that both Schmidt and Fay were major figures in the history profession. The non-replicable nature of the research does not necessarily result from some obvious flaw in the study, or some incompetence on the part of the researcher. It is intrinsic to qualitative research.

It is easy to see that the above "experiment" can be and has been undertaken many times. Norman Cantor has "described the enormous variability in historians' images of the Middle Ages and hence the absence of a single [presumably replicable] 'historical record.'"[12] In debates concerning the causes of the French Revolution or the American Civil War, there is relatively little consensus on basic issues. Often, to the extent that a consensus exists for a period of time—for example, the "consensus" that existed among American historians during the 1950s regarding the origins of the Cold War—it soon becomes apparent that what existed was really a pseudo-consensus, predicated upon a unique mindset that existed for some interval, only to be contested later. The "finding" of one qualitative researcher often resists efforts by a second to replicate it. Current debates about whether hard-line U.S. policies led to the collapse of the Soviet Union, had no effect, or merely hastened it, show few signs of definitive resolution.[13] Similarly, debates on whether or not the USSR was the primary aggressor power during the Cold War remain unresolved; while recent revelations from the ex-Soviet archives have greatly influenced and informed debate on this topic, they have not come close to settling basic issues.[14] My point is *not* that historical or qualitative research is inherently invalid or relativistic; I only note that it is not replicable.

Until now we have been emphasizing the varied interpretations expressed in diverse secondary sources, and the impediments that this poses for replicable research. Similar problems exist with primary sources, a problem Eugene Genovese acknowledges in his classic study of American slave society:

> I have readily and easily used some plantation diaries and ex-slave accounts while slighting others. Two decades of work in this history of southern slave society have helped form my own estimates of what is and what is not typical – what does and does not ring true. *Another historian ... might well interpret*

12 Lustick, I. S. 1996. 606.

13 See the following sources: Stoner-Weiss, K. and McFaul, M. 2009. Domestic and International Influences on the Collapse of the Soviet Union 1991 and Russia's Initial Transition to Democracy 1993. Working Paper 108, Center on Democracy, Development, and The Rule of Law, Freeman Spogli Institute for International Studies, Stanford University; Dudney, D. and Ikenberry, G. J. 1992. Who Won the Cold War? *Foreign Policy*, 87; Brown, A. 2007. Perestroika and the End of the Cold War. *Cold War History*, 7/1, 1–17.

14 See Leffler, Melvyn P. 1996. Inside Enemy Archives: The Cold War Reopened. *Foreign Affairs*, 75/4, 120–35. Layne, C. 2007. *The Peace of Illusions: American Grand Strategy from 1940 to the Present*. Ithaca: Cornell University Press. 223.

> *the record differently; indeed many have.* I offer my reading as one historian's considered judgment and can only warn non-specialists that all sources are treacherous and that no "definitive" study has been or ever will be written. [Emphasis added][15]

Historians and social scientists must select among conflicting primary sources, just as they must select among conflicting secondary sources. This process too is inherently subjective and non-replicable.

Finally, any *single* source of information can yield diverse, complicated or conflicting information, leading to multiple ways of reading the same material. How one chooses to read such a source will determine how one processes the information and, accordingly, what substantive conclusions to draw. This problem exists for a wide range of documentary materials, but is particularly acute when dealing with potentially controversial matters. Consider these excerpts from a forum[16] on U.S. secret interventions abroad:

> [Ralph] McGehee: … the CIA prepared a study of the 1965 Indonesian operation that described what the agency did there. I happened to have been custodian of that study for a time, and I know the specific steps the agency took to create the conditions that led to the massacre of at least half a million Indonesians …
>
> Hugh Tovar: … I am rather shattered by these allegations … I was in charge of CIA operations in Jakarta at the time, so I would have been the primary instigator of the massacres that allegedly took place. In fact the CIA served *primarily* as an intelligence collecting operation in Indonesia, and *did not engage heavily in covert action* … We certainly did not instigate the 1965 revolt. We had nothing to do with it. [Emphasis added]

A researcher might read the above in several different ways. First, one could conclude that the United States must have intervened in Indonesia to some extent, because even Tovar concedes this point (the United States "did not engage *heavily* in covert action"); Tovar's statement may sound like a denial, but under scrutiny it becomes apparent that he concedes some of what McGehee alleges. A second reader might conclude that the United States clearly was not involved in the Indonesian coup, because the charges to that effect, raised by McGehee, were firmly denied by Tovar ("we had nothing to do with it"), and the denial settles the matter. A third might conclude that alleged U.S. intervention in Indonesia could not be a very important matter, because the issue receives only a brief mention in the overall discussion (which was on covert war in general), and because many

---

15 Genovese, E. 1974. *Roll, Jordan, Roll: The World the Slaves Made*. New York: Pantheon. See A Note on Sources.

16 Moynihan, D. P. 1984 [moderator of forum] Should the CIA Fight Secret Wars? *Harpers*, September, 44.

reputable sources on U.S. foreign policy make no mention of it. Therefore it is not necessary to evaluate the validity of McGehee's allegations or to acknowledge these allegations in one's own research.

Some postmodernists[17] will view the above as an illustration regarding the existence of "multiple truths," and the need to avoid "privileging" any one truth or "marginalizing" any other truth. Such nihilistic views are both theoretically and empirically untenable and must be rejected. My point here is *not* to endorse a relativist view of empirical research; I proceed from the assumption that in any situation there is only one truth. The problem is that efforts to discover truth will in practice lead to multiple interpretations, including incorrect interpretations. For example, the above discussion of covert operations in Indonesia could yield at least three different, and mutually incompatible, interpretations about what actually happened in 1965.

Thus, the problem of multiple contradictory readings exists with a wide range of primary and secondary materials. Various sources from the same documentary collection—or even from the same author—frequently contradict one another. Different readers will generate diverse conclusions (including possibly inaccurate conclusions), and the phenomenon of multiple readings will constitute a major impediment to replication of research findings. There is no obvious way that this impediment can be surmounted.

The Problem of Biased or Incomplete Source Material

Another problem is that factual information in political science and related fields is often incomplete, owing to major gaps in the documentary record. Efforts to fill in the gaps, and the variety of ways in which researchers achieve this, can produce very different outcomes. Gaps in data records are also a problem for the natural sciences, but with a fundamental difference: in social science, the objects of our study—particularly governments, organizations and powerful individuals—often *deliberately* withhold information, if such information may be unflattering to them or contrary to their interests. That the objects of our study can act strategically and deliberately to deceive the researcher is a problem with few counterparts in the natural sciences, and this constitutes a fundamental difference between the two realms of research.

17 Terry Eagleton offers this definition for postmodernism: "a style of thought that is suspicious of classical notions of truth, reason, identity, and objectivity, of the idea of universal progress or emancipation, of single frameworks, grand narratives, or ultimate grounds of explanation." For this quote and for an extended discussion of how such perspectives often lead to an untenable form of relativism, see Gibbs, D. N. 2000. Is There Room for the Real World in the Postmodernist Universe? in *Beyond the Area Studies Wars*, edited by N. Waters. Hanover: University Press of New England. 18, dgibbs.faculty.arizona.edu/sites/dgibbs.faculty.arizona.edu/files/pomo-critique.pdf (accessed August 17, 2012).

States often withhold embarrassing or discrediting information sources through the simple expedient of classifying them as state secrets, and they actively disseminate information that is flattering to official policy. While government secrecy is often justified "in the national interest," such claims often prove, under inspection, to be mere rationalizations.[18] Official efforts to mislead the public will often mislead researchers as well. The varied ways that researchers seek to cope with this problem, and the necessarily subjective character that many coping strategies require, may further frustrate replication efforts.

Another important primary source material consists of published memoirs by officials—and these too often contain biased or misleading information. Memoir writers themselves are often aware of this bias. While writing his own memoir about experiences at the United Nations, Conor Cruise O'Brien warned his readers:

> Memoirs occupy – for quite sound reasons – a lowly place in the regard of the professional historian. They are suspect for fallibility of memory, for intent of polemic or self-exculpation and for that extra share of human vanity which must be presumed in people who trouble to write and publish the story of events in which they were personally involved. For any retrospective account the historian prefers, when he can get them, scraps of contemporary evidence, not intended for the public eye, and, above all, not intended for "posterity." Only when he has wrung all that he can from such contemporary evidence does he fall back, reluctantly and skeptically, on the memoir material and even then what he is likely to take from it will be declarations against interest, if he can find any.[19]

O'Brien writes of historians but exactly the same issues are faced by social scientists who often rely on memoirs, official histories, government press releases, presidential speeches, and the like. The problem is accentuated by the fact that the resulting distortions and omissions are not random, but systematic: participants can be expected to systematically exaggerate (or fabricate) information that favors them, while omitting unfavorable information.

Such "partial" sources present serious challenges, since there is no consensus on how to address biases and gaps in the record. Researchers tend to fall into two categories. The first category are those who readily accept O'Brien's advice; they read source materials generated by interested parties with a suspicious eye and remain alert to the possibility that the author is simply trying to cast a favorable light on his or her own conduct. Unfilled gaps in the factual record are explicitly acknowledged. The second category tends to avoid issues of partiality and interest, and accepts information from memoirs and similar sources uncritically. Quite a few

---

18 This issue is explored in Gibbs, D. N. 2009. Secrecy and International Relations, in *Government Secrecy: Classic and Contemporary Readings,* edited by S. L. Maret and J. Goldman. Westport: Libraries Unlimited, 360–80.

19 O'Brien, C. C. 1962. *To Katanga and Back.* New York: Universal Library. 6.

social scientists, whether for better or worse, fall within the second category.[20] It is not necessary to decide which research strategy is more appropriate to recognize there are two distinct, and to some extent incompatible, methods of evaluating certain types of commonly used source materials. Because different strategies of research yield different results, and because there is no reason to assume that these differences are likely to be reconciled any time soon, we have an additional barrier to efforts at research replication.

The basic problem may be illustrated with regard to the case of U.S. intervention in the Congo during the period 1960–1961.[21] A point of controversy concerns the assassination of the Congo's elected Prime Minister, Patrice Lumumba, which occurred in January 1961. The key question is whether Lumumba was assassinated exclusively by his Congolese adversaries; or if the assassination was in fact directed by the Central Intelligence Agency (possibly in cooperation with Belgian intelligence). On this issue, it might be said that we have multiple and inconsistent sources of information. On the one hand, the U.S. government has long denied that it played any role in the assassination; indeed that it had any interventionist role at all in the Congo. In 1964, the U.S. delegate to the United Nations, Adlai Stevenson, stated: "From the beginning we have opposed – and remain opposed – to foreign intervention in the internal affairs of the sovereign and independent state of the Congo."[22] Clearly, this would imply that the United States also played no role in Lumumba's assassination.

On the other hand, there is a vast body of documentary evidence suggesting that, on the contrary, the Central Intelligence Agency intervened extensively in the Congo, and that it plotted Lumumba's assassination. During a 1975 Senate hearing, for example, former CIA officer Lawrence Devlin testified that he was authorized to "eliminate" Lumumba, which led to the following exchange with the investigator:

> Question: By eliminate do you mean assassinate?
> Devlin: Yes, I would say that was … my understanding of the primary means. I don't think it was probably limited to that, if there was some other way of … removing him [Lumumba] from a position of political threat.[23]

---

20 For examples of naïve use of memoir material, see Scott, J. M. 1996. *Deciding to Intervene: the Reagan Doctrine and American Foreign Policy*. Durham, NC: Duke University Press. 125–6; Smith, T. 1981. *The Pattern of Imperialism: The United States, Great Britain, and the Late Industrializing World since 1815*. New York: Cambridge University Press. 156–7.

21 See Chapter 6, this volume.

22 Quoted in Kwitny, J. 1984. *Endless Enemies: The Making of an Unfriendly World*. New York: Congdon and Weed. 82.

23 U.S. Senate. 1975. *Alleged Assassination Plots Involving Foreign Leaders*. Washington, DC: U.S. Government Printing Office. 24. The ellipses appeared in the original report. Note that the report refers to Devlin by a pseudonym, "Victor Hedgman." For detailed discussions regarding later document releases on this topic see Weissman, S. R.

We thus have conflicting evidence, allowing researchers with different ideological and political agendas to present varying accounts. Researchers who wish to emphasize CIA intervention can cite the Senate investigation, while those seeking to exonerate American officials can cite the official denials; or they can simply avoid any mention of the issue at all.

I am tempted to take sides in this debate, and to underscore that the CIA was obviously plotting to assassinate Lumumba; the documentary record is clear on this point. Official denials by Stevenson and others—that the United States opposed all intervention—are not credible. Nevertheless, some researchers will naively accept the truthfulness of the official denials and will pretend that the United States was not running covert operations in the Congo.[24] In making these points, I am not suggesting a relativist position, nor do I imply that we cannot determine the truth regarding the Congo. My only point here is that the process of finding truth will defy notions of replicability.

Newspapers and Replicability

Many researchers have placed special faith in independent journalistic sources of information, which (in contrast to memoirs) are considered disinterested. Much source material in both qualitative and quantitative social science research is derived from newspaper or magazine articles. Yet, newspapers too can present multiple, contradictory readings.

The problem may be illustrated by this observation regarding information sources on Israeli politics:

> The Hebrew-language press is an absolutely indispensable window into Israel-Jewish society. Coverage of local politics and issues is far more hard-edged than most of what is carried in either the reports of the resident correspondents of the foreign English-language press or the English-language *Jerusalem Post.* Israelis themselves are conscious of this difference. An Israeli who immigrated from Poland in the 1950s recalled for us how his Hebrew teacher would give

2010. An Extraordinary Rendition. *Intelligence and National Security*, 25/2, 198–222; and De Witte, L. 2003. *The Assassination of Lumumba*. London: Verso. Note that the Senate report argued that the CIA *plotted* Lumumba's death, but that these plots were unsuccessful; and that the actual assassination of Lumumba in January 1961 was undertaken without any CIA involvement. However, Weissman provides considerable evidence that the CIA *did* play a role in assassinating Lumumba.

24 Two lengthy publications pertaining to the Congo published by the State Department's Office of the Historian make almost no mention of any U.S.-directed covert operations. Reading these volumes, the reader would get the impression that no covert operations existed. For an extended critique, see Gibbs, D. N. 1996. Misrepresenting the Congo Crisis. *African Affairs*, 95/380, 453–9.

> his class the exercise of translating *The Jerusalem Post* coverage of a particular story or issue into Hebrew and the *Haaretz* [a Hebrew-language newspaper at the time] coverage of the same story into English. The class soon noted that the *Haaretz* coverage was invariably far more informative and critical than the *Post*, and pointed this out to the teacher. "You must understand the function of the *Jerusalem Post*," replied the teacher. "It is to give the American ambassador a happy breakfast!"[25]

This quotation nicely illustrates what readers of the international press have long recognized: different newspapers are motivated by varied worldviews that inform their coverage and, accordingly, they may print divergent accounts of the same news. The Parisian daily *Le Monde* offers substantially different interpretations of international affairs than the *New York Times* (and the divergence is greater if one compares the *Times* Sunday Review with its French counterpart, *Le Monde Diplomatique*). Al Jazeera television presents a different picture of Middle Eastern politics than that available through American networks. Within the United States, one can discern some differences among various newspapers, especially in Washington, DC, where the unabashedly conservative *Washington Times* offers a somewhat different perspective than the more centrist *Washington Post.*

Of course, press sources do not always contradict each other and, in some cases, newspapers can present consistent versions of events. The phenomenon of "monolithic" press coverage presents a different, though equally problematic, set of issues. The fact that newspapers report consistently and support each other's coverage does not necessarily mean they are reporting in an accurate and unbiased manner. Even in democratic countries, newspapers can suffer from a variety of biases, and these may occur simultaneously in a range of different publications. The phenomenon of "pack" journalism—whereby journalists tend to reinforce, rather than challenge each other's views—may accentuate such biases.[26] The problem of press bias is widely accepted in certain fields, notably communications. According to one authority:

> It is an article of faith among virtually all scholars of communication that media in Western democracies speak with one, narrow voice and that they restrict rather than enhance political debate. It would be hard to find a paper presented at the meetings of the International Communication Association challenging this premise.[27]

---

25 Cockburn, A. and Cockburn, L. 1991. *Dangerous Liaison: The Inside Story of the U.S.-Israeli Covert Relationship*. Toronto: Stoddart. 361.

26 On the issue of bias, see Klaidman, S. and Beauchamp, T. L. 1987. *The Virtuous Journalist*. New York: Oxford University Press. 59–92.

27 Stevenson, Robert J. October 3, 1997. Letter to the Editor, *Chronicle of Higher Education*. Stevenson was Professor of Journalism and Mass Communication at the University of North Carolina. While Stevenson's statement, above, is somewhat

Newspaper coverage of warfare has been especially problematic, and journalists may become simple conduits for official propaganda. Writing of French soldiers during World War I, Marc Bloch observed:

> The prevailing opinion in the trenches was that anything might be true, except what was printed … The role of propaganda and censorship was considerable, but in a way exactly the reverse of what the creators of these institutions expected of them … The men [in the trenches] put no faith in newspapers.[28]

Such suspicion may be regarded as a perfectly rational response to newspaper complicity in disseminating disinformation. It is easy to find evidence of questionable press reporting in more recent conflicts as well. The press accounts of the Tonkin Gulf incident of August 1964 presented in U.S. papers would read very poorly if compared with information on this incident contained in the *Pentagon Papers*. Research by Daniel Hallin[29] on reporting during the Vietnam War indicated that even after 1968—when the press was at its highest level of independence—news accounts still relied heavily on official sources for information about the war. Regarding the Afghan war of the 1980s, newspaper reports on the Mujahiddin guerrillas tended to celebrate the guerillas' virtues, and to eschew their weaknesses—a point that was conceded freely by journalists after the Soviet withdrawal in 1989.[30] Retrospective analyses of press coverage during conflicts in Grenada, Panama, the Persian Gulf, and Yugoslavia revealed a high level of dependence on official information and a low level of reliability.[31] In such circumstances, the resulting inaccuracies are unlikely to be random—the press record may contain *systematic* bias.

The phenomenon of pack journalism gives rise to two very different research strategies. Some researchers assume press accounts are basically reliable, independent sources, and they assume that contrary evidence is insufficient to undermine the accounts' overall credibility. These researchers use news articles (or at least those found in reputable publications) more or less uncritically, as

---

exaggerated, it is true that a wide literature in communications accepts the idea of a systematically biased media. On this issue, see also McChesney, R. 2000. *Rich Media, Poor Democracy: Communication Politics in Dubious Times*. New York: New Press.

28 Quoted in Fischer, D. H. 1970. *Historians' Fallacies: Toward a Logic of Historical Thought*. New York: Harper Perennial. 290. The ellipses appear in the original.

29 Hallin, D. 1984. The Media, the War in Vietnam, and Political Support: A Critique of the Thesis of an Oppositional Media. *The Journal of Politics*, 46/1, 25–59.

30 Burns, J. F. February 4, 1990. Afghans: Now They Blame America. *The New York Times Magazine*; and Walsh, M. W. 1990. Mission: Afghanistan. *Columbia Journalism Review*, January/February.

31 Sharkey, J. E. 1991. *Under Fire: U.S. Military Restrictions on the Media from Grenada to the Persian Gulf.* Washington, DC: Center for Public Integrity. Regarding press distortions on Yugoslavia, see Merlino, J. 1993. *Les Vérités Yougoslaves ne sont pas Toutes Bonnes à Dire.* Paris: Albin Michel.

repositories of accurate factual information, requiring little interpretation or double-checking against primary sources. Their assumption—that whatever biases exist will not seriously affect the end results—amounts to a central, if often tacit, research assumption. Other researchers, by contrast, assume press accounts contain systematic flaws, due especially to their dependence on official sources for primary information, and that such dependence could be highly significant. Researchers from this second school of thought subject press articles to a critical reading and evaluate them for evidence of bias, over-reliance on official sources, or inherent implausibility. We thus have two distinct and to some extent mutually incompatible strategies of research. The varied strategies for using newspaper sources of information present an additional impediment to replicability in qualitative research (at least for replication at level III).

The Critical Reading Approach

The foregoing discussion is not meant to suggest that valid research through press accounts is impossible, only that it is difficult to achieve. It is possible to use even the most biased sources and come up with fairly balanced assessments, as practitioners of Kremlinology amply demonstrated during the Cold War. Barrington Moore, for example, undertook a classic study of domestic policymaking in the USSR during the Stalin era, which was based on (obviously biased) Soviet sources.[32] Allen Whiting's analysis of Chinese foreign policy during the Korean War was based on Chinese sources.[33] Similarly, intelligence analysts have long understood the art (it surely is not a science) of uncovering information based on careful reading of news stories.

The same techniques could be applied to studies of U.S. foreign policy, which could also use the technique of critically reading newspaper reports; such research would be considerably easier than was the case for the Moore and Whiting studies, given the exceptional restrictions on information in these two cases and the relative absence of such official restrictions in the United States. Through critical reading of source materials from various Western newspapers, and through systematic comparisons of information and interpretation, one could compensate for possible newspaper biases, in the way the Kremlinologists did, with a comparable (and reasonably high) degree of success. Indeed, historians such as Bruce Cumings[34]

---

32 Moore, Jr. B. 1950. *Soviet Politics: The Dilemma of Power*. Cambridge, MA: Harvard University Press.

33 Whiting, A. S. 1960. *China Crosses the Yalu: The Decision to Enter the Korean War*. New York: Macmillan.

34 Cumings, B. 1988. Preface to Stone, I. F. *The Hidden History of the Korean War, 1950–1951*. Boston: Little, Brown. For a similar approach, see also Gibbs, D. N. 2011. Sigmund Freud as a Theorist of Government Secrecy. *Research in Social Problems and*

advocate the method of critical reading of newspapers and magazines in situations where archival materials are not readily available.

There are two problems. Firstly, the method of critical reading being discussed is very time consuming. Critical reading calls for painstaking research, close attention to detail, and enough subject familiarity to set up a framework for analysis whose results will resemble reality. According to Cumings, critical reading seeks "the 'one very queer detail,' the 'one odd shaped piece that doesn't fit,' and [can] thus demolish the official logic or construct an alternative logic." Secondly, the researcher "reads a document the way Sherlock Holmes looks for fingerprints."[35] This technique of critical reading would be difficult if not impossible to replicate, even at level I. To assess even a single event requires many separate judgments, always subjective in nature, regarding the reliability of certain sources and interpretations, and the unreliability of others. Different researchers, with different assumptions and theoretical frameworks, will render such judgments in complex and largely non-replicable manners.

Conclusion

Overall, our verdict on the possibility for replication for qualitative research must be a negative one, given the subjectivity that is inherent to this genre. However, this finding does *not* mean that we lose the ability to distinguish valid from invalid theories, arguments or explanations. Even without the tool of replication, we can still assess a theory with regard to well understood criteria: we can assess the theory's internal consistency, its simplicity, and how well its predictions accord with the empirical record.[36] We can also evaluate the quality of the source materials used to test theories. Finally, we can assess how well (or badly) certain theories meet these evaluation criteria, in comparison with other, competing theories.

Thus, replication may be one of the ways to establish validity, but it is surely not the only way. Some readers will nevertheless frown upon a social science that does not include the possibility of replication. This view ignores the fact that there are many areas of inquiry that are non-replicable. For example, argumentation in the legal profession is non-replicable. Legal arguments often contain novel features, the product of a specific interpretation by a particular lawyer; a second lawyer arguing the same case, with exactly the same evidence, may present a substantially different argument. In criminal trials, the decisions of

---

Public Policy, 19. 5–22, dgibbs.faculty.arizona.edu/sites/dgibbs.faculty.arizona.edu/files/FreudArticle.pdf (accessed August 17, 2012).

35 Cumings, B. 1988. xv. Cumings is actually summarizing the approach of I. F. Stone, whose work Cumings regards as an exemplary use of the critical method of interpreting sources.

36 Hempel, C. G. 1966. *Philosophy of Natural Science*. Englewood Cliffs: Prentice-Hall. Chapter 4.

judges and juries are not necessarily replicable either. The process of evaluating the credibility of witnesses, for example, often entails a measure of subjective judgment, and this subjectivity will impede replication. Lawyers are well aware that who serves as judge and who serves on the jury can affect the outcome of a case (and thus, trial lawyers will expend considerable time vetting potential jurors). This constitutes an implicit recognition regarding the non-replicable character of the whole process, as a different judge and set of jurors may render a different verdict. Nevertheless, legal arguments and decisions can be evaluated for the adequacy of their reasoning, according to highly rigorous and well established criteria.[37] Few would argue that the non-replicable nature of legal decisions and legal argument renders the entire process invalid.

There is another analytical process that is widely accepted as valid, but is nevertheless non-replicable: tenure assessments at universities. The evaluation of a tenure candidate's record is once again a subjective process, as faculty assess research "quality" in a variety of often inconsistent ways. In close cases, such subjectivity may prove decisive in determining whether or not the candidate is granted tenure. The non-replicable character of tenure decisions is clear: a different tenure committee, composed of different members with divergent views, might well write a different report. True, the tenure process could be *altered* in ways that would make it replicable. Rules could be established that candidates must publish a certain number of articles in specified journals. Candidates who meet or exceed these criteria would automatically be granted tenure, while those who fall below would be denied. The process would then become replicable, as all subjective factors would be removed. But few faculties, even in physics departments, would consider this an acceptable procedure, as it would trivialize the process of evaluation and create an overly simplistic basis for assessing scholarship quality. The existing (non-replicable) system of tenure evaluation is clearly the superior one.

Thus, replicability is not an appropriate standard for establishing validity in certain areas of human inquiry, and these areas include both legal and tenure granting processes. Qualitative social scientific research too entails subjective features, which cannot be eliminated or simplified, and these form an insuperable barrier against replication. In qualitative research, as in law, one validates theories and interpretations through persuasiveness of argument, according to rules of logic, rather than through replicable experimentation, as might occur in the hard sciences. The expectation that replication can become a universal standard is thus unattainable. Whether for better or worse, we must accept a large measure of subjectivity in qualitative social science, with all of its implications for parapolitical scholarship.

37 Levy, E. H. 1948. *An Introduction to Legal Reasoning*. Chicago: University of Chicago Press.

Chapter 6
The Unusual Suspects: Africa, Parapolitics and the National Security State Complex

Enrico Carisch

> Humanity as such cannot wage war because it has no enemy, at least not on this planet. The concept of humanity excludes the concept of the enemy, because the enemy does not cease to be a human being—and hence there is no specific differentiation in this concept. That wars are waged in the name of humanity is not a contradiction of this simple truth; quite the contrary, it has an especially intensive political meaning. When a State fights its political enemy in the name of humanity, it is not war for the sake of humanity, but a war wherein a particular State seeks to usurp a universal concept against its military opponent … Here one is reminded of a somewhat modified expression of Proudhon: whoever invokes humanity wants to cheat.
>
> Carl Schmitt

Overview

The Congo's[1] 120-year colonial and post-colonial history of its natural resources exploitation is frequently connected with campaigns by humanitarian activists who are concerned about anti-slavery conventions, international humanitarian rights and law, and modern workplace regulations. Yet, the protagonists of such campaigns usually end up entangled—knowingly or not—in the selfish motives and policies of global industries and governments of highly industrialized states. Disparities between idealistic and actual objectives already existed 100 years ago when a coalition of British Protestant moralists, businessmen and lobbyists for the United Kingdom's New Imperialism lobbied against "Red Rubber," King Leopold II of Belgium's scandalous atrocities against rubber harvesters in the Congolese forests. Similar inconsistencies can be found in today's campaigns that go by names such as "Blood Diamond," "Conflict Minerals," "Blood Coltan" or "Dirty Gold." True to the pattern set by their British moralist predecessors—

1 Throughout this chapter, the term Congo describes the region in Central Africa that throughout its history changed its territorial extension far beyond the Congo Basin, and under changing political governance systems underwent at least four changes of name (Congo Free State, Belgian Congo, Zaire, and finally Democratic Republic of the Congo).

who in part acted for the interests of the New Imperialists—today's campaigns are driven by idealism and humanitarian concerns but end up acting as attack dogs and diversions for anyone who stands in the way of the policies of highly industrialized and resource-dependent states, the World Bank or the OECD, and the most influential Western mineral mining and trading companies.

While the campaigns against King Leopold's carnage in the Congo contributed to a shift from a purely Belgian Royal natural resource monopoly to an Anglo-Belgian monopoly, the more recent campaigns have perhaps inadvertently instigated a shift from the Western monopoly to a growing Sino-African control over the Congo's natural resource industries. While the entry of China in Africa's commodities market would appear to be a game changer, for the Congolese people and artisanal mining communities little has changed. So far, Chinese companies demonstrate the same minimal concerns for the safety and wellbeing of their Congolese workers as Western companies have during past decades.

One marked difference does prevail, however. While the management of Western companies allude to modern corporate governance principles that include respect for human rights, Chinese companies prefer modern corporate governance principles that strive toward the establishment of a "harmonious society."[2] The question is whether this Chinese approach will merely be a new round in the century-old humanitarian machinations that creates counter-productive consequences for most Congolese—and frequently life-threatening conditions.

The Four Cs

For centuries Christian and Islamic proselytizing masked the raw greed of explorers and traders from Europe and Oman who established small trading and military outposts through which they secured their share of the continent's never ending stream of ivory, rubber, gold, diamonds, exotic timber, slaves and many other natural resources. Said bin Sultan, ruler of Oman in 1700, succeeded in ejecting the Portuguese from Africa's East Coast and built his primary residence in Zanzibar. For the following 180 years Zanzibar's trading expeditions reached deep into the Congo, and the most formidable trader chief, Tippu Tip, established his own domain in Kasongo. The Swahili-Muslim presence in Central Africa was in fact the most formidable competition to all European invaders.

By the late 1800s, when the Western "Scramble for Africa"[3] was at its height, the United Kingdom had successfully claimed the largest real estate and the

2 Geis II, John P. and Holt, B. 2009. Harmonious Society: Rise of the New China. *Strategic Studies Quarterly*, winter, 177.

3 Commonly, the "Scramble for Africa" describes a time period that started a few years after Livingstone's death in 1873 and ends around 1912. Thomas Pakenham explains how he customarily uses the term, realizing that it is not clearly understood and that no one has attempted yet to research and/or offer an explanation for the scramble for Africa or in

most valuable natural resource deposits of the continent. The French became the proud conqueror of about one-quarter of Africa, which British Prime Minister Lord Salisbury sarcastically described as the "light land" of the Sahara. Portugal, the earliest of the European invaders into Africa, was joined by Germany, the latecomer, as owners of comparatively small but strategically important territories along Africa's coasts. King Leopold II finally won the heart of Africa, which is roughly today's territory of the Democratic Republic of the Congo.

The man who enabled this sudden scramble of Western civilizations onto the African continent was David Livingstone, a Protestant emissary of the London Missionary Society. He was an inspirational anti-slavery crusader, a scientific investigator and explorer and an avid advocate of European-Christian values. What the British Empire and the developed world would bring to Africa, he proudly promulgated in the three Cs: Commerce, Christianity and Civilization. As Thomas Pakenham ingeniously observed, in truth, there was always a fourth C, which dominated the others—Conquest.[4]

Before and during the "Scramble for Africa" a few simple humanitarian principles were in play. Slavery and forced labor had been outlawed by all European states for close to 100 years.[5] In Africa, the Middle East and Asia slavery was flourishing in all its forms. Unless imposed by legitimate state authorities, harsh physical punishment or causing the death of workers was against the laws of all Western countries. Caning, whipping or any corporal punishments with non-lethal intentions were tolerated by some Westerners in their own countries and were a widely accepted practice in European colonial laws. By around 1890 to 1900, Europe was at the peak of the legal evolution that brought modern labor standards, outlawed child labor and stipulated safety, health and sanitary standards.

Slavery, as practiced by Muslims in Africa, however, was a big mainstream media topic. In 1889 the anti-slavery organizations convened a big, splashy international conference in Brussels by the invitation of King Leopold II of Belgium. A *New York Times* editorial framed the issues:

> Inasmuch as this horrible trade is exclusively in the hands of Arabs who, being bigoted Mohammedans, are inaccessible to Christian arguments, the only possible way of suppressing the slave trade is by an agreement on the part of all Christian nations to lend the use of their men-of-war to patrol the African coast,

---

other words why suddenly the European nations involved suddenly rushed to take over the entire African continent. Pakenham, T. 1991. Introduction. *The Scramble for Africa*. New York: Random House. The term appears to show up the first time in a mainstream media when the *New York Times* used it as a subtitle for a January 11, 1885 update on various issues related to Africa.

4 Pakenham, T. 1991.

5 The United States of America was the last of the large Western nations to abolish slavery with the enactment of the Thirteenth Amendment on December 18, 1865.

> and by the permanent occupation of the whole of savage Africa by colonizing and trading companies.[6]

The "Scramble for Africa" was therefore eminently justified on humanitarian grounds. King Leopold II was the master player in this game of perception. His public stance against slavery made him a favorite of the leading human rights organizations of Europe and Honorary President of the highly respected Aborigines Protection Society. The King's plans for a huge swath of so far unoccupied territory in Central Africa to be managed through the recently formed Association International d'Exploration et de Civilisation de l'Afrique. The *New York Times* explained: "The Association was instituted at Brussels by a congress of distinguished geographers, whom the King of the Belgians had invited to his capital in September 1876." The King informed Henri Morton Stanley, the British-American journalist and explorer of Central Africa, that he "intended to do something substantial and of material benefit in Africa, and that he expected Stanley to assist him." The King also invited European states to become members of and financial contributors to this endeavor, while in secret he turned this Association into a holding company. The primary asset of his company would be nothing less than the entire Central African territory, with its people and treasures; the King was its sole shareholder and by force of the King's Last Will, the Belgian state would be its eventual heir. In order to gain broad international support for his charitable scheme he coerced journalists to write favorable stories about him and lobbied the governments of UK, Germany, France and the United States.

The Congo Free State

The American government proved itself to be particularly gullible to King Leopold's humanist charade. It recognized the flag of the International African Association as the flag of a friendly government. Shortly thereafter, France and Germany also recognized King Leopold's International African Association. Only the British Empire and Portugal withheld their support. During the intense negotiations at the Conference of Berlin in 1884 convened by Germany's Chancellor Bismarck to resolve all outstanding boundary issues in the Congo Basin, both powers conditionally relented. Thus, Leopold II was officially the patron of the Congo Free State, which was for political purposes a monarchy but in reality was a philanthropic corporation/non-government organization called either Association International Africaine, Association International d'Exploration et de Civilisation de l'Afrique or Le Comité d'Etudes du Haut Congo; it depended on the level of confusion Leopold wanted to spread to conceal the one fact that was essential to him—he was the single and all-controlling shareholder of the Congo.

6 As Others See Us. *New York Times*, December 28, 1889.

The British and Portuguese delegations to the Berlin Conference did not resist King Leopold out of concern for the Congolese. They insisted on what seemed a small technicality before they signed the agreement. They included a clause called the "Principle of Effectivity," which defined specific elements of evidence to determine that a territory had effectively been taken under the control of a colonial power. As a result of this clause, Leopold's man for the Congo, Stanley, cajoled, extorted and forced hundreds of Central African tribal leaders and kings into signing treaties, which in the contemporaneous European legal interpretation meant surrender of territories, people and resources. A Belgian decree dated 1885 stipulated that "vacant" land would be allocated to the Congo Free State. "Vacant" was defined as all land that was not settled or under cultivation by Europeans. However, indigenous people who happened to be living on the land would be forced to pay taxes. For Leopold's agents these taxes were ideally paid in the form of ivory or rubber.

The Free State was divided into two administrative zones. The first was a free zone that theoretically was open to any European entrepreneur wishing to acquire natural resource concessions. With this provision Leopold had allayed British concerns that the Congo would not respect free trade prerogatives of the Pax Britannica. The second zone, which included the interior of the Congo where rubber and ivory were highly concentrated, was declared *Domaine Privé* or the private economic preserve of King Leopold. In that zone King Leopold's agents would spread enlightened Western values, abolish slavery wherever it was encountered and lift up the primitives by introducing them to Christianity. Following the true and tried methods of all European colonialists, the Belgians concealed their iron grip on the Congo with the soft power of education.

The true description of events was documented in considerable detail years later, when the Belgian government was forced to publish the results of the Commission of Inquiry, which was charged with investigating the true humanitarian situation in the Congo. It turned out that the rule of law was mostly a question of interpretation. To maximize natural resource exploitation, Leopold had issued three secret decrees, which would remain the undisclosed source of absolute power for his agents. With the first issued in November 1888 he monopolized the ability to inflict violence by imposing an embargo on the importation and trade of arms; his security forces were exempted from this decree. In 1891–1892 a second decree settled that each village chief would be subject to the system of prestations that forced the requisition of workers and porters, food, construction material and predetermined quantities of ivory and wild rubber harvest for the King's agents. Finally, Leopold established the Force Publique, the police and security units composed of locals and led by European mercenaries. It was these police officers who enforced the rubber harvest quotas, wielded the *chicotte*,[7] burnt villages of

---

7 A bull whip made of hippopotamus hide. Sometimes nails were attached to its end to cause particularly deep and painful wounds.

obstinate Congolese, tortured, flogged and raped villagers, and cut off their hands or legs when they did not satisfy the harvest quota.

Rumors about ill treatment of Congolese people had been circulating throughout Europe from the very beginning of Stanley's invasion and Leopold's occupation of Central Africa. Initially, this did not impress anyone, since atrocities in colonies all over the world were understood to be unavoidable in the civilization of savages. One rumor caused particular intrigue, however. In Lisbon, an ex-Minister of the Marine inquired in parliament from the Minister of Foreign Affairs whether Stanley had appointed the infamous Zanzibar slave trader Tippu Tip to be Stanley Falls District Governor of the Congo Free State. The insinuation of a Belgian political partnership with a Swahili-Muslim slaver was very scandalous. "The debate throughout," reported the *New York Times*, "was characterized by attacks on the Congo Free State." [8]

New British Imperialism, Free Trade and Humanitarian Activists

Allegations about unseemly partnerships with Muslims did not fare well for Leopold's reputation as a humanitarian. One man who increasingly cast aspersions on Leopold whenever possible was an unknown English employee of a Liverpool shipping agency. Edmund Dene Morel was about to quit his job that had allowed him to observe the shipping traffic between Antwerp and Boma, Congo's only port. He had noted that the freighters would arrive fully loaded with ivory and Indian rubber in Belgium, but the cargo on the outgoing vessels convinced him that no orderly bilateral trade with the Congo was taking place. Rather than with goods suitable to humanitarian needs, such as medical and educational equipment, the ships left Antwerp laden with military supplies, chains and mercenaries. Morel started to inquire more deeply. He also commenced correspondence with missionaries stationed in the Congo and, thus, a human rights campaign with the most dramatic consequences was on its way.

Soon, Morel would take the role of distributing and promoting news and writing about abuses in the Congo. There were other activists, such as George Washington Williams, a maverick African-American, who wrote a harsh condemnation in "An Open Letter to His Serene Majesty Leopold II King." The unspeakable horrors in the Congo were described most famously by Joseph Conrad's three-part article published in 1899 in *Blackwood Magazine* (his account would eventually turn up as a novella better known under the title *Heart of Darkness*). Only Morel had the zeal, the organizational skills and the financing for a sustained campaign. To a large part his perseverance was made possible through his relationship with shipping and trading magnate John Holt and the intellectual engine behind the New Imperialism, Mary Kingsley. She thought that trade was the best hope for Africans

8 Stanley and Tippoo Tib The Congo State Charged with Abetting the Slave Trade. *New York Times*, June 8, 1887.

and their economic development. "As their self-appointed mouthpiece"—Morel's own description in one of his earliest correspondence with John Holt—he wrote articles in his spare time against French protectionism. In doing so, he had chosen the theme that was central to the interests of the British Empire. Maintaining and growing its far-flung empire in the face of increasing colonial interests by France, Germany, Portugal, Italy, the United States and most dramatically Belgium, became a delicate political task.

These powers expanded their reach by frequently imposing tariffs or trade monopolies. For the ruling superpower of that era, this was unacceptable, and John Holt, the principal of the leading Liverpool trading firm, John Holt & Company,[9] had to be seriously concerned. He depended upon "free trade, or more to the point, on his ability to continue the well established Liverpool merchant method of trading, which was the free exchange with native middlemen at river or coastal stations of Western cloth (or liquor – or arms) for African-produced raw materials."[10] The French government's tacit support of French concessionaires of natural resource deposits in the French Congo was a case in point that Morel took up with missionary zeal. He rallied against the French monopolies because, "in fighting primarily for himself the British merchant is indirectly fighting the new form of slavery which has been introduced into Africa with such fatal results by the sovereign of the Congo state, and in taking the stand the British merchant is rendering a great service to humanity."[11] However vital these complexities may have been for the prosperity of the British Empire, its subjects, the British people, were largely uninterested. They most certainly would not favor major confrontations or trade wars with European powers.

One very effective British strategy to galvanize the public and soon the international public were the campaigns of the humanitarian activists against Leopold's inhumane regime in the Congo and, by quiet implication, the trade monopolies in the Congo Basin. Thus, the British merchant Holt rendered a great service to humanity and to himself by providing most of the funding for the *West African Mail*, Morel's journal through which he waged his anti-Leopold campaign. Holt also sponsored the Congo Reform Association that Morel and others created in 1904. "Morel is a great asset," wrote Holt to William Cadbury in 1910, "if we know how to make use of him in our West Africa work." Cadbury was another Liverpool importer of coca, a chocolate manufacturer and financial supporter of Morel.

---

9 Cookey, S. J. S. 1966. The Concession Policy in the French Congo and the British Reaction 1898 – 1906. *Journal of African History*, VII/2, 263–78.

10 Porter, B. 2008. *Critics of Empire: British Radicals and the Imperial Challenge*. London: I. B. Tauris. 245.

11 Cookey, S. J. S. 1964. *Great Britain and the Congo Questions 1892 – 1913*. PhD thesis. University of London. 70–71.

Rhodes versus Leopold

There was also the contradiction that British businessmen, such as Cecil Rhodes, were using the British government to advance their business interests. In order to secure title to rich mining lands from indigenous leaders they routinely would call on the British Crown to install protectorates, which became thereafter the responsibility of the Colonial Office in London.

Rhodes strove to expand the hold his British South Africa Company and his many affiliates had on Southern Africa by connecting it to the other territories of the British Empire in the northern parts of Africa. His dream was a Cape to Cairo train connection—all under his and British control. Leopold's Congo stood in the way and, in any event, Rhodes also suspected rich mineral deposits in the Southern tip of the Congo, the area that by force of the Berlin Agreement's "Principle of Effectivity" would be allocated to Leopold if he were able to establish an actual presence there.

Rhodes attacked his problems with multiple strategies. To shore up political support in the British parliament for his schemes of British expansion in Africa, he "sponsored" the Irish Home Rule Party to the tune of 10,000 pounds. His foresight would net him 64 votes in parliament; votes that would become pivotal in his personal contest against Leopold's dominion over Southern Katanga. He also sent negotiators and representatives of the British Commissioner in Central Africa to Mwenda Msiri Ngelengwa Shitamb, founder and ruler of the Yeke Kingdom who ruled over the South of the Congo, the Katanga Province. The emissaries of Rhodes offered Msiri a treaty with the British Empire but in essence he was asked to cede sovereignty to the British. Of course, the British delegation did not succeed.

Learning quickly of the British failure Leopold II assembled an expedition with 400 men, led by European mercenaries. When confronted with a recalcitrant Msiri, they simply shot him. By January 1892, the Belgian ruler not only had fulfilled the requirements under the Berlin Agreement by flying the Free State's flag over Katanga, he had also displayed the cut-off head of Msiri to demonstrate to other Africans his control over them.

Copper Mines and Congo Reform Association

King Leopold's legal title to Katanga only invigorated British resolve to challenge him. Cecil Rhodes, through his close associate and friend, Robert Williams, Chairman of the Tanganyika Concession Limited, launched a clandestine exploration team to Katanga. George Grey, adventurer, geologist and brother of the British Minister of Foreign Affairs, led the expedition. By 1899 Grey found the "scandalously rich" copper fields north of the Congo-Zambezi watershed line, clearly within the boundaries of Leopold's domain. This boundary problem was not only preventing another success for Rhodes' business empire, it also had significance for those in the highest echelons of the British Empire, including the Prince of Wales—the later King Edward VII. He had an indirect stake in this discovery; his courtesan Daisy Greville, the Countess of Warwick, was a shareholder in the Tanganyika Concession Ltd, courtesy of Rhodes, who always ensured that the Prince's girlfriend was doing well.[12] In quiet overtures, Williams attempted to get King Leopold's consent for a full industrial development of the Katanaga copper deposits. But Leopold had no interest in raising capital for large industrial projects. His gamble of exploiting Indian gum and ivory by forced recruitment and a rigid quota system had begun to generate great profits. Leopold's incentive to invest large sums of capital in a new Congolese venture was also diminished for other than pecuniary reasons.

The activities of Morel as a humanitarian on behalf of the Congo and as trade warrior of the New Imperialism, and Cecil Rhodes' bare-knuckle fight with Leopold, had moved British parliament. On May 20, 1903 the British House of Commons declared:

> That the government of the Congo Free State having, at its inception, guaranteed to the powers that its native subjects should be governed with humanity, and that no trading monopoly or privilege should be permitted within its dominions, this House requests His Majesty's Government to confer with the other powers, signatories to the Berlin General Act, by virtue of which the Congo Free State exists, in order that measures may be adopted to abate the evils prevalent in that state.[13]

Rhodes' generous contributions to the Irish Home Rule Party netted him confidence when the British parliament went to vote for further actions against Leopold. It was agreed to commission the Foreign Office with a report on the humanitarian situation in the Congo. To this end, a young and idealistic Irish-born diplomat who had already excelled with a report about Boer abuses against Africans was picked: Roger Casement. His work had helped to stimulate British parliamentarians and Prime Minister Salisbury into supporting military actions against the Boers. When the account by Consul Casement was published in early 1904 it was predictably a powerful indictment of "Red Rubber" and King Leopold II. Casement stated that the Congo was depopulating and he identified four causes: "indiscriminate war" against the people of the Congo, starvation because Congolese were forced to fulfil harsh ivory and gum harvest quotas set by Leopold's men, a decrease in the birth rate, and tropical diseases.

---

12 Cecil Rhodes's Bequest to Countess of Warwick. *New York Times*, August 23, 1902.

13 Hansard. May 20, 1903. Commons Sitting. Evening sitting "Congo Free State" HC Deb May 20, 1903 vol 122 cc1289-332 1289. Available at: http://hansard.millbanksystems.com/commons/1903/may/20/congo-free-state (accessed July 7, 2012).

Pax Britannica—Belge

Intense international pressures mounted now that pitted Leopold, the Belgian government and the public against each other. At stake was the political control over the Congo and responsibility for the human rights abuses. Eventually, the Belgians would send their own Commission of Inquiry that confirmed the worst allegations and rumors.

Robert Williams, through his British-controlled Tanganyika Concession Ltd, was not distracted by these concerns from establishing a partnership with King Leopold to exploit the copper deposits in Katanga. The political ramifications left Leopold no choice but to support the scheme. He brought in Jean Jadot, a trusted senior executive of the Société Générale de Belgique to form three subsidiaries as the backbone of industrial mining of the Congo: the Societe International Forestiere et Miniere du Congo (Forminiere), La Compagnie du Chemin de Fer du Bas-Congo au Katanga (BCK) and finally the Union Minière du Haut Katanga (UMHK). None other than Rhodes' trusted ally Robert Williams of Tanganyika Concession Ltd gained a strategically crucial 40 percent stake in UMHK.

Seven years after the discoveries of the Katanga copper fields by the British, and two years after Leopold's scandalous Red Rubber production had been officially targeted by the British Empire, the exploitation of the minerals of Katanga was now a joint venture between the British Empire and Leopold II. It would take another two years until the Congo Free State of Leopold II officially went out of business and the Belgian Congo was annexed to the Belgian state as a colony. The British and the Americans withheld their official recognition of the Congo; these two states, who were most aggressively pursuing Leopold's demise, could not afford to give recognition to Belgium. Proper verification that improvements were taking place in the Congo was needed. The most important voice in that decision was Morel's and the statements by the Congo Reform Association.

King Leopold's toll on the Congolese people was horrendous. In addition to the 8–10 million dead victims, millions of Congolese survived but with severed limbs, deeply scarred bodies and hearts and had to endure traditional tribal societies that now were completely corrupted by fear. The country had no infrastructure; whatever sporadic schooling and or medical care were provided came from Catholic missionaries; the Congo *was* depopulating. By 1909, however, the stream of correspondence from Morel's informants had stopped reporting atrocities. Belgian colonial authorities announced major reforms and Morel decided to claim victory: "the atrocities have disappeared."[14] On June 16, 1913 the Congo Reform Association officially held its final meeting in London and closed down its operations. There would be no human rights monitoring or campaigning on behalf of the Congolese, neither sporadic nor sustained, for the coming 60 years.

14 Hochschild, A. 1999. *King Leopold's Ghost*. New York: Mariner Books. 273–4.

The Belgian Congo:
The More Things Change the More They Stay the Same

For the Congolese it soon became obvious that the atrocities would not disappear from their lives. Europeans and Americans however shifted their attention and interests away to new humanitarian battlegrounds. With the new political and economic order established in the Congo, transparency of the Congo Colony's natural resource business was nobody's business.

On the surface the improvements were undeniable. The Colonial Charter of the Belgian Congo stated unequivocally, "Nobody can be forced to work on behalf of and for the profit of companies or privates." This principle was more or less strengthened in the Labour Law that was adopted for the Colony in 1910.[15] The duration of labor contracts were shortened and the conditions under which they could be prematurely terminated were defined in detail including acceptable penalties that could be imposed for non-compliance with contractual terms. Physical punishment was no longer permissible and corrective measures could only be applied by imposing fines or detentions. Important drivers behind these new rules were not only the needs of the Belgian colonial authorities for a more humane image but urgent economic factors; the Congo had to shift from a barter-based to a monetized economy. Services and labor were now to be paid in a new colonial currency. The Belgian parliament had made it clear from the beginning of its annexation that the promised economic development and social services for the colony had to be paid from revenues raised by the colony. However, in order to meet the objectives massive labor contingents had to be recruited. Raising revenues was on the top of the list. Executive power rested with the Belgian Minister of Colonial Affairs, assisted by a Colonial Council with the Belgian parliament exercising legislative authority. All of them were based in Belgium. No Congolese was ever consulted or asked for his consent to this governmental structure. The Governor-General of the Congo Free State, Baron Théophile Wahis, had been in this position since 1892 during King Leopold's reign. He remained there through the transition until 1912. No one seemed to have a problem with a manager who the Congo Reform Association had once accused of complicity in covering up the most gruesome crimes of the King's mercenaries.[16]

To raise sufficient revenues to pay for the schools, hospitals, roads and other public works necessary few options were available. Potential contributions to the colonial treasury could have resulted from taking full advantage of the emerging copper and cobalt mining industry in Katanga, of the gold exploitation in the Kivu and Uele regions, of the growing artisanal diamond exploitation in East Kasai, and of the developing agricultural sector. Another source of income was the imposition of excessive taxation on all Congolese. The latter was the obvious short-term

15 Northrup, D. 1988. *Beyond the River in the Bent.* Ohio University Center for International Studies. Africa Series. Number 52. Athens. Ohio. 85.

16 Cruelties in the Congo State. *New York Times*, June 4, 1897.

solution; the colonial authorities figured that because the Congolese were already familiar with the King Leopold's system of "prestations" it would now be replaced with a "voluntary" payment of taxes in the form of labor. The tax revenues would balance the book of the colonial accounting quickly.

What looked neat on paper turned out to be a nightmare in practice. After 30 years of abuses, the Congolese were loath to serve the old masters again and moved to the jungles in large numbers rather than be industrial employees under Belgian colonialists. Epidemic sleeping sickness raced through the Congo and wiped out whole villages, which in turn prevented or stalled the movement of fresh labor forces from other parts of the Congo. In this tight and overstressed labor market, World War I and the Belgian-Anglo attempts to occupy neighboring German East Africa required the recruitment of tens of thousands of Congolese as porters and farm laborers to provide supplies and food to the soldiers. The only way forward under these conditions was to go back to legalizing forced recruitment, to imposing hundreds of hours of compulsory labor and to reintroduce the *chicolette*. The legalization of all these measures was accomplished not by changing the Colonial Charter or Labour Laws but by issuing exemptions and ordinances directly to the enterprises. Once more, the Congolese population suffered through a new cycle of brutal coercion and extortion—very similar to the measures exacted by King Leopold and universally condemned by the international community.

The copper mining industry of the Katanga was so poorly organized in respect to the protection of the welfare of its workers that, even in the internal Belgian company and colonial government reporting, the mortality rates were considered scandalous. As late as 1920, pneumonia, typhoid, tuberculosis, dysentery, meningitis and smallpox killed between 18 to 31 percent of the work force of the leading copper mines.[17] John Higginson estimated that in these same mines "somewhere between 180 000 and 250 000 men were pressed into its service" during the first 30 years of their existence. David Northrup, who has researched the labor situation in the Congo extensively, concluded that the method but not the actual abuses had changed: "a series of reforms beginning before the end of the Free State rule reduced the severity of this forced labor, but expanding demands for labour brought many more people under some sort of coerced labour system. Thus, for the affected Africans, slavery had changed its form more than its character."[18]

Compared to the international media coverage before the annexation of the Congo the silence during this time was deafening. During the 52-year Belgian colonial rule over the Congo very few reports alluded to any problems although

17 Higginson J. 1989. *A Working Class in the Making: Belgian Colonial Labor Policy, Private Enterprise, and the African Mineworker, 1907–1951*. Madison: University of Wisconsin Press. 241.

18 Northrup, D. 1988. The End of Slavery in Africa, in *The Ending of Slavery in the Eastern Belgian Congo*, edited by S. Miers and R. L. Roberts. Madison: University of Wisconsin Press.

there was a constant stream of internal reporting pointing out abuses and practices reminiscent and sometimes even worse than those under the Congo Free State administration.[19] The mining and timber companies—largely in the hands of the Belgian–British interests–the Belgian colonial authorities and the Catholic Church ran a "regime of coercive paternalism"[20] that smothered all criticism. The colonial Belgian state and the Comité Spécial du Katanga (CSK) provided the security apparatus to enforce the new order, and acted as a tax collector, a punishing agent of last resort who worked closely with the company and the military to intervene on mine properties in the case of labor unrest.[21]

Exploiting the Congo's natural resources was no longer merely the object of personal greed. The immense copper, cobalt, diamond, gold, tin and nickel reserves in addition to the timber and various animal and medicinal plant products gained importance as strategic reserves for a rapid global industrialization and for the burgeoning defense industries of the West. At the beginning of World War II Belgium was quickly overrun by Germany, and Malaysia, the traditional supplier of rubber to Europe, had fallen to the Japanese. The Belgian government sought exile in London, and the Belgian Congo became a strategic supplier of rubber and minerals to the Allies. To fulfill its managerial functions during both wars, UMHK headquarters was transferred from Brussels to the offices of the Tanganyika Concessions Limited in London. From there it organized the supply of 85,000 tons of copper to the British and American armament factories in World War I and between 1940 and 1944 Katanga's copper mines provided 800,000 tons to the Allied forces. During the Second World War Katanga's Shinkolobwe mine was also the source for uranium used in the fabrication of the atomic bombs dropped on the Japanese cities of Hiroshima and Nagasaki in 1945. Belgium prospered politically and economically, but the Congolese saw little returns from their strategic contributions.

Following World War I Belgium was rewarded for the participation of its colonial Force Publique in the East African campaign with a League of Nations mandate over the former German colony of Ruanda-Urundi. This presented a new opportunity to rule an African colony with a Belgian policy of ethnic favoritism. The Tutsi populations of Rwanda and Burundi were to become the chosen ones with the Hutu drawing the short straw.

19 Northrup provides an ongoing account of such internal reporting, pointing out very courageous Belgian colonial staff who went beyond their call of duty. Northrup, D. 1988.

20 Fetter B. 1973. L'Union Minière du Haut-Katanga, 1920–1940: La naissance d'une sous-culture totalitaire. *Cahier du CEDAF* no. 6.

21 Hönke, J. 2009. Transnational Pockets of Territoriality Governing the Security of Extraction in Katanga (DRC). *Working Paper Series*. Graduate Centre Humanities and Social Sciences of the Research Academy Leipzig. No. 2. Leipzig.

Independence and Secession of Katanga

The International Convention of Civil and Political Rights was drafted in 1954 and was still in debate at the UN General Assembly by 1960. The actual adaptation of the Convention took until 1966. However, the principles embodied in it were common sense to most European states, as were the items listed under the Universal Declaration of Human Rights or the rules that applied to all signatories of the Charter of the United Nations. Accordingly, it was widely understood in Europe that killing, torturing or otherwise physically abusing political enemies was no longer acceptable. Occupying territories of other countries without being invited to do so was not permissible either. But the dogged sense of Belgian ownership over the Congo must have skewed perception of these legal principles.

In January 1960 Congolese activists succeeded in pressing the Belgian government into allowing national elections in the Congo. Patrice Lumumba emerged as the winner of the elections and by the end of June the country officially gained independence. Rather than accepting the decision by the Congolese electorate, the Belgium government supported clandestine preparations by secessionist Katangans. Eleven days after the Congo's break away from Belgium, Katanga broke away from the Congo under the leadership of Moise Tshombe, supported by 6,000 Belgian paratroopers and representatives of major Belgian commercial interests. The strategically important copper-cobalt and uranium riches of Katanga continued to be under Belgian, British and increasingly also American patronage. Six months later Katanga's Interior Minister Godeforid Munongo delivered further proof that Katangan and Belgian interests were tightly intertwined. In a rambling announcement he revealed that inhabitants of a village had killed Lumumba while fleeing from detention. Everyone seemed to assume that this announcement was not true and that Lumumba had been illegally abducted and murdered.

Still, there was no outcry in the West and only nonaligned leaders such as Egyptian President Gamal Abdel Nasser and Ghanian President Kwame Nkumah asked U.S. President John Kennedy outright about America's role in the murder. It would take 40 years and the enterprising Belgian journalist Luddo de Witte to bring out the full truth. The revelations in his book, *The Assassination of Lumumba*,[22] were eventually confirmed by a Belgian Parliamentary Commission tasked by Foreign Minister Louis Michel to investigate and verify what had happened. The reports stated unambiguously that Belgian authorities disregarded the sovereignty of the Congolese and interfered in internal affairs, mostly due to pressures by Belgian investors in the Congo and in particular by large mining companies such as UMHK. In addition to the political sponsorship the companies were also supporting the Katanagan secessionists with 50 million francs. The investigation further revealed that King Baudouin knew that Prime Minister

22 De Witte, L. 2001. *De moord op Lumumba* [*The Assassination of Lumumba*]. London: Verso.

Patrice Lumumba was in mortal danger and that the Belgian government had pressed hard for Lumumba's arrest. It was also understood by the King and senior political leadership that no trial would be held against Lumumba, and that the Belgians would be involved in his elimination. There was also an agreement to confuse the public with fabricated accounts and to protect the Belgians who would assume responsibility for the murder. The King did nothing to prevent these acts from happening.

After the summer of 1913 when the Congo Reform Association closed its doors, no insights about the humanitarian condition in the Congo had been published. The zeal of newspaper journalists and academic researchers in the condemnations of King Leopold's atrocities had turned into apathy. As a matter of bureaucratic diligence Belgian colonial authorities and even their companies systematically gathered information and assessed various parameters of ordinary Congolese people's living conditions. Of course, they had no incentive to publish what internally was referred to as an unmitigated human disaster. For these reasons the elite and inconspicuous power structure consisting of the Belgian–British business conglomerates and colonial authorities and the clergy of the Belgian Catholic Church that ran the Congo, had very little open dissent to deal with. The Catholic Church contributed schools and health services to the overall Belgian goal of "bringing civilisation to the Congo." It appears that the clergy was either overly stern or not very successful in its civilizing work; after independence the emancipatory revelry was very frequently punctured by angry Congolese mobs targeting priests and other personnel of the Church. Under President Mobutu, the purging of Catholic values went even further, from the elimination of Christmas from the calendar of national holidays, to the ban of religious instructions at Congolese schools and to decrees to abandon Christian baptismal names in favor of authentic African names.

Mobutu and the "Congolization" of Natural Resources

After a five-year period of instability, Joseph Mobutu successfully organized a military coup in November 1965 against the leaders of the First Republic. Mobutu concentrated on many of the long overdue governmental functions and consolidation of power under Congolese leadership. He extended the campaign of Congoloization, or the *procédures d'authentification*, eventually changing his official name to Mobutu Sese Seko Nkuku wa za Banga, and the name Congo into Zaire.

As a pragmatist, Mobuto easily matched the international community's relentless political and economic expediencies over democratic and humanitarian principles. His rather spotty human rights record, his role in the removal of Lumumba and in the disappearance and killings of opposition politicians counted as mere collateral damage in the West's anti-communist drive in Africa. The West's laissez-faire attitude in respect to Mobuto's humanitarian stance was one thing. But tolerance came to an abrupt end when one year into his reign he announced the "Congolization" of many important mining enterprises. In the re-organization of the copper enterprise, all of the assets of UMHK were seized by the state and given to a new Congolese company, Général de Carrières et des Mines du Zaïre (Gecamines). Of course, the 17.95 percent shares in UMHK along with the 24.49 percent privileged voting rights, which were already in the name of Mobutu's government, were left untouched. The second largest shareholder, with 14.47 percent of all outstanding shares, the British-controlled Tanganyika Concession Ltd, was followed by Belgian conglomerates Compagnie Financière du Katanga with 8.98 percent and the Société Générale de Belgique with 4.64 percent. These stakes were now null and void because Mobutu invited new foreign investors to take 40 percent of Gecamines' shares. However, even Mobutu's attempts of nationalizing Zaire's natural resource exploitation companies stumbled on the fact that his country's mineral industry had no direct access to the international markets. SOGEMIN, a Brussels based marketing subsidiary of UHMK, had to be contracted to market the production of Gecamines. By 1976 Mobutu was forced to backtrack in his economic Zairianization. With the release of the "Decree of Retrocession" the expropriations of the past were reversed and foreign shareholders received some of their former property back.

Despite this misstep, Mobutu could not do wrong in the eyes of the West. For many years, the Bretton Woods institutions presented Zaire as their most exemplary pupil and Mobutu enjoyed if not sympathy in the Western capitals, at least the largesse of the IMF and World Bank[23] without inconvenient questions about his increasing corruption. "Mobutu is a bloody bastard, but he is the only hope,"[24] Henry Kissinger once remarked to U.S. President Ford. Only President Jimmy Carter attempted to censor Mobutu for his dismal human rights record. He proposed reduction of U.S. foreign aid to Zaire, but Congress quickly rescinded the presidential initiative. Still, human rights concerns kicked in 60 years after the end of the Congo Reform Association. However, it was not on demand of the traditional Western leadership but on the initiative of Latin American member states of the United Nations. Triggered by their own, long struggles with humanitarian abuses some Latin American countries increasingly accentuated their international politics toward the defense of human rights. Robert Garreton, a Chilean lawyer, had been appointed UN Special Rapporteur on Zaire in 1994. His statements and reports were penetrating and uncompromising: "Since Mobutu Sese Seko came to power … the United Nations has not carried out any official investigations

23 Mommen, A. Zaïre's Economic Decline and Ill-fated Liberalization Policies, in *Liberalization in the Developing World*, edited by Ales E. F. Jilbert and A. Mommen. Institutional and Economic Changes in Latin America, Africa and Asia, Routledge Studies in Development Economics.

24 *Brent Scowcroft Files* Gerald R. Ford Library Memorandum of Conversation on Monday June 16, 1975, Oval Office, President Gerald R. Ford, Dr. Henry A. Kissinger, Secretary of State and Assistant to the President for National Security Affairs discussing options on how to counter unfavorable turns of events in the civil war in Angola.

in the country. The major Western powers condoned the flagrant human rights violations because of the dictator's strategic role during the cold war."[25] Among his reporting were accounts of the disastrous consequences of Mobutu's policies on the Rwandan and Burundian settlers in the Kivus that triggered counterattacks against each other by Hutu and Tutsi groups.

While Garreton's work did offer an unvarnished and more objective view of the Congo's situation, there is no evidence that the downfall of Mobutu, which came later than for most Cold War tyrants and kleptocrats, was in any way connected with concerns over his human rights record. What is clear is that Laurent-Désiré Kabila, his successor, was actively supported by the People's Republic of China, Rwanda and Uganda. It is also obvious that the United States and the UK, powerful allies of Rwanda and Uganda, were either not able to control the situation or did not tell the leaders of these two states in clear enough language to stop teaming up with Kabila against Mobutu. Rwanda's then Vice-President and Minister of Defence, Paul Kagame, even went as far as to brag in interviews with American newspapers, "the Rwandan Government planned and directed the rebellion."[26]

The First Congolese War

The fall of Mobutu offered a long overdue break from a gory past. It was a step away from colonialism and a step toward hope for a real awakening of Africa and toward generous foreign aid. Post-Cold War revelations about past atrocities made room for feelings of guilt or at least an uneasy indebtedness; "Development aid filled this gap: it provided an outlet for young volunteers, it was in line with our paternalistic traditions, it eased our moral pains."[27] While the idealistic awakening of the West led to increased funding for conflict and post-conflict aid to Africa, it also created a rapidly professionalizing racket of non-government organizations, international advocacy groups and a proliferation of advisors and experts. Very soon, the growing footprint of Western nations in Arica's crisis regions would justify unabashed neo-colonialist attitudes, Africa-pessimism and finally donor-fatigue.

While Europeans and Americans reformulated their approach to Africa with customary arrogance, Africans took notice of new horizons. The new leader of the Congo, Laurent-Désiré Kabila, was already well in tune with the fact that China was becoming an enthusiastic sponsor of African interests after Western Europe, the United States and the Russians had lost control over many African leaders

25 Garreton, R. October 21, 1997. Mission Impossible. *Le Monde Diplomatique*.

26 Africans Use Training in Unexpected Ways Series: Special Alliances: The Pentagon's New Global Engagements. *The Washington Post*, July 14, 1998.

27 Doom, R. 2006. *Calimero in Tropical Africa: Belgium's Ethical Burden*. Centre for Third World Studies, University of Ghent Belgium.

after the Cold War. To the few observers who had taken note of Kabila during his 30-year rebel career, he was not known for his sophisticated global views. He was better known as a charismatic and hard-drinking skirt chaser who happened to be in the right place at the right time when history washed him to the surface of the armed opposition against Mobutu. Che Guevara had famously turned his back on him after he had wasted several months in Western Tanzania and in Congo's South Kivu trying to instil some revolutionary zeal in Kabila. The People's Revolutionary Party (PRP), which Kabila had founded in the 1960s, muddled through, even installing the secessionist mini-state Hewa Bora in the midst of the hillsides between Fizi and Baraka along Lake Tanganyika. He prospered by exploiting artisanal miners, mostly through gold smuggling. At the same time, Kabila and his PRP received financial support from the People's Republic of China, as did Michel Micombero, the first president of Burundi who was less than 100 miles away from Kabila's hideout and was an outspoken advocate of African socialism.

For long stretches of his revolutionary past, Kabila was assumed to be dead. By the 1990s, in the midst of mounting tensions between Tutsi and Hutu in neighboring Burundi and Rwanda, Kabila rose in the ranks of Mobutu foes to eventually assume the leadership of the Alliance des Forces Démocratiques pour la Libération du Congo-Zaïre (AFDL). In 1996, AFDL launched an armed revolt against Mobutu with the support of Presidents Paul Kagame (Rwanda) and Yoweri Museveni (Uganda). Initially, nobody took the incursion very serious. After a lightning fast and decisive six-month conquest, Laurent-Désiré Kabila gained full political and military power over the country that he now called the Democratic Republic of Congo (DRC). During his race from South-Kivu to Kinshasa, Kabila was already perfecting his proficiency in profiting from the DRC's natural resources; he had "liberated" one mining region after another. Even before he started his conquest, a major Belgian gold dealer had arranged to follow him and set up exclusive gold buying agents in every trading center of the Congo. Soon it was known that Kabila was willing to annul Mobutu-era mining deals and that the DRC's richest mineral deposits were up for grabs by the highest bidders. Hundreds of mining executives were waiting for Kabila in Kisangani, halfway to the capital, with fists full of dollars, ready to acquire concession agreements. The Presidential Palace in Kinshasa, the Ministry of Mines in the Bâtiment Gecamines in Gombe, the Grand Hotel and wherever else the newly appointed Ministers of Mines, of Finance, of Economy or of Planning happened to turn up became natural resource bazaars. The postwar rough and tumble was risky even to the highest bidders or the most loyal supporters of Kabila. Jean-Raymond Boulle, founder and majority shareholder of an upstart U.S. mining firm, American Mineral Fields, had lent his corporate jet to Kabila while the fight against Mobutu was still on. Now he cashed in by securing the mining rights for the richest copper mines in Katanga, which he lost again a few weeks later. Anglo American, the huge mining conglomerate, also cut a deal with one of Kabila's ministers and that transaction prevailed at least until American Mineral Fields sued.[28]

When Kabila revoked all mining rights issued under Mobutu in January 1998, and even those granted during the AFDL revolt in the previous year, the international community was not objecting ferociously against the wholesale reallocation of the DRC's mineral rights. Investors who felt cheated by these actions sued in the DRC's courts or requested arbitration proceedings in international legal venues. On the whole, however, there was little protest, and barely any comment about his decidedly dictatorial governance. The principal concerns of the international community had to do with the DRC's urgent need for revenues and their equally urgent interests in benefitting from the country's natural wealth. Their logic was easy to follow. Gecamines and MIBA, the two mining giants managed by Belgian interests, previously contributed on average around 60 percent to overall state revenues. Now, both operations had come to a virtual standstill. Where Kabila would find revenue sources to compensate for the badly needed reconstruction of the country was anybody's guess. Some guessed faster than others. Shortly after Kabila's takeover in 1997 the U.S. construction giant Bechtel already had a "master plan" for the reconstruction and rehabilitation of the DRC. It envisioned a comprehensive reworking of the entire infrastructure and extractive resources.[29] Its author later described how Laurent Kabila "took the plan and attempted to manipulate it into his own personal fiefdom, i.e. ownership of the DRC by various alliances with the leaders, entrepreneurs, armies and neighbouring nations who had supported his military coup against his predecessor President Mobutu Sese Seko Kuku Waza Banga."

Whatever sinister motivations Kabila may have had, he did not seem to be interested in catering to the needs of his former alliance partners. The Rwandan and Ugandan leadership charged that he had turned on them when he started to arm the Hutus who were hiding in Eastern Congo. Robert Garreton, the UN's Special Rapporteur, had reported on atrocities by Kabila's AFDL and the Rwandan re-enforcements from the Rwandan Patriotic Army against the Hutus living in Eastern Congo. With his frank and objective reports, Garreton managed to be detested by both Mobutu and Kabila. Once Kabila assumed power he blocked Garreton from resuming his investigations. A stalemate developed over the conditions under which Kabila would allow the continuation of the UN's human rights investigation and over the retribution by European governments who threatened to block all foreign aid. South Africa's Mandela backed Kabila in a show of distrust of Western

28 Westerners Angle for Mining Stakes in Congo. *New York Times*, June 17, 1997. The Curse of Riches; In Africa, Wealth Often Buys Only Trouble. *New York Times*, January 25, 1998.

29 Robert S. Stewart, author of the Plan commented on December 16, 2008 to a column by Herman Cohen in the *New York Times*. Available at: http://community.nytimes.com/comments/www.nytimes.com/2008/12/16/opinion/16cohen.html (accessed July 7, 2012).

meddling in African affairs. Bill Richardson, the American ambassador to the UN, attempted to play "godfather" to the new DRC by devising a deal that would have allowed the UN investigation to continue in "exchange for a promise of discretion and the government's right to inspect the investigation's findings."[30] By selling out the UN investigator's independence, the U.S. ambassador was going to turn the UN engagement in the DRC into a hollow shell. Happily, UN Secretary General Kofi Annan circumvented the deadlock by appointing his own Investigative Team in July 1997. The highly frustrated Garreton was allowed to retire. The new human rights investigation team led by Chief Justice Atsu-Koffi Amega from Togo took over under a slightly changed mandate; it was to include events involving all belligerent parties and their actions beginning March 1, 1993. Kofi Annan's struggle for a principled solution was in vain. When team leader Amega returned to New York with his first report he left no doubt that Kabila had paid lip service to the international community. While the UN investigators were in the DRC, he had imposed every imaginable obstacle to prevent any meaningful investigation.

There is no indication that Kabila's tug-of-war with the UN's human rights investigators was part of the reason why no Western country intervened in August 1998 when Kabila's former allies, the Rwandan and Ugandan presidents, openly backed militant opposition groups and unleashed the Second Congo War. However, it is clear that the U.S. government accepted Rwanda's and Uganda's national security rationale to start a war against Kabila. They alleged that his reversal toward favoring the Hutu population in Eastern Congo and abandoning the policy of "racial equality" was tantamount to destabilizing the entire border region to Rwanda and Uganda.[31] However, the U.S. government was too constricted in its post-Rwandan genocide remorse and could not afford to publicly state that it objected to a new Rwandan involvement in the Congo as U.S. Ambassador Griffin told Rwanda's Vice-President Kagame on August 13, 1998 in a private conversation.[32]

The Second Congo War and the Re-awakening of the Human Rights Agenda

Initially, the line-up against Kabila was straightforward. Uganda backed the Mouvement pour la Liberation du Congo (MLC) and Rwanda was behind the Rassemblement Congolais pour la Democratie (RCD). Very soon, these groups deteriorated into squabbles and internal dissension and ideological objectives gave way to control fights over natural resource deposits. Along the way, the international community lost its sense of direction and was soon paralysed by its own fracas. The human rights agenda deteriorated into a convenient political token

---

30 Breackman, C. December 1997. Pragmatic Rule in Congo-Kinshasa. *Le Monde Diplomatique*.

31 Gribbin, R. 2005. *In the Aftermath of Genocide*. Bloomington: iUniverse. 283.

32 Gribbin, R. 2005. 279.

that could be played whenever it seemed suitable. The protagonists that emerged from this chaos are for the most part still the key figures in today's DRC. Each one went to war or to combat with words and political and economic measures on a humanitarian platform, professing to fight for the best interests of this or that constituency. The combined humanitarian efforts have led to a morass in which as many as five million Congolese have been robbed, raped and killed.

RCD /RCD-Goma (Rassemblement Congolais pour la Democratie)

Some of the original founders of RCD wanted to create a Rwandan Tutsi dominated organization that would encompass a wide spectrum of Kabila-critics, from former Mobutuists to Marxist and mutinous soldiers from Kabila's own ranks, all intent on expelling Kabila as fast as they had helped him to power. The organization was intended to be political only, based in Goma. Ernest Wamba dia Wamba, a respected intellectual, Philosophy Professor at Brandeis University and History Professor at Dar es Salam University, who eventually was arrested and jailed by Mobutu, became the RCD's first leader. However, the membership of RCD soon transformed it into a belligerent organization and made James Kabarebe the military leader. Kabarebe was a former Rwandan Military Chief of Staff, who also had served as interim Chef d'Etat of the Kabila led AFDL revolt against Mobutu, and is now the Minister of Defence and National Security of Rwanda. Wamba dia Wamba left to form RCD-K, and later RCD-L-ML. The former Marxist rebel Emile Ilunga took over and RCD was renamed RCD-Goma. In subsequent elections the lawyer Azarias Ruberwa and finally the physician Adolphe Onusumba, both Banyamulenge, gained the leadership. The RCD, and its later derivatives, was a powerful military organization that at times controlled large tracts of the Congo. Under James Kabarebe it managed impressive military feats, including a direct attack against Kinshasa at the beginning of the Second Congo War. Along the way, RCD-Goma has also committed some of the worst war crimes, including the atrocities committed in 2000 during the occupation of Kisangani. Between 2002 and 2006 while the Transitional Government was in charge of the DRC, RCD-Goma assumed quasi-governmental functions in the Kivus. It exercised federal law-enforcement functions, illegally allocated natural resource rights and collected taxes and export/import duties but withheld the share of revenues that should have gone to Kinshasa. With the appointment of Eugene Serafuli, a Hutu, as Governor of North Kivu, RCD attempted to stimulate better integration of Banyarwandan groups. After the successful election of Joseph Kabila as president of the DRC, the organization soon lost its importance and much of its leadership either took on national political roles or joined the successor organization, CNDP, that was led by renegade General Laurent Nkunda Batware.

Jean Pierre Bemba and the MLC

Jean Pierre Bemba was a former assistant to Mobutu and the son of Congo's most successful businessman, Jeannot Bemba Saolona. Saolona had been Mobutu's most important business advisor, the chief reason why Kabila jailed him initially and eventually appointed him Minister of Economy. While his father served Kabila, Jean Pierre Bemba conspired with Ugandan President Yoweri Museveni and formed the Mouvement de Libération du Congo (MLC). Both father and son Bemba had long and successful histories of illegally exploiting natural resources, in particular the diamond fields of the Northern Congo and of the adjacent Central African Republic. It came as no surprise when they shared control over the Congo's richest and most renowned gold mining area, located around Watsa with the Ugandan Armed Forces. Human Rights Watch has prepared strong documentation of severe human rights abuses committed by MLC during its occupation of these mining regions.[33] After the election of Joseph Kabila as president of the DRC Jean Pierre Bemba became the leader of the most powerful political opposition. However, his new role lasted only a few weeks. In the spring of 2007, during a violent confrontation with Kabila's Revolutionary Guards, hundreds of MLC combatants were killed. Jean Pierre Bemba was forced to seek protection in the embassy of South Africa and eventually refuge in Portugal. During a visit to Belgium in early 2008 he was arrested and transferred to the International Criminal Court (ICC) in The Hague. The prosecutor of the ICC had sought Bemba's arrest for three counts of war crimes and two counts of crimes against humanity. These charges referred to Bemba's military actions when he came to the help of Central African Republic (CAR) President Ange-Felix Patasse who was under attack by Francois Bozize. Besides Bemba, the ICC has not accused any other individual for alleged war crimes in CAR.

Kabila's Countermoves

Faced with a significant mutiny among his former soldiers and an attack by the neighboring states of Rwanda and Uganda, Kabila had to organize a very comprehensive defense. One of the handicaps he faced during this new war was that the looting of the Eastern DRC took on apocalyptic dimensions. There was the collapse of the current production but there was also the loss of income from reselling mineral mining rights. In addition to the production of mineral and precious stones the belligerents also took the entire agricultural production of

33 *The Curse of Gold*. April 2005. Human Rights Watch, Haut-Commissarait pour les Droits de l'Homme de la Nations Unies 1993–2003 Août 2010 *Rapport du Projet Mapping concernant les violations les plus graves des droits de l'homme et du droit international humanitaire commises entre mars 1993 et juin 2003 sur le territoire de la République démocratique du Congo*.

Eastern DRC. The rich pastures of the Kivus on which hundreds of thousands of cows had grazed were emptied out in a matter of months. The shoe factories in Uganda were oversupplied with cowhides. Many Congolese were offended by the wholesale looting of their country by their neighbors. Even if they did not side with Kabila, latent nationalism caused many to organize Mai-Mai movements, which in many occupied regions turned out to be a formidable military factor. At the same time, Kabila equipped and organized his old foes, the Hutus, some of them surviving "genocidaires" from the Rwandan genocide of 1994. This move confirmed and further galvanized the suspicions of the Tutsi government of Rwanda. With Angola, Zimbabwe and Namibia, three members of the Southern African Development Community (SADC) responded to Kabila's request for military assistance. While officially the political obligation was cited, in reality Zimbabwe and Angola were more likely lured into the fight by the opportunity to take home some of the spoils of the natural resources of the Congo. Chad, Libya and Sudan were also contributing troops to Kabila's side. It helped Kabila that Ugandan and Rwandan troops and their proxies were by no means unified parties. Internally, tensions mounted in all factions, mostly because of the rich opportunities to plunder the natural resources. This increasing infighting was giving rise to spin-off violence in the Ituri District, the north-eastern corner of the DRC, adjoining Uganda and Southern Sudan.

The Ituri War

The *Union des Patriotes Congolais* (UPC) was created by Thomas Lubanga and others from his Gegere-Hema tribe who found themselves in disagreement with the RCD-K-ML and Antipas Mbusa Nyamwisi. UPC was the most powerful Hema organization in the Ituri conflict and with Bosco Ntaganda as army chief of staff for its military arm Forces Patriotiques pour la Libération du Congo (FPLC) Lubanga was a formidable force. Uganda recognized this upstart warlord and provided him with military support which promptly enabled him to take Bunia in August 2002. Until 2003 and later again during short intervals, UPC was thus in control of one of the principal gold trading centres of Eastern Congo, was able to extort taxes, license fees from gold traders and exporters as well as artisanal miners. Lubanga is now on trial in the ICC. In response to the rising Hema power in Ituri, their traditional enemies, the Lendu, organized the Nationalistes et Intégrationnistes (FNI) under Floribert Ndjabu. The Lendu received at times military support from Rwanda. Over time FNI also allied itself with other Ituri militias such as the Ngiti-led Front for Patriotic Resistance of Ituri Front led by Germaine Katanga and Mathieu Ngudjolo. FNI set up quasi-governmental controls over gold operations in its occupied areas. Internal documentation of the organization showed that tax revenues from natural resources have been its most important source of income. Ndjabu, Katanaga and Ngudjolo are also on trial in The Hague.

The wars in Eastern Congo generated plenty of disgruntled and disillusioned soldiers. Jerome Kakwavu was the first one who recognized the potential of these militants and organized many of them in the Forces Armées du People Congolais (FAPC), operating mainly in the strategically important border region of Aru. He also systematically organized all merchant activities in the region into an economic support network for his militia by enforcing taxations, as well as import and export duties.

UN Security Council and Soft Laws

In the face of the horrendous bloodletting in the Congo the international community produced a series of hand-wringing Presidential Statements by the UN Security Council in August 1998 and thereafter. The regional states were encouraged to take actions through the Regional Initiative for Peace in the Democratic Republic of the Congo chaired by Zambian President Frederick Chiluba. Under his guidance the Lusaka ceasefire agreement was negotiated and by July and August 1999 signed by the Democratic Republic of Congo, Angola, Namibia, Zimbabwe, Rwanda, and Uganda and MLC. Of the major belligerent parties RCD did not sign the agreement and did not abide by its stipulations. The Rwandan-backed rebels knew very well that none of the major powers were going to intervene militarily or in any other meaningful manner. Operation Palliser, the exceedingly successful British intervention in Sierra Leone of May 2000, was not going to serve as a model for stopping the vast and complex Congo war.[34] Still, the ceasefire agreement gave the UN Security Council a legal instrument and a blueprint to organize its immediate emergency response as well as to develop a long-term pacification strategy. It called for the deployment of UN peacekeepers under Chapter VII of the United Nations Charter. In the following months about 90 advance UN personnel were deployed and by February 24, 2,000 personnel were in the field. The UN authorized a force of 5,537 troops under the newly established Mission de l'Organisation des Nations Unies en République Démocratique du Congo (MONUC). But what would be the long-term response?

The eventual answer was going to be surprising in that it changed the regional dynamics and suddenly introduced idealistic ambitions into the hard-nosed extractive industries of the former colonies. The new American Ambassador to the UN, Richard Holbrooke, decided that January 2000, when the United States was taking its month-long turn for the presidency of the UN Security Council, would be the "month of Africa." He planned open meetings to discuss conflicts in Burundi, the Democratic Republic of the Congo (DRC), Angola and Sierra Leone and the effect of AIDS on Africa. On January 24, 2000, the Security Council chaired by U.S. Secretary of State Madeleine Albright welcomed the presidents of seven African nations, Laurent-Désiré Kabila among them. Kabila, a former Marxist rebel leader and gold smuggler who had engineered a bloody rampage through the

34 Eventually, there would be limited military engagements by European forces, first the French-led Operation Artemis in 2003 and then the German-led EUFOR, an over-the-horizon deployment in support of the presidential elections of 2006.

Congo, had systematically blocked UN human rights investigations and triggered a looting spree of his country's natural resources by every neighboring state and was now playing a statesman in front of the world's most senior decision-making body. In a display of extraordinary amnesia he asked: is there anyone here who is unaware of the systematic plundering of Congolese resources on and below the ground by the Rwandan, Ugandan and Burundian occupiers? Their booty—wood, diamonds, gold, cobalt and zebras—is all being sold on the open market, including in some of the countries represented here today.[35]

With his reference to "systematic plundering of Congolese resources" Kabila set into motion a new dynamic in the conflict resolution dialogue. Within a few weeks, the Security Council decided to send a mission to Central Africa led by Ambassador Holbrooke, in order to define what further steps in support of its peace-making could be undertaken. After a four-day blitz-mission, Holbrooke and his colleagues delivered the defining report for all future Security Council actions on the Congo's natural resources. The key recommendation was that the Secretary General should create a "UN Panel of Experts on the illegal exploitation of natural resources and other forms of wealth of the Democratic Republic of the Congo."[36] A critical point in the language and in the rhetoric first suggested by Kabila, and further magnified by the Holbrooke mission in the operative paragraph 77 of their report and in the statement by the President of the Security Council, was the concept that the Congo's natural resources were exploited "illegally." The choice of words, the Panel of Experts stated in its first report, presented the most contentious concept of the mandate.[37] It ended up defining illegality based on the existence of four underpinnings: violation of sovereignty; respect by actors for the existing regulatory framework in the country or territory where they operate; discrepancy between widely accepted practices in trade and business and the way business is conducted in the DRC; and the violation of international law, including "soft" law. The Panel's subsequent reports revealed that the four criteria were an overstatement since the true focus was on the fourth criteria and serious instances of the other three were not cited.

The OECD

The "soft law" approach turned out to basically be an attempt to promote the Organization of Economic Coordination and Development (OECD), a Paris-based bureaucracy with, at the time, 30 high-income countries as member states. The membership does not include a single African state, not one developing nation,

35 United Nations Security Council. January 24, 2000. *Transcript of 4092 Meeting at 10 am* S/PV. 4092.

36 United Nations Security Council. May 11, 2000. *Security Council Mission Report S2000/416*; United Nations Security Council. June 2, 2000. *Report S/2000/20.*

37 United Nations Security Council. 2001. *Report S/2001/357.* Paragraph 15.

nor Russia or China. Originally the bureaucracy was set up under the name Organization for European Economic Cooperation by the United States and Canada as a facilitator for the implementation of the Marshall Plan. By 1961 it was restructured to fit into the emerging European Economic Community and received its current name. Over time, it spun off the International Energy Agency (IEA) and the Financial Action Task Force on Money Laundering (FATF). After the end of the Cold War, the OECD attempted to become the facilitator to globalized business by offering itself as a clearinghouse for statistical trade data, as a center for the definition and harmonization of regulatory and supervisory frameworks and as a standard-setter for voluntary business principles. Thus the OECD became a prolific producer of "soft-laws." This alternative set of rules proved attractive to those who knew that their ideas would not succeed in conventional democratic settings such as national parliaments, the UN General Assembly, or the World Trade Organization. An important milestone in the OECD's soft law approach was the year 2000 version of the Guidelines for Multinational Companies. These guidelines defined ethical standards that companies domiciled in the 30 member states were asked to adhere to voluntarily or else become subject to naming and shaming campaigns.

> OECD Guidelines for Multinational Companies issued June 2000
>
> 1. Contribute to economic, social and environmental progress with a view to achieving sustainable development.
>
> 2. Respect the human rights of those affected by their activities consistent with the host government's international obligations and commitments.
>
> 3. Encourage local capacity building through close co-operation with the local community, including business interests, as well as developing the enterprise's activities in domestic and foreign markets, consistent with the need for sound commercial practice.
>
> 4. Encourage human capital formation, in particular by creating employment opportunities and facilitating training opportunities for employees.
>
> 5. Refrain from seeking or accepting exemptions not contemplated in the statutory or regulatory framework related to environmental, health, safety, labour, taxation, financial incentives, or other issues.
>
> 6. Support and uphold good corporate governance principles and develop and apply good corporate governance practices.

7. Develop and apply effective self-regulatory practices and management systems that foster a relationship of confidence and mutual trust between enterprises and the societies in which they operate.

8. Promote employee awareness of, and compliance with, company policies through appropriate dissemination of these policies, including through training programmes.

9. Refrain from discriminatory or disciplinary action against employees who make bona fide reports to management or, as appropriate, to the competent public authorities, on practices that contravene the law, the Guidelines or the enterprise's policies.

10. Encourage, where practicable, business partners, including suppliers and sub-contractors, to apply principles of corporate conduct compatible with the Guidelines.

11. Abstain from any improper involvement in local political activities.

This kind of reputational blackmail enjoyed growing popularity among activists of the Corporate Social Responsibility (CSR) movements and INGOs, while the chances of being taken through proper legal tests were very unlikely. It was precisely that set of standards that the Panel for the DRC was applying in its most controversial report S/2002/1146. It stated that a number of individuals and companies had violated the voluntary guidelines and the Panel provided certain information to that end. It further attached three lists with several hundred names of alleged violations giving the impression that these were UN-sanctioned persons and entities. Because the OECD had never managed to substantially increase its membership beyond the bracket of industrialized states the Panel's actions invigorated the impression that the UN's work was just another attempt to impose Western rules on Africa. The conclusions stiffened resistance in Africa and Asia to comply with UN Security Council decisions with some good justifications.

In its rush to judgment the Panel did not indicate the precise dates of the alleged violations of the voluntary guidelines and to what extent they may have predated the release of the guidelines in June 2000. When the report of the Panel was published on October, 16 2002 the President of the DRC's Transitional Government had already signed a modern Mining Code on July 11 of the same year into law. Why then, did the Panel ignore "hard" Congolese law in favor of "soft" OECD voluntary guidelines? Unfortunately, some valuable insights of the panel's work, such as the culpability of political-military-business leadership, were left without a chance or the political will to be bolstered with further evidence. For Congolese whose livelihood depended on artisanal mining or timber harvesting, no meaningful follow-up meant impunity to those who kept destroying their communities, their families and their lives.

Transition to the Future

Other than huge amounts of publicity and an increased awareness of the linkages between violence and natural resource diversions the UN Panel's achievements were not impressive. By adding annexes the Panel gave the wrong impression that it had a mandate to impose UN sanctions, yet it did not. Misperceptions of its reports further confused the distinction between the Security Council and the OECD. Instead of recommending sanctions, the Panel embraced the OECD process that is clearly outside the purview of the Security Council. The promotion of the OECD process over the Security Council sanctions process confused and weakened the overall effectiveness of UN sanctions.[38] The worst of it was that the OECD processes never delivered any noticeable corrective actions against the people and companies the Panel accused of illegally exploiting natural resources and funding violence. The Belgian Senate, for example, initiated elaborate hearings in order to get to the bottom of culpable Belgian firms or individuals. After 18 months of work and 71 hearings, the Commission announced that no illegal acts were committed by the people and companies investigated. Opposition senators refused to endorse the text, saying that the recommendations "without any content" are aimed at protecting "Belgian political and economic interests in the region."[39]

Joseph Kabila and the New/Old DRC

On January 18, 2001 Laurent-Désiré Kabila was assassinated by one of his bodyguards. After a short period of uncertainty his 29-year-old son Joseph Kabila emerged as the compromise leader of the DRC. A few months later, when all parties to the Congolese War singed the Sun City Peace Accord in South Africa, Joseph Kabila was confirmed as the President of the Transitional Government of the DRC. He was to lead a government in a 1+4 formula, meaning that the leaders of the most important militias, Jean-Pierre Bemba (MLC), Azerias Ruberwa (RCD-Goma), Arthur Zahigidi Ngoma and Abdoulaye Yerodia Ndobmbasi as representatives of civil opposition parties would act as Vice-Presidents. France lived up to its "superpower" status by authoring all Security Council documents pertaining to all things DRC, and by leading the way in all other matters as well. It prescribed successfully the Comité International d'Accompagnement de la Transition (CIAT) as an overlord over the fledgling Kabila government. CIAT's membership combined the major donors such as the EU, France, Belgium, the United States, as well as African partners such as the AU (Africa Union) and

38 Carisch, E., Clément, Dr. Caty and Meister, S. *Evaluating the Impacts and Effectiveness of Targeted Sanctions: DRC Case Study*. Targeted Sanctions Research Consortium.

39 Belgian Senate. February 2003. *Document législatif n° 2-942/1, 20.*

DRC's neighbours. The representatives of these countries meet once per week, in a room at the MONUC headquarters, chaired by William Lacy Swing, the chief of the UN peacekeeping mission and former American Ambassador to the DRC. The final stretch in the peace process was the signing of the Global and All-Inclusive Agreement between the DRC government, the most important rebel armies, the domestic political opposition, representatives of civil society and the Mai Mai on December 17, 2002. Now the clock was ticking toward the final resolution of the conflict by polling the Congolese. In the first truly democratic national elections the future leadership of the country was to be determined. However, there were many doubts about the integrity of this process. For those who had been observing the play between the DRC and the West the prospects looked dim.

> The forthcoming election means more to the international community, which is spending heavily on it and even sending in European Union forces to supplement MONUC to ensure that it is being held, than to the Congolese people. The major powers of the world and the international organizations under their control would like to legitimize their current client regime in Kinshasa so they can continue unfettered to extract all the resources they need from the Congo.[40]

The ICC and the Congolese War Crimes

Such negative opinions did not deter Ambassador Swing from his pragmatic approach. Surrounded by former war criminals, greedy businessmen and war profiteers, he kept promising: "First we hold our noses, then we seek justice." According to this concept, participation from the leaders of the major militias was ensured by making them part of the transitional government. The lesser leaders of the Ituri militias were offered the choice to integrate into the military forces of the transitional government as generals or to be thrown into Makala Prison outside Kinshasa. The future of these leaders had been quietly arranged when already in 2004 the Transitional Government had authorized the International Criminal Court (ICC) to investigate crimes that may have taken place in the DRC and that lay within the jurisdiction of the court. For the time being, however, six of these Ituri leaders took the bait, and waited in Kinshasa's Grand Hotel for a month to receive their deployment orders to their military units.

The Transitional Government announced that the national elections would be held on June 30, 2006; it was the final clarion call to yank the DRC into democracy, peace and security. Now, the international community exercised its complete arsenal with military option, diplomatic pressures, stepped up UN sanctions, and—for the first time ever—the arrest of alleged war criminals and their transfer to the ICC in The Hague. For the military option the German government organized a EU over-the-horizon military force. Its job was to swoop into the DRC wherever the election

40 DRC's Potential: Lighting the Continent from Cape to Cairo; *Interview with Georges Nzongola-Ntalaja*. July 21, 2006. *Pambazuka News*, Issue 261.

process was under attack. CIAT, the French, British, U.S. and Belgian diplomatic corps assumed vigilant and stern positions in their talks with the former Congolese warlords and political leaders. Through their Security Council delegations they strengthened the UN sanctions by expanding the existing embargo against deliveries of military material to all Congolese parties, except those who served under Etat Major of the transitional government. They also put over 20 warlords under targeted financial sanctions as well as a travel ban. As a warning shot to anybody still thinking about insurrection, the Transitional Government arrested Thomas Lubanga and transferred him to The Hague in the Netherlands. The former commander of the Ugandan supported Congolese Rally for Democracy-Liberation Movement (RCD-ML) and founder of the Union of Congolese Patriots (UPC) was the first individual who would stand for trial at the ICC. It was widely reported that the ICC was accusing Lubanga of having ordered an ambush in February 2005 that led to the killing of nine UN peacekeepers. However, the arrest warrant accused him of having conscripted and enlisted children under the age of 15 years and using them to participate actively in hostilities. Soon, Germain Katanga and Mathieu Ngudjolo Chui would follow Lubanga to the ICC. After the bloody Kinshasa downtown confrontation between Kabila's Revolutionary Guards and Jean-Pierre Bemba's "bodyguards," Bemba was forced into exile. A few months later, he too was transferred to the ICC in connection with crimes that he was alleged to have committed in the Central African Republic. Finally, by 2010 the FDLR Executive Secretary Callixte Mbarushimana was added to the Congolese awaiting trial in The Hague. By now, however, the use of the international judicial system was becoming somewhat suspect, since the two individuals that were most to blame for sustained war crimes in Ituri and the Kivus were Bosco Ntaganda and Laurent Nkunda. Both men had been placed on the list of sanctioned individuals by the UN, EU, and eventually also by the United States. While an arrest warrant for Ntaganda had been issued only a few months after the ones for Lubanga and the other suspects, Ntaganda enjoyed a shocking level of impunity. After having led, as the senior military leader, Thomas Lubanga's UPC, he was now the Chief of Staff of Nkunda and, as such, responsible for new atrocities that CNDP was committing. No wonder that from the deforested plateaus of Ituri and the Kivus the ICC's role in the Congo never seemed to be much more than another vanity project of well-intentioned Westerners. After the elections, any attempt to discuss the need for strengthening the military capability in the Eastern Congo was cut off in the UN Security Council and in the major capitals of the donor states. The elections were held fairly, Kabila's government now needed some time to take hold, and donor agencies were eager to spend money on reconstruction. Concerns over hard security problems were simply ignored. Among the international cadres the unspoken question was what level of violence and mayhem in the Congo was tolerable. The equally tacit understanding was that the answer depended on the level of Western media coverage.

The complete lack of political will for a thorough clean-up operation immediately after the elections was one of the most significant failures by the international community. In addition to the arming of thousands of belligerents under the charismatic Nkunda and his Congrès National pour la Défense du Peuple (CNDP), the continuing murderous roaming by Democratic Forces for the Liberation of Rwanda (FDLR) and certain Mai Mai units, there were now growing FARDC forces and other government security forces that had pillaged, raped and murdered indiscriminately. Rwanda was not showing any willingness to establish secure spaces in which Hutu communities willing to return from exile could expect to live as part of an equitable society. This obvious lack of security played into the interests of militant Hutu leaders. Ignace Murwanashyaka, was held in Germany since late 2006 and Sylvestre Mudacumura, chief of the military wing, the Forces Combattants Abacunguzi (FOCA), was soon also arrested during a visit in Germany. Thousands of FDLR troops continued nevertheless what they have been doing for years—ransacking across the Kivus, sponging off the local populations, looting minerals and extorting taxes wherever possible. Their violence served as the perfect pretext for the CNDP leaders to play up their role as protectors for Tutsis. In the process, Nkunda successfully repelled all FARDC attempts to isolate and defeat his CNDP forces. By 2008 his troops were in control of most of North Kivu's rich pastures, the traditional territory of his people. Finally, in January 2009, he was arrested in a joint Congolese–Rwandan military action. His arrest may very well have been partly engineered by his successor, Bosco Ntaganda. As the Chairman of CNDP, Ntaganda negotiated brilliant terms for himself and his troops in the Goma Peace Accord. He agreed together with his CNDP rebels to integrate into FARDC. In effect, he was strengthening Tutsi control over the Eighth military region that encompasses much of North Kivu and whose top general commander was Gabriel Amisi, another trusted Tutsi. However, Ntaganda's calculations may not add up in the end. Many CNDP combatants are unhappy with what they feel is acquiescence to Joseph Kabila.

A New Future for the DRC

Once the elections were held, and Joseph Kabila confirmed to be Congo's President, everybody was ready to move on—but not in the same direction. Kabila was quite happy to get rid of the overlord-playing foreign assistance embodied by CIAT, which was created to assist the DRC in its transition from war to an elected government. It comprised of the African Union, Angola, Belgium, Canada, China, European Commission, European Union, France, Gabon, MONUC, Russia, South Africa, United Kingdom, United States and Zambia. But now Kabila pressed hard for this project to end.

Many ministers of foreign affairs from Europe and Asia quickly learned that the game had changed. Micromanaging or lecturing the Congolese government was going to result in a strong backlash. In early 2007 Germany's ambassador had been quietly told to leave after strong condemnations of Kabila's murderous suppression of an alleged revolt by his arch-rival Jean Pierre Bemba and his soldiers stationed in Kinshasa. The then Belgian Minister of Foreign Affairs, Karel de Gucht, was warned repeatedly for his outspoken critical remarks about the Congolese government, and in the summer of 2008 the Belgian–Congolese relationship went into deep freeze when Kabila's government asked that the Belgian consulates in Lubumbashi and in Bukavu be closed.[41] After many warnings, Belgian diplomats had continued to disrespect the young Congolese president, including by referring to him as "l'élève"[42] ("student").

Congolese patience with Western condescension and patronizing policies had been approaching its limits for some time. The lack of serious follow-up actions to the UN Panel allegations about illegal exploitation was hypocritical and revealing; no one in Europe, the United States or Canada was prosecuted. Somehow the universal bill of clean health could not be true given the magnitude of abuses in the DRC. The British NGO Raid had tabulated all follow-up actions and showed that not a single case was known where criminal conviction was sought. The All Party Parliamentary Group of British Parliament, together with NGOs, kept working on the national follow-up processes on those who were not in voluntary compliance with OECD standards. In 2007 that process netted a public process against one trading company owned and operated by Indian immigrants and based in Bukavu with a small trading office in London. At the same time, the trade statistics left no doubt over how many more significant trading operations were continuing without ever being taken to task by their Western governments. A report of a new UN Group of Experts, appointed pursuant to UN Security Council resolution 1533 (2004), would make this fact known in summer 2007. This new panel was charged with monitoring violations of the arms embargo that was imposed on the DRC by the UN. Included in this monitoring mandate was the need to investigate funding to embargo violators, and thus, illegal diversions of natural resources. Regarding the trading and brokering of tin-oxide, better known as cassiterite, for the year 2006, the panel disclosed in its report published on July 18, 2007 the following data:

Belgium 2 296 Tonnes
Rwanda 429 Tonnes
Malaysia 73.8 Tonnes
United Kingdom 67.5 Tonnes
Kazakhstan 27.4 Tonnes
Hong Kong (China) 10.2 Tonnes.[43]

41 On January 10, 2010 the spokesperson of the Congolese Ministry of Foreign Affairs and Communication, Lambert Mende Omalanga, announced that Karel De Gucht, both in his national position and as EU Commission for Development, was no longer welcome in the Congo.

42 Conversations between Belgian diplomats with the author.

43 The author of this chapter was also the principal investigator for natural resource issues for that UN Group of Experts report.

As was pointed out in the same report, buyers in these end-user markets do not practice credible due diligence about the origins of the tin they are buying or brokering. This omission has entitled them to claim ignorance regarding the source of a potentially compromised delivery of minerals. Recommendations by the new UN Panel for the Security Council to support innovative Congolese legislation and due diligence schemes designed to prevent trading with conflict minerals was rebuffed by the Security Council.

Predictably, the post-election relationships with the Congo turned confrontational. Kabila's government resolutely rejected any other foreign supervision in the style of CIAT. Western governments turned decidedly aggressive by launching a barrage of demands and accusations against the Congolese leadership. With peace imminent, MONUC peacekeepers feared losing their jobs and quickly reinvented themselves as experts on good governance, on reforms of the mining industry and of how to operate a huge state such as the DRC that still had little revenues. NGOs were clamoring against corruption and for a transparent allocation of mining concessions. The World Bank also pushed for further reforms in the mining industry, and in many other areas of reconstruction. The IMF pressed the bankrupted state authorities to adhere to fiscal discipline. However, the flow of technical aid and cash to finance badly needed infrastructure improvements were as slow as the uptick in revenues from the start-up mining industrial mining activities. The Congolese people, particularly the artisanal miners, were still in dire need of security and protection. In the absence of industrial exploitation of minerals and precious stones, the artisanal communities had ballooned; by 2007/2008 it was estimated that 10 million Congolese depended directly or indirectly on artisanal mining.[44] In some ways, peace had complicated the lives of many Congolese. With the influx of international mining companies, formerly abandoned concession areas were reactivated and many artisanal miners expelled; a small number would find immediate employment, but the prospect of tens of thousands of miners finding permanent and well-paid employment was still uncertain. Senior military commanders, local agents of the security services and the police showed as little patience for disruptions as the security details of major companies. Violent eruptions involving artisanal communities became more frequent after the elections.

Confronted with an armada of post-election technocrats, development experts, accountants and post-conflict wizards, Joseph Kabila could not have possibly forgotten that his father's original and very uncomplicated sponsor had been the People's Republic of China. In March 2002 Joseph Kabila, even before the signing of the Sun City Peace Accord, had been invited to Beijing for an official visit and was welcomed by the Chinese President Jian Zemin himself. In the meantime, ministers of development or foreign technical assistance from European countries were showing up in Kinshasa, pledging hundreds of millions of dollars in aid to the

---

44 World Bank. May 2008. Growth with Governance In the Mining Sector. *Report No. 43402-ZR*. 10.

DRC. However, these generous-sounding packages were always contingent upon achieving certain benchmarks. The demands for democratization and economic liberalization sounded suspiciously like yet another colonial straightjacket. In Kabila's mind there was always a much less complicated avenue to prosperity and growth. Announcing 2006 "The Year of Africa," the Chinese government had demonstrated the meaning of its doctrine of non-interference by either blocking or abstaining from international sanctions against the regimes of Sudan, Zimbabwe and Eritrea.

Shockwaves reverberated through the international community when in September 2007 the signing of a memorandum of understanding between the Congolese and Chinese parties was announced for mineral-for-infrastructure transactions worth over U.S.$6 billion. This was the largest Chinese investment in Africa by far and nobody had expected it; nobody had even been aware of such negotiations taking place. In January 2008, another shockwave was triggered when an additional U.S.$3.5 billion deal was added. The rich "Marshall Plan" for the reconstruction of basic infrastructure[45] was secured with a loan of over U.S.$9 billion by the Export-Import Bank of China. The China Railway Group, Sinohydro Corporation, and the Metallurgical Group Corporation are together 68 percent shareholders in the new joint venture called Sicomines. The DRC government and Gecamines hold the remaining shares. The deal promised the DRC the construction of thousands of kilometers of railway systems connecting mining areas with seaports, two hydroelectric dams and the rehabilitation of two airports. In exchange, the Chinese partners secured the right to extract 6.8 million tons of copper and 420,000 tons of cobalt from the Mashamba, Dikuluwe mines and from other mining sites beginning in the year 2013. According to World Bank estimates, the planned extractions will require an additional U.S.$2 billion in investments. Although some aspects of the deal underwent modifications, the DRC National Assembly approved the agreement in May 2008. "For the first time in our history, the Congolese people can see that their nickel and copper is being used to good effect," was Kabila's comment.

Once the Western world recovered from this seismic shift, a chorus of critics demanded full transparency of the agreements with China. Allegations of corruptions and non-transparent allocations for mineral deposits now reached hyperbole. While these charges may have their justifications, it is interesting that only in the face of a massive Chinese deal did Western activists voice concerns over the ethical and commercial consequences. The World Bank, cautiously playing the referee, declared in a pivotal report on the Congo's mining industry that legitimate investment from private companies of whatever nationality is to be welcomed. This introduction is followed with a long list of doubts and questions. Among them the possibility that Chinese companies may benefit from tax exemptions and incentives, all of them in contravention of the Mine Law. Additional concerns

45 Description by DRC Minister for Infrastructure Minister Pierre Lumbi during the announcement ceremony.

involved the possibility that the DRC government may have entered into obligations of non-concessional debt and that the terms of the agreements need to be fully disclosed in order to be vetted by the Bretton Woods institutions. Kabila was not holding back his disappointment with the West when he stated that after having been turned down by all major Western states when he requested funding for the urgently needed infrastructure project in his country, the same parties who had denied the lifeline were griping that the Chinese got a sweetheart deal and began pressing him to revise the terms; "What revolted me was the fact that there was resistance to this agreement and there was no counterproposal."[46]

Regardless of the motivations and hidden meanings of the political wrangling over the deal with the Chinese, there are real caveats for Congolese people. Artisanal miners and others living close to the future Chinese mining areas in the DRC must have concerns that there has not been any conclusive evidence on how Chinese companies deal with foreign laborers or how they address environmental concerns. Experiences in other African countries with large Chinese industrial engagements are so far mixed, and if there are any early indications, Chinese enterprises are not meeting the standards European and American companies have set. Given the more than 100-year history of Western companies in the Congo, these standards are not difficult to surpass. What is certain is the proliferation of voluntary standards even among Chinese companies and industry associations and that they operate in the same manner as their Western counterparts. However, unlike their Western rivals, not much public information has emerged as to how or whether compliance with these standards has been tested or challenged either by their shareholders, their regulatory and supervisory agencies or by their judicial authorities. Therefore, for Congolese workers the uncertainty remains whether they will receive protection or whether the abuses continue as they have been part of their lives ever since King Leopold's agents contracted village chiefs for rubber and ivory harvesters.

46 For Congo's Leader, Middling Reviews. *New York Times*, April 4, 2009.

Chapter 7

State Hierarchy and Governance: Of Shadows or Equivalence in Regulating Global Crisis

Mark Findlay

Introduction

The nation-state has had its day. Not just as a governance context but as an analytical tool, the state has failed most those who are in desperate need of good governance. In the resource rich and regulatory poor world the state has collaborated in its own demise. Created as a shelter for the common good, the state is now a shell for sheltering self-interest. From this deontological demise grows crisis and in a globalized world such crisis is beyond the territoriality which states treasure.

Regulating global crisis sounds like a contradiction in terms. If ever there was an era of crisis worldwide, man-made and natural, it is now. At the same time as global warming, epidemic poverty and disease, international financial meltdown, and the erosion of self-determination and privacy reveal, regulatory strategies are failing the challenge. Then why attempt to address crisis with regulation at anything more than an aspirational level?

The reasons for regulation's perceived and recurrent failure are both simple and profound. Over a decade ago I argued in *The Globalisation of Crime*[1] that the myopic focus of the West on globalization as its problem and its unique opportunity to monopolize socioeconomic development denied the pressing significance of its impacts on cultures in transition. A driving motivation behind these critical reflections expands on a realization[2] that:

> consolidated statehood is the exception rather than the rule in the contemporary international system … outside the world of developed and highly industrialised democratic states most countries contain what we call "areas of limited statehood."

---

1 Findlay, M. 1999. *The Globalisation of Crime: Understanding Transitional Relationships in Context*. Cambridge: Cambridge University Press.

2 As well summarized in Borzel, T. and Risse, T. 2010. Governance Without a State: Can it Work? *Regulation and Governance*, 4, 113–34.

> While areas of limited statehood still belong to internationally recognised states … it is their domestic sovereignty which is severely circumscribed.[3]

The regulation literature (policy included) is vastly over-concerned with the Western, Westphalian socioeconomic contexts. For instance, the debate about non-state centered regulation evolves from the assumption of a functioning, strong Weberian[4] state framework. Most modes of governance, however, domestically and particularly internationally today do not exist in any such sophisticated counter-regulatory shadow.[5] As such, the top-down or bottom-up hierarchies of regulation[6] which rely on eventual state institutionalized enforcement capacity are relevant only to a select hegemony of states and economies:

> The language of hierarchy, hegemony and empire has become the analytical prism through which scholars explain the emerging politics of globalization.[7]

This emphasis in the analytical literature may arise from the conviction that preferred governance modes (state, international organizations, NGOs, MNCs, public/private partnerships (PPPs)) reside in capitalist, neoliberal socio-politics. As such, contemporary considerations of international political economy "such as neo-liberalism or neo-realism are too state-centred in their assumptions to fully appreciate the growing importance of non-state actors and various transitional networks."[8] An argument to justify the disciplinary deficit when it comes to imagining non-Western, non-capitalist regulatory frameworks might consist of stating the obvious: these are the dominant political and economic models and as such should drive the global regulatory mission. This dogmatic differentiation might be a convincing argument were it not for the realization that:

- the conditions of global crisis are created by both the developed and the developing world;
- the negative consequences of global crisis are felt much more profoundly in the developing world;
- the failure of regulation is not limited to areas of weak or limited statehood;

---

3 Borzel, T. and Risse, T. 2010. 118.

4 Gerth, H. H. and Wright Mills, C. 1946. *From Max Weber: Essays in Sociology*. Oxford: Oxford University Press; Lassman, P. and Spiers, R. 1994. *Weber: Political Writings*. Cambridge: Cambridge University Press.

5 For a discussion of this in terms of global governance and new politics see, Teubner, G. 1997. Global Bukowina: Legal Pluralism in World Society, in *Global Law Without a State*, edited by G. Teubner. Dartmouth: Brookfield. 3–28.

6 Braithwaite, J. 2008. *Regulatory Capitalism*. London: Edward Elgar.

7 Cooley, A. 2003. Thinking Rationally about Hierarchy and Global Governance. *Review of International Political Economy*, 10/4, 672–84 at 673.

8 Cooley, A. 2003. 673. Also see Strange, S. 1996. *The Retreat from the State*. Cambridge: Cambridge University Press.

- regulatory failure is not always corrected under the shadow or within the hierarchies of strong states; and
- the modes of social coordination and embedded social markets essential for good governance in non-consolidated state terrain are at the heart of regulating global crisis, whatever the context.

The task for a more inclusive analysis of incentives to confront global crisis is to disentangle and reveal the contextual relationships between these modes of social coordination in order that regulating global crisis can be given a flatter and wider sweep. This will take our thinking away from hierarchies and more toward relationships in which the incentives to minimize and avoid crisis are stimulated. In these relationships it is the role of "functional equivalents" for a state-based shadow of hierarchy that enable the "effective and sustainable non-hierarchical modes of governance involving non-state actors in areas of limited state-hood."[9]

This perspective leads to a more organic and harmonious shift from crisis to ordering. Beyond the rehabilitation of configurations of limited statehood (and more broadly the place of transitional cultures in contemporary globalization) within current governance scholarship, is the purpose of understanding and maximizing incentives to cooperation in the prevention and management of global crisis. Like it or not, state-focused or otherwise, we are obliged to reflect on styles and situations of governance which are multi-layered beyond consolidated state hierarchies. Aligned with this is the inescapable need to reflect on the state beyond Western constellations or muffled by cosmopolitan dreaming.

Realistic Reflections on the Global State

For the purposes of the analysis to follow I am greatly assisted through conceptualizing the state (local and global) as a constellation of power and authority placed somewhere on a continuum between deep consolidation and weak fragmentation. Progressing along that continuum it is fair to assume that the influence of governance hierarchies diminishes and the enforcement shadow of the state fades. So too as we move from consolidation to fragmentation, governance relocates from within to beyond the state. This shift should not be confused as governance without government. Rather it means that the analyst needs to stop struggling to find the institutions of the strong state as evidence of good governance and governability, and delve more deeply into what Borzel and Risse (2010) refer to as "functional equivalents" of the state's imminence.

While there are many configurations of limited statehood (not confined to failed states or to a failure to control territory), the modern liberal democratic notions of the state exhibit a consistent and almost universal emphasis on:

---

9 Borzel, T. and Risse, T. 2010. 120.

- the ability to enforce collectively binding decisions;
- ultimately through a monopoly over the means of legitimate violence;[10]
- operating through hierarchies of authority with sanctioning at the apex;
- demonstrating an institutionalized authority structure and a bureaucracy for its execution; and
- authoritatively making, implementing and enduring central decisions for a collectivity.

Universals characterizing limited statehood are more difficult to identify as even some consolidated states may contain areas of limited influence. Identifiers may include:

- weak domestic sovereignty;
- loss of monopoly over the use of force;
- partial enforcement powers;
- non-hierarchical authority structures;
- reduced administrative capacity;
- loss of control over territorial or functional space; and
- evidence of traditional or new non-hierarchical modes of governance.

A function of the consolidated state is law-making. Law diminishes in governance significance as it moves to the supranational[11] or it fails to endorse private rights and public obligation when the enforcement shadow of the state is faint or fragmented.

Is Law Beyond, Not Without, the State?[12]

The role of law as a regulator in a world where the reach of domestic jurisdiction is becoming more and more constrained and where supranational law is not yet achieved is a reason for discussing law's relevance in general. In systems theory terms autopoetic considerations of private law systems in particular offer a new vision of what some think of as being a false dichotomy between law within and beyond the state.[13] The contract, for example, can create its own legal order

10 This has been diminishing in recent times of global conflict in particular to where the state outsources the means and delivery of violence and as such can only claim to authorize this process of agency.

11 For a general discussion of this at both expressive and facilitative levels see Morgan, B. and Yeung, K. 2007. *An Introduction to Law and Regulation: Text and Materials*. Cambridge: Cambridge University Press. Chapter 6.

12 This is a question asked by Michaels in his critique of considering Lex Mercatoria as law beyond the state. See Michaels, R. 2007. The True Lex Mercatoria: Law Beyond the State. *Indiana Journal of Global Legal Studies*, 14/2, 447–68.

13 For a richer discussion of this see Teubner, G. 1997.

through its internal hierarchies of obligations and rights, combining primary norms (contractual rights and obligations) with secondary norms giving these primary norms their validity. In this way a legal system in microcosm, including objective law and possible adjudication, emerges out of, and applies to, the contract. Such a contract can well explain how commercial arrangements can be regulated through contracts prevailing even in limited or fragmented state settings where legal hierarchies are impotent and where political and economic enforcement administrations of the state cast little or no deterrent shadow over contracting parties.

Perez suggests[14] that it is not simply inevitable but in fact to be preferred that public interests can be absorbed into the otherwise sacrosanct interests of contractual private parties; in particular, it is where communities are directly influenced by large-scale construction, the argument goes, that community interests have a place within private contractual negotiations, intersecting public and private goods. In similar fashion, Michaels argues against state parallels when trying to imagine the future of supranational legal regulation:

> Authors endorsing the a-national or non national character of lex mercatoria, I argue, are barking up the wrong tree. In perpetuating the state/non state dichotomy, the lex mercatoria without state remains within a state focused legal paradigm.[15]

But for Michaels, as with Brandt, the state referent for supranational legal regulation is not inevitable or perpetual. In the sense that the legal system creates itself in separation (but not away from) the influences of the institutions of politics, law can be seen as without the state. At the global level however the internal differentiation of legal systems applying supranationally is not so easily or ideally divorced from politics or economy. At the global level law as regulation still represents a segmentary differentiation, linked hard or soft to the functioning of state interest. That is the immediate barrier to Brandt's *new politics* or Teubner's *global law*. In later writing on non-state governance[16] Michaels provocatively suggests that for law and governance as state indicia, it is not about state/non-state divides, but that the analyst must "put the state in perspective in order to overcome it."[17] Here is where the challenge emerges for considerations of governance to detach from hierarchies with the state, characterized by its sanctioning capacity toward the apex.

---

14 Perez, O. 2002. Using Public-Private Linkages to Regulate Environmental Conflicts: The Case of International Construction Contracts. *Journal of Law and Society*, 29/1, 77–110.

15 Michaels, R. 2007. 452.

16 Michaels, R. 2010. The Mirage of Non-State Governance. *Utah Law Review*, 1, 31–45.

17 Michaels, R. 2010. 44.

Governance from Afar

Governance can be considered, from the perspective of regulation, as the various institutionalized modes of social coordination to collectively produce and implement binding rules or provide collective "goods."[18] Governance is a dynamic and evolutionary phenomenon, particularly at the global level,[19] involving process and structure, and sometimes calling on the creation of new political manifestations and languages.

I do not see conventional discourse on sovereignty as helpful in understanding the nature of modern governance, particularly at the global level. A reason for this resides in the incapacity of some regulatory paradigms, such as public international law, to break free from the referent of the liberal democratic state in the conceptualization of sovereignty, authority, power and obligations. In replacing a discourse of sovereignty when looking at the manner in which regulation determines governance (and vice versa), an examination of frames and actions of particular governance styles is rewarding. Take, for instance, the determination of governance by examining the actors which advance it. Therefore, liberal democratic state governance is governments, resting on personalities and alliances, not on compatibilities, while in multinational global networks governance assumes life through negotiation and competition (between firms, consumers, shareholders, managers, etc.). As a process, governance is a different mode of social coordination. How then is "sociability" for the purpose of a common good, to act as a powerful motivation for regulatory collaboration even where enforcement shadows diminish and alternative self-interest prevails?

Coordination and collaboration includes:

> the involvement of non-governmental actors (companies, civil society) in the provision of collective goods through non-hierarchical co-ordination. This co-ordination range [*sic*] from consultation and co-operation, delegation and/or co-regulation/co-production to private self regulation inside and outside the control of governments. Non-hierarchical co-ordination can involve governmental actors so long as they refrain from using their coercive powers.[20]

Sociability is a concept which can deflect the analytical focus of governance away from distinctions based on hierarchical coordination. As a dominant mode of coordination, I will argue, sociability offers a way of adjusting regulatory strategies to confront global crisis whether the governance model relies on a coordinated (or suffers a fragmented) state. This said, sociability neither replaces nor diminishes

---

18 Borzel, T. and Risse, T. 2010. 114.

19 Brandt, U. 2005. Order and Regulation: Global Governance as a Hegemonic Discourse of International Politics? *Review of International Political Economy*, 12/1, 155–76.

20 Borzel, T. and Risse, T. 2010. 115.

the regulatory significance of hierarchical coordination; it just does not depend on hierarchies or even their strong and impending shadow.

The problem facing any consideration of regulation absent a long hierarchical shadow is sufficient alternative sanctioning capacity to deter and deal with opportunistic self-interest and free-riding. As the discussion of collaborative motivation (summarized below) illustrates, the transformation of self-interest into common good is a crucial precondition to any diminishing reliance on hierarchical sanctioning capacity. It might be no more than the recognition of a common positioning in a community of shared risk, and the impending anarchy that agreement and compliance violation on a large scale would precipitate, which helps achieve such a transition without sacrificing the interest fundamentals of a capitalist liberal democracy. A central plank in the reasoning of collaborative (flat) regulation is the diminished reliance on sanction or threat in a climate where minus efficient impending sanction machinery, friendship and trust, and not deterrence and fear, become actualized market relationship essentials rather than being confined to normative best practice. Even in consolidated states and certainly in those where their authority and reach is limited or fragmented, governance is multi-level and multi-layered. As Borzel and Risse conclude, the diversity of state constellation is not a sign of its withering. Michaels sees the state as mythical as non-state governance but both views would accept that "At stake then is the transformation of the state rather than its disappearance."[21] In collaborative (flat) regulation the consolidated state can facilitate dialogue, but its role even at this level is on par with any other alternative functional equivalent.

Shadow of Hierarchy

The shadow of hierarchy provides an important incentive structure for cooperation, particularly between non-state actors. Whether the state is weak or strong it appears that for differing reasons such as compromised autonomy/capture, and a reluctance to share governance authority, states are not keen to coordinate with non-state actors unless:

- the regulatory terrain is specialized beyond the knowledge and capacity of the state;
- the regulatory terrain has large supranational reach;
- there operate successful and pre-existing non-state regulatory networks;
- pressure groups are urging such collaboration;
- the state is otherwise reluctant to manage the regulatory challenge for political or economic reasons; or
- the crisis to be managed is either largely caused by state action/inaction or it is beyond state capacity to resolve.

21 Borzel, T. and Risse, T. 2010. 128.

Where state-centered foundations for the shadow of enforcement hierarchies are weak or absent, alternative frameworks of regulation may emerge explained by what March and Olsen (1998) distinguish as the logic of consequences or the logic of appropriateness.[22] As an essential part of the logic of consequences actors and agencies whose self-interested behavior is otherwise essentialist and defines their mission, and whose prime purpose is the attainment of private rather than public good, become constrained into governance concerns. In contexts of global crisis, the need to invest in the common good in situations of economy and political dysfunction and instability (Braithwaite's regulatory "window" in boom/bust regulatory cycles[23]), and where legal and property rights are shaky, the inducement into collaborative regulation is strong and immediate. This is so even where the shadow of hierarchy is weak and distant either for the period of the crisis or prevailing as a consequence of the limited and fragmented existence of the state, or other important equivalent regulatory frames.

Incentive Structures

The bulk of my examination of regulating global crisis will be concerned with creating conditions and incentivizing relationships which ensure that non-state actors and agencies engage in effective and sustainable regulatory governance in areas of limited statehood. I argue that the dominant governance terrain in which crises are formed and in which they will largely be met in the medium term is where the reach and shadow of the state remains indistinct. This does not exclude the role of strong states and hegemonies in crisis regulation. On the contrary, the under-utilization of effective hierarchical governance, particularly when it comes to environmental regulation, is a significant reason for how the world became crisis ridden. Rather, the argument goes that while the failure of state-centered regulation is a failure of will and not capacity, the disengagement or avoidance of a massive reserve of regulatory potential (and crisis generating reasoning) in non-state sanctioned hierarchical regulatory modes needs critical reflection and policy empowerment.

The logic of consequences suggests that motivations for contributing to regulatory governance can be stimulated by repositioning self-interest into the common good. One path to such repositioning is the fear which emerges from a realization of positioning within communities of shared risk. Through the lens of sociability another forceful and under-recognized incentive toward participatory regulatory governance (without the strong shadow of hierarchical enforcement) emerges when key self-interested actors become embedded in normative structures that induce them to do *the right thing*. While it might be hoped for the sake of good

22 March, J. and Olsen, J. 1998. The Institutional Dynamics of International Political Orders. *International Organisation*, 52, 943–69.

23 Braithwaite, J. 2008. Chapter 2.

governance and the proliferation of corporate social responsibility that altruism brings this conviction about, it could equally or more realistically be that the investment in, say, community health, is to ensure a productive workforce and not merely to seek the betterment of mankind. Whatever, the regulatory outcome may well be the same and the benefit as individually valuable. This regulatory ethos will be more effectively ensured through a mix of self-interest and commitment to the common good as it would be in situations where the hegemonic enforcer is standing by. If commercial interests in particular wish to do business in the vast world of limited or fragmented state influence it is not a question of preferring enforcement based hierarchical shadows, but adapting to the reality of faint or far off external intervention.

For instance, where multinational corporations intersect with large NGOs and PPPs in contexts where states are limited and fragmented in their authority and reach, traditional norms can be employed (even where they may be conservative and reactionary) toward the creation of "socially embedded markets."[24] In socially embedded markets we see evidenced a consolidation of both "logics" for collaboration, where the consequential and the appropriate meet for mutual stakeholder benefit. In this respect, the state is not the sponsor of social responsibility; in fact it is often essential that it should not be so for reasons of conflict of interest or cultures of corrupt administration.[25] Socially embedded markets can provide a functional equivalent for the shadow of hierarchy and, as will be argued later, the collaborative nature of socially embedded markets flattens the need for, or attractiveness of hierarchical regulation once state sanctions are bypassed.

The argument here relies on a confidence in regulatory cooperation, however attained, not only to address global crisis in a more responsible and responsive fashion, but to do so where the shadow of regulatory hierarchy is faintest or most distant. While regulatory competition can precede cooperation, unlike with the regulatory co-opetition literature,[26] discussion of regulatory cooperation to follow will not tie itself to concerns for inter-, intra- or extra-governmentality.[27] To do so necessitates some linear order of regulatory status again with state government at the top (or at least positioned recurrently in situations of key influence).

Regulatory reformers in the United States have called for decentralization in the name of "federalism." In Europe, a similar sentiment advances under the banner of "subsidiarity." One of the underlying and critical theoretical

24 This term infers a process where even the most self-interested firms are turned to the common good not through altruism but pragmatism which reveals the commercially consolidating potential of corporate social responsibility and community investment.

25 See Findlay, M. 2007. Misunderstanding Corruption and Community: Comparative Cultural Politics in Corruption Prevention in the Pacific. *Asian Criminology*, 2, 47–56.

26 Borzel, T. and Risse, T. 2010. 123–6.

27 Jordana, J. and Levi-Faur, D. 1994. *The Politics of Regulation: Institutions and Regulatory Reforms for the Age of Governance*. London: Edward Elgar. Chapter 1.

premises of these two movements is the suggestion that "regulatory competition" among horizontally arrayed governments will generate pressures for improved governmental efficiency in the regulatory realm. Critics have suggested that rather than welfare-enhancing competitive pressures, divergent regulatory standards may instead trigger a welfare-reducing "race toward the bottom." Esty and Geradin argue[28] that both race-toward-the-bottom and regulatory competition theories are overstated from a descriptive point of view and unsatisfactory from a normative perspective. Regulatory theory (they argue) must reflect the diversity and complexity of the world. When global crises are located beyond the shadow of the state, much more than for crises in consolidated states I assert, optimal governance requires a flexible mix of competition and cooperation between government actors as well as between governmental and non-governmental actors, along both horizontal and vertical dimensions. That said, as the state hierarchical shadow diminishes, the regulatory order flattens and cooperation is not only more essential but more attractive even if difficult to establish and maintain through trust and friendship bonds. Esty and Geradin plump for an enriched model of "regulatory co-opetition"[29] recognizing that sometimes regulatory competition will prove to be advantageous but in other cases a greater form of collaboration will produce superior results. In a world that is pluralistic, not simplistic, a combination of regulatory competition and cooperation will almost always be optimal. Again where my preferred analysis moves on from co-opetition models is by leaving the bond of consolidated state hierarchies in favor of social citizenship and socially embedded regulatory environments.[30]

Social Citizenship—Pathway to Flatter Regulation

Social citizenship, whether in the form that this chapter develops sociability, or in more conventional discussions of corporate social responsibility (CSR), is a perspective on regulation which helps us understand the limited choices available in any regulatory mix:

> the degree of control that regulators have in the design and enforcement of a particular regulatory regime varies. Regulators' capacity to shape an effective regime may be extremely limited if concerns about political legitimacy dominate decisions about what legislative or regulatory tools are made available …

---

28 Esty, D. and Geradin, D. 2000. Regulatory Co-opetition. *Journal of International Economic Law*, 3/2, 235–55.

29 Defined by Esty and Geradin as an optimal business strategy requiring a mix of competitive and cooperative actions. Also see, Brandenberg, A. and Nalebuff, B. 1996. *Co-optition*. New York: Currency Doubleday.

30 Taylor-Gooby, P. 2008. *Reframing Social Citizenship*. Oxford: Oxford University Press.

> A focus on human agency is timely and intrinsic to the concept of a regulator as a "sociological citizen" reflecting and acting creatively to bring about beneficial outcomes. According to proponents, sociological citizens are creative and self-directed, they draw on a broad canvass to achieve regulatory goals.[31]

According to Silbey et al. "sociological citizens" view "their work and themselves, as links in a complex web of interactions and processes rather than as an office of delimited responsibilities and interests."[32] Sociability, which is the mark of the social (or "sociological") citizen regulator does not emerge or is not sustained in some purely normative abstract. It is deeply contextual. The more we move that context away from the shadow of the consolidated state, the more sociability is actualized through lateral relationships which neither depend on but indeed avoid the need for a state-topped regulatory hierarchy.

Sociability is a process where potential mutual regulators gain a level of perspective which is influenced deeply by their experience of crisis and their role within it which enables them to exercise a more profound understanding of regulatory responsibility and its implications. This deeper understanding allows the mutual regulator to see both crisis and ordering as they, are rather than as they should be, prompting them to engage in regulation in a more responsive and responsible fashion. As C. Wright Mills may have it, such understandings translate into a *sociological imagination* that prompts the mutual regulator to improve rather than subvert the larger system of common good through norm experimentation.[33] They do not wait on state compulsion or on state agency for better regulatory outcomes.

Michaels, in his denial of the essentialist state hierarchy when imagining new governance forms, suggests a novel trajectory of thinking.[34] Much of the recent discussion concerning governance where the state is essentially at a hierarchical peak has been influenced by Michel Foucault. But as Selby points out[35] the limitations of Foucault as a theorist of world politics is explained by his lack of interest in supranational and international realms. Even so, the state or supranational context in which, as Foucault would argue, knowledge is power, explains the currency of hierarchy: the capacity to ensure social differentiation through who regulates knowledge.

Michaels further projects:

31 Haines, F. 2011. Addressing the Risk, Reading the Landscape: The Role of Agency in Regulation. *Regulation and Governance*, 5, 118–44.

32 Silbey, S., Huising, R. and Coslovsky, S. 2009. The Sociological Citizen: Relational Interdependence in Law and Organisations. *L'Annee Sociologique*, 59/1, 201–29.

33 Mills, C. W. 1967. *The Sociological Imagination*. Oxford: Oxford University Press.

34 Michaels, R. 2010. 44–5.

35 Selby, J. 2007. Discourse, Liberal Governance and the Limits of Foucauldian IR. *International Relations*, 21, 324.

> A more important step concerns the very hierarchy of levels. If it is correct that we are observing a move in the world from a political segmentary differentiation along state borders to a functional differentiation along different societal groups then this suggests that the methodologically central position of the state is wavering too. Note in a world that shifts from territoriality to functionality, the state does not automatically lose its role on functional grounds. A trajectory of theoretical accounts of governance should enable us to overcome this focus on the state … a more specific analysis of modes and structures of hybridity, or of the particular mix of public and private governance. This makes it possible, at least, to deny the state its central position in the analysis and to develop, on a fourth level, a governance theory beyond the state. On that level, the state's institutions exist on an equal level, analytically, with non-state institutions … A governance concept that transcends the distinction between state and non-state laws, by contrast, should enable us truly to imagine governance not only outside the state, but outside even the dichotomy of state/non-state, outside the state framework altogether.[36]

Such an analytical progression when directed to the regulation component of governance offers the possibility of laterally (rather than hierarchically) viewing collaborative regulation in limited or fragmented state contexts. Having moved so far away from the shadow of state hierarchy in regulation, it is appropriate to return to the reality of modern regulatory trends, whether they are seen in the context of consolidated states and global capitalism, or as I would prefer, in a world where regulation relies on alternative functional equivalents which explain the potential of regulatory collaboration in the face of global crisis.

The Ubiquity of Regulation

Along with socioeconomic development comes the regulation of most aspects of daily life. This age of regulation is both driven by and transcends modern market economics, in the same way it transcends a mono-cultural, mono-political or mono-economic conception of the state. Whether it is through the advance of supranational mega-corporatism, economic globalization, or conversely market failure, regulation imbues developed Western legal traditions, cultures, governance and much that gives contemporary society its form and vitality. Why is this so? Why is it also the case that an orientalist, or myopic regulatory discourse which exists in the shadow of consolidated states has for too long ignored the consequences for and appropriateness of other regulatory agendas where the state shadow is faint or distant? Perhaps the answer lies in a century and a half of triumphant market

36 Michaels, R. 2010. 44–5.

capitalism and an age of globalization where materialist economic development and modernization is the dominant global frame.[37]

Even the market failure welfarist critics see the common sense of extensive state regulation:

> Markets fail, a Pigouvian (1938)[38] would say, because of externalities, asymmetric information, and lack of competition, and governments need to regulate them to counter these failures. Regulation is ubiquitous because market failures are.[39]

The case for regulatory capitalism explains epidemic regulation particularly at the global level as the essential economic and political context in which mega-corporatism thrives. In this we can identify the symbiotic relationship between regulation, new capitalism and the growth of state regulatory capacity.

> [R]egulation, particularly anti-trust and securitisation of national debt, enabled the growth of both provider and regulatory states. Regulation did this through pushing the spread of large corporations ... the corporatization of the world increased the efficacy of tax enforcement, funding the provider and regulatory state growth. The corporatization of the world drove globalization ... this was a very different capitalism and a very different world of governance than existed in the early twentieth century capitalism of family firms.[40]

This would seem to run contrary to the law and economics tradition which suggests that the relentless drive of competition and the strategic intervention of contract arrangements and tort actions address market failure, leaving little space for regulation.[41] If this is so, and if it is looked at against the empirical evidence of the recent exponential regulatory growth explosion,[42] is it fair to suggest that the ubiquity and efficiency of regulation may not go hand in hand?

---

37 Findlay, M. 1999.

38 Pigouvian market analysis saw market failure not as a failure of markets but of market conditions. For a development of these views see Carlton, D. and Loury, G. 1980. The Limitation of Pigouvian Taxes as a Long Run Remedy for Externalities. *The Quarterly Journal of Economics*, 95/3, 559–66.

39 Shleifer, A. 2010. Efficient Regulation. *NBER Working Paper No. 15651*. Issued in January 2010.

40 Braithwaite, J. 2008. 28–9.

41 Coase, R. 1960. The Problem of Social Cost. *Journal of Law and Economics*, 3, 1–44.

42 Levi-Faur, D. and Jordana, J. eds. 2011. *The Rise of Regulatory Capitalism: The Global Diffusion of a New Order*. London: Sage.

Smart regulation,[43] meta-regulation,[44] responsive regulation,[45] really responsive regulation,[46] problem solving regulation[47] and regulatory competition[48] are recent approaches to the regulatory agenda which indicate a compatible explosion in scholarship and critique of contemporary regulatory thinking. Despite this regulatory renaissance the person in the street could be left wondering at the incredulity from those responsible for managing global crisis, when crises take hold.[49]

This chapter asks why we live in a world of such intrusive and expanding public and private regulation, outside the limits of the law. This critical approach is adopted in explaining regulatory ubiquity for several reasons. Not least of which it is recognized that as social, commercial and political relations move beyond the nation-state, the jurisdictional character and confines of domestic law and its essential place in command/control regulation and enforcement need to be re-envisioned. It is argued that with regulation operating de-centered from the state,[50] and more and more in networks of private interest, the inextricability of law (expressive or facilitative) and regulation cannot be taken for granted. For the regulation of global crisis in particular, law and lawyers, local and international, have a job arguing their relevance in meaningful regulatory responses beyond an expressive or supportive role. The critical analysis of crisis regulation will put the place of law into a sharp regulatory perspective. The test of whether crisis can be transformed to orderliness is asserted as a more convincing measure of regulatory efficiency than market success or failure.[51]

---

43 Gunnigham, N. and Grabosky, P. 1998. *Smart Regulation: Designing Environmental Policy*. Oxford: Oxford University Press.

44 Parker, C. 2002. *The Open Corporation: Effective Self-Regulation and Democracy*. Cambridge: Cambridge University Press.

45 Ayers, I. and Braithwaite, J. 1992. *Responsive Regulation*. Oxford: Oxford University Press.

46 Baldwin, R and Black, J. 2008. Really Responsive Regulation. *Modern Law Review*, 71/1, 59–94.

47 Sparrow, M. 2000. *The Regulatory Craft*. Washington, DC: Brookings Institution.

48 Jordana, J. and Levi-Faure, D. 1994.

49 An example of this is the common response of economic analysts that they did not foresee the financial meltdown of 2008 continuing beyond the limited context of American mortgage failure.

50 Black, J. 2001. Decentring Regulation: Understanding the Role of Regulation and Self-Regulation in a "Post-Regulatory" World. *Current Legal Problems*, 54/1, 103–46.

51 In proposing this alternative we would be foolish to ignore the economic (and more particularly, market) objectives for regulation. The assertion is intended, however, to allow for situations where a regulatory fixation on market failure may itself lead on to related and non-related global crisis regulatory challenges.

Sociability—New Non-State Relations

This analysis considers *regulatory sociability* as both the characteristic and consequence of relevant regulation, countering the criticism of modern regulatory intervention as reflecting little more than politicized popular responses to economic crisis. In the richest, most representative and benign governance structures regulation abounds, charged as it is with obtaining and retaining the quality of life for citizens and civil society. That said, we need to interrogate beyond self-interest in the direction of forces that achieve mutuality revealing what makes regulation efficient in achieving any such political and social aspiration.

Legal tools such as contracts and damages claims are themselves heavily regulated. Well-functioning courts manage and enforce legal remedies and resolve disputes, but when litigation is expensive, unpredictable or biased, regulatory capacity and efficiency is at risk. In addition, market failure and information asymmetries are not always essential triggers for regulation. Regulatory intervention often precedes market failure, and goes well beyond market need. In these respects I consider whether regulation is driven more by political imperatives than by efficiency or outcome-based motivations. Recognizing the reality that regulatory regimes are vulnerable to capture by the commercial, political and social interests which they are set to regulate,[52] the chapter has revealed those foundational social bonds which are strained in crisis and restored in orderliness. This is the framework of *regulatory sociability*.

The outcome of *regulatory sociability* should reflect culturally sensitive and contextually efficient institutional and process adaptations of governance to a complex and globalized world. The measure of this at the sharp edge is the way in which conciliatory and collaborative (not just responsive or reflexive) regulation moves chaos and crisis to orderliness. An essential precondition for sociability, and for the effectiveness of collaborative regulation, is trust.

Cooperative compliance as a cause and consequence of regulatory sociability entails the creation of regulatory relationships based on trust. Only where externalized incentives to cooperate trump the need for trust, and these could include legal compulsion, will such trust relationships recede and sociability diminish in any organic form. But in conclusion, mechanical and imposed regulatory regimes of re-ordering crisis are unsustainable due to a variety of critical reasons. For crisis, particularly global, to be convincingly converted to orderliness that lasts, regulation wherein players can be taken at their word, and dialogue between them is honest; where interests are mutualized and agreed rules are fair and applicable; and there is a resultant preference for cooperative regularity, are required if sociability is to emerge.

52 Stigler, G. 1971. The Theory of Economic Regulation. *Bell Journal of Economics and Management Science*, 2/1, 145–85.

However, the aspirations for regulatory sociability expressed in this chapter are neither naïve or altruistic. Much is said about the externalization of risk to communities who do not share in the private (and legally endorsed) interests and protections of regulated commercial environments. The need to break into that legalized, privatized domain in order to advance through pluralist regulation strong and shared notions of public (general) good is well recognized.[53] The inducement to collaborate, not from the acceptance of mutual as opposed to self-interest, at least in the short-term, is explored in communities of shared risk. The fragility of cooperative compliance if it depends on best practice or good corporate citizenship is critically anticipated. From within the conditions of regulatory sociability, a hard look is cast at the possibility of realigning global preferencing from economic wealth and material profit to sustainability in all its life forms. Finally, risk aversion and crisis reduction are not causally assumed, and orderliness not naturally expected as a consequence of sociability without a very critical appreciation of the vulnerable conditions which create and continue any collaborative regulatory frame.

Regulation's Reality

Regulation can take many forms. Within broad regulatory frames there can exist and operate a variety of styles ranging from:

- conversations and dialogue
- behavioral incentives
- inducements
- persuasion
- precautions
- inspections
- rules, agreed or imposed
- licenses to act or associate
- boundaries within which enterprise can be achieved
- best practice
- compliance
- sanction to command and control.

What often determines the choice and mix of these styles, or the manner in which they may be graduated or escalated, is whether the purpose of the regulator is for intentional change, or rather expressive governance. These intentions need not be exclusive and the selection of regulatory strategy to follow, not integrated,

53 For a discussion of this in the context of promoting general interests into construction contracts where agreements for advancing the built environment, risk the quality of life for non-contracting communities see, Perez, O. 2002. 77–110.

balanced or inclusive. Regulation all too often is a struggle between, rather than a reconciliation of, competing interests. That is where the chapter's commitment to sociability comes in: to influence purpose; to assist in the selection of strategy; to construct modes of operation; and to calibrate outcomes and measures of efficiency. Regarding the latter, efficiency as I see it is impacted upon by institutional choices and not dependent on the maintenance of public–private distinction.[54]

Regulation is neither just a "thing" nor a "result." In appreciating truly dynamic regulatory frames in transitional state contexts I advocate examining institutions and technologies of regulation. This is preceded by the critical consideration of regulation as theory. Then we need to look particularly at regulatory authorship, and regulatory space, followed by contextual considerations of regulation as change agents. Next the legitimacy of regulation for various locations of governance is particularly reflected against accountability and as such it is inevitable to consider the preferred regulatory regime and regulation outcome of sociability. All this is for the larger purpose of appreciating the big picture transition of global crisis to orderliness in specific places and stages of political economy.

In an age of globalization, moving out of a terror-risk focus into considerations of risk and securitization with a broader world focus, the need for collaborative internationalist engagement is no longer an aspiration. Transnational and international regulatory conversations and strategies have taken the context of regulation beyond the interests and boundaries of the nation-state. No longer is collaborative regulation limited to compliance in narrow corporate settings. The operation of risk and securitization within global governance is producing collaboration as a result of bio-political normalization and not simply through normative accession.[55]

As Cooley observes, too much recent analytical focus on globalization, particularly from the perspective of political economy, is constrained in a way:

> that globalization should be viewed as s hierarchical set of structures, institutions and processes. Of course there are various strands of the "globalization as hierarchy" approach … Even those who make the case that this new global system is not comparable to previous political economic orders find it difficult to discard altogether the hierarchy and imperialism analogies … even if we reject state-centred accounts of international political economy in favour of a more globalist or hierarchical understandings of economic governance, rationalist

54 While maintaining such distinction throughout their analysis Morgan and Yeung accept and advance a hybridization of theory and practice such as Braithwaite's Tripartism which undermines in action the public and private regulatory domains. Morgan, B. and Yeung, K. 2007.

55 Findlay, M. 2008. *Governing through Globalised Crime: Futures for International Criminal Justice*. Columpton: Willan.

> formulations still offer invaluable insights into the political dynamics of the contemporary international system.[56]

Rationalist engagement with the manner in which the state is or is not essential in confronting global crisis precipitates a richer discussion of alternative functional equivalents to the shadow of state hierarchy as a regulatory enforcer. As with law, and its problematic relationship with consolidated states, and from there its questionable relevance in regulating global crisis, the measure of a capacity to move crisis to ordering without the shadow of the state depends not on an institutional analysis of state-dependent governance forms but rather a functional understanding of what motivates embracing the common good. Regulation is an essential purpose and a critical challenge for the state, law, supranational governance and alternative functional equivalents to the shadow of the hierarchical consolidated state in the modern age.

56 Cooley, A. 2003. 672–4.

Chapter 8
Dual State: The Case of Sweden

Ola Tunander

The Concept of a Dual State: Illustrations from Turkey and Italy

In 1955 in the *Bulletin of Atomic Scientists*, Hans Morgenthau wrote about a U.S. "dual state" in a study of the U.S. State Department. According to Morgenthau there was in the United States, on the one hand, a regular democratic state hierarchy that acts according to the rule of law, and, on the other hand, a more or less hidden security hierarchy, or what I will call a "security state" or "national security state," that monitors and controls the former, or at least is able to "exert an effective veto over [its] decisions," to quote Morgenthau. This article was also published as a chapter, "The Corruption of Patriotism," in Morgenthau's 1962 volume *Decline of Democratic Politics*.[1] While the democratic state or what Peter Dale Scott has called the "public state"[2] deals with political alternatives, with elections of governments and apparent political choice, the "security state" enters the scene when "no alternative exists," when a certain activity is defined in terms of life and death, when this activity, in Ole Wæver's words, is "securitized."[3] In fact, this parallel security structure, the "security state" or what some would call the "deep state," is the very apparatus that defines when and whether a "state of emergency" will emerge. This aspect of the state is what Carl Schmitt in his work *Political Theology* from 1922 referred to as the "sovereign."[4]

The existence of such a parallel security structure has often been denied. Political scientists including proponents of "political realism" usually speak about *the state* as if it was a unified entity despite the fact that Morgenthau, strongly influenced by Carl Schmitt, has been described as the father of "political

1 Morgenthau, H. J. 1962. *Politics in the Twentieth Century, Vol. 1: The Decline of Democratic Politics*. Chicago: University of Chicago Press. Chapter 29. This article has previously been published in 1955 in the *New Republic* and the *Bulletin of the Atomic Scientists*.

2 Scott, P. D. 2007. *The Road to 9/11: Wealth, Empire, and the Future of America*. Berkeley: University of California Press.

3 Wæver, O. 1995. Securitization and Desecuritization, in *On Security*, edited by R. D. Lipschutz. New York: Columbia University Press; Wæver, O. 2000. European Security Identities, in *European Security Identities – Contested Understandings of EU and NATO*, edited by J. P. Burgess, and O. Tunander. Oslo: International Peace Research Institute Report 2. 29–56.

4 Schmitt, C. 1985 [1922]. *Political Theology*. Cambridge, MA: MIT Press.

realism." However, in contrast to the writings of today's political scientists, this is not the way many political leaders themselves *speak* about the state. They often *speak* about the state as a divided entity: a dual state. In certain countries, this is obvious. In Turkey, the existence of a dual state has been admitted at the highest level. The "security state," or what in Turkey is called the deep state,[5] is always present, and every political leader knows that it intervenes in case of "emergency." Turkish Prime Minister Recep Erdogan and former Turkish presidents Kenan Evren and Suleyman Demirel have all confirmed the existence of a Turkish deep state, a hidden and parallel state structure that in certain respects exists above the regular state with direct links to the protecting power: the United States.[6] "In our country there are two [states]," President Demirel said; "There is one deep state and [one legal state]," adding that the "state that should be the real is the spare one, the one that should be spare is the real one."[7] The deep state with the CIA-linked Grey Wolves and death squad leader Abdullah Çatli carried out bomb attacks in the 1980s that justified or provoked General Kenan Evren's military coup on September 12. Former CIA Station Chief in Ankara, Paul Henze, told President Jimmy Carter: "Our boys have done it."[8] After the coup, a Turkish-American Defense Council was established to guarantee total Turkish loyalty to the United States.[9] In a car crash in Susurluk close to Istanbul in 1996 a black Mercedes hit a truck. Çatli's body was found together with a Turkish government MP Sedat Bucak (still alive), whose militia forces had been used by the Turkish government to fight the Kurdish rebels in the southeast, along with the corpses of an important police chief, Husseyin Kocadag, who commanded Turkish counter-insurgency units, a beauty queen (Çatli's girlfriend, Gonca Us), and a large amount of narcotics and weapons, including pistols with silencers and machine guns. Çatli, who was a contract killer and a major heroin trafficker on Interpol's wanted list, was carrying six different identity cards with

5 In Turkey but also elsewhere the concept of deep state is used frequently for a kind of security structure able to operate outside the law. See for example RAND Conference Proceedings, Chubin, S. and Green, J. D. *Turkish Society and Foreign Policy in Troubled Times*. Geneva, Switzerland, April 25–27, 2001, Center for Middle East Public Policy and Geneva Center for Security Policy.

6 Gorvett, J. Turkey's Deep State Surfaces in Former President's Words, Deeds in Kurdish Town. *Washington Report on Middle East Affairs*, January/February 2006; Kanli, Y. January 29, 2007. The Turkish Deep State. *Hürriyet*. Available at: http://arama.hurriyet.com.tr/arsivnews.aspx?id=-598627 (accessed July 12, 2012).

7 President Demirel quoted from Turkish NTV, November 15, 2005.

8 Ganser, D. 2005. *NATO's Secret Armies: Operation Gladio and Terrorism in Western Europe*. London and New York: Frank Cass. 239; Lee, Martin A. 1997. On the Trail of Turkey's Terrorist Grey Wolves. *The Consortium*. Available at: www.consortiumnews.com/archive/story33.html (accessed July 12, 2012).

9 Private conversation with former Defence Minister Ümit Haluk Bayülken, who signed the deal. May 2004; see also http://en.wikipedia.org/wiki/1980_Turkish_coup_d'%C3%A9tat (accessed July 12, 2012).

different names; one "passport" for the exclusive use of Turkish officials was signed by the Minister of Interior.[10] When Turks speak about the deep state (*derin devlet*), they speak about the link between organized crime, security forces, other government agencies and the U.S. intelligence and Special Operations Forces. However, while Demirel focused on the military as a veto power, General Evren and former Prime Minister Bulent Ecevit have focused on the Stay-Behinds and their connections to organized crime and U.S. intelligence as the real actor. But all of them seem to emphasize the role of the United States. U.S. security forces intervene when "necessary" in collaboration with the local security forces, the Turkish deep state, by planting bombs and provoking military coups or by the use of military coups like the ones in 1960, 1971, 1980 and 1997. Special police officers were used for killing a large number of dissidents.[11] Threats of military coups are always taken seriously by the political leaders.

The same was the case in Cold War Italy as well as in Greece in 1967, when a coup was organized by the Greek–U.S. liaison officer Colonel Georgios Papadopoulos to "veto" the anti-NATO policy by the Greek Prime Minister Georgios Papandreou. The CIA's former Chief of Station in Athens and Rome, Thomas Karamessines, played an instrumental role.[12] In Italy, U.S. forces in collaboration with Italian intelligence and local fascists "initiated" military coups in 1964, 1970, 1973 and 1974.[13] Elected governments were forced to modify or change their policies to make the coup forces withdraw from the political scene. The 1964 coup was led by General Giovanni de Lorenzo, Italy's former Chief of Military Intelligence, who had been appointed on recommendation of the U.S. Ambassador Clare Boothe Luce. De Lorenzo later became MP for the fascist party MSI (Movimento Sociale Italiano).[14] His collaborator in 1964, and leader of the 1970 coup, Prince Junio Valerio Borghese, had been Benito Mussolini's most trusted officer, a former commander of the fascist Naval Special Forces Decima MAS and later Honorary President of the MSI. At the end of the war, he

10 Komisar, L. April 1997. Turkey's Terrorists: A CIA Legacy Lives on. *Progressive*. April 1997 Available at: www.scribd.com/doc/54065954/Turkeys-Terrorists-a-CIA-Legacy-Lives-On (accessed July 12, 2012); Lee, Martin A. 1997. Gatto, A. November–December 2006. The Susurlik Legacy. *Druglink*. Available at: http://oraclesyndicate.twoday.net/stories/3213126/; Wikipedia. http://en.wikipedia.org/wiki/Susurluk_scandal (accessed July 12, 2012); Ganser, D. 2005. 242–4.

11 Available at: http://en.wikipedia.org/wiki/Ayhan_%C3%87ark%C4%B1n (accessed July 12, 2012).

12 McKenzie Bale, J. 1994. The "Black" Terrorist International: Neo-Fascist Paramilitary Networks and the "Strategy of Tension" (doctoral dissertation). Ann Arbor, UMI Dissertation Service. 272–3; Ferraresi, F. 1996. *Threats to Democracy: The Radical Right in Italy after the War*. Princeton: Princeton University Press. 74–83; Ganser, D. 2005. 212–223.

13 McKenzie Bale, J. 1994. 403–7, 459; Ferraresi, F. 1996. 74–83; Ganser, D. 2005. 63–83.

14 Ferraresi, F. 1996. 77–83; Ganser, D. 2005. 63–83.

had been rescued and then recruited by a U.S. intelligence officer, the later CIA Chief of Counter-Intelligence and CIA liaison to Italy, James Jesus Angleton.[15] De Lorenzo had used his counter-insurgency plan Piano Solo (or Plan Solo) for the opposite purpose similar to what Colonel Papadopoulos did three years later with the Prometheus Plan.[16]

In 2006 the shadow Foreign Minister during the 1970 Borghese coup, Adriano Monti, said that he had received the "green light" for the coup from the CIA's Otto Skorzeny in Madrid.[17] Skorzeny had been Adolf Hitler's most trusted lieutenant, who had saved Hitler's and Mussolini's lives at critical moments 1943–1944.[18] In 1970, Skorzeny represented the CIA after having been recommended to the Agency and its Director Allan Dulles by Hitler's intelligence chief for the Eastern front, General Reinhard Gehlen, at that time the CIA's man for West Germany.[19] In the preparation for the coup in 1970, the CIA and Skorzeny only had one condition: Giulio Andreotti should be prime minister.[20] However, sources argue that Angleton had aborted the coup after the Italian government had given its "assurances of a total pro-American loyalty." Others argue that it was President Richard Nixon himself, who intervened and stopped the coup through his man in Italy, Hugh Fenwich, who also was close to Monti.[21] At that very moment, Borghese's people—along with the fascist leaders, the shadow Minister of Foreign Affairs Adriano Monti and his colleague Stefano delle Chiaie (Abdullah Çatli's Italian collaborator)—had already taken control over the Ministry of Interior and sized a large amount of machine guns from its weapons depot.[22] In all these cases, the fascist coup plotters, often inside the intelligence and security services, collaborated with their U.S. counterparts, but the fascist activists and leaders, who were part of the security state or deep state, were rather instruments of a high-level network of Italian liaison officers to the United States. On several occasions, Italian governments were forced to modify their policies in line with U.S. demands. Franco de Felice argued in his *Doppia lealta e doppio stato* (1989) that the dual state was born from the incapacity of the Italian state to reconcile its domestic policies with its foreign policies. The elected

15 BBC documentary "Gladio: Part 1," June 1992; McKenzie Bale, J. 1994; Ferraresi, F. 1996.

16 Ferraresi, F. 1996.

17 Monti, A. 2006. *Il "Golpe Borghese": Un golpe virtuale all'italia*. Bologna: Il Scarabeo. Available at: www.amazon.es/%C2%ABgolpe-Borghese%C2%BB-virtuale-allitaliana-Documenti/dp/8884780926 (accessed July 2012).

18 Annussek, G. 2005. *Hitler's Raid to Save Mussolini: The Most Infamous Commando Operation of World War II*. Cambridge, MA: Da Capo Press; Infield, G. B. 1981. *Skorzeny – Hitler's Commando*. New York: St Martin's Press.

19 Cookridge, E. H. 1972. *Gehlen – Spy of the Century*. London: Corgi Books.

20 Monti, A. 2006.

21 Ganser, D. 2005. 76–7; McKenzie Bale, J. 1994. 250–511.

22 Ganser, D. 2005. 237–8.

government had to be disciplined to accept total U.S. loyalty.[23] Paolo Cucchiarelli and Aldo Giannulli (1997) have written about the dual state or "parallel state" as a state that operates both inside and outside the law.[24]

Some would argue that the Italian state or the Greek state at the time—and even more the Turkish state—had not yet developed a democratic culture. Turkey had a limited democratic experience and Italy came directly from its fascist experience of the 1920s, 1930s and 1940s. Similar to other Mediterranean states like Spain and Portugal and former fascist states like Germany, they were not yet considered mature in their democratic development; the recurrent patterns of military coups and coup attempts were explained by the comparative immaturity of their nascent democracies. But there were also similar coup attempts and a similar parallel security structure in traditional democracies like France,[25] and, surprisingly for many, similar coup attempts and dual state structure are to be found in states like Sweden, which has had a most excellent democratic reputation. It is not enough to look at the history of the state, its autocratic origin in the monarchy or aristocracy; one may also have to look at the structure of the type of democratic state that we know from the Western world.

This chapter will deal with Sweden, and it will show that a state that often is considered to be a most respectable democracy also has had a hidden parallel security state that in Morgenthau's words is able to veto the decisions of regular democratic state.[26] This hidden deep state defines when a "state of emergency" will emerge. It "decides on the exception," to quote Carl Schmitt,[27] and during the Cold War it was linked to the protecting power: the United States with its Western security apparatus. Thus, the Schmittian sovereign here is the parallel hierarchy of informal Western structures with their military/intelligence center in the United States. It has been this informal security structure, or security state or deep state, which has intervened if necessary to guarantee U.S. or "Western" interests. Indeed, the central actors of this Western security network appear as the real sovereign, in the Schmittian sense, that decides on the exception in the Euro-Atlantic area, or in what Schmitt would call a *Grossraum*.[28] By letting the security aspect of the state invade the public sphere and "securitize" the political life, the

---

23 De Felice, F. 1989. Doppia lealtà e doppio stato. *Studi storici*, 3, 493–563; Tunander, O. 2009. Democratic State vs. Deep State – Approaching the Dual State of the West, in *Government of the Shadows: Parapolitics and Criminal Sovereignty*, edited by E. Wilson. London: Pluto Press. 56–72.

24 Cucchiarelli, P. and Giannulli, A. 1997. *Lo Stato Parallelo: L'Italia "Oscura" Nei Documenti e nelle Relazioni delle Commissione Stragi*. Rome: Gamberetti.

25 Cookridge, E. H. 1972; Henissart, P. 1970. *Wolves in the City – The Death of French Algeria*. New York: Simon & Schuster.

26 Morgenthau, H. 1962. 400.

27 Schmitt, C. 1985. 5.

28 Schmitt, C. 1939. *Völkerrechtliche Grossraumordnung mit Interventionsverbot für Raumfremde Mächte: Ein Beitrag zum Reichsbegriff in Völkerrecht*. Berlin: Deutcher Rechtsverlag.

democratic state loses its influence; the deep state or security state is able to "fine tune the democracy."[29] I will discuss these problems, especially the divide between the nation-state aspect and the protecting power, using Sweden as an example.[30]

The Origin of the Swedish Dual State

In 1941 Ernst Fraenkel published a book about the dual state in Nazi Germany. He located the roots of the dual state in the ambivalence of the democratic breakthrough, in its divide between the new democratic *Rechtstaat* and its traditional aristocratic *Machtstaat* (power state). Fraenkel describes this duality as typifying the German state of the 1930s.[31] In the German case, however, this duality was overt, combining the "regular" legal state with a parallel *SS-Staat*, an autocratic emergency state operating outside or "above" the legal system, with its philosophical foundation in the Schmittian "sovereign." Fraenkel refers to Emil Lederer, who argues that this *Machtstaat* has its historical origin in Europe's aristocratic elite, which still played an important role after the triumph of democracy.[32]

In the Swedish case, we know that the revolutionary chaos in Russia and Germany after World War I and the simultaneous hunger demonstrations in Sweden made the Swedish industrial and financial elite, particularly the influential Wallenberg family,[33] turn to the Conservative Party to force it to accept general and free elections for women as well as for men.[34] Democracy was introduced as a concession primarily to the Social Democratic labor movement to avoid the dramatic events on the continent. The Social Democratic Party was voted into power and they strongly favored a neutral policy in foreign affairs, while the industrial and aristocratic military elites kept their traditional ties to Germany. Germany had from the early 20th century been described as the protecting power of Sweden.[35] During

---

29 One Turkish "general famously called it the 'fine tuning of democracy'." Bouton, R. January 30, 2003. Turkey's New Govt Faces Challenge. *Dawn*.

30 Some sections of this article use material from Tunander, O. 1999. The Uneasy Imbrication of Nation-State and NATO – The Case of Sweden. *Cooperation and Conflict*, 34/2, 169–203 and from Tunander, O. 2005. Swedish Geopolitics: From Rudolf Kjellén to a Swedish "Dual State." *Geopolitics*, 10, 546–66.

31 Fraenkel, E. 1969. *The Dual State: A Contribution to the Theory of Dictatorship*. New York: Octagon Books.

32 Fraenkel, E. 1969. 167–9.

33 Olsson, U. 1986. *Familj och företagande. Stockholms Enskilda Bank 1946–1971 Bank, Family and Enterprise*. Stockholm: SEB and The Institute for Economic and Business History Research, Stockholm School of Economics.

34 Söderpalm, S. A. 1969. *Storföretagarna och det demokratiska genombrottet. Ett perspektiv på första världskrigets svenska historia*. BHL 21. Dissertation, Lund University.

35 Bengtsson, R. 2000. *Trust, Threat and Stable Peace: Swedish Great Power Perceptions 1905–1939*. Lund University: Lund Political Studies 114. Department of Political Science, Lund University.

World War I, Sweden and Germany used the same intelligence net in Finland, and the close Swedish–German collaboration continued into the 1930s.[36] Chief of Defense General Olof Thörnell, Chief of Defense Staff Lieutenant General Axel Rappe, his successor Lieutenant General Samuel Åkerhielm and several other top generals wanted Sweden to enter World War II on the side of Germany.[37] Commander of the Northern Military District, later Chief of Army, General Archibald Douglas, was, together with Herman Göring's friend and brother-in-law in Sweden, Eric von Rosen, a co-founder of Nazi Party, the National-Socialist Bloc.[38] In 1940 Douglas invited the Nazi Party leader Per Engdahl to speak to the troops. Protesting soldiers "were immediately sent to Vitvattnet" (Douglas' concentration camp), to quote Engdahl. Other pro-Nazi generals—Hjalmar Falck, Commander of the Northern Military District Nils Rosenblad, Commander of the Eastern Military District Rickman von der Lancken, and Chairman of the Swedish-German Society Henri de Champs—all belonged to the Swedish aristocracy.[39] In 1939 the Wallenbergs had negotiated a deal with major German companies, Bosch A.G. and I.G. Farben, to buy their assets in Allied countries and, according to a secret agreement, let the Germans have the right to regain these assets after the war to avoid confiscations by U.S. and British authorities.[40] Sweden's signal intelligence FRA (Försvarets Radio Anstalt) was ordered by General Åkerhielm not to report to the Cabinet about the communication between Swedish generals (and colonels) and their German counterparts. Not until late 1943 did the Chief of FRA inform the Minister of Defense.[41] The elected government, the political elite, was supposed to be kept in the dark. In July 1942 a Swedish–Russian military phrasebook was printed for a Swedish military attack against the Soviet Union as part of the Nazi German offensive.[42] The phrasebook was signed at Stockholm Castle by the Conservative minister K. G. Everlöf and Lieutenant General Henry Kellgren, the liaison officer between the Defense Minister and the Defense Staff and close friend to the German Defense Attaché.[43] Later Defense Minister Torsten Nilsson wrote that General Archibald Douglas wanted to move his army forces in Northern Sweden into

36 Ottosson, J. and Magnusson, L. 1991. *Hemliga makter: Svensk militär underrättelsetjänst från unionskrisen till det kalla kriget*. Stockholm: Tiden. 46–78.

37 Agrell, W. 2000. *Fred och fruktan: Sveriges säkerhetspolitik 1918–2000*. Lund: Historiska Media. 53, 77–8; Nilsson, K. 1996. *Svensk överklassnazism 1930–1945*. Stockholm: Carlssons Bokförlag.

38 Nilsson, K. 1996. 104.

39 Nilsson, K. 1996. 76.

40 Aalders, G. and Wiebes, C. 1996. *The Art of Cloaking: Secret Collaboration of Neutral States with Nazi-Germany*. Amsterdam: Amsterdam University Press.

41 Agrell, W. 2000. 77.

42 Svensk-Rysk Militärparlör (Förkortad del), Stockholms Slott July 13, 1942 (private archive).

43 Olsson, S. 2001. Beyond Diplomacy: German Military Intelligence in Sweden 1939–1945. *International Journal of Intelligence and Counter Intelligence*, 24/2. 338–51.

Finland to annex a considerable portion of Soviet territory.[44] General Rappe, who was the most outspoken supporter of the war, presented maps to the Cabinet for the Swedish operation into the Soviet Union in his briefing to the government. He wanted to move two-thirds of the Swedish Army to the Finnish–Soviet front, but Prime Minister Per Albin Hansson (1933–1946) turned down his request.[45] According to Chief of Navy Admiral Stig H:son-Ericson, General Axel Rappe tried to recruit officers for a military coup in Sweden already in March 1940. Admiral Ericson was himself in doubt;[46] Rappe wanted to get rid of the "neutralist" government, but he did not receive enough support. According to Gunnar Pettersson, the aristocratic coup-plotters turned to King Gustav V several times during the spring of 1942, but despite the young Prince Gustav Adolf's ties to Herman Göring and the Nazis and, despite the King's pro-German attitude, the King did not support a military coup.[47] However, the seriousness of the military coups proposed by the aristocratic elite indicates that the Swedish state was not a unified entity; this military-security elite was primarily loyal not to the elected government but to the King and to Germany as a protecting power. This parallel security hierarchy kept its informal ties to the Germans and kept the elected government in the dark. The origin of this *Machtstaat* in parallel to the Swedish *Rechtstaat* was not just the continuous political ambitions of the aristocratic elite after the democratic breakthrough, as proposed by Emil Lederer and Ernst Fraenkel. Rather, the origin should also be sought in the split between the state's democratic hierarchy and its security hierarchy linked to the protecting power: Germany. The origin should also be seen in light of the fact that the domestic policies of Sweden were impossible to reconcile with the policy of the protecting power, in a manner similar to what Franco de Felice had stated about Cold War Italy.

It is interesting to note, however, how easy it was for Sweden's pro-German military elite to switch to U.S. loyalties after the war. In November 1945, General Archibald Douglas, who had been the founder of the National-Socialist Bloc, invited the U.S. General George Patton for a dinner at the Wallenberg residence. The leading Swedish generals were primarily anti-Soviet and now the United States turned out to become the new protecting power. They kept the Americans fully informed, while certain figures still kept the elected government in the dark. Swedish Waffen SS officers and officers from the Nazi Sveaborg, who had been fighting as volunteers at the Finnish-Soviet front, including the commanders

44 Nilsson, T. 1986. *Utanför protokollet.* Stockholm: Tidens förlag. 176.

45 Andersson, G. 1955. *Från bondetåg till samlingsregering: Politiska minnen.* Stockholm: Tiden. 217.

46 Ericson, S. H. 1966. *Knopar på logglinan.* Stockholm: Bonnier. 135.

47 There were a lot of rumors of a possible pro-German military coup in winter–spring 1942. A pro-British general was intensively preparing for the Defense of Stockholm, and the illness of the pro-German Swedish King Gustav V put the coup-plotters in a difficult situation. Pettersson, G. 2000. *Mannen som kom tillbaka från det döda.* Stockholm: Ordfront. 241–7.

Anders Grafström and Otto Hallberg, established parallel Swedish Stay-Behinds, the former under the Defence Staff (in collaboration with the CIA representative in Stockholm, William Colby).[48] In 1949 Prime Minister Tage Erlander (1946–69) appointed Alvar Lindencrona, Director for the Swedish insurance company Thule (bought by the Wallenberg company Skandia in 1963) as Chief of the Swedish Stay-Behinds. Anders Grafström headed the department for recruitment, military training and arms caches. In the early phase, however, the government knew very little about the people involved. From 1957 the Swedish Stay-Behinds were put under the Ministry of Interior and from 1967 under the Ministry of Defense, but still, according to the Assistant Under-Secretary of Defense Ingmar Engman, only a couple of people at the Ministry knew about them.[49] The headquarters was located in the Thule Building on Sveavägen 44 in Stockholm.[50] Swedish representatives participated in NATO's Allied Clandestine Committee (ACC) meetings that supervised the European Stay-Behinds. The major difference between the ACC and the CPC (the Clandestine Planning Committee) according to a participant in both committees was that the "neutrals," including Sweden, participated in the ACC but not in the CPC. The latter committee was chaired by SACEUR (Supreme Allied Commander Europe). The decisions in the CPC were supposedly more interesting.[51] After the war, the Swedish "secret army" became firmly integrated into the U.S. and British sphere of influence.

The Swedish Dual State: A Neutral State vs. a State under the U.S. Nuclear Umbrella

During the war, the Wallenberg family had sold ball-bearings and steel to Germany and had had secret deals with German companies (see above, p. 177). Jacob Wallenberg had collaborated with the Germans (secretly supporting the Carl

48 Ganser, D. and Deland, M. 2010. NATO's Secret Army in Sweden. *Journal for Intelligence, Propaganda and Security Studies*, 4/2. 20–39.

49 Conversations (1996-97) with the Swedish former Assistant Under-Secretary of Defense Ingemar Engman (1972–79). See also SOU. 1994:11 *Om kriget kommit–Förberedelser för mottagande av militärt bistånd 1949–1969.* Betänkande av Neutralitetspolitikkommissionen (Neutrality Policy Commission) Statens Offentliga Utredningar (SOU). Stockholm: Statsrådsberedningen. 1994; Colby, W. 1978. *Honorable Men: My Life in the CIA*. London: Simon & Schuster; see also Ganser, D. and Deland, M. 2010. According to former Chief of Staff General Carl Eric Almgren (1961-67) Colby's parallel Stay-Behinds were closed down around 1960 (Carl Eric Almgren for the Neutrality Policy Commission, December 3, 1993, Swedish Government Offices Records Centre, Stockholm).

50 Ganser, D. and Deland, M. 2010.

51 Conversation with a German former member of both committees. The statement about the difference between the ACC and the CPC was made at the intelligence conference in Oslo in 2005.

Gördeler and Stauffenberg coup attempt against Hitler in 1944), while Marcus Wallenberg worked with the Americans and with British intelligence.[52] After World War II, the Wallenbergs continued as usual thanks to the support from their lawyer, later Secretary of State John Foster Dulles, and their representative in the United States, Deputy Secretary of State Robert Lovett.[53] Sweden's aristocratic and military elite abandoned its historical German ties for a pro-U.S. stand, whereas the Social-Democratic government officially kept the Swedish West-leaning policy of neutrality, which enjoyed popular support. After the war Marcus Wallenberg was the "liaison" for the Swedish Chief of Defence General Nils Svedlund and senior U.S. officers. General Svedlund met U.S. State Secretary John Foster Dulles at the home of Wallenberg.[54] After the war, the Wallenberg brothers kept their liaison with the Dulles brothers (also with Allan Dulles as Director of the CIA). Similarly in the 1980s, Peter Wallenberg, Marcus's son and successor as head of the Wallenberg empire, acted as a "liaison" between Sweden's Chief of Defense General Lennart Ljung and the U.S. leadership (including Henry Kissinger and George H. W. Bush, Snr.).[55] A significant segment of the aristocratic military and industrial elite appeared as an informal network of power with its own loyalties and international ties distinct from the elected government with the ruling Social-Democratic political elite. Here we may find the historical roots of the Swedish dual state.

However, the economic success of Swedish industry, in particular of the Wallenbergs, was a precondition for the Social-Democratic welfare state, which became the foundation of the postwar compromise between Social-Democratic neutralism and pro-U.S. industrial and military elites. Prime Minister Hansson's successor, the Social-Democratic Prime Minister Tage Erlander, supported the concealed Swedish–U.S. military ties as long as these were kept secret. The military leadership was informally given the right to act—and secretly cooperate with the United States and NATO—as long as the government had the right to speak, to define publicly what was official policy. This "historical compromise" of the 1950s and 1960s seems to have been acceptable to both sides. The Swedish power elites were as divided as before, but while the Social Democrats officially kept their West-leaning neutrality, some conservative and military elites exchanged their German ties for U.S. ones.[56]

52 Nylander, G. 1999. The German Resistance Movement and England: Carl Goerdeler and the Wallenberg Brothers: Banking and Enterprise at No.2 Stockholm.The Foundation for Economic History Research within Banking and Enterprise. Available at: www.wallenberg.com/arkiv/german.doc (accessed July 12, 2012).

53 Aalders, G. and Wiebes, C. 1996.

54 SOU. 1994.

55 Ljung, L. 1978–1986. *Dagbok (Diary).* Stockholm: Krigsarkivet (Swedish Military Archives).

56 Tunander, O. 1999.

In Sweden, the prime minister had to bridge this conflict as a supreme leader, which gave him much the role of a "president." In the early 1960s, Sweden's top-secret nuclear weapons program, headed by the then Prime Minister Erlander, and by his secretary Olof Palme, was shut down (or rather cut down and put to sleep) possibly as a "deal" with the United States, making the United States extend its nuclear umbrella to Sweden.[57] According to a U.S. National Security Council document from the 1960, the United States was to "assist Sweden … to resist Soviet Bloc attack" and this provided "the basis only for unilateral US planning and not for planning within NATO."[58] This was not to be known by NATO commanders. The State Department document, "Guidelines for Policy and Operations—Sweden" (June 1962) uses the same language, including U.S. unilateral planning for the same contingency; "This document was in force through the 1970s, and probably in one form or the other up to 1989."[59] General Carl Eric Almgren (Chief of Staff 1961–1967 and Chief of Army 1967–1976) told a government inquiry that, already from the 1960s, Swedish airbases were prepared to receive U.S. aircraft.[60] Ingemar Engman (Advisor to Defense Minister Sven Andersson 1967–1972 and Assistant Undersecretary of Defense 1972–1979) stated that in case of a Soviet military attack on the continent, the prime minister, the defense minister and the chief of defense intended to give the green light for U.S. aircraft to be evacuated from West Germany to Sweden on the very first day of hostilities. To the Swedish leadership in the 1960s, this was a primary option.[61] The U.S. aircraft in West Germany were under U.S. and not under NATO command, and in case of a war these aircraft could be re-deployed to Sweden as part of a bilateral Swedish–U.S. arrangement. From the early 1960s, a top-secret secure line was established between the Swedish Defense Staff and the U.S. Air

57 At least, this occurred at the time when the United States was launching its non-proliferation policy and discouraging Sweden from procuring nuclear weapons (see for example Agrell, W. 1985. *Alliansfrihet och atombomber – Kontinuitet och förändring i den svenska försvarsdoktrinen 1945–1982*. Stockholm: Liber).

58 SOU. 1994. Supplement. 140.

59 SOU 2002:108. *Fred och säkerhet – Svensk säkerhetspolitik 1969–89*. Stockholm. Statens Offentliga Utredningar. Utrikesdepartementet. 2002. 221–34.

60 Almgren for the Neutrality Policy Commission SOU. 1994. Swedish Government Offices Records Centre, Stockholm.

61 Engman said that he received this information as a close adviser to Defense Minister Sven Andersson (1957–1973), not as a senior official at the Defense Ministry. He believes that no civil servant was informed, only the military supreme commanders and chiefs of staff and a handful of political leaders. In 1967 Engman came in from the secret Military Intelligence Service IB (later SSI) to the Defense Ministry as advisor to Sven Andersson. In 1972, he became responsible for defense material, research and the classified accounts. In 1974, he was a candidate to replace Birger Elmér as Chief of IB (1957–1974), but he continued as Assistant Under-Secretary of Defense for Defense Material. Tunander, O. 1999. 178–9; Tunander, O. 2000. A Criticism of Court Chroniclers. *Cooperation and Conflict*, 35/4, 451–60 at 434–5.

Force Headquarters in Wiesbaden to facilitate this operation.[62] U.S. attack and fighter aircraft would be re-deployed from West Germany and the USA to the "forward deployed unsinkable aircraft carrier" of southern Sweden with direct access to the Central Front and the Soviet heartland rather than to the "defensively deployed unsinkable aircraft carrier" of Great Britain. With this option, the Soviet Union would suddenly be extremely vulnerable, and it would have to divert its forces and go for a more defensive strategy. This option was of vital importance to the United States. Sweden was not believed to be able to stay out of a war in the long run, and Engman argued that early deployment of U.S. air forces in Sweden would have been the only possibility for Sweden to receive American support.[63] In 1970, in the middle of the Vietnam War, when Prime Minister Olof Palme (1969–1976 and 1982–1986) compared the U.S. bombing in Vietnam with the war crimes of Stalin and Hitler, he told his Chief of Defense General Stig Synnergren (1970–1978) that he was a great friend of the United States and that "the positive Swedish relations with the USA including the US nuclear umbrella and so on will be kept as before."[64]

This double-talk was appreciated neither by the U.S. president nor by a significant part of the Swedish security elite. President Nixon spoke in less diplomatic terms about Prime Minister Palme as "that Swedish asshole,"[65] and the U.S.-leaning Swedish elite was becoming increasingly worried about government policy. During the 1970s and the first half of the 1980s, this conflict developed into an exceedingly grave split between a U.S.-linked industrial-military-security elite on the one hand and a neutralist Social-Democratic government led by a strong prime minister, Palme, on the other. Sweden was a neutral and "sovereign nation-state," but Sweden was also a state "plugged in to NATO," to quote John Owen

62 Swedish former Chief of Staff, General Carl Eric Almgren, stated in interviews for the Neutrality Policy Commission (SOU. 1994) that the secret secure line from the U.S. Air Force Headquarters in Wiesbaden to the Swedish Defense Staff originated in a room at the U.S. Air Force Headquarters under Swedish disposal. However, this room was normally staffed by a U.S. officer (Carl Eric Almgren for the Neutrality Policy Commission December 3, 1993, Swedish Government Offices Records Centre, Stockholm); Lieutenant-Colonel Arvid Cronenberg, up to 1967 directly responsible for this line at the Swedish Defense Staff, told me in December 1998 that it was set up by the Americans (possibly in 1963) to enable the Swedes to communicate with the U.S. Air Force in Wiesbaden to receive U.S. military aircraft in a crisis or war situation.

63 See the interview with former Assistant Under-Secretary of Defense Ingemar Engman for the Neutrality Policy Commission. SOU. 1994. Swedish Government Offices Records Centre, Stockholm. See also Tunander, O. 1999. 178–9; Tunander, O. 2000. 451–60; Holmström, M. 2011. *Den dolda alliansen.* Stockholm: Atlantis. 439–50.

64 Skoglund C. 1995. Svensk försvarspolitik, strategiskt och operativt tänkande under efterkrigstiden. *Kungl. krigsvetenskapsakademins handlinagar och tidskrift*, 3, 16.

65 Elmbrant, B. 1989. *Palme.* Stockholm: Författarförlaget. 148.

at the North European Office of the U.S. State Department.[66] This underlines the dual structure of the state: the contrast between nation-state aspect and the supranational U.S.-leaning aspect of the state.

While the Swedish government often carried out an anti-U.S. and anti-NATO policy in the developing world and in the UN, Sweden was, in certain respects, "plugged in to NATO" or included in the "US *Grossraum*," to use Schmitt's concept. The former chief of the Swedish Navy, Vice-Admiral Bengt Lundvall (1970–1978), has stated that his wartime position was to be Swedish liaison to NATO and, in the event of an occupied Sweden he would be Chief of Defense at the Swedish Headquarters in Exile in Great Britain. These positions, however, were so secret that "nothing was written down on paper." The information was transferred "orally" to his successor Vice-Admiral Per Rudberg (Chief of Navy 1978–1984).[67] Swedish–U.S. agreements were made "orally," according to Lundvall's opposite number and friend in Washington, Admiral Elmo Zumwalt, Chief of Naval Operation (1970–1974). Zumwalt was quoted by later Assistant Under-Secretary for Defense Dov Zakheim as saying that there was an "unofficial alliance" with Sweden.[68] The option of sending U.S. aircraft to Sweden, as discussed above, was guaranteed by a Swedish–U.S. mutual understanding, apparently not by a formal agreement on a piece of paper. Former Chairman of the Joint Chiefs of Staff, General John Vessey (1982–1985), told me in 1989 about the Swedish–U.S. military ties, declaring that "when it comes to Sweden, there was only one rule: Nothing on paper." This was confirmed by several other high-ranking officers.[69] General H. F. Zeiner-Gundersen, former Norwegian Chief of

---

66 Leifland, L. 1997. *Frostens år – Om USAs diplomatiska utfrysning av Sverige*. Stockholm: Nerenius och Santérus Förlag. 108. According to the Swedish former Commander-in-Chief, General Stig Synnergren (1970–1978) and the former Chiefs of Navy, Vice Admiral Bengt Lundvall (1970–1978) and Vice Admiral Per Rudberg (1978–1984), the wartime position of the Swedish Chief of Navy was not to be Chief of Navy but Chief of the Supreme Headquarters in Exile in London, where he would have the position of a Swedish liaison to NATO and act as Commander of the Swedish resistance movement in an occupied Sweden. Plans for a Headquarters in Exile in London were made already in the late 1940s." (Holmström, M. March 22, 1998. Marinchef i exil skulle försvara riket. Svenska Dagbladet; Holmström, M. 2011. 383–9).

67 Holmström, M. March 22, 1998.

68 Zakheim, S. D. 1998. *The United States and the Nordic Countries During the Cold War*. Lecture to the Nordic International Studies Association Seminar, Copenhagen. March 6; Zumwalt said on Swedish TV: "It was always an informal relationship with understanding on both sides that there should be no record in any formal way … because of Sweden's neutrality." Interview with Admiral Zumwalt Reportrarna *Swedish TV2*. Aired September 9, 1998.

69 At the Third Oslo International Symposium on the High North Towards 2010 June 18–22, 1989, Dr. Paul Cole presented some U.S. documents and some archival evidence indicating a Swedish–American collaboration (see Cole, P. M. 1990. Neutralite du Jour – The Conduct of Swedish Security Policy since 1945. Ann Arbor, MI. UNI Dissertation

Defense (1972–1977) and Chairman of NATO Military Committee (1977–1980) said that his ties to his Swedish counterpart General Stig Synnergren were built on trust; continuity had to be guaranteed by close ties and absolute trust.[70] General Synnergren told the Neutrality Policy Commission:

> I never asked the Government for advice. The responsibility was mine. I took the decisions. The Government – the Defence Minister or the Prime Minister – was not informed about all decisions. And in the single cases when I briefed them about something, I did that when there was a risk of a leak to the public.[71]

Several interviewed Western generals expressed an absolute trust in their Swedish military colleagues, but not in Sweden's political representatives. At a lunch talk with James Schlesinger, former Director of the CIA (1973) and former U.S. Secretary of Defense (1973–1976), I asked him about his views on Sweden during his time in the government. His answer was short and concise: "Which Sweden? The 'Political Sweden'? or the 'Military Sweden'? The military were planning to get the USA involved as soon as possible."[72]

Whereas political views in Sweden may, as in all countries, have represented a continuum of ideas from far left to extreme right, the political–military power structure was not only divided but, to a certain extent, polarized. Why? Because the more or less neutral Swedish nation-state—as expressed in popular tradition and official government policy—was in conflict with secret security hierarchies

---

Service). I asked General Vessey afterwards about Cole's paper. Vessey pointed out that you would never find anything important in the archives, because "when it comes to Sweden, there was only one rule: Nothing on paper." General Vessey has also served in the NATO Military Committee and as Vice Chief of Staff of the U.S. Army. General Vessey confirmed this statement in September 1998. Also in September 1998, Lieutenant-General Wilhelm Mohr, former Norwegian Chief of Air Force (1964–1969) and Deputy Commander of NATO's Northern Command (1969–1972), told me the same. Lieutenant-General Kjeld Hillingsø, former Commander of NATO's BALTAP Command (1993–1995), told me that there was only one rule in the cooperation with the Swedes: "Nothing on paper."

70 General Zeiner-Gundersen also said: "within NATO, the most important things were not always written down on paper. What was most secret was decided orally and guaranteed by the trust between individuals. What is written on paper – in a document – can always be leaked to the press. A verbal commitment, however, cannot be proved."

71 General Stig Synnergren for the Neutrality Policy Commission April 29, 1993, Swedish Government Offices Records Centre, Stockholm.

72 Discussion with James Schlesinger at the PRIO International Conference on Nuclear Technology and Politics at Rjukan, Norway, June 16–18, 1993. In my notebook I wrote that Mr. Schlesinger said: "Which Sweden? The 'Political Sweden' or the 'Military Sweden'? The military wanted us to come as soon as possible." I called Mr. Schlesinger on November 16, 1998 and asked him if I could quote him on that. He confirmed this statement but wanted to change the last sentence: "The military were [*sic*] planning to get the USA involved as soon as possible."

that informally were linked to the United States or "plugged in to NATO." After looking into this secret collaboration, it may seem that this was the true Swedish security policy. Sweden's official neutrality, however, would not necessarily be easy to change: it possessed its own inertia. The long tradition of neutrality had created its own justifications and its own discourse. And the prime minister and his close advisers would not necessarily accept U.S. military plans. If Sweden were to receive U.S. attack and fighter aircraft at Swedish airbases, Sweden would also be inviting Soviet nuclear attacks on these bases. According to Lieutenant General Vladimir Cheremnikh, Deputy Chief of Staff Leningrad Military District (chief of military plans North-western Military Theatre), Swedish airbases used by U.S. Air Force operations would be eliminated.[73] But this seems to have presupposed the use of nuclear weapons, certainly one reason for Prime Minister Palme's preoccupation with a Nordic Nuclear-Weapons Free Zone in the early 1980s. Perhaps Palme started to believe in Swedish neutrality for an early phase of a war, which would save Sweden in case of a short war, while the U.S.-linked security elite still favored an immediate deployment of U.S. forces. It seems as if the "Political Sweden" existed with its own pride, its own vision and its own hierarchies, while other, and, partly overlapping or imbricating, hierarchies were directly linked to the United States, and to what Carl Schmitt called a *Grossraum*.[74]

Sweden has, like most Western states, been both a sovereign nation-state and a state under the U.S. nuclear umbrella, a state belonging to the *Pax Americana*. The Neo-Realist idea of a unified state is not able to explain such a divided state or dual state. There seem to have been two conflicting "Swedens": one national state structure, and one shadow structure, primarily linked to the United States, and this dual structure—which exists in every NATO state but is more pronounced in the case of Sweden—indicates that NATO is not merely something in between an alliance of sovereign states and a super-state, but is, in fact, a "both–and": both a formal alliance and something of an informal U.S. "super-state." Former National Security Agency Director William Odom argued that the United States was something of a "supranational political-military authority."[75]

---

73 Stated by Lieutenant General Vladimir Cheremnikh during his presentation at the International Peace Research Institute in Oslo in 1994. My report from this event, a now declassified Swedish Military Intelligence and Security Service (MUST) report, has been published as an attachment to Bengt Gustafsson 2010. *Sanningen om ubåtsfrågan: Ett försök till analys*. Stockholm: Satnérus. 366–70.

74 Tunander, O. 1999.

75 Odom, W. E. and Dujarric, R. 2004. *America's Inadvertent Empire*. New Haven: Yale University Press. 204.

The Swedish Dual State and the Sovereign

In Sweden and probably also in other West European states, Morgenthau's dual state, its divide between "regular state hierarchy" and "security hierarchy," had been fused with the *Grossraum* divide between the hierarchy of the nation-state and the security hierarchy of the protecting power or *Reich*. U.S. intelligence and security forces would always be present in the local states to guarantee the security of the *Grossraum*. In other words, the U.S. security hierarchy would intervene if "necessary" as a veto force or an "emergency power," or what Carl Schmitt called the sovereign. It might intervene to influence the nation-state hierarchy or with operations able to manipulate policies of this hierarchy or, in the final analysis, veto its decisions by replacing its leaders. This has certainly been typical for some Mediterranean countries but also for other European states, not least Sweden.

Sweden's role in U.S. military strategy depended on trust, and the new Swedish "political line" would have been unacceptable to the Americans in a crisis or even more so in a pre-war situation. Mikael Bentler from the Swedish Security Service (SÄK) told me that in the beginning of 1970s, at the time of the military junta in Greece, the Swedish government supported its Social-Democratic colleagues in the Greek resistance movement. However, at the same time, SÄK bugged the same Greek resistance activists in Sweden and copied their documents, including their telephone books, for the Greek military junta. Or rather, the material was sent to Greece via West Germany, and it was used to arrest Greek Social Democrats when they arrived back home. Bentler held that information on political refugees from South Africa, Chile and Argentina had been passed on to the CIA by the SÄK and that the CIA then forwarded it to these regimes, making possible the arrest and torture of the relatives of the same political refugees. It is a fact, in most civil wars or military coups from the 1960s to the 1980s—in Greece, South Africa, Angola, Mozambique, in Chile, Argentina, Nicaragua, in Vietnam and in Palestine/Israel—the Swedish government and its security services were supporting different sides in the conflict. The Swedish government collaborated with states or national movements at war with U.S.-financed forces, while individuals inside the Swedish security service and within the Swedish military forces collaborated closely with their U.S. or UK counterparts. Olof Frånstedt, Chief of Counter-Intelligence and Chief of Operations at SÄK (1967–1978), said in an interview that inside SÄK "we had a serious traitor, Mikael Bentler." According to Frånstedt, Bentler had gone directly to Prime Minister Palme and informed him about SÄK's activities. Frånstedt also said that he had been informed in the early 1970s by James Jesus Angleton, the CIA's Chief of Counter-Intelligence, and by Peter McKay of MI6, that Palme was believed to be an agent of influence. Palme, according to Angleton, had contacts with a professor, a CIA double agent, who also was working for the KGB. Frånstedt said that he was briefed about it by "James Jesus at his office in Langley."[76]

In the early 1980s, Palme supported the Sandinistas in Nicaragua and the ANC in South Africa, and when President Ronald Reagan tried to isolate the Soviet Union, he worked for a dialogue that included important Western and Soviet representatives. He chaired the Independent Committee for Disarmament and Security,[77] which launched a program for "Common Security" strongly in conflict with U.S. policy.[78] The Committee also proposed a Nuclear Weapons-Free Zone in Europe which would include the Nordic countries and the two Germanys. From the 1980s, Palme's neutrality policy may have led Sweden to try to stay out of an early phase of a NATO–Soviet war, which would seriously have weakened NATO's Northern Flank. At the very outset of a war, Palme could have tried to block U.S. access to Swedish airbases, from which U.S. aircraft would be able to gain air superiority on the Central Front, be able to strike Soviet air defense systems in the Soviet Baltic Republics and provide U.S. long-range bombers with air support. Palme might have been able to block U.S. operations from Swedish territory, including U.S. air strikes against Leningrad and Moscow, and the use of Sweden for landing of the U.S. Marines in the Soviet Baltic Republics,[79] which might have set free a considerable quantity of Soviet forces for use on the Central Front. In November 1983, Peter Wallenberg handed over a British intelligence report to the Swedish Chief of Defense General Lennart Ljung, which indicated that there might be "a Swedish-Soviet pact in the near future" (something Ljung considered totally unfounded). In November 1984, Ljung wrote in his diary that SACEUR, General Bernard Rogers, had told the Volvo Director P. G. Gyllenhammar that he was worried about Sweden's "political line." Henry Kissinger had told Gyllenhammar

---

76 Jallai, A. Interview with Frånstedt, O. April 12, 2011. Available at: http://www.jallai.se/2011/04/palme-misstankt-landsforradare/ (accessed August 18, 2012).

77 Palmekommissionen. 1982. *Gemensam säkerhet – ett program för nedrustning*. Report of the High Commission on Questions of Disarmamernt and Security, chaired by Olof Palme, Stockholm, Tiden.

78 A member of the Committee, later Norwegian prime minister Gro Harlem Brundtland criticized NATO for deploying medium-range nuclear missiles in Europe. According to Norwegian Conservative Prime Minister Kåre Willoch, she "proposed to the Parliament to make decisions that in practice meant that the Norwegian government should support the Soviet Union in the negotiations with NATO." Willoch, K. October 4, 1997. Sovjetunionen, KGB og Arbeiderpartiet. *Aftenposten*, 9.

79 In November 1989, in a conversation I had with Robert Komer, former U.S. Under-Secretary of Defense, he said: "One option for the US Marine Corps was to land three divisions on the Soviet Baltic coast. These forces would have to be transported over the Baltic Sea, for example, from Karlskrona in Sweden."

the same. Sweden was, according to Kissinger, "denied essential information." The problem was the "Political Sweden," not the "Military Sweden."[80]

It is not clear what Kissinger and Rogers refer to, but it is quite likely that they speak about the "Swedish submarine war" in the 1980s. A report from the U.S. Rand Corporation wrote that with 17 to 36 submarine operations (with regular subs, mini-subs, and combat swimmers) per year, "*Soviet intruders began to penetrate into the heart of Sweden's coastal Defense zones*, including the harbours and naval bases" (italics in the original).[81] Milton Leitenberg wrote for the Washington-based Centre for Strategic and International Studies (1987) that these operations were "the first Soviet military-political initiatives against a Western European state since the Berlin crisis of 1960–1961."[82] In three years, the number of Swedes that perceived the Soviet Union as a direct threat increased from 8 percent to 42 percent and the number that perceived the Soviet Union as a threat or unfriendly toward Sweden increased from 33 percent to 83 percent.[83] Prime Minister Palme and his Cabinet could not understand why the Soviets did this, but false "evidence" presented by his admirals forced him to protest strongly against Moscow. The intrusions forced Palme to terminate his foreign policy, his policy for "common security" and his dialogue with Moscow. Local naval commanders received ceasefire orders from the Chief of Defense Staff immediately before passages of submarines they believed originated from the Soviet Union. They blamed Prime Minister Palme. They were furious.[84] Soviet leader Yuri Andropov asked why the Swedish admirals did not use more force; they should sink every submarine that enters Swedish waters so that the Swedes could find out for themselves who was responsible for the intrusions.[85] In 2000, former U.S. Secretary of Defense Caspar Weinberger (1981–1987) and British Minister of Navy Keith Speed (1979–1981) stated on Swedish TV that they had operated submarines both "regularly" and "frequently" in Swedish waters after U.S.–Swedish/UK–Swedish Navy-to-Navy

80 Ljung, L. 1978–1986. See also Mörth, U. and Sundelius, B. 1998. *Interdependens, konflikt och säkerhetspolitik – Sverige och den amerikanska exportkontrollen*. Stockholm: Nerenius och Santerus Förlag. 148.

81 McCormick, G. H. January 1990. *Stranger than Fiction – Soviet Submarine Operations in Swedish Waters*. R-3776-AF. A Project AIR FORCE report prepared for the United States Air Force, Rand Corporation. v.

82 Leitenberg, M. 1987. *Soviet Submarine Operations in Swedish Waters*. New York: Praeger. 155–7.

83 Stütz, G. December 1987. *Opinion 87 – En opinionsundersökning om svenska folkets inställning till några samhälls- och försvarsfrågor hösten 1987*. Stockholm: Styrelsen för psykologiskt försvar. 64.

84 Tunander, O. 2004. *The Secret War against Sweden – US and British Submarine Deception in the 1980s*. London: Frank Cass. The book was published by the Naval Policy and History Series, edited by Geoffrey Till.

85 President Mauno Koivisto. 2008. *Grannar – Frändskap & friktion*. Stockholm/Helsinki: Atlantis/Söderström. 168–72.

consultations.[86] Speed also said: "It was a Navy-to-Navy issue. The Chief of Defense Staff or the Flag Officer Submarines told his Swedish counterpart and it was up to them to inform their government."[87] But they never did. In 2007, at a conference in Norway, I gave Weinberger's Secretary of Navy, John Lehman (1981–1987), a printout of the Weinberger interview. Lehman told me that these operations in Sweden were decided by a "Deception Operation Committee" chaired by Director of the CIA William Casey (1981–1987), which was also mentioned in an interview conducted by the German TV-channel Arte.[88]

In autumn 1985, a number of furious naval officers staged a "revolt"; they went public with their criticism of Prime Minister Palme's handling of the submarine issue. One of these officers, Commander Hans von Hofsten, had participated in a meeting with police officers, according to his superior Commodore Cay Holmberg. They had "discussed the problem [of whether] one could trust Palme or not, and how it would be possible to manage this by removing Palme in one way or another."[89] Defense Minister Thage G. Peterson said that "military circles directed a well-organized attack against Olof Palme" in the months before his trip to Moscow in April 1986.[90] In his memoirs, Peterson writes that he reported the information about the naval officers to the Palme Murder Inquiry.[91] Palme was shot dead at 23:20 on the street outside the Skandia House (the former Thule building) at Sveavägen 44 on February 28, 1986. "Sveavägen" was the street of "mother Sweden"; Thule was the Palme family company, which had been taken over by the Wallenberg family and been turned into the headquarters for the Swedish Stay-Behinds. Ministers, senior military officers and security service officers thought in terms of a dual state and they had a total lack of confidence in each other. The SÄK collaborated closely with its U.S. counterpart, and former Social-Democratic Minister and Ambassador Carl Lidbom—investigating the SÄK after the murder of Palme—told the Chief of SÄK Sune Sandström that it was important that the

86 Interview with Caspar Weinberger on Striptease, *Swedish TV2*. March 7, 2000. Interview with Keith Speed, Striptease, *Swedish TV2*. April 11, 2000.

87 Neroth, P. Email to the editor of *Sunday Times* forwarded to Ola Tunander, February 8, 2008.

88 Conversation with John Lehman, U.S. Maritime Strategy Conference, Bødø (Norway), August 2007. See also Huchthausen, P. and Sheldon-Duplaix, A. 2009. *Hide and Seek: The Untold Story of the Cold War Espionage at Sea*. New Jersey: Wiley. 285; Tunander, O. 2012. Subs and PSYOPs: The 1982 Swedish Submarine Intrusions. *Intelligence and National Security*, forthcoming. Available at http://www.tandfonline.com/doi/pdf/10.1080/02684527.2012.699294 (accessed July 15, 2012).

89 Commodore Cay Holmberg interviewed in Striptease, *Swedish TV2*. March 31, 1999.

90 Interview with Defense Minister Tage G. Peterson Norra Magasinet, *Swedish TV1*. February 21, 1996.

91 Peterson, T. G. 1999. *Resan mot Mars – Anteckningar och minnen*. Stockholm: Bonniers. 557.

government had confidence in the SÄK. According to Lidbom, Sandström replied that "it is equally important that SÄK has confidence in the government."[92]

In early and mid 1980s, the U.S. security state no longer trusted "Political Sweden" and signaled its discontent to its Swedish security elite. "Political Sweden" was playing around with trust and there was a strong pressure for removing the dissident element. Former Chief of Operations at SÄK, Olof Frånstedt, argued that the Palme Murder Inquiry should primarily have focused on Palme as a possible traitor; the killing was most likely a political murder, he claimed. When the Palme Murder Inquiry ignored this aspect, it either did not know what it was doing, Frånstedt said, or it ignored this fact precisely because it knew what it was doing.[93] In other words, it knew that it had to present a cover-up. Former Swedish Foreign Minister Sten Andersson stated that it was a group within SÄK that operated against Prime Minister Palme and looked upon him as a "threat to Swedish security."[94] At a press conference in 1985, Bertil Wedin, a London-based consultant and South African intelligence operative, as well as a former Swedish intelligence officer, editor of the Wallenberg bank newsletter and a Swedish representative to the World Anti-Communist League (WACL), said:

> I am working against Palme and the Swedish Government. I am doing that in cooperation with the intelligence services in the Scandinavian countries. For me it is important to work against Palme. SÄK and the Swedish military are clearly in conflict with its own Government.[95]

The South African colonel and death squad leader Eugene de Kock told the Truth and Reconciliation Commission in 1996 that South African agent Craig Williamson as well as his subordinate Bertil Wedin had been involved in the Palme murder.[96] Two English-speaking men, with an accent believed to be South African, had told two witnesses in Stockholm two weeks before the murder that they were in Sweden to kill Palme. They had displayed several weapons, one a gun equipped with a silencer that corresponded to the weapon that was used for the murder.[97] But there were also a number of other warnings. Eight days before the killing, a

92 Lidbom, C. 1990. *Ett uppdrag*. Stockholm: Wahlström and Widstrand. 50.

93 Jallai interview with Olof Frånstedt 2011.

94 Sten Andersson interviewed in Striptease, *Swedish TV2*. March 31, 1999.

95 Bertil Wedin quoted in Poutianen, K. and Poutianen, P. 1995. *Inuti labyrinten – Om mordet på Palme*. Smedjebacken: Grimur Förlag. 726.

96 South African History Online. September 26, 1996. Available at: www.sahistory.org.za/dated-event/de-kock-alleges-sa-secret-agent-shot-olof-palme (accessed July 12, 2012); Daley, S. September 27, 1996. South African Links Top Spy to the Slaying of Palme. *The New York Times*. Available at: http:en.wikipedia.org/wiki/Bertil_Wedin (accessed July 12, 2012).

97 Borgnäs, L. 2006. *En iskall vind drog genom Sverige: Mordet på Palme*. Stockholm: Norstedts. 374–7.

former representative of the then CIA-led WACL,[98] Anders Larsson, handed in a warning to Palme and to Foreign Minister Sten Andersson about the upcoming killing of Palme. The information supposedly came from right-wingers close to SÄK; they wanted to stop Palme's trip to Moscow. The decision had been taken by the CIA's Covert Action Department, Larsson argued.[99] The Governor of the city of Norrköping, Henry Eriksson, reported to the Prime Minister's Office six weeks before the killing that SÄK/police officers (linked to the WACL) were preparing a coup d'état against Palme before his meeting with Mikhail Gorbachev in Moscow in April 1986.[100] In December 1985, a MI6 officer, "Mack" Falkirk, was able to copy the agenda for Palme's meeting with Gorbachev. According to Falkirk, this agenda had then been used by the CIA in Stockholm to agitate before Swedish officers for the removal of Palme.[101] Five weeks, three weeks and one week before the murder, a Swedish-Yugoslav mercenary, Ivan von Birchan, reported to the Stockholm local government and to the police that he had been offered two million dollars for the killing of Palme, by a comrade in arms from Rhodesia, a CIA agent "Charles Morgan," who also worked with the Contras in Honduras, who were, in turn, financed by the WACL.[102]

The killing of Prime Minister Palme is still not solved, but at the time the degree of conflict between the democratic state and the security state was certainly unacceptable to both sides, and the serious Cold War tension led the United States and UK to consider the Swedish government a threat to the Northern Flank. While the Military Sweden, according to James Schlesinger, was "planning to get the USA involved as soon as possible," the Political Sweden was seemingly blocking U.S. access to Sweden, which was more than just problematic because of the increasingly tense relations with the Soviet Union throughout the early 1980s. The Swedish political idea of "neutrality," a nation-state with different options, may have created a Swedish illusion of "freedom of choice." Former Swedish Minister of Defense Anders Thunborg told me in November 1998 that "In case of a war, we had several options and the decision-making was in our hands."[103] However,

98 Major General John Singlaub, who had worked for the CIA already from 1947, became the leader of WACL in 1981. WACL was at the time strongly linked to South-American death squads. Anderson, Scott and Anderson, Jon Lee. 1986. *Inside the League: The Shocking Expose of How Terrorists, Nazis and Latin-American Death Squads have Infiltrated the World Anti-Communist League*. New York: Dodd Mead.

99 Borgnäs, L. 2006. 368–71; Poutianen, K. and Poutianen, P. 1995. 507–35; International Foundation for Contemporary Studies [Anders Larsson] 1990. Aktuell information (4 pages), Buggningsmålet i Stockholm (private archive).

100 Borgnäs, L. 2006. 360–366.

101 The *Dagens Nyheter* journalist Olle Alsén's interview with E. O. "Mack" Falkirk (private archive).

102 Interview with von Birchan. Available at: http://www.youtube.com/watch?v=2mvXwYqp1kM (accessed July 12, 2012).

103 My interview with former Swedish Minister of Defense Anders Thunborg in November 1998.

letting the access to Swedish airbases depend on "pure chance," on the views of a Swedish prime minister and his Cabinet, may not have been a U.S. preference. And then, when U.S. plans for assisting Sweden depended on ties not defined in written documents but solely on trust between individuals, the lack of trust in the prime minister became a major security concern. The U.S. security state may have considered the Swedish government an internal Swedish problem as long as the Swedish security state was able to take necessary measures to remove the threat to the Northern Flank.

Here, the sovereign is, in the final analysis, the U.S.-led security hierarchy that demanded a change in Swedish policy. The Schmittian *Reich* had primacy over the nation-state, and the security state had primacy over the regular democratic state, which implies a divided state, or in Morgenthau's words, a dual state. The conflict between the Political Sweden and a U.S.-linked Military Sweden had become unacceptable. Carl Schmitt recognized that, in the final analysis, the sovereign is not "double." The dual state represents a real duality, but in the final analysis, in case of emergency, it is not the democratic state but the security state that will intervene and veto a certain policy, and in the Western world the U.S. security state and its networks inside the single states have had the last word. Or to quote Carl Schmitt: "The sovereign is he who decides on the exception."

Chapter 9
Canadian Stalking Horse: "A Parallel Power"[1]

David MacGregor

> After one century, homo canadiensis remained hazy, incapable of defining himself in any convincing fashion … In a country that lacked consistency to this point, Trudeau was far from being the only one to refuse to recognize two nations, that is, the tough reality of ours compared to the non-existence of the Anglo-Canadian one. The new Quebec bothered them. It was beginning to make them all frightened.
>
> Rene Levèsque[2]

> I think the society must take every means at its disposal to defend itself against the emergence of a parallel power which defies the elected power in this country and I think that goes to any distance. So long as there is a power in here which is challenging the elected representative of the people I think that power must be stopped and I think it's only, I repeat, weak-kneed bleeding hearts who are afraid to take these measures.
>
> Pierre Trudeau[3]

> It is my hope that some day the full details of the intelligence upon which the government acted can be made public, because until that day comes the people of Canada will not be able fully to appraise the course of action which has been taken by the government.
>
> John Turner[4]

In world-historical consciousness, Canada is mostly present by its absence. As time drifts from epoch-making events, Canada's formerly acknowledged contribution

---

1 The research assistance provided by Ms Julie Richardson and Ms Samantha Scheepers has been vital to the completion of this chapter.

2 Levèsque, R. 1986. *Memoirs*. Toronto: McClelland and Stewart. 228.

3 Trudeau's "Just Watch Me" Interview with Tim Ralfe of CBC and Peter Reilly of CJON-TV. October 30, 1970. Available at: http://faculty.marianopolis.edu/c.belanger/quebechistory/docs/october/watchme.htm (accessed July 15, 2012).

4 Minister of Justice John Turner. 1 October 16, 1970. "The Explanation given by John Turner, Minister of Justice, for Invoking the War Measures Act." House of Commons. Available at: http://faculty.marianopolis.edu/c.belanger/quebechistory/docs/october/turner.htm (accessed July 15, 2012).

tends to shrink and disappear—or was barely recognized in the first place.[5] I want to suggest that Canada may be more significant in global affairs than usually admitted—a kind of stalking horse. The *Front de libération du Québec* (FLQ)—our story in this chapter—may have functioned as a model for advanced capitalist terrorist groups, though it is now almost forgotten. Contiguous to the Russian bear and the American eagle, direct offspring of the British lion and the Gallic rooster, the reclusive Canadian beaver thrives on secrecy and guile, a geopolitical pivot for a covert union of espionage, crime and commerce. Pierre Elliott Trudeau said that living next to the United States was "like sleeping with an elephant." Among mammals, the elephant and the beaver—like Pinocchio's nose—continue growing until they die. But rather than the eagle/elephant, Canada may well be still sleeping with the lion.

In the late 1940s American sociologist Everett C. Hughes published an epochal book called *French Canada in Transition*. The book reached a large audience in both Canada and the United States, appearing in multiple editions. Hughes wrote in the Preface to the 1963 edition that:

> French Canadians are … now the senior national minority in the western world; perhaps, instead of being proud of that position, they are wounded to think that minorities—younger, poorer, less educated and cultivated than they—have achieved a national status which they, the French Canadians, have never really sought in large number and with continued determination. Quebec remains a crucial spot for observing changes of a kind which are now occurring in many parts of the world.[6]

Hughes' words might have served as an announcement for the FLQ, which began its campaign of bombings in 1963.

Carl Schmitt formulated the "theory of the partisan" in 1962, one year before the first FLQ bombs exploded. Schmitt defined a new form of irregular warfare that would replace conventional wars between states with desultory but deadly conflict pursued by guerilla groups: shadowy figures occupying a liminal space between the soldier and the civilian. Like Schmitt's classic partisan, the FLQ believed in a war of "absolute enmity"—but the "concrete absolute enemy" was not only the "class enemy" postulated by Schmitt, but an ethnic opponent—*les canadiens anglaises* and their fraternal allies, the British. The key issue for the

---

5 For example, Canadian troops made up a large contingent of the Expeditionary Force sent into Russia after the armistice of November, 1918. Dieppe featured the deliberate mass sacrifice of Canadian troops so that Britain could prove to the Russians that a second front in the West was impossible in 1942. The Cold War started in Ottawa with the desertion of Soviet cyber clerk Igor Gouzenko. Gouzenko's defection led directly to Churchill's Iron Curtain speech, the Second Red Scare and Senator McCarthy. Pearson's interventions over Egypt/Suez in 1956 signaled that the British Empire as a visible entity at least was finished.

6 2009. *French Canada in Transition*, Oxford: Oxford University Press. vii–viii.

partisan is to remain legitimate, to avoid falling into the category of the criminal. For purposes of investigating the FLQ, Schmitt's definition of the partisan is useful: "The modern partisan expects neither law nor mercy from the enemy. He has moved away from the conventional enmity of controlled and bracketed war, and into the realm of another, real enmity, which intensifies through terror and counter-terror until it ends in extermination."[7]

FLQ terrorism reached its peak in October 1970, when terrorist events were hardly underway in Italy and elsewhere in Europe. The Piazza Fontana bombing in Milan, for example, took place on December 12, 1969. Daniele Ganser in *NATO's Secret Armies*[8] suggests that the "strategy of tension" characterizing European politics in the 1970s and 1980s was a product of terrorism carried out by NATO's "stay behind" armies, originally set up to offer resistance to an expected Soviet invasion of Europe. From this perspective, state-sponsored provocations in Europe, disguised as left-wing or right-wing terrorism, may have headed off socialist and communist electoral victories. While the "stay behinds" thesis may not explain the FLQ (no one credibly feared a Soviet invasion of Canada), the overt Marxist leanings of the notorious Québéçois terrorist group may have encouraged belief in Europe (subsequently disproved) that terrorism emanated mainly from the left: perhaps, once again, Canada affirmed its role as a stalking horse.

Quebec's State of Exception

On October 17, 1970, two reporters discovered a late model, green Chevrolet containing the body of Laporte, Liberal cabinet minister in the Quebec provincial government. FLQ kidnappers evidently strangled Laporte after holding him for a week. A day before, Prime Minister Trudeau proclaimed the War Measures Act, suspending civil liberties and proscribing the FLQ. In an early morning sweep police jailed more than 450 Québéçois. Laporte's death represented the climax of seven years of terrorism, though the release on December 3, 1970 of another kidnap victim, British trade commissioner James Richard Cross, and a strange assassination in Paris a few months later finally concluded this incredible Canadian saga.[9]

---

7 Schmitt, C. 2007. *Theory of the Partisan: Intermediate Commentary on the Concept of the Political*, trans. G. L. Ulmen. New York: Telos Press Publishing. 10–11.

8 Ganser, D. 2005. *NATO's Secret Armies: Operation GLADIO and Terrorism in Western Europe*. Frank Cass: London. 6–7. Available at: http://sandiego.indymedia.org/media/2006/10/119640.pdf see pp. 6–7 (accessed February 26, 2012).

9 McLoughlin, M. 1998. *End Game in Paris: The Assassination of Mario Bachand and the Death of the FLQ*. Toronto: Viking. The FLQ lumbered forward after December 1970, but mostly as a (belatedly acknowledged) vehicle of the Royal Canadian Mounted Police (RCMP). See below.

The FLQ story involves more than "a history of Canadian unpleasantness," to borrow a phrase from the American comic novel *Infinite Jest*, which partly revolves around an FLQ-style double agent working for U.S. intelligence.[10] The FLQ claimed inspiration from Third World Liberation groups, such as the Tupamaros of Uraguay. The group's name, and its de-colonization strategy was inspired by the Algerian Front de libération nationale (FLN), and the Vietnamese Front Nationale de Libération.[11] We shall see that many intelligence services became involved in some way with the FLQ affair. Paris, in particular, worried about "a French connection" with the FLQ. The French ambassador to Canada "conceded that the style of FLQ tracts and actions suggested these could have been inspired by advice from French nationals."[12] Although French officials denied it—pointing to the FLQ's revolutionary rhetoric—another probable model for the FLQ was the far-right OAS (l'Organisation de l'armée secrète), founded in 1961 and mostly destroyed a year later with the arrest of its leader. The OAS included top French military and intelligence officers opposed to a settlement with insurgents in Algeria. The OAS waged a bloody terrorist war in the French colony, often disguising its attacks to enable attribution to anti-colonialist forces. The OAS sponsored several assassination attempts against President De Gaulle, who ordered French withdrawal from Algeria in 1962. The revolutionary victory in Algeria "triggered a seismic wave of anti-colonial movements across the Third World, serving both as a millennial image of freedom and a more practical lesson in the violent means necessary to win it."[13] Pontecorvo's striking 1966 film version of the Algerian revolution, "The Battle of Algiers," likely had little impact on the development of the FLQ, but it influenced the Black Panthers in the United States, and other 1960s resistance groups.

Franz Fanon's anti-colonialist writings, grounded in the Algerian experience, struck a chord within the intellectual milieu of the FLQ.[14] Armed resistance,

10 Wallace, D. F. 1996. *Infinite Jest*. New York: Little Brown. Foster's novel may be an exception to the rule that the FLQ has disappeared from literary-political consciousness.

11 See Fournier's discussion in Fournier, L. 1984. *FLQ: The Anatomy of an Underground Movement*, trans. E. Baxter. Toronto: NC Press Limited. 21–2. See also Meren, D. 2007. *Les sanglots longs de la violence de l'automne*: French Diplomacy Reacts to the October Crisis. *The Canadian Historical Review*, 88/4, 624–5.

12 "Canada's Joint Intelligence Committee (JIC) was convinced that close links existed between the FLQ and French intelligence services, and that the activities of these services and related agencies – at least in the form of moral support – during the FLQ's formative years were an important factor in facilitating its growth." Meren, D. 2007, 624.

13 Matthews, P. 2004. The Battle of Algiers: Bombs and Boomerangs, in *The Criterion Collection: Film Essays*. Available at: www.criterion.com/current/posts/342-the-battle-of-algiers-bombs-and-boomerangs (accessed October 30, 2011).

14 Brian Palmer suggests that Fanon's global influence was first felt in Quebec, where his writings made a huge impact" "at least when the influence is discussed in terms of Canada and the United States." Palmer, B. 2009. *Canada's 1960s: The Ironies of Identity in a Rebellious Era*. Toronto: University of Toronto Press. 544.

taught Fanon, offered an escape route from "alienation and helplessness." Québéçois writer Herbert Aquin's revolutionary separatist protagonist of the classic *Prochaine épisode* believes that "the terrorist act is the first act of the people's autonomous history … 'Our history will begin at the unknown moment when the revolutionary war begins … That day, with open veins, we will enter the world … Actions will prevail.'"[15] The FLQ also bore close resemblance to the U.S. Black Panthers (with whom the FLQ allied itself at one point)—and not just because of Pierre Vallières' *White Niggers of America*, published in 1968:

> Black nationalism—like French Canadian separatism—is of inestimable service to revolutionaries in that it forces them to envision the liberation of the whole man and enables them to avoid the half-revolutions which, as soon as they are victorious, change into the oppression of racial, linguistic, religious or other minorities.[16]

Quebec terrorists shared important linkages, including "a crude sort of marxism,"[17] with revolutionary groups that emerged later in highly industrialized capitalist countries. Chilling similarities, such as the fate of Laporte and the assassination almost eight years later of Italian Prime Minister Moro, emerge between the FLQ and various groups operating in Europe, such as the Red Brigades and the Red Army Faction. In the case of both the murdered French Canadian and Italian politicians, for example, the government suspended civil liberties, instituting a classic Schmittian state of exception. Seven years almost to the day of Laporte's death, on October 18, 1977, police discovered the bullet-riddled body of Red Army Faction kidnap victim, German industrialist Hanns-Martin Schleyer in the trunk of a green Audi 100—a critical event in the "German Autumn."[18] Similar

15 Aquin, H. 2001. *Next Episode*, trans. S. Fishman. Toronto: The New Canadian Library. 65 cited in Kostash, Myrna. 1980. *Long Way from Home: The Story of the Sixties Generation in Canada*. Toronto: Lorimer. 213.

16 Vallières, P. 1971. *White Niggers of America*. Toronto: McLelland and Stewart Limited. 52.

17 The Only Way. *Economist*, October 24, 1970. Issue 6635. 13.

18 In *Year of the Gun*, a novel about Moro's kidnapping, the protagonist is "overcome by déjà vu" while reconnoitering the home of the Italian leader. "When he circled around Via Camillucia and returned to the intersection, he experienced the same uncanny certainty of having seen the place before. This time, however, he understood why. Although he had never seen this neighborhood, he had studied photographs of a spot just like it—the one in Germany where Hanns-Martin Schleyer had been abducted … [Moro's] was a community of no charm, no personality. That was its point, its reason for being. People who lived there were tired of Italy's excess of personality, sick of Rome's charming eccentricities, and more than willing to trade the *centro storico* for cleanliness, quiet, and privacy." Mewshaw, M. 1984. 185–6. Laporte's modest suburban neighborhood in St Hubert on the outskirts of Montreal, so remote from the lively European ambience of downtown, may have also signaled a desire for privacy and quiet.

to Laporte and Moro, German authorities refused to negotiate with Schleyer's abductors. Terrorist kidnappers in Quebec and Rome—as in Germany—did not receive the expected surge of support from among the broad masses. Instead, most people turned away, disgusted and frightened by the spectacle of senseless murder. Moro wrote Italy's leaders anguished letters pleading for rescue; seven years earlier Laporte had done the same, appealing to Prime Minister Trudeau and Quebec Premier Bourassa. In the case of both Moro and Laporte grieving families opposed a state funeral, believing that authorities betrayed their loved one. And in both instances lavish state funerals occurred despite family opposition. While the Moro kidnapping on Rome's Via Fani engendered a growing critical literature about "Italy's JFK," the official story of Laporte and the FLQ is rarely questioned, especially in Anglophone Canada.

The FLQ chronicle has at least as many alternative versions as *Last Year at Marienbad.*[19] Indeed like Alan Resnais' film, the history of the FLQ "toys with our expectations regarding plotline, character development, continuity, conflict, resolution."[20] It is not for nothing that the literary classic emerging from the FLQ years, Hubert Aquin's *Next Episode*, concerns a conflicted separatist double agent operating in Lausanne whose mirrored loyalties leave him in the final analysis with "several open-necked Hathaway shirts [and] some books scattered here and there" in an apartment on Montreal's Sherbrooke Street West.[21] Aquin's novel is no ordinary feat of the imagination. A widely known Quebec media commentator and literary analyst, he joined the FLQ at its inception. Arrested and jailed in 1964 for carrying an unregistered handgun, he wrote *Prochaine Episode* in a psychiatric ward while serving his sentence. Aquin shot himself 12 years later.

A critical aspect of the FLQ chronicle is that its founding preceded the period of 1960s activism in Canada and the United States, and may have served as a detonator for political protest in North America. Four major variations on the FLQ theme are rehearsed in the literature concerning the 1970 October Crisis that climaxed the terrorist group's history. There is the official account that a daring seven-year-long series of sensational provocations by a rag-tag group of *Felquistes* caught politicians and police flat-footed. From a more critical perspective, the RCMP and Quebec police knew more than they claimed at the time. In a third rendering, intelligence services desperately tried to alert elected officials to imminent FLQ danger, but a feckless political class ignored them with fatal results. All three of these approaches take for granted that the FLQ (at least until after the October Crisis) was an autonomous terrorist group, and was solely responsible for murdering Laporte. A fourth, mostly samizdat, narrative insists

19 Polizzotti, M. 2009. "Which Year at Where?" *Last Year at Marienbad.* DVD Booklet. The Criterion Collection. 7.

20 Polizzoti, M. *Last Year at Marienbad: Which Year at Where?* From Criterion. Posted June 23, 2009. Available at: www.criterion.com/current/posts/1177 (accessed July 7, 2012).

21 Aquin, H. 2001. 112.

that the federal power under Trudeau deliberately fomented the crisis in order to severely weaken its separatist opponents.

This chapter tentatively offers a fifth possibility: that the FLQ episode may have been part of a global terrorist "strategy of tension" aimed at tilting advanced capitalist governments in an authoritarian direction. (A much bloodier version of this strategy occurred in Latin America, where manufactured terrorist violence justified mass disappearances in Argentina, Chile and Bolivia.) Guido Preparata capsulizes the leftist version of the "strategy of tension" as applied to domestic Italian politics: "the string of bomb attacks that went off (from 1969 to 1974) are to be seen as manifest acts of provocation secretly promoted by the regime itself in order to fend off, insulate, and fight back the mounting tide of progressivism sparked by the protests of 1968."[22] Prime Minister Trudeau famously observed on the eve of the War Measure Act (apparently referring to the FLQ) that a "parallel power" had appeared on the Canadian scene. Trudeau's impromptu remarks in response to unscripted queries from an aggressively inquisitive reporter in a scrum at the entrance of Parliament deserve quotation:

> I think the society must take every means at its disposal to defend itself against the emergence of a parallel power which defies the elected power in this country and I think that goes to any distance. So long as there is a power in here which is challenging the elected representative of the people I think that power must be stopped and I think it's only, I repeat, weak-kneed bleeding hearts who are afraid to take these measures.[23]

In retrospect, this "parallel power" may have been Canada's shadow government among its intelligence and military networks operating in concert with British, U.S. and other foreign security services, together with organized crime. Perhaps this may explain the occult resemblances between high profile kidnap operations that seized Laporte and Moro. Following a brief sketch of Quebec politics in mid-century, and a glance at the history of the FLQ, my chapter offers a critical examination of the official story of October, and its revisionist sequels. I turn then to Pierre Vallières' radical deconstruction of October and his views on the meaning of the crisis. Concluding sections present an alternative thesis that takes into account recent research on police infiltration and control of terrorist groups, in the 20-year period, 1963–1983.

---

22 Preparata, G. The Bogeyman: The Story of a Political Soldier and Elements for the Sociology of Terrorism. Available at: www.guidopreparata.com/chpg/Bogeyman.pdf (accessed July 7, 2012).

23 Trudeau's "Just Watch Me" Interview with Tim Ralfe of CBC and Peter Reilly of CJON-TV. October 30, 1970. Available at: http://faculty.marianopolis.edu/c.belanger/quebechistory/docs/october/watchme.htm (accessed July 7, 2012).

Duplessis = Duplicity

Premier Duplessis' Union Nationale party, in alliance with the Roman Catholic Church, dominated Quebec after World War II. Except for a scattering of predominantly Anglophone towns, rural communities were solidly Francophone and heavily influenced by the Church. English-speaking big business, including U.S. and British firms, monopolized the province's vast resources in mining, forestry and hydroelectric power. An English Canadian elite held sway over Montreal. In the remote capital of Quebec City, a conservative French-speaking petit bourgeoisie leveraged powerful government institutions. Except for the Maritime's Acadian community, and a few Francophone islands elsewhere, Quebec was an isolated outpost of French culture, "the largest French-speaking population … outside France."[24] Duplessis took advantage of Quebec's unique status and distinct institutions, making the fabulously rich province his own personal fiefdom. Deference to the "French fact" largely inhibited criticism from English Canada. In his remarkable 1960 biography, Laporte, then a political columnist for *Le Devoir*, highlights Duplessis'

> brutality when election time came around, or, if one wishes to put it another way, his ferocious electoral battles to keep the reigns of power he had wrested from the Liberals in 1944. Some opponents were so roughly handled by the Duplessis machine that they might have wondered whether they were candidates for a parliamentary riding or a jail cell.[25]

During Duplessis' years in office, rapid industrialization transformed Quebec's agricultural and resource-based economy and new social layers, including a strong Québéçois working class, emerged that shunned the Church and repressive values trumpeted by the premier, who died in 1959. Duplessis' successor, the charismatic Paul Sauvé, launched the "Quiet Revolution" with an extraordinary radio address ("From now on …") pledging an end to "Duplessism," and a new horizon for Quebec. In July 1960, provincial elections projected a Liberal government under Jean Lesage, whose motto was "Maîtres chez nous" (Masters in Our Own House).

By 1963, urbanization in Quebec had caught up to the province of Ontario, after a 10-year time lag. While the two provinces shared an equal urban:rural split (91:9 percent), transformation in Quebec had been more dramatic and intense than in the rest of Canada. Unemployment in the province stood at more than 10 percent. According to demographer Nathan Keyfitz, writing in the same year, Quebec was caught up in:

---

24 Bosher, J. F. 2000. *The Gaullist Attack on Canada, 1967–1997*. Montreal: McGill Queens University Press. 4.

25 Laporte, P. 1960. 140.

> the *politique de grandeur*, which has its roots in these demographic facts and draws on French Canadian history and aspirations. It is reflected in the pride of Montrealers in the accomplishments of Hydro-Quebec, in the *metro* which is being built, and in the World's Fair of 1967 [Expo 67]—their way of celebrating 100 years of Confederation. Many of them hope that this anniversary will also celebrate the advent of a larger constitutional position for what in anticipation they will call the *Etat du Quèbec*.[26]

Duplessis set the stage for an "autonomous Quebec," introducing a provincial flag and inventing a tradition of pomp and circumstance for parliamentary gatherings.[27] Indeed, the epochal slogan employed by Jean Lesage's Liberals ("maîtres chez nous") was invented at the beginning of the 20th century and became a rhetorical mainstay under Duplessis. However, the Lesage government would be the first Quebec administration to refuse to take part in programs developed and funded by the federal government. Often Quebec initiatives would differ only mildly from the federal model (e.g. the Quebec Pension Plan versus the Canada Pension Plan) but the precedent was set for Quebec opting out of shared cost programs. "This produced an asymmetry between Quebec and the rest of Canada, conceding to the government of Quebec in effect, if not in theory, what came to be called special status—all this within the context of the existing Canadian constitution."[28]

Nationalization of the province's massive power grid was an important accomplishment of the Lesage government, under Minister of Natural Resources, René Lévesque.[29] However, the Liberals soon divided amongst "federalists," like Laporte, who opted for keeping the province within a united Canada, and "indépendantistes," such as Lévesque, who turned toward a sovereign Québéçois state, and became leader of the newly formed Parti Québéçois in 1968. A radical separatist group founded in 1960 and headed in the mid-1960s by Pierre Bourgault called Rassemblement pour l'indépendance nationale (RIN) later spawned, among others, a nationalist-Marxist fringe calling itself the FLQ. The FLQ's original members included Pierre Vallières—who had been appointed in 1962 by Pierre Elliott Trudeau, as editor of *Cité Libre*, the anti-Duplessis, anti-clericalist and socialist journal co-founded by Trudeau in 1950. Within a few years of the Liberal victory, FLQ terrorism grabbed newspaper headlines in the province and the rest of Canada.

---

26 Keyfitz, N. 2009. Foreword to Hughes, E. C. ed. *French Canada in Transition*. xiv.

27 Black, C. 1998. *Render Unto Caesar: The Life and Legacy of Duplessis*. Toronto: Key Porter Books Limited.

28 Bothwell, R. 1999. *Canada and Quebec: One Country, Two Histories*. Revised Edition. Vancouver: UBC Press. 119.

29 Levèsque, R. 1986. 168–78. Lévesque's autobiography provides a fascinating look at Quebec politics in the mid-20th century.

Five Scenarios in Search of a Perpetrator

There are at least five major variants of the FLQ narrative leading to the October Crisis of 1970. The first is the widely summoned official version, already mooted above, that a sporadically active, seven-year-old Quebec terrorist group surprised politicians and police in October 1970 with daring kidnappings that shook the established order. At first the FLQ attacked the hated emblem of the British crown inscribed on every government mailbox. "In May 1963, mailboxes were blown up, and one attempt to dismantle a bomb led to the death of Army demolition expert, Sergeant Walter Leja." Police work rapidly brought results. Within a month authorities arrested 16 members of one cell. "The leader, Georges Schoeters, turned out to be a Belgian who had trained in terrorism in Belgium and Cuba."[30] Schoeters founded the FLQ along with two young Québéçois, one still in his teens.

> Schoeters, age 33, was a Belgian-born immigrant to Quebec. Schoeters, who had met Fidel Castro when Castro came to Montreal in 1959, and who had travelled extensively to Cuba, drew his motivation from Third World Marxist humanism. Cuban and Algerian flags and pictures of Castro and Che Guevara hung on the walls of his apartment on Côte-des-Neiges Boulevard, 26 and, when appearing in court after being arrested for his FLQ activities, he insisted on swearing on *The Wretched of the Earth* rather than the Bible.[31]

Despite the arrest of its leader, new iterations of the group sprang up like mushrooms, only to be destroyed or deactivated by the authorities.

In 1964, raids on armouries equipped the terrorists with machine guns, rifles and pistols, and ammunition. Again arrests followed, and this time the leader was one François Schirm, a Hungarian who had served in the French Foreign Legion and had established an FLQ training camp in the Laurentians. Two years later, yet another cell of the FLQ, led this time by an intellectual and writer named Pierre Vallières (who had for a time, been editor of *Cité Libre*, Trudeau's magazine), stole dynamite and rifles and, in bombing a factory, killed a 64-year-old woman, Therese Morin.[32]

Experts imputed the repeated survival of the FLQ to its "classic cellular organization." Organized into "very small cells, some as tiny as two or three members," no member knew any FLQ militants except the ones in his or her cell. Accordingly, "Montreal police chief Marcel St. Aubin said he was having trouble investigating the FLQ because of 'the internal organization of the movement, as it

30 Granatstein, J. 1998. *Spy Wars: Espionage and Canada*. Darby, PA: Diane Publishing Co. 206.

31 Mills, S. 2010. *The Empire Within: Postcolonial Thought and Political Activism in Sixties Montreal*. Montreal: McGill-Queens. 66; Laurendeau, M. 1990. *Les Québécois violents: la violence politique 1962–1972*. Montréal: Boréal. 121–2.

32 Granatstein, J. 1998.

is divided into numerous small cells.'"[33] The RCMP estimated that the entire FLQ membership including peripheral sympathizers amounted to 2,000 individuals. Official conspiracy theories abounded.

Canadian political leaders and the military believed that the FLQ relied heavily on foreign support. Two or three thousand French conscripts doing duty as language teachers and assistants in business offices in Canada fell under suspicion. But suspects also included agents from Algeria, the Soviet Union, Cuba and other Latin American countries.[34] The CIA and British intelligence joined the list of foreign agencies suspected of having some connection with Québéçois terrorism.

Although estimates of FLQ strength were subsequently ratcheted downwards to about 10 or 20 individuals, the official version suggested nonetheless that the FLQ represented a real threat to democracy. Speaking in the midst of the national emergency, Federal Minister of Regional Economic Expansion Jean Marchand offered: "We know there is an organization that has thousands of rifles and machine guns in their possession, and dynamite enough, about two thousand pounds, to blow up the heart of the city of Montreal."[35] In his October 16 television address to the nation on the War Measures Act, Trudeau confided, "The kidnappers' purposes would be served equally well by having in their grip you or me, or perhaps some child."[36] Once alive to the FLQ threat, authorities duly apprehended the culprits of October and sentenced them to long prison terms, thus erasing the movement that had been extensively penetrated anyway by the RCMP in the aftermath of the crisis.

Interestingly, the mainstream account of October differs little from the line penned later by Francis Simard, convicted member of the Chenier cell that kidnapped and murdered Laporte and later, an author of several books on the FLQ.[37] Theories (like those of Vallières and Lévesque) suggesting infiltration by security services are "downright stupid and dishonest," Simard writes. There is no reason to suspect that "the Army, the police or the mob" finished Laporte. "Sincerity," offers Simard, is a watchword of the FLQ. "Without going into all the details, we always took responsibility for Laporte's death. After our arrest and during the trial that followed, we admitted we were totally responsible …

33 Chodos, R. and Auf der Maur, N. eds. 1972. *Quebec: A Chronicle, 1968–1972.* Toronto: Lorimer. 51.

34 Bosher, J. F. 2000. 149.

35 Levèsque, R. 1986. 247.

36 "P. Elliott Trudeau's Televised Statement on the War Measures Act." October 16, 1970. Available at: http://faculty.marianopolis.edu/c.belanger/quebechistory/docs/october/trudeau.htm (accessed July 7, 2012).

37 Simard, F. 1987. *Talking It Out: The October Crisis from Inside*, trans. D. Homel. Toronto: Guernica Editions. Originally published as *Pour en finir avec Octobre. Éditions International Alain Stanké.* Simard's book was made into a motion picture called *Octobre* in 1994.

We never said it was an accident. We never claimed it was someone else." Sentenced to life in prison in 1971, Simard was paroled 11 years later.

In scenario two, a more critical version of the official story outlined for instance by Nino Ricci in his recent biography of Trudeau, the RCMP and Quebec police knew more than they claimed at the time of the October Crisis. They had sufficient warning of FLQ plans to prevent the kidnapping of Cross, and the murder of Laporte. Prime Minister Trudeau did not initially trust RCMP claims about the FLQ, and resisted extra-constitutional action. Events in Quebec, including calls for a coalition government to replace Premier Bourassa's faltering regime—for security reasons, Bourassa "in panic" and "showing signs of shock"[38] had moved his entire cabinet from Quebec City to the Queen Elizabeth Hotel in Montreal—and public support for so-called FLQ political prisoners, pushed Trudeau to invoke the Act, following an official request from Premier Bourassa. Trudeau was correct to reject negotiations with the kidnappers, "on the legitimate grounds that conciliation would only encourage further terrorist acts. In future years, this logic would in fact come to define the official response to terrorism around the world."[39] (As we have seen, among authorities so encouraged were Italian Christian Democrats who refused to bargain with Moro's abductors.) For this account of the FLQ, the RCMP role assumes in retrospect a darker cast.

> Most damning were the revelations that the RCMP had carried out a number of actions after the crisis to indicate continuing FLQ activity, including false FLQ communiqués, stealing dynamite and infamously burning down a barn that belonged to an imprisoned FLQ member's mother … Given that anti-terrrorist police had so infiltrated the FLQ by that point as to constitute virtually its only members, the RCMP activities seemed aimed not at terrorism but at discrediting the separatist movement as a whole.[40]

A third scenario, in some ways a polar opposite of scenario two, claims that intelligence services of the RCMP tried to warn elected officials of imminent FLQ danger, but a feckless political establishment ignored warnings until too late. Unfairly blamed for October, and bulldozed by vengeful politicians into extreme measures following the crisis, the now-tainted RCMP intelligence service lost a subsequent bureaucratic battle to newcomer CSIS (the Canadian Security Intelligence Service—apparently named after its British counterpart, SIS), which captured most of the RCMP's intelligence function. From this perspective, the great irony is that the authoritarian mandate of CSIS normalized the "dirty tricks" and widespread spying on the Canadian public that had brought the RCMP into disrepute. Important to this interpretation is the idea that the RCMP was initially

---

38 Levèsque, R. 1986. 244.

39 Ricci, N. 2009. *Support Canada's History In Other Ways*. Toronto: Penguin Canada. 120.

40 Ricci, N. 2009. 118.

spellbound by Cold War ideology and saw only communist infiltration as a threat. Accordingly, the RCMP was unable to deal properly with a separatist movement that was highly suspicious of this federal force.

Serious barriers faced the RCMP Security Service as it turned its attention to the emergent terrorist problem. There was a pronounced ideological disposition on the part of the Security Service to see security threats primarily, if not exclusively, in Cold War terms: espionage, terrorism, sabotage and subversion were all instinctively linked with communism, and foreign interference almost always meant Soviet bloc machinations. It was initially hard for these veteran Cold Warriors to grasp the significance of an entirely domestic revolutionary movement. Another barrier they faced was cultural and linguistic: the RCMP of the 1960s was very much an "'Anglo' force, with few Francophone officers, an organization not especially 'at home' in the Quebec milieu."[41]

There are glaring problems with scenario three. In reality the roots of the FLQ, and its slogans and organization, came from the Canadian Communist Party. Communists were the first theorists to articulate "the national question" in Quebec. Instead of a deficit, the RCMP focus on communism likely was an asset. Moreover, the Canadian secret police had extraordinary success in infiltrating the Quebec separatist movement. The long-time chief adviser to key separatist leader Levèsque was a man named Claude Morin, revealed decades later as an RCMP intelligence asset. No doubt there were many other successes, though not made public. Although reports suggested only five men in the so-called Liberation Cell of the FLQ took part in the kidnapping of Cross, it was later revealed that the cell included as many as seven members, one a woman. The sixth member of the cell, Nigel Hamer, a community college teacher, was arrested in 1980 and held for only four months. Hamer spoke no French and may have been working for the intelligence service—in which case, police would have known the whereabouts of Cross from the beginning of his months-long captivity.[42]

The first three scenarios surveyed above take for granted that the FLQ (at least until the October Crisis) was an autonomous terrorist group, solely responsible for kidnapping Richard Cross and murdering Laporte. A fourth, mostly underground variant, propelled by Vallières, insists that the federal power under Trudeau deliberately fomented the crisis in order to severely weaken its bitter opponents among the *indépendantiste* movement in Quebec.

Valliéres himself is a fascinating figure. In his early career, he was a writer for the leftist newspaper *La Presse* and *Cité Libre*, the journal founded by Trudeau. A former seminarian, Valliéres scolded the Liberals under Lesage for failing to follow through on a real Quebec revolution. Later he founded *La Révolution Québéçois*, a Marxist periodical that celebrated nationalism and the Algerian experience, but

41 Whitaker, R. 1993. Apprehended Insurrection? RCMP Intelligence and the October Crisis. *Queen's Quarterly*, 100/2, 383–406.

42 Crelinsten, R. D. The Internal Dynamics of the FLQ during the October Crisis of 1970. *Journal of Strategic Studies*, 10/4, 59–89.

was diffident about the value of separatism for the workers of Quebec. Valliéres was part of a hard-core leftist movement that succeeded in tying up Jean Lesage's plans for industrialization in Quebec with bitter strikes and lockouts, leading to the Union Nationale victory in 1966. He joined the FLQ in 1965.

Partly based on Vallières' account, Ian Adams' novel, *End Game in Paris* (1979) recommends a larger role for the CIA in the October events. In this variant, which has supporters among the *indépendantiste* community and sections of the French government, the FLQ was compromised and penetrated early in its existence by federalist secret police. Likely with assistance from organized crime, intelligence agencies orchestrated the crisis, including the kidnapping of Cross and murder of Laporte. This was also the view of former Quebec Premier René Levèsque, who writes: "'War Measures' are brought into force by P.E. Trudeau who imprisons all those opposing his federalist ideas. According to certain information received, this violence is remote controlled by the RCMP in the service of the politicians in power."[43] In his *Memoirs* Lévesque refers to the federal government's "campaign of intoxication launched as soon as the second kidnapping had provided the pretext that had been so impatiently desired. From the start the federal government had been frenetically seeking a way to condition public opinion."[44]

According to Vallières, the terrorist group's storyboard was constructed almost from the beginning by Canadian military intelligence, which by 1966 had:

> "systematically" infiltrated separatist groups, the labour movements and student circles in Quebec. Valliéres goes so far as to suggest that such police and military operations and particularly the use of *agent provocateurs* in the demonstrations, strikes, et cetera, of the period manipulated the developing "revolutionary consciousness" of the Quebécois and manipulated it into a "revolutionary threat."[45]

Vallières notes also that Montreal police had uncovered two FLQ kidnapping plots in February and June 1970 that presaged the events in October. "During the October Crisis most of the policemen in the Montreal and suburban forces … were to be diverted away from significant investigations and relegated to diversionary tasks." Kidnap victim James Cross received training from British intelligence, whose representatives may have been among the large international intelligence presence in Montreal in 1970. In a strange echo of *Next Episode*'s Swiss plotline, James Cross' family secretly left Montreal for the residence of the British Ambassador in

43 Levèsque, R. 1986. 175.

44 Levèsque, R. 1986. 244.

45 Kostash, M. 1980. 228. Interestingly, Kostash does not attempt to integrate Vallières' testimony into her celebratory account of the FLQ. For example, what if the FLQ Manifesto, with its memorable description of the Prime Minister as "Trudeau the faggot" was actually a product of the busy studios of Canadian intelligence?

Berne after the death of Laporte. In London the British Foreign Office disclosed Cross' kidnapping by the FLQ two hours before the FLQ delivered four ransom notes stating responsibility for Cross' disappearance.[46]

Manipulation by intelligence services may explain the strange character of the FLQ Manifesto. News reports obtaining global distribution emphasized the FLQ's Marxist orientation while underplaying its Quebec nationalist claims. As part of its bargaining strategy following the kidnapping of Cross and Laporte, the government permitted television and radio stations to air the lengthy and tendentious FLQ Manifesto. The document's extensive use of Anglicisms was a rather odd feature of a supposedly *nationalist* manifesto. René Lévesque, who is used "as a sort of witness"[47] in the FLQ Manifesto mentions its "coarse language" in his *Memoirs*.[48] It is as though General DeGaulle had intoned "Vivre Free Quebec" rather than "Vive le Québéc Libre" (as he did famously before large crowds from a balcony in Montreal on July 24, 1967).

From this alternative perspective, federalist forces, led by Prime Minister Trudeau, and assisted by U.S. and British intelligence agencies, manufactured the October Crisis in order to crush separatism in Quebec. However, the matter of attribution remains a problem: Trudeau did not manufacture the October Crisis and the War Measures Act predictably set the stage for Parti Québéçois growth that eventually led to a PQ government in 1976.[49]

The Indeterminacy of Parapolitical Being

I can offer no decisive scenario for the FLQ events. However, there are factors that complicate or deepen the mystery surrounding the emergence, success and demise of this unlikely band of terrorists. None of the previous scenarios really account for the manifold presence of active foreign intelligence agencies in Quebec at the time of the FLQ. Something was happening in Quebec that concerned many powerful interests outside Canada. The number of domestic and international intelligence agencies interested in some way with the FLQ may outnumber the total count of core militants belonging to this terrorist organization. Levèsque wryly observes that "In December, with Cross's kidnappers in exile and the assassins of Laporte locked up and their accomplices identified, [the FLQ] came to the grand total

46 Vallières, P. 1977. 50–51.

47 Levèsque, R. 1986. 244.

48 Levèsque, R. 1986. 243.

49 For example, Levèsque, R. 1986. 25. The October crisis "affected the reputations as defenders of individual liberties that Trudeau and especially Bourassa at the provincial level, boasted … The provincial government emerged even weaker in respect to Ottawa. The federal government appeared the stronger of the two. Quebec was finding out that it had real power."

of some twenty-odd desperados."[50] In *End Game in Paris*, a fictional CIA field operative confides that, "Montreal is better than Berlin or Vienna these days. Everybody is here; if all the intelligence offices got together, we would have a small army." The officer continues:

> Just to mention a few, there is of course, yours truly, the Company—the CIA. Our friends and competitors, the KGB. The French are in here meddling around with SDECE. Then because the [FLQ] has snatched a British diplomat, MI6 is huffing and puffing around. The Israelis are here with MOSSAD. SAVAK to keep an eye on their Iranian students, the South Africans with BOSS, the Argentinians with SIDE.[51]

Issues at stake may clearly have involved more than Trudeau's reputation or the fate of separatism in the province. The unsettled political scene is itself of interest, including a number of early deaths of political leaders, and multiple connections with drugs and organized crime.

> Montreal in 1968 was a thoroughly cosmopolitan, corrupted and corruptible city, a gateway to the United States for heroin. Several drug organizations—Corsican, French, and American—were active in the city, using the docks, the Montreal-New York corridor, and body-packed couriers to make drug shipments. Almost every major international drug-trafficking investigation—whether Canadian, American, or Italian—would uncover a Montreal connection.[52]

Mostly operating in and around Montreal, the FLQ was part of a hive of underground activity in the city, featuring incessant political change and extreme gangland violence. Indeed, the October Crisis seriously disrupted a major investigation by the RCMP narcotics squad into the famed French Connection that smuggled heroin into the United States via Marseilles.[53]

Whatever else one can say about modern Quebec's premiers, longevity was not a strong point. Three Union Nationale premiers died in office, including Duplessis (1890–1959) at 69 and Paul Sauvé (1907–1960) who collapsed at 52, four months after succeeding Duplessis. Daniel Johnson (1915–1968) defeated Jean Lesage's Liberals in 1966 but died unexpectedly in office at age 53, barely two years into his term. While surviving the premiership, Quebec's remaining provincial leaders perished in their sixties, or earlier. Sauvé's brief replacement as premier, Antonio Barrette (1899–1968), succumbed at 69. Jean Lesage (1912–1980) fell

---

50 Levèsque, R. 1986. 249.

51 Adams, I. 1980. *End Game in Paris*. Markam ONT: PaperJacks Ltd. 65.

52 Lamothe, L. and Nicaso, A. 2002. *Bloodlines*. Toronto: HarperCollins. 28.

53 Charbonneau, J. P. 1976. *The Canadian Connection: An Expose on the Mafia in Canada and its International Ramifications*. Ottawa: Optimum Publishing Company Limited. 280–281.

at 68; Jean-Jacques Bertrand (1916–1973)—Daniel Johnson's *Union Nationale* successor—died at 56, less than three years after his defeat by Liberal Bourassa in 1970. Bourassa (1933–1996), who served twice as Premier, expired at 63. Parti Québéçois leader Lévesque (1912–1987), who defeated Bourassa in 1976, barely reached 65.[54] In *My Quebec*, Lévesque observes that 70 "is an age when one begins to do one's summing up."[55]

A repressed and mysterious element in Canadian politics highlighted by the birth and demise of the FLQ is the overwhelming, if indirect, influence of organized crime in the process of political selection. To cite only a couple of examples, Prime Minister Lester B. Pearson's Quebec chief, Guy Favreau, a respected lawyer and accomplished jurist, was caught up in the scandal regarding legendary French Canadian drug trafficker Lucien Rivard. The latter's miraculous escape from a high security prison in March 1965 eventually led to the end of Favreau's career. Favreau's exit cleared the way for the "three wise men" from Quebec, Jean Marchand, Gérard Pelletier and Pierre Trudeau. Trudeau went on to win the Liberal Party leadership in 1967 following Pearson's retirement, and scored a huge victory in the 1968 federal election. Organized crime's influence in the Quebec construction industry—which was engaged, among other things, in the world's largest hydro-electric project at James Bay—led to the founding of the Cliche Commission on Organized Crime.

Intense publicity in Quebec (including live TV airing in Quebec of the hearings) surrounding the commission sent some reputations into orbit (except for Cliche himself, another victim of the Quebec early death syndrome—who died at age 57). The representative of big business on the highly publicized Commission was lawyer Brian Mulroney, later to become Prime Minister of Canada. The Commission's chief counselor was a then-obscure barrister, Lucien Bouchard, eventually Brian Mulroney's Quebec chief, and then founder of the Bloc Québéçois, and Premier of Quebec. Narcotics trafficker Rivard was never called before the Commission on Organized Crime, which bypassed the Caruana-Contrera mafia organization, focusing instead on the Contronì mafia, which was directly linked to New York's Bonanno crime family.[56] It is perhaps not coincidental that Laporte, as Quebec Immigration and Manpower Minister, was given the task of settling the crime-ridden Quebec construction strike of summer 1970, only a few months before he was shoved into a green Chevrolet in front of

54 The toll of early death for political leaders of Quebec during the turbulent FLQ years also applied to some of the province's most important writers and commentators. Aside from Laporte, who doubled as politician and journalist, Andre Laurendeau, one of the co-chairs of the Bilingualism and Bicultural Commisson, died in 1968 at age 58, Robert Cliche, distinguished jurist and leader of the NDP in Quebec, died at 58, Hubert Aquin killed himself in 1977, age 47. As a chronicler and member of the FLQ, Aquin's death itself might stand as the decisive finish of the period of the FLQ in Quebec.

55 Levèsque, R. 1986. 67.

56 Lamothe, L. and Nicaso, A. 2002. 34.

his home by FLQ kidnappers. Earlier in that year Laporte's brother died suddenly after an altercation with a top Liberal bagman. Shortly before his death Laporte met with drug kingpins who earlier financed his failed campaign for leadership of the provincial Liberal Party. In October 1970, these same crime leaders offered to help rescue Laporte from his FLQ kidnappers.[57] For some reason, Quebec Premier Bourassa, enjoying an unassailable majority government, appointed Jean Cornoyer, a former Union Nationale Labour Minister (1969), to Laporte's vacated post.

Why did the FLQ choose Laporte as its victim? A fiery columnist for *Le Devoir*, the nationalist Quebec newspaper, Laporte was first protégé and then thorn in the side for Duplessis. Laporte's book on Duplessis is a small masterpiece, the product of a deeply inquiring intelligence. Following Duplessis' death, Laporte joined the Liberals under Lesage, who won the historic 1960 election. A hard-working cabinet member, concentrating on files including relations with Quebec and France and federal/provincial affairs, Laporte was always a dedicated federalist and Lesage loyalist. While his friend Levèsque chose separatism, Laporte was adamant that Quebec must remain within Confederation. When Lesage threw in the towel, sparking the Liberal leadership race of May 1970 that included Laporte, Bourassa and right-winger Claude Wagner, the Liberal leader was saddened to have to jettison his firm friend Laporte for the upstart, quasi-separatist, Bourassa. Lesage was convinced that Laporte could not win. There were rumors that Laporte was close to the Montreal crime world. His Quebec nationalism was questionable as well; some said he was too doctrinaire as a federalist. Lesage's support for Bourassa assured the rookie politician's success in the race against Wagner and Laporte.[58] According to Vallières, senior officials in Ontario and Quebec suspected at the time that Laporte's killing by the FLQ was actually a gangland execution resulting from a power struggle in the notoriously corrupt Quebec Liberal Party.[59]

The October saga is rife with sloppy police work that evidently allowed the FLQ kidnappers to seize their victims without incident and then avoid capture multiple times. The RCMP had the best "watcher" units in the world, capable of following highly trained secret agents without raising suspicion in their quarry. Yet blundering amateurs in the two FLQ kidnap cells managed repeatedly to avoid detection and arrest in high surveillance areas of Montreal and its suburbs. Indeed, the green Chevrolet carrying the lifeless body of Laporte was found inside the maximum security area maintained by the RCMP.[60] Again there are echoes with Moro, whose corpse was discovered in the heart of Rome's intelligence

57 Charbonneau, J. P. 1976. 444–5.

58 Thomson, D. C. 1984. *Jean Lesage and the Quiet Revolution*. Toronto: Macmillan of Canada.

59 Vallières, P. 1977. 101.

60 Vallières offers a detailed analysis of the incredible misadventures of police investigators of Laporte's abduction and murder. Vallières, P. 1977.

community. Canadian police later admitted that they had indeed penetrated the FLQ—but unfortunately they succeeded in doing so only *after* the October Crisis![61] Government employment of agents provocateurs both within the FLQ and among student and other opposition groups could explain the sudden manifestation of radical oppositional zest accompanying the twin kidnappings and government authorized release of the clumsy FLQ Manifesto on television and radio. Kidnap victim Cross' long association with British intelligence might offer additional insight about the FLQ saga.

I suggested earlier in this chapter that Prime Minister Trudeau's comment about a "parallel power" may have referred to a shadow government, a force behind the democratic façade of Canadian politics. The celebrated media scrum on October 14, 1970 also features the Prime Minister's memorable "Just watch me" response to the interviewer's query about Trudeau's willingness to discard civil liberties in pursuit of terrorists. Whatever the interviewer's motivations, he was relying in his questioning on Trudeau's background as a prominent guardian of civil liberties. A remarkable feature of this interview is the Prime Minister's brief discomposure when the interviewer inadvertently suggests the Canadian leader himself might become a target of kidnappers.

Lévesque and other *indépendantistes* felt that Trudeau's famous remark about a "parallel power" referred to the "provisional government" mooted in Quebec that would have included Lévesque, Quebec Liberal savant Claude Ryan and other leading lights in Quebec politics. And this might have been what Trudeau had in mind. A related possibility is that Trudeau suspected the work of French intelligence in the October Crisis. Trudeau's circle certainly worried about a French hand in Quebec affairs, especially after DeGaulle's 1967 speech in Montreal. Possibly, however, the events in Quebec reflected the old strategies of the British Empire: keep the colonies and lesser states weak by fomenting divisions and encouraging antagonism among old foes; encourage trade in destructive substances (such as opium and cocaine) that are noxious for community life; stifle attempts at unity (such as those of charismatic Union Nationale leader Paul Sauve, Quebec Liberal leader Jean Lesage and Prime Minister Trudeau) and, wherever possible,

61 RCMP recruitment and staffing of FLQ cells became common knowledge in the late 1970s, especially following testimony of FLQ infiltrator Carole DeVault. But for years the official story was that the RCMP only managed this penetration after the October Crisis, not before. Accordingly, police intelligence supplied to key officials to deal with the FLQ during the kidnappings was "inadequate" and failed to reveal "how little support the FLQ really had, and how disorganized they were." Police bumbling merely started with 400 plus arrests in Quebec in October; then it got worse. Once "the Mounties realized after the crisis how inadequate their security operations had been in Quebec that they tried to correct the problem, and this is what led to 'excesses and abuses' known commonly as the 'Dirty Tricks' era of the RCMP." Clearoux, R. 1990. *Official Secrets: The Story Behind the Canadian Security Intelligence Service*. Toronto: McGraw-Hill Ryerson. 87–8. See also Littleton, J. 1986. *Target Nation: Canada and the Western Intelligence Network*. Canada: Ian Adams.

discourage large-scale industrial development that might ultimately pose a threat to the ruling monetarist powers. If this was the game plan, it obtained some success in Canada, taking the wind out of Trudeau's activist federal government, fracturing Canada around linguistic and ethnic lines, thereby throwing the country into a series of constitutional crises, and slowing economic progress in Quebec. As a reproducible model of an urban guerrilla enterprise meant to confound and divide political systems—a Canadian stalking horse—the FLQ was extraordinarily successful. Germany's Red Army Faction and Italy's Red Brigades, both emerging around 1970, likely took their inspiration from the FLQ. Others were to follow. These terrorist units introduced to the continent the familiar wrecking strategies of Empire brought up to date by the Canadian stalking horse: divide and rule, intimidate, foster political suspicion, and discourage industrial progress. Forty years later the legacy of disorder remains more or less in place.

Chapter 10
A Study in Gray: The *Affaire Moro* and Notes for a Reinterpretation of the Cold War and the Nature of Terrorism

Guido Giacomo Preparata

The abduction and assassination in March 1978 of Christian-Democrat statesman Aldo Moro—Italy's "JFK mystery"—is treated by the managing establishment of collective memory in two different ways. One—the so-called "reductionist" (i.e. anti-conspiratorial) approach takes the whole *affaire* at face value—in other words, it regurgitates the episode through the black-and-white rendition of a crisis-stricken government that, for the length of roughly a decade (the 1970s), became so untiringly sieged by popular grievance that such collective revulsion eventually degenerated into pathological forms such as terrorism. Of these terrorist acts, the elimination of Moro came to represent the epitomic and symbolic climax. Whereas the other—a conspiracy theory of the Left, and a highly popular one (hereafter referred to as "the vulgate")—imputes the elimination of the statesman to highly sophisticated scheming, ultimately directed by foreign powers (the United States and/or Britain according to a few variants), which were bent on denying Italy any kind of political autonomy. In particular, this script maintains that Anglo-American circles conspired to foil a proto-nationalist alliance, led by Aldo Moro from the Catholic center and by Enrico Berlinguer from the Communist Left, whose common vision would have animated a far-sighted policy of international independence in the Mediterranean basin. Being "reductionism" not worth the critical effort, it is here argued that "the vulgate," instead, is a myth; that this proto-nationalist alliance was never contemplated. Rather, what seemed to have occurred from 1969 until the early 1980s was an unrelenting attack of different factions (with foreign ramifications) against Italy's Catholic tenure. One such onslaught appears to have been launched by way of Italian Communism in the late 1970s, and it was in one of the defining episodes of this ruthless fight that Moro came to be "sacrificed."

The Chronology of the *Affaire*

March 16, 1978, 9:02 a.m. A commando of the Red Brigades (Brigate Rosse, BR), consisting of 10, possibly 12 individuals,[1] ambushes Moro and his security detail—a total of five men, riding in two cars—in Via Fani, not far from the politico's residence, a middle-class suburb in the north-western corner of the capital. All five bodyguards are slaughtered by a hail of bullets; Moro, miraculously ungrazed, is said to have been extracted from his vehicle and swiftly transferred to a similar one. Escorted by two additional cars, this vehicle vanishes in the early morning traffic and conveys Moro to the hiding place(s).[2] Shortly thereafter, in the heat of the moment, a new government led by Giulio Andreotti obtains the vote of confidence; among the declared supporters, for the first time in nearly thirty years of the Republic's history, are the Christian-Democrats' relentless enemies of yesteryear: Enrico Berlinguer's Communists. The event—the abduction followed by the Communist rallying to the flag—is sensational, unprecedented. With a phone call to one of Rome's main newspapers, the Red Brigades claim responsibility for the carnage in Via Fani and the abduction of Aldo Moro.

17 March. The BR are silent. There is a massive, conspicuous deployment of police officers in Rome, seen everywhere patrolling the streets and blocking intersections in search of the missing Moro.

18 March. The BR release the first communiqué (in total, nine such proclamations will be issued over the length of the affair): in it, they announce that their hostage will be subjected to a "people's trial."

19–24 March. The searches yield no result. Meanwhile, the government solemnly reiterates its pledge to abide by a stance of unbending non-cooperation vis-à-vis the terrorists (so-called *linea della fermezza*).

25 March. The second communiqué is issued and it features a tirade against the putative ravages of world capitalism. It makes no mention of Moro's health.

29 March. The media are now busy diffusing excerpts from the third communiqué as well as three missives by Moro himself, respectively addressed to his wife, Minister of the Interior Francesco Cossiga, and one of Moro's close aides, Nicola Rana.

4 April. Parliamentary debate corroborates the government's resolve not to give in to any eventual request on the part of the BR. These, in turn, send out their "postmen" to deliver a new document accompanied by a plaintive letter from Moro destined for Benigno Zaccagnini, the secretary of his own party, the Democrazia Cristiana (DC).

10 April. The terrorists guide journalists to their fifth communiqué and another letter from Moro, a bitter one, penned against a former minister and DC colleague

1 To this day many details surrounding the number and identity of the actors as well as of the actual sequence of events remain hazy.

2 Whether the planners of the operation had readied a single hideaway, as maintained by the official narrative, or several, is still a matter of controversy.

of his, Paolo Emilio Taviani. The tone of these letters is increasingly perceived as "desperate."

11 April. Slowly and peripherally, the wall of "*fermezza*" (no negotiations) appears to be fissuring; voicing their dismay at the coalition's impassibility, Bettino Craxi's Socialists, echoed by the green libertarians of the Radical Party, argue overtly that such intransigence may have catastrophic repercussions.

15 April. With the sixth communiqué, the BR announce the closure of the trial. Though they had promised to divulge any embarrassing state secret that might have emerged from Moro's "interrogation," no such classified information is mentioned, let alone leaked. Past the customary rounds of revolutionist verbiage, the audience is finally apprised that, for his culpable collusion in the Republic's exploitative and nefandous deeds, the people's court has condemned the hostage to death.

18 April. A seventh dispatch surfaces; it informs the public, this time, that Moro has been killed and that his body lies at the bottom of the lake Duchessa in the environs of the city of Rieti, 45 miles to the north-east of Rome. Though the origin of the communiqué is dubious, the authorities nonetheless send a rescue team to the lake, whose divers skim the basin in view of dredging up the body, which, however, is nowhere to be found.

20 April. This queer obituary turns out to be a hoax,[3] which the BR themselves unveil with the guided disclosure of a new *comunicato*. Along with a photograph of Moro holding the front page of a newspaper announcing his death, the authentic seventh communiqué outmatches the *coup de théâtre* at the lake by advancing the possibility of a "prisoners' swap": Moro in exchange for 13 imprisoned *brigatisti*. The government is given a 48-hour ultimatum to accept the bargain.

21 April. The secretary of the Socialist Party (the PSI, Partito socialista italiano), Craxi, distances himself ever more conspicuously from the hardliners: emphatically, he demands that a concrete initiative be taken to save Moro's life.

22 April. In the name of "humanity," Pope Paul VI implores in an open epistle "the men of the BR" to let Moro go—to go free, that is, the Holy Father underscores, "without conditions."

---

3 Not until his mysterious death in 1984 would it be ascertained that the author of the fake was Antonio Chichiarelli, a career delinquent and professional *faussaire* of art (especially of De Chirico's) associated with Rome's premier criminal association, la *banda della Magliana*. Chichiarelli is supposed to have been hired for the job by components of the secret services, all the while C. Vitalone—a magistrate and *fedelissimo* of Giulio Andreotti—still claims that the idea of the hoax was his and that he conceived it to flush, confuse and force thereby the BR into making a misstep the government could leverage to its advantage. The plausibility of Vitalone's rather suspect late, post-factum rationale, not to mention the ways in which it might have been relayed to Chichiarelli, are adjacent facets of yet another unsolved enigma, one of the great many quilting this unbelievable tale. See, e.g., Flamigni, S. 2003. *La tela del ragno. Il delitto Moro*. Milano: Kaos Edizioni. 288–9.

24 April. The BR admonish in their eighth pronouncement that further "dirty" maneuvers such as the ruse of the lake are bound to compromise any possibility to find an agreement around the prisoners' exchange.

30 April. Mario Moretti, the commander of the BR, places a phone call to the home of Moro enjoining his family members to pressure the leadership of the DC into finding an immediate and "clarifying" solution to the stalemate.

2 May. Divergences at the top become more strident: knowing that Moro's hours are numbered, the Socialists upbraid the Christian-Democrats loudly for temporizing. The Communist Party (PCI, Partito communista italiano), on the other hand, remains utterly inflexible, bent to the last not to cede to the BR's "vile blackmail."

5 May. The BR's ninth statement affirms that, as the margin for maneuver has been entirely used up, they will be "*executing* the sentence." The inapposite use of the past participle is widely interpreted as the terrorists' very last aperture for negotiation.

6 May. There appears to be some last-minute, frantic consultation at the summit over the eventuality of releasing one or more political convicts for the life of Moro, but the attempt just as suddenly fizzles out in a puddle of indecisiveness, legalistic quibbling and overall unwillingness to alter a course that appears to have been set two weeks earlier.

9 May. Moro's machine-gunned body is found in the trunk of an automobile in Via Caetani, in the historical center of the capital.

Some Preliminary Considerations

Here we are, in 2012, discoursing about "security"; global crises; Sino-centric imperialism; the perennially elusive, but academically enticing, "loose networks" of the usual Islamist suspects, or the crazed solo Norse terrorist; the menace from Iran; Afghanistan … and also the crucial experiences of days past, like, say, the Cold War: chunks of a recent history, which have irremediably flowed past us, and which we aver to have fully, "readily understood."[4]

The truth is that, as far as the official historiography is concerned, the long and contorted twists of the 45-year-old so-called "Cold War" (ca. 1945–1990) have yet to be arranged in a single, elegant and coherent narrative, which is to say that we have not comprehended a thing about it. That history has yet to be written, *in toto, ab ovo*.

To pretend to utter anything profound about the role of Islamist terror, or terrorism *tout court* in the overall configuration of America's "War on Terror" without possessing a systematic and historically grounded knowledge of what terrorism was and how it operated in the 1970s is comparable to discussing the performance of a steam engine without any notion of thermodynamics. For example, how can we even aspire to sketch a geopolitical fresco of the beginning

4 Horgan, J. 2005. *The Psychology of Terrorism*. London: Routledge. 31.

of the Third Millennium, if we do not possess a single clue as to the significance and functional meaning of, say, Carlos, the Mogadishu/Schleyer case, the FLQ, the warped schisms of Palestinian partisan organizations, the RAF, the Red Brigades, ETA … or, indeed, the *fantasque* abduction and murder of Aldo Moro?

This is difficulty #1, namely our "complete ignorance of thermodynamics": we do not have anything even resembling a condensed primer of the Cold War. We only have the official documents and their academic glosses, which is to say, virtually nothing. Without such knowledge, without an interpretative key and at least a few decisive leaks from the realm of classified information, we are perfectly compassless. This penury forces us, therefore, if write we must, to rely on journalistic collages and/or soporific archival compilations (of official, unrevealing papers). In other words, the reading public is unfailingly sold … scenarios; it is asked to sit and consume all manners of scripts, "stories," *fables convenues*. The disjunction between the actual management of political affairs and the image thereof that is fed to us is complete: "their game" is one thing, what we see of it, entirely another. The virtual entirety of what we are given to perceive of the political game is *theatrics*. The *comptes-rendus* of such pantomimes are what we call "history books" (aye, so-styled "non-fiction" books are, more often than not, the most fictional of all): they are screenplays drafted by scriveners faithful to the various bastions of what is, in the end, a *monolithic* "Castle" (after Kafka).

This brings us to difficulty #2: i.e. the structure of such screenplays, which is invariably identical across the board regardless of the specific subject. Up to the presidency of Bush Jnr. (2001–2008), which witnessed especially in the aftermath of 9/11 a thunderous re-scripting of history in the key of "patriotism," Western historiography has been virtually monopolized by a leftist interpretation of world affairs (and despite the Neo-cons, the influence of the Left in U.S. academia remains dominant; in Europe, as Neo-conservatism could not have left any durable footprint, the Left's quasi-monopoly is still in force). A tested form of division of labor seems to have been at work here for quite some time: the rulers—whom we conventionally subsume under "the Right"—seem to be perfectly content to have left thus far the management of "cultural affairs" and indoctrination to leftish luminaries and publicists. The schematism endorsed thereby propounds a vision according to which the world is equally divided between villains and heroes, and all heroes are basically progressives, i.e. leftists. In this regard, America's conscience—the usual imperial suspect emerging for this basic hermeneutic application—has had no problem reckoning with her questionable behavior in Mossadegh's Iran, or even in Vietnam—to cite only two instances that have been given ample exposure in the literature.[5] America's

5 For the unseating of Mossadegh, see, e.g., Dorril, S. 2002. *MI6: Inside the Covert World of Her Majesty's Secret Intelligence Service*. New York: Free Press; Kinzer, S. 2008. *All the Shah's Men: An American Coup and the Roots of Middle East Terror*. New York: Wiley.

honor—that of her (governing) "Right"—was in any case saved. Saved because (1) the skullduggery in Iran could ultimately be imputed to the avid wishes of despicable oil companies; whereas (2) the Vietnam War, whatever the true motives of U.S. intervention, had provided the big, progressive heart of America a splendid, historical occasion to hold to task a brutish administration (Johnson-Nixon) for the brief, yet glorious length of the Season of Love. So with these two passing illustrations, we have already singled out three of the leftist playwright's stock characters: (1) the evil corporations (America herself does no wrong, by definition); and even if America does wrong, as she did in South-East Asia, it was the exclusive fault of (2) Mephistophelian, meteoric monads such as Henry "Dr. Strangelove" Kissinger, "Tricky Dicky" Nixon, or the blow-hard Texan LBJ. Pitted against these stood: (3) the sane forces of society—incarnated by the heroic Bobby Kennedy, Martin Luther King, etc.—who made such a show of civil resistance as to give the spectator undying hope in "his country." In sum, most (leftist) historiography uses the same casting template: an unholy entente of corporate interests[6] and power-hungry mavericks or debauched "Colonels" challenged by an alliance of tribunician patricians (e.g. the Kennedys as the Gracchus brothers), featuring, preferably, the appearance of a token Spartacus (the Campesino, Che Guevara or Martin Luther King). (Again, all of this is here presented by way of example; to argue then that the massive anti-war protest of 1968 was itself entirely piloted from above, would be to digress far beyond the scope of these notes.)

Interestingly—and this is of fundamental significance—throughout the duration of the Cold War, Moscow remained enveloped in a mantle of mysteriousness. Because of difficulty #1, the role of the USSR in "the story" has remained so unfathomable that screenwriters have never been capable of fashioning Soviet or Communist protagonists that were not caricatures. In fact, almost all fiction works of that era, cinematographic and otherwise, are nowadays, with a few notable exceptions (namely Richard Condon's *The Manchurian Candidate*,[7] and Frankenheimer's cinematographic adaptation thereof), indigestible.

After 9/11, the art of American scripting changed somewhat, but that is another story, whose analysis in every respect was bound to suffer, yet again, from the orthodox, lacunose treatment of Cold War history.

Difficulty #1 in a Nutshell

Simply put, the Cold War could not have been what we have been told—namely, a stark contraposition between two perfectly antagonistic systems of life, between two opposite spiritual tendencies, as it were—Socialist East vs. Capitalist West. This doctrinal falsehood strikes its roots in the very myth of Bolshevism itself,

6 On Nixon's lobbying for Pepsi, see Summers, A. 2000. *The Arrogance of Power. The Secret World of Richard Nixon*. New York: Viking Press. 266.

7 Condon, R. 1959. *The Manchurian Candidate*. New York: McGraw-Hill.

whose true account, also, awaits a proper, truthful reconstruction. From its very beginning, Soviet Communism has served, at the highest strategic level, Anglo-American hegemonic aspirations—and that was, first of all, in connection with the destruction of Germany. It is a formidable story, fragments of which I have attempted to recount in my *Conjuring Hitler*, and which shows that, essentially, from the Rapallo Treaty of 1922 to the Molotov-Ribbentrop Pact of August 1939, by way of Tukhachevsky's execution in 1937 and Stalin's "appeasement" of Nazi Germany in the mid-1930s, this "Soviet enigma" was more than anything an exquisite foil for Britain's anti-German designs.[8] Spiritually, indeed, the "Collectivist East" differed very little from the "Consumerist West"—something the sophisticated fathers of postmodernism, Georges Bataille and Ernst Jünger above all, had understood.[9] Bolshevism was but a form of materialistic society, like ours, yet resting upon an extremely inefficient form of state-capitalism, whose technological recipes were, for the most part, imported from the West. *The need for brutal social control and all manner of bureaucratized violence exercised from within was obviously predicated on the Soviet Union's glaring state of organizational rudimentariness in the face of the enormous geopolitical responsibility, which the West had, so to speak, forced Moscow to undertake.* Nothing more, nothing less. The USSR was, as Anwar Sadat would poignantly aver at a much later phase of the Cold Game, an "imaginary foe": too weak, too poor (relatively to the West), too clumsy, and too *artificial* to be that arch-fiendish, archetypical adversary that was putatively bent on bombing the West out of existence and rebuilding Man from scratch. Evidently, it was all propagandistic bluster.

We would need one of Borges's imaginary *bibliothèques* to canvass every single chapter of the Cold War with a view to debunking the official narrative, and showing that behind the various "crises" (the Korean War, the Rosenbergs,[10] H. D. White[11] and Alger Hiss, Cuba, the U2s, JFK, the arms race, Kim Philby[12] and the spying saga of the "Cambridge Five," Vietnam, Terrorism, détente, Watergate … all the way to the epilogue with Reagan and Gorbachev) there lay other stratagems, other power struggles. All such crises were not the outcomes of policies more or less tortuously engendered by a principled hostility toward the Soviets, but, rather, maneuvers concealing the imperatives of managing empire

8 Preparata, G. G. 2005. *Conjuring Hitler. How Britain and America Made the Third Reich*. London: Pluto Press.

9 Preparata, G. G. 2011. *The Ideology of Tyranny. The Use of Neo-Gnostic Myth in American Politics*. New York: Palgrave Macmillan.

10 Radosh, R. and Milton, J. 1997. *The Rosenberg File*. New Haven: Yale University Press.

11 Craig, R. B. 2004. *Treasonable Doubt. The Harry Dexter White Spy Case*. Kansas City: University Press of Kansas.

12 Page, B., Leitch, D. and Knightley, P. 1981. *The Philby Conspiracy*. New York: Ballantine Books.

from Washington over the vassals, with—*or eventually without* (such would be the dilemma)—the theatric connivance of Soviet Russia's circus bear. After all, it is inconceivable that there could not have been a tacit U.S./USSR co-management of world affairs (particularly) after Yalta. Especially considering, again, how much weaker one partner (the USSR) was vis-à-vis the other (the United States). This opens a whole new perspective on the problem, whose focus then appears to be, above all, America's preoccupation *with keeping things together within the Atlantic Alliance while having the USSR as some kind of safety buttress (the indispensable Oriental bugaboo) strategically erected behind the Iron Curtain.* The different approach makes new, interesting room for other key, intermediate players such as Britain, Germany and France, of course, and also Italy, each of whom, quite organically, did bring to the arcane and constraining altars of the Cold Game the fruits of her political volition.

The Screenplay for Italy

> To an observer who takes the trouble to look at the total picture [of contemporary jurisprudence] there appears a huge cloak-and-dagger drama, in which the State acts in many disguises but always as the same invisible person. (Carl Schmitt)[13]

> We know it: information does not exist at a certain level. What exists, instead, is the leakage of information. (Mino Pecorelli)[14]

In eight, if not nine, out of ten books devoted to the deep politics of Italy's First Republic, one is bound to read, worded almost identically, the following story. This we call the "vulgate."

In the last stages of World War II, it had already been decided at the Anglo-American pie-sharing summits that Italy would be one of America's spoils: her "aircraft-carrier in the Mediterranean," not-so-metaphorically speaking.[15] Ever since—and this remains true today—Italy has been a country of "limited sovereignty." The trouble in 1945—if it ever was one in the strategic sense of the word—was Italy's *Left*: large (altogether ca. 40 percent), sympathetic to Moscow, and with a hefty progressive axe to grind. From the U.S. viewpoint, something serious had to be done forthwith, especially in view of the political elections of April 1948, which were going to decide the political shape of things to come. So, the Establishment, under close American watch and expert management, regrouped.

13 Schmitt, Carl.1985. *Political Theology: Four Chapters on the Concept of Sovereignty*. Chicago: The University of Chicago Press. 38.

14 Flamigni, Sergio. 2006. *Le idi di marzo. Il delitto Moro secondo Mino Pecorelli.* Milano: Kaos Edizioni. 22.

15 Fasanella, G., Sestrieri, C. and Pellegrino, G. 2000. *Segreto di Stato, Le verità da Gladio al Caso Moro*. Torino: Einaudi. 12.

Over the next 10–15 years, multitudes of diehard Fascists ("*Repubblichini*") were given security clearance and redeployed not just as politicos or aldermen, but also, more ominously, as fully-armed gang-leaders within a tentacular, ever-expanding, and super-secret network of spies, army generals, shock troops, saboteurs and agents provocateurs.[16] This eldritch, Europe-wide *réseau*—whose central is variously ascribed to NATO[17] (viz. the infamous "Gladio," presumably created in 1956)[18] and/or a Black International, or to even wider, more submerged and haunting structures such as one phantomatic *Anello* ("the Ring")[19]—was developed, it was later averred, in view of forestalling a potential invasion of Europe by the Red Army.[20] Of course, the contention sounded implausible; in truth, said the vulgate, the function of these networks was to prevent and neutralize any attempt on the part of the Left to assume power, in any form, at any level. Throughout the 1950s this Neo-Fascist panic, which went by the acronym of FODRIA,[21] inspired Communist publicists with a quotidian supply of alarmist flashes enjoining the working class to beware of the odious plots the Blacks were interminably devising against it.[22] On the other hand, it was known that cohorts of *partigiani*—the heroic backbone of war-time anti-Fascist resistance—who acted also as the semi-tolerated, semi-clandestine armed militia of Italy's Communist Party (PCI), were sharpening their teeth and bayonets, and oiling their machine-guns with an eye to the reckonings of Election Day.[23] But Stalin[24] had enjoined Palmiro Togliatti, the PCI's unchallenged leader, to lie low, not to provoke, and to keep his "troops" on alert for the exclusive purpose of self-defense.[25] So the aggressors were indisputably the Right-wingers, who lived in perennial fear of

16 Barbacetto, G. 1993. *Il Grande Vecchio. Dodici giudici raccontano le loro inchieste sui grandi misteri d'Italia da Piazza Fontana a Gladio*. Milano: Baldini and Castoldi. 82.

17 Laurent, F. 2006. *Le cabinet noir. Avec François de Grossouvre au cœur de l'Élysée de Mitterrand.* Paris: Albin Michel. 220–224.

18 Galli, G. 2007. *La venerabile trama. La vera storia di Licio Gelli e della P2.* Torino: Lindau. 130–131.

19 Limiti, S. 2009. *L'Anello della Repubblica*. Milano: Chiarelettere.

20 Riva, V. 2002. *Oro da Mosca. I finanziamenti Sovietici al PCI dalla Rivoluzione d'Ottobre al crollo dell'URSS.* Milano: Arnoldo Mondadori. 350; de Simone, A. and Nardiello, V. 2004. *Appunti per un libro nero del comunismo italiano. Dalla resistenza al Dossier Mitrokhin, tutti i crimini nascosti del PCI.* Napoli: Controcorrente. 133–86.

21 "Forze oscure della reazione in agguato" ("Obscure forces of Reaction waiting in ambush").

22 Cecchini, L. 1987. *Il palazzo dei veleni. Cronaca litigiosa del pentapartito (1981–1987)*. Soveria Mannelli, Catanzaro: Rubettino Editore. 37.

23 Turi, R. 2004. *Gladio Rossa. Una catena di complotti, dal Dopoguerra al Caso Moro*. Venezia: Marsilio. 240.

24 Di Giorgio, L. 1979. *Berlinguer o le ambiguità*. Pisa: Giardini Editore. 29.

25 Finetti, U. 2008. *Togliatti e Amendola. La lotta politica nel PCI, dalla Resistenza al terrorismo*. Milano: Edizioni Ares. 114–20.

losing their oligarchic privilege to the progressive aspirations embodied by the PCI, and, to a minor degree, by the PSI (the Socialists).

Owing to profuse CIA funding, the ceaseless application of the Vatican and the staunchly-conservative Azione Cattolica,[26] the enthusiastically pro-American Mafia in the South,[27] and the ciphered threats of the "Gladiators," the Right, coalesced around the national-populist core of the DC, eventually won the elections by a reassuring margin, and the danger of a civil conflagration was averted. Togliatti, too, was relieved.[28]

From then on, and throughout the following two decades, Right-wing propaganda, abetted by the United States, kept agitating the scare of a Red uprising. The PCI-PSI opposition was thus forestalled until the early 1960s, when the DC resolved to co-opt the Socialists through a tactical curving to the Left designed to assuage its rightist image at a time it could well afford to do so: the halcyon days of the "Italian boom" (1955–1964). Aldo Moro, as premier of several of these center-Left governments, was the strategist in charge of the operation, which was judged alternatively: either as a rather cynical ploy to declaw the reformist platforms of the Socialists, or as an overly prudent, fully compromissory, yet frank overture to genuine progressive exigencies.[29] Actually it was possibly more the former than the latter, as a red flag was raised in 1967 by the leftist press, which tentatively lifted the curtain on what appears to have been a putschist conatus—the very first of several to come—in 1964. The timing seemed perfectly consequential: as the upswing, owing to a credit crunch, was dampened, the trade unions began re-displaying some of that rambunctiousness that always makes elites twitchy.[30] A "plan" (*Piano Solo*) had then been devised by the commander of the Carabinieri—General Giovanni De Lorenzo—at the instigation of the President of the Republic—the Christian-Democrat and vehement anti-Communist, Antonio Segni—to neutralize the Left through a series of surgical offensives, including the forcible evacuation of PSI and PCI leaders to a prisoners' camp in Sardinia.[31] The truth of the whole affair has never fully emerged. But the late "confessions" of one its protagonists indicate that this coup, *like all the others that were to follow,*

26 Rumor, P. 2010. *L'altra Europa. Miti, congiure ed enigmi all'ombra dell'unificazione europea*. Verona: Hobby and Work. 84.

27 Marino, G. C. 1998. *Storia della Mafia*. Roma: Newton and Compton Editori. 142–57.

28 Flamini, G. 2005. *L'amico americano. Presenze e interferenze straniere nel terrorismo in Italia*. Roma: Editori Riuniti. 43; Fasanella, G. Sestrieri, C. and Pellegrino, G. 2000. 86.

29 Mosse, G. L. 1979. L'opera di Aldo Moro nella crisi della democrazia parlamentare in occidente, in *L'intelligenza e gli avvenimenti—testi 1959–1978*, edited by A. Moro. Milano: Garzanti. xxv.

30 Addario, N. 1982. *Una crisi di sistema. Economia, classi sociali, e politica in Italia, 1960–1976*. Bari: De Donato. 52–3.

31 Flamigni, S. 2006. 9–10.

was a mere threat,[32] in this case addressed to the Socialists, to moderate their progressive agenda (especially anti-speculative zoning laws).[33] The general in menacing charge of the grandstanding, De Lorenzo, was, in fact, most devoted to Moro—and Moro himself eventually proceeded in a parliamentary investigation to cover up the scandal,[34] for the pragmatic sake of republican stability and peace, it was said.[35]

So runs the account of the leftist "vulgate." To this we may interject the following: whatever the net value of the center-Left, it was too little too late as the chickens would eventually come home to roost in the torrid biennium of 1968–1969. At that point, small-time tactical shifts would prove no longer expedient. The tables had turned. Notoriously, it was a time of significant change, which happened to coincide with the first sizeable quake of the postwar order as it was originally conceived at Bretton Woods in 1944. No longer capable of funding its empire by printing dollars galore, which the ever more industrious Western allies had come to accumulate as reserves ever less willingly (America's so-called "tearless deficit"), and faced with the certainty of a disastrous defeat in Vietnam, the United States appeared to give way. As America floundered about in search of palliatives that would enable her to weather the storm—which would come, to begin, in the form of détente and the imposition of the U.S. dollar through the threat of competitive devaluations (the "U.S. Treasury-Bill Standard"[36])—the West at large seemed to have been given some sort of political breather. It seemed as though "the people" had been granted an intermittent recess from vassalage, in which they took to the streets to vent their dissatisfaction, demanding some form of change. In Italy that meant also higher wages, which, indeed, would come. As had been the case for the other parties, yet more surprisingly so, the sudden popular surge caught the Communists unawares; actually, by its novelty and indiscipline, it made them nervous.[37] Electorally, 1968, in fact, gave the PCI *nothing*,[38] but the Party would be quick enough on its feet to capitalize on it and ride the wave of protest with founded expectancy. This, admittedly, was their chance: to reap, as chief opposition party, the easy rents of suddenly manifest, pent-up dissent. And they would, of course, but gradually at first. Doubtless, the situation was chaotic, but the political configuration that was to emerge from the quake of the *autunno caldo* ("hot autumn") was not yet clear. In 1968–1969, Italy's economic position

---

32 Fasanella, G., Sestrieri, C. and Pellegrino, G. 2000. 50–52.

33 Galli, G. 2003. *Il prezzo della democrazia. La carriera politica di Giulio Andreotti*. Milano: Kaos Edizioni. 74.

34 Moro, A. 1979. 131–5.

35 Cossiga, F. and Cangini, A. 2010. *Fotti il potere. Gli arcana del potere e della natura umana*. Roma: Aliberti Editore. 101. 121–2.

36 Hudson, M. 2002. *Superimperialism. The Origin and Fundamentals of US World Dominance*. London: Pluto Press. 16.

37 Valentini, C. 1997. *Berlinguer, l'eredità difficile*. Roma: Editori Riuniti. 141.

38 Valentini, C. 1997. 178.

was by no means endangered, quite the opposite, in fact: it featured strong exports, solid industrial growth, a pacified labor movement, and a per capita income on a par with Britain's.[39] Productive investment was slacking[40]—the harbinger of serious trouble to come—but all this lay submerged for the time being.

Piazza Fontana

Then, bombs went off throughout 1969, beginning in Padua, on January 1, with a conflagration near the respective domiciles of the chief of police and the university's president. Successively, Milan, Trieste and Rome witnessed a string of explosions; in fairs, public edifices (the ministry of justice and town hall), movie theaters, and numerous trains all over the country (August). Until mid-November, 200 bombings in total, no victims, a few injuries;[41] no one "messenger" of all such explosive signals could be identified, but, for a few incidents, the authorities had jailed a number of "anarchists."[42]

On December 12, 1969, there were four more explosions, three in Rome, and one, *this time lethal*, in Milan: at Piazza Fontana, 17 people were killed and several scores wounded. At this juncture, things changed. Italy was about to enter her darkest decade—the 1970s, *gli anni di piombo* (the "Years of 'Lead'"). To this day, the dynamics behind Piazza Fontana have remained a mystery. Initially—unsurprisingly, considering their previous arrests for this type of crime—the authorities blamed the attacks on unknown, marginal and highly improbable Milanese anarchists: one of them, Piero Valpreda, a 37-year-old "dancer" and drifter, was initially splashed on the front page as Italy's new "monster." Valpreda was said to belong to a bedraggled coven of bomb-toting maniacs that called itself the circle of "March 22nd."[43] The anarchists' involvement, in connection with what appeared to be blatant provocation on the part of the police led—a few hours after the bombings in Milan—to the detention and subsequent inexplicable death of another anarchist, the train-conductor Giuseppe Pinelli. Pinelli flew out of a window of the fourth floor of Milan's police headquarters. No one has been able to reconstruct the scene. Yet, progressively, "people" began to talk; new "truths" were emerging: for one, the press eventually learned, and revealed, that "March 22nd" was a nest of spies; it was infiltrated by military intelligence, the police and

39 Salvati, M. 1984. *Economia e politica in Italia dal Dopoguerra ad oggi*. Milano: Garzanti. 106.

40 Forte, F. 1974. *Odissea dell'economia italiana. Tra recessione e inflazione*. Roma: Buffetti Editore. 100.

41 Giannuli, A. 2008. *Bombe a inchiostro*. Milano: Rizzoli. 11.

42 Boatti, G. 2009. *Piazza Fontana. 12 dicembre 1969: il giorno dell'innocenza perduta*. Torino: Einaudi. 83.

43 In remembrance of the day which witnessed the beginning of France's popular uprisings of 1968.

… a Nazi-Fascist provocateur.[44] Which connection led to a deeper, and far more disquieting, layer of political complicities.

To resume the narrative of the vulgate, the idea thus suggested itself that these absurd anarchists had been, in fact, framed by young Neo-Fascist fanatics, who had orchestrated the entire bombing set-up. Manipulated by agents of the Italian Services, these blackguards, in turn, were following the instructions of the masterminds of a "Black International," which allegedly had been given the go-ahead by NATO's High Command.[45] It appeared beyond a reasonable doubt[46] that these (Neo-)Nazi-Fascist cells led directly to (conspicuous segments of) Italy's Military Intelligence and the Ministry of the Interior.[47] Judicially, 17 of the *attentati dinamitardi* of 1969 have been undisputedly attributed to the Black cell of the "traditionalist" ideologue Franco Freda.[48] As the story goes, the blueprint for a conservative revolution needed to counter Communism's new wave of progressivism, freedom and peace was laid out in 1965, in Rome, at a conference sponsored by pro-U.S. military circles. The conference was attended by a variety of arch-conservative personages later implicated in the slaughter of Piazza Fontana.[49] It so seemed that the clandestine anti-Communist squadrons of the 1950s had been resurrected for their original purpose at the proper time.

The intriguing aspect in all this is that five days *prior* to the bombings, on December 7, 1969, British intelligence, behind the façade of *The Observer*, insinuated that a coup molded on the Greek model[50] was afoot in Italy. On December 14, two days *after* the murderous detonation, the same source stated that the coup's putative leader was Italy's President, Giuseppe Saragat. Saragat, backed by U.S. President Nixon, was said to be fronting a movement of hidebound Neo-Gaullists that were presently pursuing a "*strategy of tension*." The dictatorial goal of such a strategy was to declare a state of exception after having fomented a season of anonymous terror.[51] More specifically, *The Observer* intimated that Saragat stood as the catalyst of a military-industrial junta bent on bullying the DC into joining its (Rightist) ranks instead of rerunning a despicable entente with the Socialists, which was tacitly buttressed by the Communists.[52] Sizzling with indignation, Saragat publicly rejoined that, actually, the orchestrators of the massacre were themselves British spies[53]—spies who had conspired with the

44 Boatti, G. 2009. 387.

45 Cucchiarelli, P. 2009. *Il segreto di Piazza Fontana*. Milano: Ponte delle Grazie. 58.

46 Fasanella, G. and Pellegrino, G. 2005. *La guerra civile*. Milano: Rizzoli. 64–5.

47 Giannuli, A. 2008. 46.

48 Boatti, G. 2009. 186.

49 Fasanella, G., Sestrieri, C. and Pellegrino, G. 2000. 43.

50 The so-called regime of the "Colonels" 1967–1974.

51 Giannuli, A. 2008. 41–2.

52 Bellini, F. and Bellini, G. 2005. *Il segreto della Repubblica. La verità politica della strage di Piazza Fontana*. Milano: Selene Edizioni. 16–20.

53 Fasanella, G. and Priore, R. 2010. *Intrigo Internazionale*. Milano: Chiarelettere. 33.

cabal of Giangiacomo Feltrinelli, the *richissime* Red editor turned Maecenas of the Marxist-Leninist brigades of the world.[54]

Officially, Italy had to protest, and the Foreign Office to apologize … but the suggestion was out. Even more interestingly, politicos in-the-know would later aver that those bombs—originally placed by the young "Blacks" behind the anarchist cover—*were not meant to cause any deaths,*[55] *but that an eleventh-hour, surreptitious intervention of American military intelligence*[56] *by way of Germany (NATO)*[57] *so altered the bombs' timer that blood was deliberately spilled.* Why? In order, so confessed a Black terrorist, to derail the original plan, and propitiate thereby "social peace." Social peace? How does the vulgate interpret this tangle of information? By leveraging another revelation, according to which there existed two orientations among the conspirators: a traditionally reactionary current, embodied by Saragat's "American Party," which only sought to exploit fear, and a maximalist fringe of *golpistas*—the industrial-military handlers of the terrorists—who were willing to take lives. The spilling of blood in Piazza Fontana was thus the contrasted outcome of the ideological divergence within this faction, which, in one form (bloody) or the other (bloodless), was attempting to establish "social peace" through a swerve to the Right, and the concomitant persecution of the Communist Party. How were the Catholic center (the nominal "Left" of the DC) and the reformist Left expected to deport themselves under the state of exception? The answer: by one compromise after another all the way to self-dissolution.[58]

As the story went, after the slaughter, the politicians in collusion with the putschists could not muster the nerve to proclaim the state of emergency, and so on Christmas Eve an "armistice" was swiftly arranged with the moderate center through the patient offices of the usual Aldo Moro, the unchallenged master of negotiation.[59] As a visible result, some (mostly intelligence chiefs)[60] were demoted, others were shuffled around, a few went underground, some rhetoric was toned down, and the truth, of course, was safely filed away.[61] What was evident at this crossroads was that the Christian-Democrats were back at center-stage, as always; and the Communists, for their part, came out strengthened from the shock. They did not stray from the pack: like the "others," they had initially demonized the anarchists,[62] and were now enthusiastically sleuthing the "*pista nera*"

54 Bellini, F. and Bellini, G. 2005. 21.

55 Cucchiarelli, P. 2009. 86.

56 Via a commando of four, possibly five, men.

57 Boatti, G. 2009. 269; Cossiga, F. and Cangini, A. 2010. 118; Sceresini, A., Palma, N. and Scandaliato, M. E. 2010. *Piazza Fontana, Noi sapevamo. Golpe e stragi di Stato—Le verità del Generale Maletti*. Roma: Aliberti Editore. 99.

58 Giannuli, A. 2008. 44.

59 Moro served at the time as Foreign Minister.

60 di Giovacchino, R. 2005. *Il libro nero della Prima Republica*. Roma: Fazi Editori. 85.

61 Cucchiarelli, P. 2009. 88, 377, 429, 452–53, 531.

62 Giannuli, A. 2008. 25.

(the Black trail).[63] Speaking of Blacks, interestingly, the legitimate façade of the MSI[64] loomed larger and feistier than usual: after the great commotion, it had risen to ca. 15 percent of the electorate—up by more than five points over its historical average. Altogether, this precarious equilibrium had been tortuously achieved by scapegoating the bomb-throwers (the extra-parliamentarian expendables in this particular episode).[65] Keeping in mind the rising success of the Right after Piazza Fontana, one realizes—as Moro did[66]—that there was something to Italy's "monarchism" after all, and it was, for the time being, making everything complicated, and unstable.

The connections and secret alliances discussed hitherto were bared in the course of numerous trials, all of which, however, ended with the full acquittal of the several defendants. The system, recites the vulgate, always protects itself. In sum, the Italian screenplay maintains that these ultra-Right-wing disposables had been manipulated by a partnership of Italian and U.S. intelligence on behalf of reactionaries camouflaged in coalitions of the center-Right, again, to pre-empt the mass-appeal of the PCI. In the name of anti-Communism, the *golpistas* were hoping to subvert what they perceived as a patently non-cohesive and increasingly Bolshevized "partito-cracy" and replace it with a strong Presidential Republic—a *Ve République* Italian style. On the international plane, it seemed, then, that Piazza Fontana marked the high-point of the clash between two adversarial factions: a Nixonian, authoritarian party versus a "Lib-Lab-technocratic" faction led by Britain's Labour Party and its European Social-Democrat satellites (above all, Germany's SPD).[67] With the attacks on the press (and other non-descript covert action), the latter had resolved to burn Saragat. According to the vulgate, they did so because they thought that the kind of adventurism he was putatively vouchsafing was not only doomed to failure, but that in this very failure the Communists might find the sterling occasion to fashion themselves as Italy's last standing bastion of political virtue.[68] An untoward outcome, to be avoided at all costs. Yet this is dubious because Saragat's small party (the PSDI)[69] had been, at least since 1966,[70] the very protégé of those British Laborite clubs that were now drawing heavy fire upon it. Why? We will attempt to answer the question in the course of the exposition.

63 That is, in pursuit of the Nazi-Fascists.

64 *Movimento sociale italiano*, the party of Mussolini nostalgics, which stood furthest to the Right in the constitutional arc.

65 Giannuli, A. 2008. 145.

66 Moro, A. 1979. 241.

67 Barbagallo, F. 2006. *Enrico Berlinguer*. Roma: Carocci Editore. 128.

68 Bellini, F. and Bellini, G. 2005. 33.

69 Partito social-democratico italiano (approximately 5 to 6 percent of the electoral vote in the 1960s).

70 Casanova, A. G. 1991. *Saragat*. Torino: ERI. 132.

1969–1974: The "Black Trail"

Be that as it mysteriously may, the official pose to assume thenceforth was obvious. The DC moderates and the PCI set out to decry publicly and sensationally what they described as an unprecedented "reactionary" assault on the constitutional integrity of the country's democratic institutions.[71] Black terrorism, nonetheless, continued until 1974, with several other bloody bombing ambushes, amid an escalation of street fights, feuds, and random extremist violence pitting "Reds" vs. "Blacks." Italy was going the way of Argentina.[72] In this first quinquennium of the leaden years (1969–1974), all in the key of Black subversion, as many as *five* soon-to-be-aborted coups were spread through the insiders' grapevine.[73] The vulgate believes each one to have been genuine, and serious. The most famous of these trumpeted conspiracies, which allegedly availed itself of the logistical support of the Sicilian Mafia,[74] was Borghese's "monarchist" uprising of December 8–9, 1970. A Communist newspaper broke the scoop in March 1971.[75] This coup, recounts the vulgate, was some kind of reloaded sequel to Piazza Fontana: it was planned to seal militarily in the capital what could not be sealed through terror in Milan the previous year. It is said that, in the dead of night, after the "occupation" of a few strategic positions by a handful of Borghese's men, the final assault was called off at the last minute—it is not clear by whom. The leader himself, Junio Valerio Borghese—once a glorious commander of the Navy's special forces—had been saved from the post-bellum Fascist-hunt by legendary CIA mastermind James Jesus Angleton and redeployed in the aforementioned gladiatorial nets of anti-Communist subversion during the early 1950s. Angleton was also a godfather to Federico Umberto D'Amato, the chief of the ominous Ufficio Affari Riservati (Uaarr) within the Ministry of the Interior, which the vulgate pinpoints as one of the definitional loci of state-organized terrorism[76] since Piazza Fontana.[77]

Eventually, the assizes would nullify, once more, the inquests launched in those days by few daring magistrates: the *golpe Borghese*, they sentenced, was at best a fancy and a rumor, the rumor of an *opéra bouffe* fantasized by a senile platoon of be-medaled retirees. The vulgate's intimation in the face of such arrogant verdicts, again, was that the Nixon administration—itself enthralled by the Gaullist allure—

71 Limiti, S. 2009. 88–9.

72 See, e.g., Lewis, P. H. 2011. *Guerrillas and Generals: The "Dirty War" in Argentina*. New York: Praeger.

73 Cucchiarelli, P. 2009. 543.

74 Camillo, A. 2004. *Colpo di Stato*. Milano: Rizzoli. 50–55.

75 Flamigni, S. 2005. *Trame atlantiche. Storia della loggia massonica segreta P2*. Milano: Kaos Edizioni. 44.

76 Of the strategists of (State-) terror, D'Amato was one of those that that had to be "transferred" for having become too exposed; see, e.g., Giannuli, A. 2008. 323.

77 Flamigni, S. 2005. 44–5. De Lutiis, G. 2007. *Il Golpe di Via Fani: Protezioni occulte e connivenze internazionali dietro al delitto Moro*. Milano: Sperling and Kupfer. 11.

must have been mulling over the possibility of playing the "Greek trump" for this other Mediterranean country on the verge of socio-political breakdown. When the several attempt(s) to do so failed, the young Neo-Fascist hands—many of whom, feeling betrayed and sacrificed, had suddenly begun to die, or disappear in jail or abroad—engaged in one last vindictive[78] bombing campaign against their former back-stabbing employers in the "Palazzo" (politicians, career officers, intelligence handlers and policemen).[79]

1974 was a critical divide. The timeline corresponded, indeed: the year Nixon was ousted, the Neo-Fascists were beaten back, and the Black bombings ceased altogether. Afterwards, the Establishment, always with an eye to the destruction of Italian Communism, switched tactic. In the three-year transition, with the consummate skill that was its trademark, the DC managed to outmaneuver the MSI,[80] divesting it eventually of the electoral premium and the legitimist petulance it had momentarily acquired in the wake of the bombing season. Now, having disposed of the Neo-Fascist Right—center and (illegal) fringe—with the specter of the "*pista nera*," the true anti-Communist underground was about to conjure up the "Reds" (i.e. self-styled Communist urban warriors) with the same objective in mind: namely to arm and manipulate squads of such dazed Che Guevara-wannabes with a view to defaming and thwarting Italian Comunism .[81] The era of "Red terror" was in the offing. Admittedly, the oligarchs were clever and resourceful, extremely so. Meanwhile, under Ford's new executive team, the United States vowed officially nevermore to use assassination as a means to altering the political course of nations, as it theretofore had culpably done according to a fresh congressional inquiry (the Pike Commission). It was black on white. Boy-scout's honor.

"I Rossi" and Aldo Moro

> Perché io credo nella DC; io amo la DC … . (Aldo Moro)[82]

The Red Brigades (Brigate rosse, BR) were born in 1970 from a nucleus of former Communist zealots (young students, party activists, intellectuals, and a minority of working-class desperadoes) and a handful of ex-Catholics *pasionarios*. It was an organism that somewhat resembled Argentina's ERP (Ejercito Revolucionario

78 Cucchiarelli, P. 2009. 449.

79 Fasanella, G. Sestrieri, C. and Pellegrino, G. 2000. 78.

80 Fiori, G. 1989. *Vita di Enrico Berlinguer*. Bari: Laterza. 221.

81 Willan, P. 1991. *Puppet Masters: The Political Use of Terrorism in Italy*. San Jose: Authors Choice Press. 180.

82 "Because I believe in the DC; I love the DC …" (From a speech given in Bari, January 31, 1969). Moro, A. 1969. *Una politica per i tempi nuovi*. Roma, Agenzia "Progetto." 72.

del Pueblo).[83] The beginnings of the BR—i.e. the deeds of the so-called "first generation" of Renato Curcio (Catholic upbringing, formation at the sociology department of the University of Trento) and Alberto Franceschini (former militant of the Federation of the Communist Youth)—were bloodless exploits (incendiary attacks, kidnappings mostly of industrial bosses, hold-ups, propagandistic bravado, and various other acts of provocation), avowedly seeking to jumpstart the accumulated revolutionary potential of the disaffected masses. The "masses" would not respond as the BR would have wished, but there was no doubt that the peaceable voters of the PCI (the vast majority)[84] all harbored an undisguised sympathy for these latter-day Robin Hoods. Interestingly, and we shall return to this, the image—and far more importantly, the electoral weight—of the PCI itself did not suffer as a result of the terrorist bloodletting, quite the opposite.

The BR escalated to the "second phase" when, between March 1972 and December 1973, they carried out four blitz-abductions of "class enemies": three mid-level corporate officers[85] and a Right-wing trade-unionist. These were hit-and-run kidnaps whose spectacular purpose was to expose the "regime" by diffusing humiliating photographs of the victim's distress as he stood prostrated at gun-point in front of the terrorists' insignia. The culmination of this intensifying course of action was reached in April 1974, when Franceschini's commando executed the abduction of Judge Mario Sossi, a declared enemy of the extra-parliamentarian Left. This was no blitz, however: Sossi was detained *sine die*; meanwhile the BR attempted to project their politics onto the next level by demanding a prisoners' swap. As the government categorically refused to parley and impeded Sossi's wife from appearing on television,[86] Franceschini, via his early connections to influential Catholic radicals, managed nonetheless to reach the Vatican, which appeared willing to intercede with Fidel Castro for the extradition of the designated political detainees to Cuba. Even the pope, Paul VI, weighed in the matter, acknowledging explicitly the importance of the Church's mediation.[87] As it went, it was the Secretary of the PCI, Enrico Berlinguer himself, who sank the whole enterprise by pressuring Fidel Castro to desist, in exchange for 60 FIAT tractors.[88] A phenomenal story. Clearly, it was a vital matter for the PCI to disjoin terrorism from (international) Communism in the collective perception.[89] Despite

83 Bellini, F. and Bellini, G. 2005. 52.

84 Santanchè, G. 1978. *La rivoluzione fallita. I "metodi" di Boris Ponomariov in Europa*. Milano: Mursia. 19–20.

85 From Fiat, Alfa Romeo and Sit-Siemens.

86 Valle, A. 2008. *Parole, opere e omissioni. La Chiesa nell'Italia degli anni di piombo*. Milano: Rizzoli. 197.

87 Giovagnoli, A. 2005. *Il caso Moro. Una tragedia repubblicana*. Bologna: Il Mulino. 134.

88 Fasanella, G. Sestrieri, C. and Pellegrino, G. 2000. 142; Valle, A. 2008. 94.

89 Bartali, R. 2009. Il PCI e le Brigate Rosse, in *Le vene aperte del delitto Moro. Terrorismo, PCI, trame e servizi segreti*, edited by S. Sechi. Firenze: Mauro Pagliai Editore. 83.

the tactical miscarriage, Franceschini was immensely satisfied with the PR effect of the operation, so much so that after slipping a few telephone tokens in Sossi's coat pocket to make his call, he dropped the judge in the vicinity of a train station. The rapt had lasted 40 days. The BR were at the summit of their popularity.

It was precisely at this point in time, the spring of 1974, in concomitance with the defeat of the DC on the symbolic issue of the Divorce Law (May) that the fortune of Berlinguer's party took off. In three years, the quota of the PCI would climb from the traditional quarter to more than a third of the electorate. Dented and bruised, the DC suffered the Communist assault, but managed to stay the course. Christian-Democrats and Communists were neck-and-neck: there began anxious talk of a possible Communist "*sorpasso.*" Since 1973, Berlinguer, in fact, had been proposing an alliance between Communists and Christian-Democrats,[90] the epochal *compromesso storico* ("Historical Compromise")—a hyper-pragmatic solution dictated by the need to "save" Italy by governing it "together," as it were, for the duration of the crisis. To that effect, Berlinguer called all progressives—*lay and Catholic*—to join forces in a common front against Reaction.

On the other side of the fence, peering from that thicket of inoxidizable DC sphinxes, someone seemed to be listening. No less a personage than Aldo Moro had invited his colleagues since the beginning of 1969 to bestow upon the eager Communists a "strategy of attention." Moro, as everyone knew, was a conservative.[91] He had never liked the Left—the Communists least of all[92]—and the Communists, of course, had never liked him: verily, how could they feel any attraction to what they used to disdain as the "degenerative" symbol of Italy's First Republic?[93] Moreover, no one could have forgotten that Moro had been the tactician-in-chief responsible for engulfing the Socialists in the early 1960s—sundering them, that is, from his personal enemies, the Communists.[94] But Moro was no friend of the Right either: to him, *la destra*, whose cult of violence he proclaimed to loathe,[95] was the "inner demon."[96] And on the personal level, he was incontrovertibly reputed honest and modest—a clean, pious and square Christian-Democrat, by no means assimilable to those other nasty clichés of the DC party boss: either crass, corrupt and retrograde, or quintessentially hypocritical, cagey and cynical. Moro was, or had been, a political adversary all right, but he was decent—the "least implicated of them all."[97]

---

90 Galloni, G. 2008. *30 anni con Moro*. Roma: Editori Riuniti. 180–181.

91 Cossiga, F. and Cangini, A. 2010. 38–9.

92 Moro, A. 1979. 22.

93 Coppola, A. 1976. *Moro*. Roma: Feltrinelli. 152.

94 Preti, L. 1975. *Il Compromesso Storico. Un problema che divide gli italiani*. Milano: Rusconi. 8–10.

95 Moro, A. 1979. 242.

96 Guerzoni, C. 2008. *Moro*. Palermo: Sellerio Editore. 69–77.

97 The judgement is P. Pasolini's, cited in Sciascia, L. 1972. *L'Affaire Moro*. Milano: Adelphi. 13–14.

So this was the statesman that after the fires of 1968–1969 had undergone some kind of "conversion."[98] In light of the traumatic upheaval among workers and students, it was high time in his view to effect a "painful, yet fecund operation" of dissent, of "opposition" within the DC itself[99] so as to sensitize the establishment to the pressing exigencies of the times.[100] "Confounding"[101] a number of colleagues, he had thus drifted to the "Left," *solo* and placidly, in search of a zone of "autonomy" that would have afforded him the lucidity with which to gauge the changing situation. Concomitantly, Pope Paul VI—to whom Moro was extremely close—counterbalanced Moro's leftward drift with the conservatism[102] of his encyclical *humanae vitae.*[103]

The Left was accustomed to these fissiparous maneuvers. Given the presence of a vast Communist party, which the constraint of the Cold War prevented from governing, the DC, as ruling party, periodically used the numerous "currents" within its fold to give off a diverse and mobile image of itself. Yet, for all that, Moro's Left-turn and the "strategy of attention" were worthy of the greatest consideration from the Communist standpoint—furthermore, he was known to be pro-Arab.[104] The shift was promising. Indeed, the vulgate relates that while on a mission to Washington as Foreign Minister in 1974, Moro had been "warned." He had suffered a dressing-down by Henry Kissinger on account of his manifest overtures to the Communists, and some faceless interlocutor at a subsequent reception, *sottovoce*, had threateningly conveyed to the Italian Minister that such a policy was going to be the end of him.[105] Now, just as Moro seemed to be conceiving in his heart a rebellious veering away from Italy's Atlantic commitments, so was Berlinguer, yet far more formidably, seeking to set his Party and himself free from the shackles of Moscow.[106] In this connection, the world of progressivism would soon be abuzz with slogans downright "heretical,"[107] those of "Euro-communism" (July 1975).[108]

So while Europe's Communist parties—chiefly those of Italy, France and Spain, all of them, not by accident, Latin, Catholic countries[109]—were beginning to wow world audiences in a synchronized, sensational breach from the hoary

98 Cucchiarelli, P. 2009. 432.

99 Moro, A. 1979. 214.

100 Moro, A. 1979. 173–6.

101 Mosse, G.L. 1979. lx.

102 On the matter of contraception.

103 Bozzo, G. B. and Tassali, G. 1983. *Aldo Moro, il politico nella crisi, 1962–1973.* Firenze: Sansoni Editore. 320.

104 Fasanella, G., Sestrieri, C. and Pellegrino, G. 2000. 92–3.

105 Flamigni, S. 2003. 82–94.

106 Fiori, G. 1989. 268.

107 Fabien, J. 1985. *La guerre des camarades*. Paris: Olivier Orban. 65.

108 Chiara, V. 1997. 252.

109 Fisichella, D. 1979. *Quel Giano bifronte del PCI, da Togliatti a Berlinguer.* Milano: Editoriale Nuova. 61.

pretensions of a decrepit Soviet Union no longer hip amongst the majority of Western lefties, Italy's law-enforcing apparatus had been busy infiltrating the Red Brigades. There is no controversy on this count: throughout the tenure of Curcio and Franceschini, (the "first" generation), the BR had been permeable as could be, hosting as they did at least four unwelcome "guests" respectively from the Ministry of the Interior (the Uaarr, as uusual),[110] civil and military intelligence, and the Carabinieri.[111] Which fact also implied, amongst a variety of disturbing side-reflections, that the group could already have been easily dismantled in 1972, yet was not, deliberately so.[112] It was thanks to one of the Carabinieri's agents—Silvano Girotto, a former juvenile delinquent turned Franciscan priest turned Chilean *guerrillero*, known as "frate Mitra" ("Brother Machine-Gun")[113]—that the BR's old guard was decapitated, or, at least, two-thirds thereof. Rendezvoused by Girotto at a train station of a locality in Piedmont where the Carabinieri lay in ambush, Franceschini and Curcio were apprehended in August 1974. The "other third" of the BR's executive, Mario Moretti, by sheer luck (or possibly forewarned by Ministry of the Interior),[114] managed to elude arrest—on this decisive occasion, as he had on others before.

Hyperion

> There are a great many stories of this country that are passed under silence and will never be clarified on account of some kind of spell ... Some sort of complicity between us and the powers that be that prevent us and them to say what really happened. (Renato Curcio)[115]

Moretti's psycho-sociological template was different from that of the other BR leaders. Neither an intellectual (like Curcio), nor a utopian fugleman (like Franceschini), he was an intransigent with a knack for management, whose inoffensive complexes, bourgeois and Catholic, cast a tame if elusive shadow. His, however, was not exactly an unremarkable profile in that family ties did avail him, when he came to Milan for college education, of the tutelage of an aristocratic household with somber connections to the ultra-Right.[116] After being

110 Fasanella, G. and Franceschini, A. 2004. *Che cosa sono le BR? Le radici, la storia, il presente*. Milano: Rizzoli. 136.

111 Flamigni, S. 2003. 61, 101–3.

112 Fasanella G. and Franceschini, A. 2004. 116.

113 Girotto, S. 2002. *Mi chiamavano Frate Mitra. La prima autobiografia dell'uomo che è stato frate, guerrigliero, testimone contro le BR*. Milano: Edizioni Paoline.

114 De Lutiis, G. 2007. 84.

115 Renato Curcio [cited in Flamigni, S. 2003. 99].

116 Flamigni, S. 2004. *La sfinge delle BR. Delitti, segreti e bugie del capo terrorista Mario Moretti*. Milano: Kaos Edizioni. 14.

hired by Sit-Siemens and joining the aggressive vanguard of its labor union, he eventually gravitated toward the subversive orbit and came into contact—by which specific channels, is not said—with a mysterious leftist sub-sect known as the "Superclan." The Superclan's leading organizer, Corrado Simioni, was even more enigmatic than the congregation itself. The "Simioni mystery" was born in 1963.[117] He was said to have studied theology in Bavaria, and to have been a former militant of the Socialist party, from which he was expelled for reasons hitherto unknown. Some insiders contended he was a CIA asset,[118] while others averred he worked as an informant for the Italian police.[119] In the early days, given a penchant for expensive sports cars, Simioni would be seen driving to BR gatherings in a Ferrari or Maserati to impart these groups of aspiring terrorists the ABC of anti-capitalist subversion. At the time, Franceschini had found the whole vignette weirdly jarring, but tried not to think too much of it.[120] Eventually, as suspicions grew against him, Simioni migrated to Paris (1974), where he would conceal his impenetrable activity behind the façade of an improbable language school named Hyperion (formerly "Agora," nowadays, "Kiron"), in Quai de la Tournelle 27,[121] with offices in Brussels, Bonn and London.[122] That Simioni would elect the French capital as his sanctuary was not so strange if indeed Paris was, as hinted by Giulio Andreotti himself, the home to the Terrorist International.[123] To this day, no one knows for sure, but the surmise is that Hyperion was a covert station of the CIA, or maybe the KGB or "both."[124] In any event, Moretti was Simioni's man from the outset. Simioni died in 2008, swaddled by the sort of discreetness that only true power may dispense, and with a cross of *Chevalier de France* pinned on his shroud. Yes, because he had also been an intimate of France's popular holy man and self-proclaimed prophet, the Abbé Pierre,[125] who, lo and behold, had a niece married to another Italian with a past of Red terror. Paris did shelter a multitude of such refugees,[126] and would function as a sanctuary for Red terrorists well into the 1980s.[127] To this day, the Hyperion dossier continues to

117 De Lutiis, G. 2007. 47–59.

118 Zupo, G. and Recchia, V. M. 1984. *Operazione Moro. I fili ancora coperti di una trama politica criminale*. Milano: Franco Angeli. 269.

119 Zupo, G. and Recchia, V. M. 1984. 28.

120 Fasanella, G. and Franceschini, A. 2004. 64–5.

121 Zupo, G. and Recchia, V. M. 1984. 266–8.

122 Allainmat, H. and Lecavalier, G. 1987. *Affaires d'État. Des dossiers très spéciaux, 1981–1987*. Paris: Albin Michel. 37.

123 Flamigni, S. 2006. 102.

124 Caruso, A. 2007. *Il lungo intrigo. Dal 1943 a oggi: per una storia segreta d'Italia*. Milano: Longanesi. 259–60.

125 Secular name: Henri Antoine Grouès (1912–2007).

126 Imposimato, F. and Provvisionato, S. 2008. *Doveva morire. Chi ha ucciso Aldo Moro: il giudice dell'inchiesta racconta*. Milano: Chiarelettere. 172.

127 Jacquard, R. 1985. *Les dossiers secrets du terrorisme. Tueurs sans frontières*. Paris: Albin Michel. 223.

mesmerize all those that have attempted to plumb the depths of the Moro *affaire*, replete as this meager dossier is with gaping lacunae constellated by isolated, astounding leads. Most astounding of all is possibly the final entry, according to which, the peculiar duo Simioni/Grouès—the erstwhile Maserati-driving terrorist spin-master and the monastic crusader for communal low-income housing[128]—had been received in a highly-reserved audience by the Pope, John Paul II, in November 1992.[129] On what account, one can only wonder.

With Moretti in command, and all potential rivals of the old guard safely out of the way (courtesy of the Carabinieri),[130] the BR were transformed. The reorganization of the "new BR"[131] was completed by 1975—with near-perfect parallelism to the initial point of the PCI's historical, three-year acceleration. Moretti's BR was sanguinary. From 1976 onwards, even beyond 1981—the year of Moretti's arrest (April)—they would strike like a plague: a hail of murderous shootings, kneecappings, kidnaps; hundreds of attacks in the center-north of the country coordinated by the several "columns" of the organization, all of them inflicted in a state of mounting social psychosis. The BR's stated ambition? To paraphrase Moretti: to shatter the prospects of a DC–PCI *rapprochement* and steer thereby the PCI to its radical roots by exasperating the contradiction between the revolutionary aspirations of the people ("the base") and the pusillanimous conservatism of the Communist leadership.[132] *Vaste programme*. To the PCI (and the vulgate), on the other hand, the picture was clear: even though they professed to be hailing from the seedbed of Marxism-Leninism, these repulsive *brigatisti* were frauds, Fascist provokers disguised as comrades.[133] It was patent: they were deviously instigated by Italy's undying reactionary elites, as always, to smear the integrity of the PCI and, therefore, ruin its chances to save Italy from its villainous aristocracy.

Casting a good look all around, in fact, it was hard to suppress the impression that everything was conspiring against the PCI's rightful bid to govern the country. The Communists were truly besieged. Not only had they had to fend off the Neo-Fascists, but presently, *on their left*, they also found themselves forced to deflect the insidious provocations of the BR as well as the patient work of heinous harassment woven by the abundantly-funded (by whom?) and fiendish Foucauldian fringe of Toni Negri and *Autonomia Operaia* (the intractable,

128 Falcone, P. 2004. *L'Abbé Pierre. La construction d'une légende*. Villeurbane: Éditions Golias.

129 Flamigni, S. 2003. 212.

130 Fasanella, G. and Franceschini, A. 2004. 110, 155–9.

131 Galli, G. 1993. *Il partito armato. Gli anni di piombo, 1968–1986*. Milano: Kaos Edizioni. 125.

132 Moretti, M. cited by Galli, G. in his introduction to Arlati, R. and Magosso, R. 2003. *Le carte di Moro, Perché Tobagi?* Milano: Franco Angeli. 18.

133 Galli, G. 1993. *Storia del PCI. Il Partito Comunista Italiano: Livorno 1921-Rimini 1991*. Milano: Kaos Edizioni. 265.

chaos-minded segment of the extra-parliamentary Left)[134]—all of them ragingly opposed to the "historical compromise." Such supplemental defensive effort was, of course, required over and beyond the archetypical fortification against the enduring aversion of the DC's Right-wingers, behind whom lurked no less a force than the United States itself. And, to top it all off, the PCI had moreover to shield itself as best as it could from the superadded enmity of Moscow, which had taken a sublime dislike to Berlinguer's breakaway "Euro-communism"—the new brand leftism with a friendlier, Italian, democratic and "*pluralistic*" visage.[135]

Despite these oceans of adversity, Berlinguer & Associates soldiered on. Their courageous perseverance would pay off. In 1975, at the administrative elections, the PCI jumped to 34.4 percent, gaining almost four points over the polling of 1972. In the political elections of June 1976—a crucial date—the PCI anted up, scoring a remarkable 37.4 percent: the dreaded "passing" (of the DC, which held on to a solid 38 percent) did not occur, but it was close. America and her European loyalists were officially on red alert. Italy, Moro said, had "two winners." What now? Well, there appeared no choice but to "open" to the PCI in some fashion. The DC thus left the door ajar by contriving a peculiar formula whereby the PCI would be given some posts of institutional prestige, and, de facto, a greatly boosted stake in the legislative and the administrative stock of the country. QED, nodded the PCI: there was no governing without them. In exchange, the PCI forebore from casting a vote of no-confidence against Andreotti's new, strictly-DC executive. This byzantinism, presumably fished from Moro's bag-of-tricks, was termed the government of "non-no-confidence,"[136, 137] and it inaugurated the so-called season of "National Solidarity" (August 1976). It was somehow understood that this was the first baby step toward the end-goal of the "historical compromise." Conservatives panicked and the realm of printed matter was soon flooded with books, tracts, pamphlets, essays and articles decrying hysterically a state of Communist siege, which would have dragged Italy into a downward spiral of terror, economic chaos and the progressive and traumatic absorption of the country into the Soviet bloc.

1977, the most violent year of the decade: 1,400 episodes of violence, 23 dead and 38 injured. The BR were on a rampage. National Solidarity, however, proved to be a double-edged sword for the PCI. If, on the one hand, the party saw its democratic legitimization greatly magnified, on the other it was, in fact, held hostage: hostage to Andreotti's stridently unpopular austerity decrees and hostage to the overall dismal condition of the Italian state. They were all in the same boat, and the boat was sinking. Understandably, the (Communist) "base" was

---

134 Zupo, G. and Recchia, V. M. 1984. 187–91.

135 Gentiloni, S. U. 2009. *L'Italia sospesa. La crisi degli anni Settanta vista da Washington*. Torino: Einaudi. 123.

136 *Governo della "non-sfiducia."*

137 Gismondi, A. 1986. *Alle soglie del potere. Storia e cronaca della Solidarietà Nazionale*. Milano: SugarCo Edizioni. 81.

confused:[138] hardcore PCI militants, who lived and voted to run the DC into the ground, were now seeing their leaders consorting with the enemy[139] and begging them, the faithful, to be patient. To what end, they questioned? Was it not obvious that National Solidarity was the DC's kiss of death? What was the PCI gaining from this senseless concession? Indeed. In November 1977, Berlinguer rescinded this questionable contract and caused Andreotti's government to fall. He wanted more. He wanted a better deal;[140] several more months of this diet, and the PCI would have started hemorrhaging votes, this much was evident.

Thus we reach the critical caesura: 1977–1978. Berlinguer, followed by a team of councilors, and Moro, accompanied by a handful of confidants, began to meet repeatedly in a series of frantic and intense super-secret negotiations.[141] Furtively, for a fortnight, they shuttled back and forth from one private apartment to another, at night, bargaining, bearing messages, emendations, proposals and counter-proposals to each other, and cross-arguing some more. And, finally,[142] they agreed on something.[143] They agreed that the new executive, that was scheduled to appear before the Houses on March 16, 1978 for the vote of confidence, was going to be … a near-perfect replica of its predecessor: Andreotti as Prime Minister, and the usual pack of staunchly anti-Communist ministers in his train. Record has it that when Berlinguer made bold to suggest three names of his liking as ministerial candidates—not Communists, but merely respected, Left-leaning "technicians"—Moro himself refused,[144] even though Andreotti was favorable. Visibly miffed by what seemed an overt "provocation,"[145] Berlinguer suspended the parleys, postponing his fatal decision to the very day of the formal presentation of Andreotti's governmental program. "Then we'll see," he curtly concluded.

The rest is history. On March 16, Moro was abducted in a spectacular commando operation, which was footed with the murder of his five bodyguards. For nearly two months he would be held captive in the course of what is one of the most twisted political episodes of the 20th century. On 9 May, his body, riddled with bullets, would be found in the trunk of a car parked in an alley not far from the headquarters of the PCI. In the heat of those days, Berlinguer, in a strained and emotionally-laden indictment of the system, unveiled the rationale of the maneuver: it was, he said, to date the most outrageous counter-thrust of

138 Giglio, T. 1982. *Berlinguer o il potere solitario*. Milano: Sperling and Kupfer. 154.

139 Barbagli, M., Corbetta, PierG. and Sechi, S. 1979. *Dentro il PCI*. Bologna: Il Mulino. 15.

140 Chiara, V. 1997. 277.

141 Chiara, V. 1997. 270.

142 On February 16, 1978.

143 La Rocca, F. 2001. *L'eredità perduta. Aldo Moro e la crisi italiana*. Soveria Mannelli, Catanzaro: Rubettino Editore. 145.

144 Finetti, U. 2009. *Storia di Craxi. Miti e realtà della sinistra italiana*. Milano: Boroli Editore. 107–8.

145 Gismondi, A. 1986. 171.

Italy's Right and of its foreign accomplices aimed at swatting the only form of entente—*the compromesso storico*—that could have saved Italy from the abyss. For something truly exceptional had come to pass on that fateful March 16: upon receiving the news of the kidnap, *the PCI had immediately resolved to vote for the government*. For the first time in 30 years (since the ousting in 1947) the Communists had become part of a governmental majority. They had entered a coalition instinctively hostile to them only to abandon it, dejected and disappointed, a little less than a year later. With Moro gone, they had lost their patron-friend in the lion's den; with Moro, gone forever was also the mirage of the "historical compromise." Italy's grand opportunity to become something else, something better—a respectable democracy—was irremediably missed. The vulgate is, in short, Berlinguer's synthesis.[146]

Throughout this indescribable adventure, the "network" had not lain idle, of course—far from it. Not only did it "steer" the fully-infiltrated BR into ramming the left flank of the PCI—and, eliminating Moro himself, of course—but it also foiled from within all judiciary, intelligence and investigative initiatives promoted by the sane portions of the apparatus to locate and free Aldo Moro from terrorist captivity. In 1981, when the scandal of the secret Masonic lodge P2 imploded, Italians discovered that a vast assortment of Italy's chief political, military and intelligence executives—all of them in positions of top responsibility during the Moro ordeal—was affiliated to the lodge. P2 itself was, seemingly, a direct emanation of NATO's most fanatical anti-Communist clubs.[147] All the pieces clicked into place. In June 1979, Italy's subsequent appointment with the electorate, the PCI lost a million and a half votes.

"The Party with Clean Hands"

The foregoing scenario has all the ingredients of a good movie. First of all, the ambiance: it is dreary and rife with presages of impending tragedy. The narrative is punctuated by long silences, which grow into suggestions of grave, enormous crimes. It is under such gloom and through the mists of Cold War intrigue that we make the acquaintance of our dramatis personae: the heroes, who file in from the left, and the criminals, already on stage, lying in wait on the right. Narratively, scene follows scene in a crescendo of suspense. The tension escalates until it finds

---

146 Colombo, A. 2008. *Un affare di Stato. Il delitto Moro e la fine della Prima Repubblica*. Milano: Cairo Editore. 52; Satta, V. 2006. *Il caso Moro e i suoi falsi misteri*. Soveria Mannelli, Catanzaro: Rubettino Editore. 401–2.

147 Ganser, D. 2005. *NATO's Secret Armies: Operation GLADIO and Terrorism in Western Europe*. London: Routledge. Ganser, D. 2009. Beyond Democratic Checks and Balances: The "Propaganda Due" Masonic Lodge and the CIA in Italy's First Republic, in *Government of Shadows. Parapolitics and Criminal Sovereignty*, edited by E. Wilson. London: Pluto Press. 256–76.

release in an extraordinary, spectacular stunt: *il sequestro*, the abduction. The theatrics of the kidnapping fuel a second, gripping act. In the finale, all hopes come crashing down; the villains triumph, but the heroes will not have fought in vain—their bravery will be forever remembered, as a testament. The curtain is drawn. But there is still hope. Long live Berlinguer, long live Moro, and long live the Left.

It is a tale of many things, especially of idealism and irredentism, which is incarnated by two upright, proto-nationalist leaders in a "cold" era of blocked, stunted longings: the meek and reflective Moro, the martyr, and the prophet[148] Berlinguer, the David of the Left who had taken on the Goliath of International Oligarchism, both of them victims of a 30-year hideous and murderous conspiracy.

It is a good story.
'Tis a pity it doesn't hold water.

Even assuming that all the facts up to Piazza Fontana may be interpreted according to the vulgate, there is one major problem with its script. *And that is the role and behavior of the PCI, and, therefore, of the USSR itself.* We keep finding ourselves butting ceaselessly against difficulty #1. Yes, the oligarchic elites of Anglo-America might very well have been recruiting secret armies *locally* and organizing these super-clandestine organizations such as Gladio for decades in the name of anti-Communism. But why do so if a Russian invasion of Europe was never a realistic possibility? This leads us, therefore, to surmise that all such conspiratorial activity was a gigantic pretext ultimately designed by NATO and its satraps to: (1) mortgage the colony's resources and; (2) keep under close surveillance eventual *nationalist* pushes within the vassal states—spontaneous motions, that is, which might have rocked the *foreign* order so painstakingly established after 1945. So far so good: this much was safely acknowledged early on even by an intelligence executive of the Ministry of the Interior.[149] Now, the vulgate extends this sensible hypothesis by arguing that in the late 1960s progressives from all walks of life attempted a mutinous merger to free Italy from Russian and American control. Specifically, this meant that each of the two major parties came to split into a servile, conservative faction and its rebellious counterpart. Thus, Moro, in the DC, was faced with the hostility of the powerful pro-American partisans, whereas Berlinguer, to a minor extent, found himself obstructed by the Stalinist diehards of the PCI.

Though suggestive, this entire scenario is a fabrication.

Let us start with Moro, the Church and the putative "*sinistra DC*." That Moro was a leftist at heart, who began rethinking his position in 1968 and drifted thereafter

148 Paragreco, S. 2001. *La Guerra delle sinistre. Dal frontismo alla diaspora.* Soveria Mannelli, Catanzaro: Rubettino Editore. 121.

149 Flamini, G. 2005. 68–9.

toward an entente with the PCI is entirely unsupported by the record. Moro was a skilled politician, five-time Premier, and an operator well-known, despite the fashionable phlegm, for his *tough* pragmatism: a "mystical Machiavelli," as one Communist leader captioned him. He had been in power for nearly 40 years,[150] and served as a most reliable custodian of the Atlantic order *for 30.*[151] Among the many services rendered, he vouched for Mafia dons (Genco Russo in 1960),[152] showed "understanding" for the United States in Vietnam,[153] and protected each and every secret of the First Republic by deep-sixing all parliamentary inquests and redacting their released transcripts.

1. Gladio. How could Moro have ever been a target of the network, when, if we are to believe Francesco Cossiga,[154] he had been one of the very founders of the organization?[155]
2. "Piano solo." General De Lorenzo had planned no coup whatsoever in 1964. De Lorenzo did not even believe that a coup was remotely feasible in Italy: too many sleepy generals presiding over too slothful an army, a wholly recalcitrant Church, and no charismatic leader in a war-defeated country.[156] De Lorenzo had merely proffered his uniform to clothe an act of pure intimidation vis-à-vis the Socialists, with which Moro was fully complicit.
3. Kissinger, 1974. The chronicle of the crisis Moro suffered in the United States is far from clear. If it was (and still is) impossible to be Foreign Minister in Italy without Washington's approval,[157] how could Moro have assumed that office repeatedly from 1969 to 1974, and suffer to boot *public* American reprimands? After that "incident," it was said that he nearly

150 Since 1939, in fact, when, under Fascism, he was elected president of the federation of young Catholic universitarians (FUCI). It was through this association that Moro became intimately acquainted with Mgr. Montini, the future Pope Paul VI.

151 Costantini, C. and Moltedo, G. 1976. *Messaggi di fumo. Aldo Moro: i pensieri di un cavallo di razza*. Milano: SugarCo. 11–12, 93.

152 Caruso, A. 2000. *Da cosa nasce cosa. Storia della Mafia dal 1943 a oggi*. Milano: Longanesi and Co. 173.

153 Barnet, R. J. 1983. *The Great Alliance. America, Europe, Japan—Makers of the Post-war World*. New York: Simon & Schuster. 265.

154 F. Cossiga (1928–2010): unquestionably one of the most conspicuous among Christian-Democrat leaders and a symbol of the First Republic. He was in power for 34 years; several times Minister, Premier for the first time in 1980; and elected as Italy's 43rd president in 1985. It is unanimously recognized that his role, essentially, had been that of Italy's chief curator of British Interests.

155 Farina, R. 2010. *Cossiga mi ha detto. Il testamento politico di un protagonista della storia italiana del 900*. Venezia: Marsilio. 123.

156 Beltrametti, E. 1975. *Colpo di Stato militare in Italia*. Roma: G. Volpe Editore. 15–104.

157 Cossiga, F. and Cangini, A. 2010. 180.

> swooned, and had thereby to foreshorten his visit by taking to his bed as soon as he was back in Rome. He then swore to a close collaborator he would abandon politics for good. Two weeks later, however, he was on his feet, ready to lunge into the forthcoming electoral campaign, which he would conduct aggressively on a strictly anti-PCI platform.[158]

Moro, like all the other DC muckamucks of that epoch (Andreotti, Cossiga, Fanfani, Piccoli, etc.), is utterly undecipherable. Not a single *scholarly* monograph worthy of the appellation is available on the political and cultural importance, if any, of these Christian-Democrat doges.[159] The little we know is that Moro was a hypochondriac suffering from sleeplessness[160] that could not start a car uphill. He loved silk ties,[161] wrist-watches and liquor-doused vanilla ice-cream,[162] was repulsed by germ-oozing pocket change,[163] smoked Muratti and Turmac cigarettes, and feared thunder. Never a crowd-charmer, he was unpopular and generally disliked:[164] "Dr. Divago," the "anesthetist-in-chief," they called him. He bored everybody;[165] he forever "temporized," speaking hours to "complicate everything" and say nothing—nothing which the mortals could fathom. However, what was truly remarkable, according to a doyen of Italian journalism, was how perfectly *lackluster* had been his tenure as Minister—from Education to Foreign Affairs by way of Justice: one shining instance of *aurea mediocritas*.[166] Yet Cossiga said he was "*intelligentissimo*": therefore, Moro, a man of power, through and through, and one just right for the times. The reason why he could afford to pass off as "clean" was, of course, the reliance on a wingman, Sereno Freato, his fixer, who took care of all the sooty work—such as collecting slush-funds from the CIA, or kickbacks from Italy's Big Oil cartel (all of it for a good fee, which bought Freato Tuscan estates, Rembrandts, Boccionis, and more).[167]

---

158 Galli, G. Introduction to Arlati, R. and Magosso, R. 2003. 20–21.

159 Clementi, M. 2009. La memoria difensiva di Aldo Moro, in *Le vene aperte del delitto Moro. Terrorismo, PCI, trame e servizi segreti*, edited by S. Sechi. Firenze: Mauro Pagliai Editore. 39.

160 Bernabei, E. and dell'Arti, G. 1999. *L'uomo di fiducia. I retroscena del potere raccontati da un testimone rimasto dietro le quinte per cinquant'anni*. Milano: Mondadori. 73.

161 Giacovazzo, G. 2003. *Moro 25 anni dopo. Misteri*. Bari: Palomar. 26, 115–16.

162 Scarrano, M. and De Luca, M. 1985. *Il mandarino è marcio. Terrorismo e cospirazione nel caso Moro*. Roma: Editori Riuniti. 17.

163 Ferrara, G. 2003. *Misteri del caso Moro*. Bolsena: Massari Editore. 8.

164 Zupo, G. and Recchia, V. M. 1984. 9.

165 Gismondi, A. 1986. 61.

166 Pietra, I. 1983. *Moro. Fu vera gloria?* Milano: Garzanti. 8–9.

167 Riva, V. 2002. 423; Flamigni, S. 2006. 185 and 193; Scarrano, M. and De Luca, M. 1985. 44.

At the time of the National Solidarity,[168] the only near-certainty to watchful outsiders was that Moro had been delegated by his *amici* to implement versus the Communists the self-same stratagem he had performed against the Socialists in the 1960s—namely, luring them into the DC swamp, and *slowly wear them down* (i.e. erode their electoral share).[169] If the set-up was blatant to the seasoned publicists of the Left,[170] how could Berlinguer and the master-tacticians of the PCI not have known?[171] How could they not have known it was a *trap*?

Moreover, there was something deeply amiss in Berlinguer's impassioned call to unite in a crusade "*catto-comunista*." Faction-wise, where were these "Christian-Democrats of the Left"? Where were these belligerent Catholics itching to collude with Rome's ultra-disciplined Stalinists?[172] Indeed, the manifest response of the DC to Berlinguer's systematic exposition of the "compromise" in the Party's weekly, *Rinascita*, and all subsequent vocal pleas was, at best, cold. Moro himself, of all people, was, from the start,[173] declaredly inimical to the suggestion of there being elective affinity between his beloved party and the PCI:[174] as said, he founded his 1975 campaign on the categorical rejection of all advances from the Communists.[175] The Vatican, for its part, barring a few insignificant exceptions, was thoroughly unresponsive and uncooperative as well:[176] to the *Osservatore Romano*,[177] the gambit smacked of sheer opportunism.[178] The picture that emerged from this dance was, therefore, odd: it was as if the PCI had cast itself in the vestments of an ardent suitor, whose incessant advances were making no impression whatsoever on the graces of milady DC. Was it a charade? Were they all acting? That they were playing, there is no doubt; but what game exactly?

And now to come to the part of the Italian Communists.
Absolutely puzzling, to say the least.

Theirs, allegedly, was the party of honesty, high ideals and culture: "the party with clean hands." Truth be told, they sustained that part well. From what is known, it is unanimously agreed that the levels of personal corruption affecting Communist politicians—bosses and rank-and-filers alike—were on a

168 Which began in August 1976 and would end in January 1979.

169 Guerzoni, C. 2008. 98; Galli, G. 2003. 155.

170 Gismondi, A. 1986. 86.

171 di Giulio, F. and Rocco, E. 1979. *Un ministro ombra si confessa*. Milano: Rizzoli. 59.

172 Barbagallo, F. 2006. 168.

173 Autumn 1973.

174 Coppola, A. 1976. 134.

175 Castoldi, L. 1978. *E se Fanfani avesse ragione?* Milano: Everest Edizioni. 71.

176 Fiori, G. 1989. 345–6.

177 The Vatican's official press organ.

178 Faller, U. 1976. *Berlinguer: Il marxismo in doppiopetto*. Milano: Edizioni Everest. 148–9.

scale by no means comparable to those, positively anguishing, prevalent amongst their Christian-Democrat and Socialist equals.[179] Not to mention the leadership *fascinosa* of Enrico Berlinguer, whose sudden ascent from obscurity was in all likelihood the production of hidden great electors.[180] In 1969, when it was certain that Berlinguer would soon take charge, the fuzzy outline of a totally unknown apparatchik[181] was chiseled overnight *from scratch*[182] into the effigy of a latter-day Sufi, a cross between Cola di Rienzo and Gandhi. Ever since "Berlinguer" has become the object of such reverence that to this day no one dares to impugn this sacred icon of Italian politics. As there is not a single penetrating study on Moro's political legacy, there is not one of the multitudinous biographies of Berlinguer that is not a gushing hagiography.

The Communists had played their part competently and deserved credit for it because they had, indeed, been *co-governing* the country for 30 years (they called it "consociativismo"): how could they not with such numbers behind them? In a nutshell, consociativismo functioned thus: the majority proposed a bill the Communist opposition shot it down and then proceeded to emend it.[183] And for all their self-victimizing moans, Italian Communists had, all in all, an easy life: widely and deeply hooked into the management mazes of communal administrations—including some of Italy's wealthiest—the PCI could avail itself of an editorial empire, a national TV channel (out of three),[184] the near entirety of the country's academic establishment, and a glowing constellation of business connections.[185] What besiegement?[186] The open issue, rather, was that, in view of the Catholics' weakening grip, Berlinguer and his simply wanted more power, or power *tout court*.

The Communists had much going for themselves, yet they failed to seduce all the way. Problematic was first of all their unshakable allegiance to Moscow, of course:[187] now, how can the party of high ideals be so staunchly and bigotedly loyal to a regime so drably undemocratic, inefficient and repressive? Berlinguer himself acknowledged that no Italian laborer would ever want to live in a place like the USSR.[188] The PCI had indeed suffered massive defections after the Soviet invasion of Hungary in 1956, as well as strong opposition and more desertions

179 Galli, G. 1991. *Affari di Stato. l'Italia sotterranea, 1943–1990: storia, politica, partiti, corruzioni, misteri, scandali*. Milano: Kaos Edizioni. 168.

180 Lanucara, A. 1978. *Berlinguer Segreto. Carriera e lotta interna al PCI*. Roma: Talerio. 151.

181 Mafai, M. 1996. *Dimenticare Berlinguer. La sinistra italiana e la tradizione comunista*. Roma: Donzelli. 8–15.

182 Interview of Massimo Caprara in de Simone, A. and Nardiello, V. 2004. 279–80.

183 Fasanella, G., Sestrieri, C. and Pellegrino, G. 2000. 30–32.

184 RAI 3, since 1979.

185 Finetti, U. 2009. 101–2.

186 Fiori, G. 1989. 336.

187 Paragreco, S. 2001. 115.

188 Giglio, T. 1982. 212.

following Brezhnev's crushing of the Czech Spring in 1968. Despite these setbacks, Berlinguer's Party remained dedicated to the Soviet cause, as it would until the very end, in fact—*past the bloody days of Moro*.[189] Vis-à-vis manifest Soviet malfeasance, Berlinguer caviled, protested, distinguished, admonished, and even thundered at times, but the disappointing truth was the PCI was a Russian possession, and for as much as the Communists played up their warm-hearted *italianità* it was clear to all that this was a proprietary affair and that there was only so much Berlinguer could do or say. The USSR *owned* the PCI; I will return to this key issue shortly.

This aspect takes the discussion back to Gladio and the Red Scare in the 1950s. If it was true that enterprises like Gladio were being organized in earnest, it was not less true that the PCI did precious little to mitigate the anxiety that was more or less deceitfully fostered by anti-Soviet propaganda. For Communist propaganda, on the other hand, stayed aggressive, menacing and unyielding throughout this time, and, what is more, the PCI itself, as said, appeared to have harbored paramilitary cells, reliant, like their enemies, on a web of arms caches.[190] The subversive urge of the partisans within "Red Gladio" (or "*Apparato*")[191] was said to be so menacing that between 1950 and 1952 Italian authorities had temporarily readied counter-measures to parry what they perceived as the pangs of a nation-wide Communist uprising. The Americans, too, were alarmed, "but not that much … ."[192] As for the Communists, it is said they knew of Gladio at least since 1965.[193] Were, then, these cross-alarms of *wholly spurious* Red and Black uprisings part of a coded language wherewith the warring elites signaled to one another, swapping threats and/or warnings? Cossiga, again, suggested obscurely that they were all part of a generalized exchange of "artillery fire,"[194] which is to say, then, that it was all smoke—or, rather, psychological devices, to be primed regularly in order to create the environment (i.e. psychosis) of choice. And, for the little that we know, the same reasoning should apply to the explanation of Italy's five phantasmagoric coups (1970–1974), which an insider described as "farces."[195]

---

189 Gardner, R. N. 2005. *Mission Italy: On the Front Lines of the Cold War*. New York: Rowman & Littlefield. 238.

190 Finetti, U. 2008. 115.

191 Flamini, G. 2005. 26–7.

192 Riva, V. 2002. 350–353.

193 Satta, V. 2006. 264.

194 Beccaria, A. 2010. *Piccone di Stato. F. Cossiga e i segreti della Repubblica*. Roma: Nutrimenti. 99.

195 For instance, reference is here made to the claim by G. Giannettini—a contractor of Military Intelligence in the late 1960s—that Borghese's coup was a farce staged by Giulio Andreotti. See di Giovacchino, R. 2005. 89.

> In this game, how could one conceive an invasion of the European democracies by the forces of the Warsaw Pact and thereby wager on the masochism of the Kremlin, if not by crafting hollywoodesque scenarios of WWIII liable to win the favor of audiences already consumed by nuclear angst? And yet Gladio is not a fiction and the gladiators are not understudies. For nearly fifty years [American agents] have operated in the shadow of the Western democracies while the Red Star marched in the streets of the People's Republics in the name of a common destiny: the consolidation of empires. During the Sixties, the Russo-American condominium is fully operative.[196]

In any event, neither militarized faction ever denounced the other *formally*, exposing it in broad daylight before the public with a view to a peaceful resolution in the name of democratic stability. Of course not: because what these simulations were designed to achieve was to reproduce on a reduced, national scale the main tension of the Cold Game. Yet, as posited at the beginning of this section, this was obviously not Anglo-America's plan to neutralize the Left, but rather to subjugate the Italian vassal, period. And—hypothesis number 2—the means employed for the purpose was a simple scheme of *divide-et-impera* applied with *the full complicity of both adversarial parties*: Black gladiators *and* Red Partisans.[197] The hands might not have been aware, but the cadres on both sides perforce were. Which means that all of them had consciously deceived the whole country for the entire duration of the game.

In this sense, the DC was no more an enemy of Italy or of progressivism than the PCI itself: *both*, coerced by the exigencies of a bigger pretense than they, nullified the country's chances for a better future.

The Big, Mangy Soviet Bear

The USSR was a giant with feet of clay, and the Communists were perfectly aware of it.[198] Yet, as noted above, its geopolitical valence was of the essence. Vis-à-vis the Soviets, this particular configuration was such that when Italy's powers dealt in Moscow, the Catholics laid the political groundwork, the Liberals took care of (industrial) business,[199] and the PCI—figuring as a fiduciary liaison of sorts—took its "Iron Curtain" cut (customarily of 3 percent). The distribution to the Communist coffers was facilitated by a fluent circuit of offshore accounts coursing from London to Cyprus via Liechtenstein, Vienna and Malta. The fattest,

196 Brozzu-Gentile, J. F. 1994. 210.

197 A. Ronchey cited in Silj, A. 1978. *Brigate Rosse-Stato, lo scontro spettacolo nella regia della stampa quotidiana*. Firenze: Vallecchi. 109. Ronchey, a conservative, chiefly blamed the PCI for Italy's lack of democratic renewal.

198 Bernabei, E. and dell'Arti, G. 1999. 159.

199 Bernabei, E. and dell'Arti, G. 1999. 7.

epochal deals in this context were FIAT's plant of Togliattigrad (1966), which Premier Moro fully endorsed, and ENI's giant pipeline[200] (1969),[201] which Foreign Secretary Moro attempted, instead, to sabotage in every way for fear of seeing the Communists excessively strengthened by it (they would cash in 12 million dollars for their mediation).[202] The United States, oddly but surely, did not seem to have had much to object to any of this; the Italians, since the 1950s, had tranquilly traded with the Russians[203]—as had everybody else, indeed.[204]

This was the situation when Nixon became President. It is no accident that the *anni di piombo* overlapped perfectly with détente: 1970–1979.[205] Those years were "the bottom of some kind of trough";[206] they were a manifest reflection of the United States' decade-long hegemonic crisis, a time when the superpower had run aground on the shoals of Vietnam and the gold suspension of 1971. As we know, it was not until Reagan's Neoliberal "redress" in the early 1980s that the organizational stalemate would be unblocked. All the socio-cultural friction experienced in the interim throughout the Western block was thus the direct repercussion of this time of *indecision*—especially of its final, and most dramatic quinquennium, which was aptly dubbed the "long vigil."[207]

The postwar mechanism of imperial exaction, whereby the United States maintained the empire through the export of quality manufactures and the manufacturing of exportable greenbacks, had run its course in the late 1960s. Nixon sought to replace it with a protracted mercantilist skirmish waged against the Europeans, leaderless as ever, whose attrition he would compensate by opening up, on the other hand, a diplomatic triangulation with Russia and China. The tactic yielded the United States significant savings (by scaling down the arms race) and, most importantly, enabled it to keep all three rival blocs in check. However, by having to decrease the pitch of ideological animosity—now that détente was on—especially within a global setting characterized by economic anemia was bound to cause supervisory difficulties over the political drift of the colonies.

However that might have boded for Europe, what is certain is that, thanks to détente, the USSR began to accumulate a fantastic debt versus the West: between 1970 and 1977 it would end up owing upwards of 40 billion dollars and the rest

200 ENI: *Ente Nazionale per gli Idrocarburi*, Italy's Petroleum State Enterprise.

201 The contract was signed two days before the slaughter of Piazza Fontana.

202 Riva, V. 2002. 403–4, 484–95.

203 Galli, G. 1993. *Repubblica delle Nebbie*. Milano: Rusconi. 39.

204 For the mirror image of such transactions in France (namely the role of Jean-Baptiste Doumeng), see, e.g., Robrieux, P. 1982. *Histoire intérieure du Parti Communiste (1972–1982): Du Programme Commun à l'échec historique de Georges Marchais*. Paris: Fayard. 69.

205 Luciani, G. 1977. *Il PCI e il capitalismo occidentale*. Milano: Longanesi. 43.

206 Harbutt, F. J. 2002. *The Cold War Era*. Oxford: Blackwell Publishers. 237.

207 Hart, G. interviewed in Brancoli, R. 1976. *Gli USA e il PCI*. Milano: Garzanti. 124.

of the Eastern bloc roughly three times as much.[208] Much of what the Soviet bear borrowed for was grain: and so it was that the West, along with Argentina (perennially in the clutches of U.S. multinationals),[209] found itself relaxingly feeding the arch-fiendish Communists, whom, discursively, it had solemnly pledged to annihilate. Not only was it incongruous (not to worry), but it was expensive—foolishly so. Was Soviet Russia worth it? Was it a fair price to play the Cold Game? The beauty of this engaging flow-chart was that Italy was in a position of chief responsibility in the whole process—on account of the size of its Communist Party, of course: the West's largest. And for good measure, the PCUS[210] re-channeled, annually, at least five billion dollars to the PCI, essentially earmarked for the pro-Communist press; as far as we know, the last of such payments was wired in November 1980.[211] By 1977, the Italian Republic appeared to be the creditor of roughly a tenth of the entire Soviet foreign liability, and of a smaller fraction of the much heavier indebtedness of the Eastern satellites. It was not all Italy's money: the usurious transfusions from the Allies and the IMF, which she had made a humiliating habit of periodically begging at world summits, were in this fashion conveyed to the Soviets—again, with full American acquiescence. It is difficult to establish percentages—who gave how much—but, doubtless, the Italians were sinking torrents of their own cash into the Communist East without any faith of ever recovering it. Why they did is not hard to guess: seeing at the turn of the 1970s no outlet for the expansion of productive investment in their own saturated economy, which, like that of most other Western partners, sought to preserve corporate profits and social peace (wages) by *inflating* the general price level,[212] the Italians wagered their economic future on the Second World—and there was cheap energy to be had as well.[213] The Italians were not the only ones. France and Germany were in the running too, but for untraceable motives, the competition amongst Europeans for the Socialist markets and the United States' imperial capacity for coordinated oversight were such that Berlinguer and his were in a tremendous rush to finalize.[214] Finalize what? Their *seizure of power*, for as much as détente had opened new spaces for inter-European rivalry *it was at home*

---

208 Massari, R. 2007. *Rapimento Moro e declino della sinistra. L'avvio della mutazione genetica della sinistra (1978–1980)*. Bolsena: Massari Editore. 196. Andre Gunder Frank reports a cumulative debt figure for the USSR between 1971 and 1981 (20 billion) that is half of that quoted by Massari (40 billion), and 60 billion dollars for the Eastern satellites as a whole: Frank, A. G. 1983. *The European Challenge – From Atlantic Alliance to European Entente for Peace and Jobs.* Nottingham: Spokesman. 57, 59.

209 Miller, N. 1989. *Soviet Relations with Latin America, 1959–1987*. Cambridge: Cambridge University Press. 159.

210 The acronym of the Communist Party of the Soviet Union.

211 Riva, V. 2002. 350, 508.

212 Frank, A. G. 1980. *Crisis in the World Economy*. London: Heinemann. 53.

213 Chenkin, K. 1983. *Andropov. Abbozzo di un ritratto di uno zar*. Milano: Rizzoli. 142.

214 Lanucara, A. 1978. 15–21.

that the pressure to secure a head start was most acute.[215] Hence the progression from mass agitation (1968–1969) to terrorism via political violence: the sequential preamble to civil war, which is quite obviously the superficial expression of the war of the elites.

Transversal Factions

Which elites? That is the question. Nationality or party affiliation is, as a discriminating category, of no use whatsoever in discerning the contours of the warring factions. For instance, even conceding that the DC (or any political party), by overtly partitioning itself into "Left" (Aldo Moro's) and "Right" (e.g. Amintore Fanfani's current, see below), was merely playing "tricks,"[216] it is nonetheless difficult to deny that the deeper lines of allegiance ran along other sorts of tracks. This is admittedly the most forbidding piece of the puzzle not only because to attempt the identification of the actual parties perforce collides with the wall of silence dutifully opposed by the adepts of power, but also because such lines of allegiance could have shifted over time.

We will nevertheless venture the following scenario.

The story according to which Italy's Catholic Party, the DC, was the wholesale mouthpiece of America's most retrograde authoritarianism is essentially inaccurate. On account of its centrality to the spiritual management of the Mediterranean zone and (far) beyond, the Church (also via the DC) was in no position to reject the closest of rapports with the postwar ruling entity of the world, namely the Washington–London axis. But even so, trite as it might sound, Anglo-American puritanism is constitutionally alien to, and thus mistrustful of, the Latin/Catholic psyche.[217] And such underlying mistrust,[218] and *incomprehension*,[219] on the part of the Anglo-Americans vis-à-vis the Christian-Democrats, was never truly overcome, despite the multitudinous expressions of financial dependency, scheming collusion, xenophile enthusiasm, and subalternate dealings tying (often tightly) the ones to the others in the context of post-military-defeat. Hence the troubled season.

The desire to dethrone the Catholics from their position of political command can be dated to the mid-1960s, during the Johnson administration, which came to fund profusely a project dubbed "re-suture of the Socialist Party." The idea

215 G. Amendola cited in Luciani, G. 1977. 175.

216 Di Giorgio, L. 1979. 18–19.

217 Schmitt, C. 1923. *Römischer Katholizism US und politische Form*. Stuttgart: Klett-Cotta. 27.

218 Beccaria, A. 2010. 99

219 Lanucara, A. 1978. 134.

was to reincorporate into a de-radicalized Socialist Party (ca. 12 percent of the electorate), its former Rightist and unabashedly pro-Atlanticist schismatic wing, the PSDI.[220] This was the 6-percent bastion of our acquaintance Giuseppe Saragat.[221] It was hoped in 1966 that, merged as the new PSU,[222] the two parties could poll several million votes at the political elections of 1969. Then, consolidating its expected gains as a modern, Anglo-Saxon-looking Liberal outfit, the PSU would have gradually upstaged the insufferable Catholics of the DC, some of whom, indeed, were convinced that the labor agitations of 1969 had been methodically orchestrated precisely with a view to setting the scene for the triumph of the PSU and the concomitant fall of the DC. More specifically, the Catholics contended that Saragat had been talked into this plan by the Social-Democrat Helmut Schmidt, who was for the occasion acting as some kind of German consul for an "Anglo-Dutch" Party with deep American ramifications.[223] In any event, nothing came of it, for the Socialists and Social-Democrats, now merged in the PSU, foundered miserably at the elections, polling fewer voices, together, than they had done separately (14.5 vs. 19.9 percent).

But the situation evolved. The Unified Party was torn apart in July 1969 as the Socialists re-became themselves, and Saragat, regaining control of its 6-percent fief, named it Partito Socialista Unitario.[224] It was around this refurbished PSU that, putatively, the conspiracy of Piazza Fontana would revolve. What truly happened? It is hard to say. It could be that the bombing campaign that had raged throughout 1969 had been indeed conducted for the sake of the first PSU. Having that flunked, the Anglo-Dutch patrons of Saragat might have egged him on with a new solution: the proclamation of the state of exception in the aftermath of a more powerful (yet bloodless) deflagration—the putsch, in short. The problem, however, seems that by late 1969 Saragat would no longer have been alone in this. *Trasformisti* to the bone as the Christian-Democrats were, and keen on not losing an ounce of power, they (or an influential segment thereof) must have: (1) joined the conspiratorial bandwagon early on and (2) effected the maneuver so deftly as to have assumed in the course of the preparations their usual strategic preeminence. The faction of the DC Rightists allegedly on board was that of Amintore Fanfani, who was supported by the economic brawn of Eugenio Cefis, the super-boss of ENI[225] and of a squad of financiers, industrialists and oil men such as Carlo Pesenti and Attilio Monti.[226] Cefis was sensed at the time to be preparing his advent as Italian *pontifex* of a

220 Partito social-democratico italiano; the PSDI fissured from the PSI in 1947.

221 Pecorelli, F. and Sommella, R. 1994. *I veleni di "OP." Le "notizie" riservate di Mino Pecorelli*. Milano: Kaos Edizioni. 61.

222 Partito Socialista Unificato.

223 Bernabei, E. and dell'Arti, G. 1999. 84–6.

224 Engendering a bit of confusion in that the new outfit had the same acronym as the dissolved one (PSU).

225 See note 200.

226 Cucchiarelli, P. 2009. 546.

grand-duchy of multinationals; for his praetorians, the man had already picked the best Italy had to offer in the way of intelligence and journalism.[227] But there was more: the Neo-Fascists were on board, too. And these do not seem to have played in the affair so marginal and auxiliary a role as the vulgate would suggest.[228] Ideologically, possessed as they were with all manners of anti-Liberal beliefs on sacred hierarchy and the centrality of Eurasia, these circles were bringing to the cauldron spices that could have irreversibly altered the flavor of the mix. Altogether this congeries of forces sought to organize itself into an Italian replica of the operation that brought De Gaulle into power in 1958 (codename "Résurrection"). It is known that the campaign of metropolitan bombings covertly carried out by French Intelligence was instrumental in reaching the objective.[229] Whatever the sum of these heterogeneous forces might have truly amounted to by December 1969, it appears that whoever had sponsored the putsch at the international level had second thoughts about it all and therefore resolved to abort it, *murderously*. After all, it was an established reality that the U.S. Democrats "fretted over the Gaullist model for Europe … and viewed a stable center-Left government as a barrier to a potential Italian De Gaulle."[230] This would explain (1) the last-minute dispatch of a NATO commando from Germany to detonate the bombs with the intent of killing innocents, and (2) the provocation of British Intelligence in *The Observer* five days before the slaughter. Saragat was exposed, but the ultimate recipients of the message were probably Fanfani and Cefis. In sum, it so seems: (1) that this putsch was real and had high chances of succeeding[231] and; (2) that it was someone else's project, which had been turned into something entirely *different* (and acceptable to Nixon), hence the slaughter. As said, the Blacks were scapegoated, and the parallel (false flag) exposure of the anarchists (in addition to the Neo-Fascists) throughout the preparatory bombing phase followed the standard procedure whereby an additional sacrificial layer of expendables affords a cover behind which to regroup and hide higher connivances.[232]

At this conjuncture, and for the next four years, the DC would attempt to salvage the wreckage, but in vain. It managed to deflate the far Right (of the

---

227 D'Archangelo, M. and Ricci, T. L. 1993. *Nel nome della P2*. Milano: Edizioni Nuova Italia. 730–731.

228 Anonymous (Freda, F.) 2005. *Piazza Fontana, una vendetta ideologica*. Padova: Edizioni di AR. 25.

229 Brozzu-Gentile, J. F. 1994. *L'Affaire Gladio. Les réseaux secrets américains au cœur du terrorisme en Europe*. Paris: Albin Michel. 223.

230 Di Scala, S. 1988. *Renewing Italian Socialism: Nenni to Craxi*. Oxford: Oxford University Press. 124.

231 Saragat would later ruminate (self-servingly) that for as much as he had personally admired De Gaulle, he did not think that a course such as that undertaken by the General in 1958 would have been possible in Italy. Cucchiarelli, P. 2009. 444.

232 Cucchiarelli, P. 2009. 89.

MSI)[233]—small consolation—but Eugenio Cefis's grand-strategy to harness Italy's economic growth to a consortium of giant state enterprises, fronted by the chemical pole (his own domain) failed.[234] His direct antagonist,[235] Gianni Agnelli of FIAT, carried the day with a different platform, one no less autocratic and exploitative than Cefis's, but allegedly axed on seeking an entente with the unions in view of a "global" competitive outlook.[236] Along with Cefis's empire, came to grief another extremely bold endeavor on the part of a controversial financier,[237] Michele Sindona,[238] to build—some surmised also on behalf of the Vatican[239]—a banking/financial cluster[240] that could rival those of older, established moneyed potentates.[241] It is no coincidence that all such efforts took place in the shadow of the Nixon administration and that, with the latter's abrupt demise, they, too, sank. Dismissed were also the spies of yesteryear: as James Jesus Angleton was, after a savage fight,[242] thrown out of the CIA in 1974, so fell his protégés, General Vito Miceli[243] of Military Intelligence (a devotee of Moro's)[244] and, as mentioned above, Federico Umberto D'Amato of the Ministry of the Interior—both of them implicated in Piazza Fontana. Politically, this plausible Neo-Gaullist front appeared to have been definitely vanquished in May 1974 with the referendum on divorce (whose institutionalization it had opposed).

Past the fumes of propaganda, notice, ultimately, how thoroughly *immobile* the PCI had stood throughout this interlude. Not only did its functionaries systematically refrain from questioning the official version or attempt to dig deeper in any direction,[245] but they also kept themselves on the sidelines, untouched by

---

233 At the political elections of 1972 the MSI polled 8.7 percent; it had garnered nearly 14 percent the previous year.

234 Turani, G. 2004. *La nuova razza padrona*. Milano: Sperling and Kupfer Editori. 99.

235 Addario, N. 1982. 102.

236 Gualtieri, R. 2006. *L'Italia dal 1943 al 1992. DC e PCI nella storia della Repubblica*. Roma: Carocci. 183.

237 Flamigni, S. 2005. 131–86.

238 Guarino, M. 1998. *I mercanti del Vaticano. Affari e scandali: l'industria delle anime*. Milano: Kaos Edizioni.

239 Massimo, T. 1994. *Ladri di democrazia. Dalla P2 a tangentopoli, il malaffare politico che ha portato alla fine della Repubblica*. Napoli: Tullio Pironti Editore. 53.

240 Gianadelio Maletti interviewed in Sceresini, A., Palma, N. and Scandaliato, M. E. 2010. 224. Vasile, V. 2005. *Michele Sindona, Troppo caffè può far male*. Roma: L'Unità. 20–40.

241 Galli, G. 1991. 166.

242 Limiti, S. 2009. 123–4.

243 Miceli subsequently retired from the Army and continued his political career as an MP for the MSI, the most conservative party of the constitutional arc.

244 Galloni, G. 2008. 158; Fasanella, G., Sestrieri, C. and Pellegrino, G. 2000. 50; Barbagallo, F. 2006. 204.

245 Cucchiarelli, P. 2009. 317; Massimo, T. 1994. 30; Massari, R. 2007. 209–10.

any scandal, as if lying in wait, their electoral share barely moving. Significantly, in the second installment of that mysterious warning published in *The Observer*, it was written that the conjurors had underestimated the prudence of the PCI, which, in the crisis, had deported itself as a responsible party for law and order.[246] As a hint dropped from across the Channel, this was a not a sign of hostility, as the vulgate would have it, but the very opposite.

The PCI's Chance

> That of the "dialogue" between the PCI and the Americans is a story entirely to be written, and who knows if one will ever find out the whole truth about it. (Gaddo Melani)[247]

Having successfully leveraged for three years the (farcical) "psychosis of the *golpe*," "*le trame nere*" (the "Black conspiracies") and above all, the proverbial corruption of the DC, Berlinguer's PCI finally pushed forth in the spring of 1974. The shift roughly corresponded to the rise[248] of the Trilateral Commission,[249] of which, incidentally, the aforementioned patron of FIAT, Agnelli, was also an important member. This appears to have been the highly influential group that longed to see Nixon removed from power, holding him responsible for the deplorable conditions prevailing amongst the Western partners as a result of the unrelenting commercial cannonades his administration had fired upon them ever since the end of Bretton Woods in 1971 (e.g. devaluation of the dollar, the oil shock as an instrument of pressure, etc.).[250] Nixon had a vision and motives for doing so, to which we will briefly return in the conclusions, but for the *hic et nunc*, he had raised considerable enmity, which would prove fatal to his presidency.

The Trilateralists, who, in essence were the forefathers of modern-day Globalists, would not come to power, with their presidential shoo-in Jimmy Carter, until 1978. But their strategy for Italy was already perceptible soon after Nixon's demise: while officialdom kept uttering the ritualistic anti-Communist pronouncements, a reputable portion of the United States' intelligence, industrial and political circles was openly contemplating the option of putting Berlinguer

246 Bellini, F. and Bellini, G. 2005. 102.

247 Gaddo, M. 1977. *Dal Moro-colore alla Non-sfiducia. Due anni di vita italiana visti dalla porta accanto*. Milano: Edizioni Il Formichiere. 134.

248 1972–1975.

249 Giglio, T. 1982. 125. The initial gatherings of the Trilateral Commission coincided with Berlinguer's drafting for *Rinascita* of the three famous articles on the historical compromise in the fall of 1973.

250 Frieden, J. 1980. The Trilateral Commission. Economics and Politics in the 1970s, in *Trilateralism: The Trilateral Commission and Elite Planning for World Management*, edited by H. Sklar. Boston: South End Press. 68–85.

and his in charge of the Italian colony. These circles had become convinced of the DC's utter unreliability on the occasion of the divorce referendum.[251] What began thereafter was the usual Cold War pantomime, which featured, on the one hand, the official spokesmen, say, Kissinger, thundering against Italian Communism, and the token Communist lieutenant, on the other, assuring the base that Kissinger's was "not the only voice we [Communists] hear from America."[252] The pantomime was not a mere gimmick: it actually mirrored the clash of views existing within the U.S. establishment over the immediate political fate of Italy, and ultimately over the question of whether it was worthwhile to wage the Cold War at all.

Nothing conveyed the precariousness of the entire setting better than the transitoriness of Gerald Ford's presidency. Indeed, it was through this palliative administration that the first Neo-Cons—names such as Donald Rumsfeld and Dick Cheney[253]—would emerge: operatives that, under Reagan, would contribute to the erasure of the Soviet Union as a world player.[254] In the Trilateral camp, which, instead, was attempting to keep the USSR within the game, it was only consequential that, in 1975, its leaders would address the possibility of doing business with Berlinguer & Co. In principle, no spiritual obstacle militated against it: these Italian Communist leaders were bourgeois, for the most part Anglophiles, and thoroughly pro-capitalist—the Marxist-Leninist pose was just that. The success of the PCI at the regional elections of 1975 only strengthened the Trilateralists in their conviction.[255] There thus began a flurry of pro-PCI studies and papers sponsored by Zbigniew Bzrezinski at Columbia University,[256] by the CIA,[257] and by a variety of other well-connected American associations seeking to establish contact with the PCI by inviting its most presentable elements, such as Giorgio Napolitano, to extensive tours of American academia and other posh politico-cultural foundations.[258]

All of which signified that, de facto, the USSR had put up the PCI for sale.[259] The Soviets were so bankrupt and desperate to obtain foreign aid that they were willing to sell the Americans the juiciest chunk of the franchise. Allegedly, they had tried to do so before, in 1971, by offering the PCI to Germany's SPD, but the

---

251 Flamigni, S. 2006. 32.

252 Gismondi, A. 1986. 78.

253 Under Ford, Rumsfeld served as Secretary of Defense and Cheney, succeeding Rumsfeld, as the White House Chief of Staff.

254 And, under G. H. W. Bush Jnr., to the post-9/11 strategy of the War on Terror.

255 Albonetti, A. 1978. *Gli Stati Uniti e il PCI. Da Kissinger a Carter*. Roma: Circolo Stato e Libertà. 4.

256 Faller, U. 1976. 160–161, 204.

257 Giglio, T. 1982. 121–5; Satta, V. 2006, 347; Gatti, C. 1990. *Rimanga tra noi. L'America, l'Italia, la "questione comunista": i segreti di 50 anni di storia*. Milano: Leonardo Editore. 141.

258 Barbagallo, F. 2006. 258, 265.

259 Lanucara, A. 1978. 17, 123.

transaction fell through for one vote.[260] Doubtless, this was a splendid opportunity for the Italian Communists. And in 1975 Berlinguer felt power within his grasp. He was ideally placed to make a go of it: (1) his party was worth over a third of the electorate; (2) détente had reached its climax with the Summit of Helsinki;[261] (3) FIAT was backing him up;[262] (4) he had successfully mediated, with stealth, all the agreements that went into making the *Ostpolitik* (acting as confidential emissary between Moscow and Bonn);[263] (5) he could avail himself of (undisclosed) top financial expertise,[264] including that received from his uncle, Stefano Siglienti,[265] who had been the chief of IMI, the banking powerhouse formerly in charge of allocating no less a package than the Marshall Plan funds for Italy[266] and; (6) he now had the Trilateral plus the CIA courting him.

The barometer of situation was given by the PCI's official stance versus Italy's allegiance to NATO: in 1969 the Communists had been vehemently opposed to it; in 1972, the year Berlinguer became Secretary, he began to change his mind;[267] in 1974 he favored it; and in 1976 he went so far as to declare that "NATO could represent even for the forces of the Italian Left a guarantee against Soviet aggression, and a useful shield for building the Socialism of Freedom"(!).[268] What more could the Americans want? To complement duly this phenomenal about-face, he coined inane slogans—"we must be both conservative and revolutionary!"[269]—and made the reformist content of his "historical compromise" as vague and (disappointingly) amorphous as possible.[270]

Euro-Communism—the allegedly *frondiste* push on the part of Southern Europe's Communist Left to break away from the ideological clutches of the Soviets—was officially inaugurated in July 1975.[271] In reality, it was an electoral ruse, fully coordinated with the USSR.[272] Euro-Communism's "refreshing" anti-Soviet jeremiads, which so pleasurably impressed the radical chic, were

260 Bernabei, E. and dell'Arti, G. 1999. 226.

261 Lebec, E. 1997. *Histoire secrète de la diplomatie vaticane*. Paris: Albin Michel. 196.

262 Sklar, H. 1980. 546.

263 Selva, G. 1974. *Brandt: L'Ostpolitik*. Bologna: Cappelli Editore. 152–5.

264 Gismondi, A. 1986. 269.

265 Gracchus. 1974. *Il sistema Sindona. Scandali bancari e manovre politiche nella crisi italiana*. Bari: De Donato Editore. 69.

266 Lanucara, A. 1978. 133.

267 Chiara, V. 1997. 249.

268 Barbagli, M., Corbetta, Pier G. and Sechi, S. 1979. 19–21.

269 Fisichella, D. 1979. 9.

270 Barbagallo, F. 2006. 191. Galli, G. 2007. 264.

271 It will fizzle out in March 1977.

272 Cossiga, F. and Cangini, A. 2010. 251; Santaché, G. 1978. *Una rivoluzione fallita. I "metodi" di Boris Ponomariov in Europa*. Milano: Mursia. 121.

choreographed in Rome (and Paris[273] and Madrid) according to an identical script. The objective was to pilfer centrist (i.e. middle-class) votes from the DC and the Socialists during the interval most auspicious for the task: the late phase of détente (1975–1979)[274]—it was now Musketeers vs. "Moscowteers."[275] If it worked, Moscow could raise the price, a bit. To Amintore Fanfani, who, semi-retired, had time to pay them a visit, the Chinese plainly explained that the Soviets were devising all such propagandistic artifacts (Euro-Communism, freedom from Moscow, revisionism, etc.) in order to keep their foot in the door: they were but acts of the same "tragi-comedy."[276] The tragi-comedy would reach its surreal apex in Moscow, on the occasion of the sixtieth anniversary of the Bolshevik Revolution (November 2, 1977), when the "musketeer" Berlinguer froze in horror the mummies of the Soviet Supreme with a six-and-a-half minute speech extolling the "universal" value of "democracy."

> The chiefs of the Communist Parties are anything but naïve. All in all, they believe in one thing only: that without the help of the Nomenklatura they will not be capable of seizing power in their respective countries ... Contrary to the common opinion diffused in the West, The Soviet Nomenklatura looks with favor upon the coming to power of the Euro-Communists.[277]

This is the crucial transition of our story—crunch time for Berlinguer. In the arm-wrestling match with the Catholics, he was about to cause the demise of the first of National Solidarity government; meanwhile Jimmy Carter was being elected. The contrasts dividing the Americans over the situation in Italy were tangible: it was plain that a part of the administration—the very Trilateralists that had started the process—were still encouraging the Communists. It was no less patent, however, that the hawks, who would storm the White House four years later with Reagan's conservative jolt, had clout enough to stall all such advances.[278] Being torn internally, the posture of the American establishment was qualified on all corners of the chroniclers' quad as thoroughly "ambiguous."[279] Indicative of this state of affairs was the uncomfortable position of the U.S. ambassador in Rome, the Trilateralist Richard N. Gardner. Gardner floundered to prop up the official

273 Lecoeur, A. 1980. *La stratégie du mensonge. Du Kremlin à Georges Marchais*. Paris: Éditions Ramsay. 182.

274 Massari, R. 2007. 178–9.

275 Fabien, J. 1985. 17.

276 Castoldi, L. 1978. 204.

277 Volensky, M. 1980. *Nomeklatura. La classe dominante in Unione Sovietica*. Milano: Longanesi. 398–408.

278 Gardner, R. N. 2005. 22–63, 163.

279 Wolfe, A. 1984. *The Rise and Fall of the Soviet Threat*. Boston: South End Press. 35, 36; Albonetti, A. 1978. 19.

line of his government, which was hostile to the PCI, while the foxes of the DC[280] were certain that he was secretly abetting the cause of Berlinguer. It was precisely at this historical conjunction that the abduction and murder of Aldo Moro were consummated.

An Anonymous Novel

Before we proceed to the finale of this study, it might be worthwhile to mention that in 1975, Gianfranco Piazzesi, a journalist for the *Corriere della Sera*, had published anonymously a *roman-à-clef*, entitled *Berlinguer e il Professore*, which became a bestseller.[281]

Here is the story. In 1974, Italy's Old Money is frightened by an epidemic of kidnappings, which aggravates the disquiet of an environment already roiled by economic troubles. This epidemic marks the rise of an unforeseen wave of *nouveaux riches*. In response to the kidnaps and the *parvenus*, the representatives of Old Money resolve to import, as private security guards, an army of gurkhas. The only rich man who is neither afraid nor in a fix is Eugenio Cefis, the royal leader of the state chemical enterprise. As the kidnappers are eventually repressed, the old rich seek to rid themselves of the gurkhas, who are no longer useful. On the economic front, Cefis, whom the crowds suspect of putschism, offers the unions the following deal: if the laborers' demands are contained, he is willing to pay their salaries in gold. The Church offers to mediate by offering to stow away all the gurkhas inside isolated churches. Meanwhile, to bridge over Italy's insolvency, the Christian-Democrats beg Washington for a loan, which they intend to secure with the country's artistic patrimony. Kissinger meets DC conservative leader Amintore Fanfani and retorts that the Americans will not advance any money, since they know that the Italians will convey it to the Soviets. Fanfani gives Kissinger the lie by rejoining that everyone knows that the Americans are in cahoots with the Italian Communists. Thereafter, face-to-face with Berlinguer, Fanfani offers to congeal the "the match" sine tempore: this "historical compromise" of yours, he sneers, what is it if not a co-management funded by U.S. dollars? Berlinguer declines the offer and enjoins Fanfani, instead, to play by the following scenario: on a certain day he is to go on TV to announce to the people that, subsequent to the discovery of a putschist conspiracy, he is about to proclaim a state of emergency and assume thereby full powers. Thus, concludes Berlinguer, the Communists will have reached their goal: namely to seize power surreptitiously via a coalition specially assembled by the beleaguered Christian-Democrats under an imaginary state of exception.

280 Carlo Donat and Giulio Andreotti; see Gardner, R. N. 2005. 77; Satta, V. 2006. 362.

281 Anonymous (Gianfranco Piazzesi). 1975. *Berlinguer e il professore*. Milano: Rizzoli.

(Easily) decrypted: a rising Liberal and anti-Catholic vanguard (*the nouveaux riches*) is seeking to harness to its agenda the electoral base of the PCI, and the working class (the kidnappers), with a view to toppling the Catholic leadership (Old Money). Feeling baited and blackmailed by organized labor, the old bourgeoisie hires Neo-Fascist thugs (the gurkhas) for self-defense … and provocation. Cefis oversees the maneuver. After the work is done, the Blacks are buried away in the crypts. Meanwhile, the United States, alienated by the whole business, decides to bet on the Communist horse. The DC tergiversates, but Berlinguer is in a rush to break the stalemate and so plans an "inciting incident" that would clandestinely enable his Party to gain access to the control panel. The United States approves.

Saying the Ineffable

> A political agreement that would introduce the Communist Party in full political solidarity with us is not acceptable in our view […]. We do know that a most delicate game of foreign policy, which I merely touch on, is afoot. (Aldo Moro)[282]

To return to the vulgate. Was it really the case, then, that all terrorist acts from Piazza Fontana onwards were planned and effected by Blacks (dissembling as Reds since 1974) to derail the PCI? As we have stated above, in 1969, the propagandistic accusation by the conservative milieu that the bombings were inspired by the PCI was *never* made. The conspirators did frame and sacrifice those unlikeliest of all suspects—the anarchists—and when that cover melted, they ditched without afterthought the Neo-Fascists (the "gurkhas") as well. But the Communists came unscathed out of the whole affair. No organ of the center-Right pointed the finger at them. *The strategy of tension actually boosted the Communists' institutional legitimacy*,[283] as they increasingly began to assert themselves as the only reliable and righteous force in the constitutional arc. *The Observer*, indeed, had appreciated this much.

Same story with Red terror. According to the vulgate, the putative forces of Reaction—say, the spectral triad of: DC Right-wingers, the CIA, and pro-Fascist Atlantists—secretly armed and manipulated groups such as the BR, and delegated to the complicit Socialists (PSI) the no less covert task of fomenting the extra-parliamentary Left (fronted by Toni Negri and the Foucauldians),[284] both actions being the prongs of a single maneuver aimed at spearing the PCI from its left. Fortunately, the exegetes add, Berlinguer and his lieutenants adroitly dodged the offensive—at least for a time. Admittedly, either the terror-masters were incompetent or the PCI was just too virtuous, or possibly both. But something does not quite add up, because these self-same banaghans of the vulgate affirm

---

282 From Moro's last speech, February 28, 1978. Moro, A. 1979. 387.

283 Fasanella, G., Sestrieri, C. and Pellegrino, G. 2000. 14.

284 Fiori, G. 1989. 325–6.

adamantly, following Berlinguer, that the Right was eventually able to sink the *compromesso storico* with a single shot (i.e. the abduction of Moro). They argue that Moro, as the chief, compassionate mediator of the conservative bloc was the only politician capable of ferrying both sides of the "compromise" to a full-blown democratic solution—in other words, that he was irreplaceable. Yet two years of uninterrupted BR-slaughter (1976–1977) had apparently done nothing to compromise the strength of the party. And that is revealing. Actually, the more the BR struck the more votes Berlinguer garnered.[285] Was it just a freak correlation? Were the BR ultimately helping the cause of Berlinguer?[286]

They were—in two ways. The labor of the BR may be configured, in essence, as a psyop, which came to affect the instinctive responses of two different cohorts of the leftist electorate. First, by targeting *exclusively* Christian-Democrat, conservatives and industrial executives,[287] the *brigatisti* were performing some kind of masked-avenger cleansing, which law-abiding and DC-hating PCI voters were intimately relishing yet were too coy to applaud overtly. Second, and most important, by intensifying the level of violence, and enabling thus *Communist* spokespersons to *criminalize* and disown *Communist* terrorism ever more vehemently, Moretti and his gang were de facto legitimizing the PCI *and pushing it further to the center*.[288] And that is exactly where Berlinguer wanted it to be in order to fish the extra votes with which he could "force" the DC to come to an understanding (namely the unrequited advances of the *compromesso storico*).

Otherwise, if it was true that the BR thought Berlinguer a "sellout"[289] and his "revisionism" a sacrilege; if it was true that in the eyes of the *brigatisti* the *embourgeoisement* of the PCI represented the supreme, most insufferable betrayal of Marxist-Leninist revolutionary ideals, *then it would have been perfectly coherent on their part to maim, ravish and assassinate Communist captains as well*. If it was true, as Moretti would later confess, that he had planned the abduction of Moro to trigger some kind of rupture between the "base" and the leadership of the PCI, well, then, why not kidnap Berlinguer, the hated arch-traitor himself? The "base" did not care a fig about Aldo Moro.

But, could the base be ever expected to riot, massively? It did not in 1969, and it would not take to the streets after the first BR in the early 1970s either, although part of it mutedly cheered for them. By early 1978 it was obvious:

285 Solé, R. 1979. *Le défi terroriste. Leçons italiennes à l'Usage de l'Europe*. Paris: Éditions du Seuil. 139, 160; Fisichella, D. 1979. 94.

286 Raufer, X. 1982. *Terrorisme: maintenant la France?* Paris: Éditions Garnier Frères. 145–6.

287 With the notable exception of two Communists, both of them shot in the legs—the journalist Nino Ferrero (September 18, 1977) and Carlo Castellano (November 17, 1977), a senior director of the Ansaldo conglomerate—the BR concentrated their fire upon the conservative bloc.

288 Lanucara, A. 1978. 139.

289 Fasanella, G., Sestrieri, C. and Pellegrino, G. 2000. 31.

no matter how tense the environment, the Italians were, in the final instance, a docile lot. So no revolution for or against Moro; but what if Berlinguer himself had been snatched? One could argue that the ravishment of the party's secretary or of another popular Communist bigwig would have caused, nation-wide, such an upsurge of sympathy that the PCI would have found itself further boosted by the event. But the more veracious supposition is that the spectacle of a Left senselessly cannibalizing itself across the legal divide would have been positively lethal for the quotation of the Party. Had they taken Berlinguer the BR would have so completely disoriented the electorate of the PCI as to have played themselves out of political existence. If Italy's CIA-fueled "puppet-masters" were so diabolically anti-Communist as the vulgate assures they were, *to have the BR sequester, or better, assassinate Berlinguer* could have been, therefore, the perfect (political) crime. It might have killed with one stone all three birds—the PCI's electoral dynamism, the icon Berlinguer, and the not inconsiderable, if modulated, popularity enjoyed by the BR.

Mario Moretti, of course, was deliberately talking stupendous nonsense—as he would most of the time, he, no less a sphinx than his fellow power-brokers at the top. Following the logic of this sub-game, to kidnap Berlinguer was never an option, even though some dubious rumors, circulated by Berlinguer himself, suggest that it had been contemplated.[290] Moro, then, was the chosen victim. Was the public emotionally devastated by the abduction? Not in the least[291]—shocked for certain by the slaughter of the five innocents in Via Fani and by the high profile of the victim, but not intimately touched. And at both extremes of the spectrum, the news of his abduction was actually greeted with gloating ovations.[292] Despite the fluttering of red and white banners in the trademark corteges of the day and other customary displays of civil indignation, not a tear was shed for a member of that class that had concerned itself exclusively with the strict management of the *arcana imperii*. Moro had always made short shrift of popular affection.[293]

Be that as it sorrowfully may, the glossers of the vulgate invest the figure of Moro, notwithstanding his lack of mass-appeal, with capital significance. Not just for standing out as a representative of the old guard that had, like some sort of modern Walter Rathenau,[294] morphed into a pro-Arab, recalcitrant mutineer[295]

290 Pecorelli, F. and Sommella, R. 1994. 215.

291 Arbasino, A. 1978. *In questo Stato*. Milano: Garzanti. 8.

292 For a testimony of the reaction from the Right see Bruni, P. 2008. *Il perduto equilibrio nei giorni tristi di Aldo Moro*. Castrovillari: Il C. 87; and from the Left, Guerzoni, C. 2008. 15.

293 Cossiga, F. and Cangini, A. 2010. 39.

294 Feldbauer, G. 2000. *Agenten, Terror, Staatskomplot. Der Mord an Aldo Moro, Rote Brigaden und CIA*. Köln: Papy Rossa Verlag. 39; Pietra, I. 1983. 179–80.

295 The parallel with Rathenau and his association with the putative existence of a "National Bolshevist" conspiracy—a sort of *compromesso storico avant la lettre*—is literarily suggestive, but wholly unwarranted (for a treatment of that particular episode, see my *Conjuring Hitler*, 112–21).

(against the Atlantic Alliance), but also for being the keeper of a great many filthy and most delicate secrets of the Republic. In short, he had to die; he was too dangerous. If that was the case, the question has been asked before: why run the immense risk and undertake the extraordinary cost of spiriting Moro away in broad daylight, and keeping him captive for two months when there was every reason to believe that the policing apparatus of the state would have been looking for him under every stone with guns drawn? Why not shoot him dead in Via Fani?[296] Second, if Moro's pro-Arab policy was such a nuisance, he should have been discretely removed from his post, as it is generally done, at least four years earlier, when he was still Foreign Minister. Why wait until 1978, when as President of the DC (a purely honorary title) he could do no harm in that sense, and eliminate him to boot in the most convoluted and sensational of manners? And third, why should the reactionary conspirators, who by definition are the most informed of all people, take such indescribable pains merely to extract from their prey information they certainly already possessed?

Clearly, the choice of Moro was not *ad personam*, but strictly instrumental. It was not his individuality that mattered, but his being kidnapped. It was the inciting incident, which had to feature a high-priest of the DC that was needed by the schemers at this critical conjuncture of Italian politics. But what for?

A number of commentators have remarked that in the aftermath of the kidnap, the position of Berlinguer's PCI presented a striking change from that of the past: of the state they had so vehemently vilified for three decades, the Communists were presently posing as the fiercest, most uncompromising stalwarts—more royalist than the king. Roaring against the BR in the name of National Solidarity, they unleashed in the streets of Rome shortly after the kidnap a presidium of red-clad militants and trade-unionists. Evolving in patterns clearly suggestive of a military drill,[297] they marched as if claiming the governmental perimeter, suddenly thrown in a state of emergency, as their own turf. In parliament, the Neo-Fascists of the MSI (Movimento Sociale Italiano)—part of the exiguous minority that had refused to vote for the new executive on March 16—grew so frightened by what they trepidatiously decried as a Communist takeover that Vito Miceli,[298] who had thereupon flown to Washington, begged the U.S. cavalry to come to the rescue.[299] Why do so if, as the vulgate still suggests, "America" was allegedly in on the operation?

Equally suspect is the episode of the emergency meeting that took place in the premier's (Giulio Andreotti's) office immediately before the confidence vote, an hour or so after Moro's disappearance. The party secretaries of the traditional allies of the DC were present, along with Berlinguer and his lieutenants. The story

296 Satta, V. 2006. 378. Flamigni, S. 2006. 275. Carr, M. 2006. *Unknown Soldiers. How Terrorism Transformed the Modern World.* London: Profile Book. 156.

297 Fisichella, D. 1979. 96.

298 The former Chief of Military Intelligence (1970–1974), most loyal to Aldo Moro.

299 Feldbauer, G. 2000. 80; Flamigni, S. 2006. 69.

has it that in the tense atmosphere of the room the Communist secretary turned earnestly toward Andreotti and requested that, given the exceptional gravity of the situation, several Communists be given key ministerial posts in the executive soon-to-be sworn in.[300] Andreotti refused. Piazzesi's tale had been prophetic: an inciting incident had indeed occurred, yet it seemed that the Catholics were not holding up their end of the bargain.

But most topsy-turvy of all was the actual dénouement of the whole affair. The mainstream press—with *L'Unità* at the forefront[301]—pounced on the news of the kidnap with truculent libido and fermented it into a symphonic and voyeuristic blast the likes of which the discursive sphere has seldom witnessed since. At first they blared that it was all a Soviet, then a German, conspiracy. On a separate track, they then proceeded to "beatify" the victim: Moro, the foe of yesteryear, was presently depicted as "meek and hieratic," "a solitary St George slaying the dragon of the BR."[302] And to render the drama even more grotesque, there were these ghostly "postmen of the BR" that delivered missives and communiqués in abundance, coming and going wherever and however they pleased, always undetected.[303] It was senseless: for so serious an emergency, elementary *raison d'état* demanded that an information shutdown be enforced as stringently as possible. Why did the authorities not impose on papers and newscasts a complete black-out[304] or some form of scrambling, as they did when Sossi had been taken? In fact, the regime not only refrained from muzzling the media, but ratcheted things up, deeming it opportune to give news agents and publicists free rein, full-time, to indulge scandalizing speculations and politological imbrications to paroxysmal heights. It seemed as though the media were shooting a film, which the BR had scripted.[305] Terrorism could not have hoped for a more efficient soundboard.[306] Even *before* the BR would issue their "hallucinating" communiqués, the *Corriere della Sera* titled that the Republic would not be blackmailed, and that there would be no dealing with the terrorists under any circumstances. Which meant that, unless the Special Forces rapidly managed to flush him from the "people's prison," Moro was doomed. But who had yet heard the *brigatisti* demand ransom or to negotiate anything?[307] In any case, the audiences were informed that this was, beyond any reasonable doubt, a shameful assault on the "historical compromise." And this was merely the beginning, for this "baroque"[308] insanity would produce one vertiginous

300 Colombo, A. 2008. 53.

301 The press organ of the PCI.

302 Silj, A. 1978. 9–17, 28, 29.

303 Flamigni, S. 2006. 270.

304 Solé, R. 1979. 227.

305 Silj, A. 1978. 43.

306 Girotto, S. 2002. 351.

307 Da Rold, G. 1982. *Da Ottone alla P2. Sei anni di Compromesso Storico al Corriere della Sera*. Milano: SugarCo. 58.

308 Solé, R. 1979. 62.

absurdity after another, such as the surprise that of the "no-negotiations" party, the most inflexible hardliners were the Communists themselves.[309]

Admittedly, the inexplicably counter-intuitive and cynical stance of Berlinguer vis-à-vis Moro's ordeal and chances of survival is still one of the most perplexing aspects of the mystery. Pro-PCI apologists have promptly excused their hero, protesting that the new hyper-legalistic course of the PCI was leaving its spokespersons no alternative; the Party *had* to defend the State, whatever the cost.

Disingenuous argument. Had not the Liberal press, presently favorable to the Communists,[310] averred that Moro was the pivot of the "compromise"? And now that his life was at stake, his Communist "allies" turned their back on him without a moment's hesitation, recoiling into what could pass as the stiffest of traitorous behaviors. How could the integrity and the electoral capital of the PCI have in any way suffered if Berlinguer had hinted that he was ready to seek bargaining avenues to save the priceless life of his cherished "partner"? Not only would Berlinguer not lift a finger for Moro, but he would actually wait out the foretold execution with disturbing aloofness.

We have reached a provisional point where we may recapitulate the facts and restate our alternative screenwriting treatment of the events of March 16, 1978.

Between 1975 and late 1977 segments of the U.S. and the USSR must have settled for some kind of pact intended to roll over the lease of the Soviet Union. Some of the main conduits for the purpose unsurprisingly ran through Italy. This makeshift arrangement had determined opponents from the first hour; these would rise and carry the day with the neo-liberal coup (1979–1981), which eventually nullified this late "compromise," and consequently the geostrategic usefulness of the Soviet Union. In this interval of critical instability, which does reach, in point of fact, as far back as Piazza Fontana (December 1969), ascendant financial/economic interests wishing to unclench the DC's feudal choke-hold on Italy's economy were pushing their way to the fore of political decision. It was as if Italy had three levels of bourgeoisie: B1, the traditional Catholic-conservative bloc; B2, the new Liberal-technocratic elite; and B3, the Mafia: B2 came to challenge B1, and B3, coming in the wake of B2, merely sought to advance its interests by scavenging the scraps of the fight.[311] To pre-empt B2 it is likely that B1 invented (or appropriated) the putschist strategy of 1969. The Red Brigades, instead, seem to point to B2: we know that the "first generation" of the BR was closely monitored by the PCI,[312] and that it was presumably funded by an industrial/financial clan of the north, that of Pirelli, Falck and Feltrinelli ("the infernal trio"),[313] which, itself, could have been part of the wider "Anglo-Dutch" faction mentioned earlier.

309 Giovagnoli, A. 2005. 121.

310 Preti, L. 1975. 39.

311 De Lutiis, G. 2007. 220–24.

312 Fasanella, G. and Franceschini, A. 2004. 44.

313 Hallier, J. L. 1991. *Le dandy du grand chemin. Conversations avec Jean-Louis Remilleux*. Paris: Éditions Michel Lafon. 41, 77.

There remains, then, to shed light on Moretti's new BR. There is yet no judicial proof that they "worked for" the PCI, and in support of their independence and impermeability, some claim that they were not infiltrated during the *affaire* Moro,[314] while others have countered that they certainly were, mentioning at least one documented case, which was handled by Military Intelligence.[315] As a further installment of *dezinformatsia* (produced in 1974 by the Carabinieri), it was also rumored that the BR were directed by Czech Intelligence. Rolling cunningly with the canard, the Communists regularly sent to Prague an envoy[316] to "dissuade" the Czech comrades from pursuing such dangerous games;[317] and even five days before Moro's assassination (May 4), one of the PCI's generals made a show of summoning the Czech ambassador to "warn" him that the eventual disclosure of his government's responsibility in the *affaire* might have disastrous consequences.[318]

Proof or no proof, it is difficult not to see that the BR were created, and refitted, to fuel the PCI's "drive toward the center." As stated earlier, what is characteristic of the Italian Communists in this phase is their *attendismo*, their wait-and-see attitude in the war of the Bourgeoisies. It seems as though they watched the duel intently, hoping eventually to get an engagement, an engagement that would arrive in mid-1974, when the first BR were dismantled in view of the escalation. In this sense, the true target of terrorism in the seventies was the DC, and certainly not the PCI, which, in the final analysis had offered itself for hire to overthrow the Catholics. That is why the DC rejected the *compromesso storico* from the first, and selected Moro as commander-in-chief to conduct the great Christian-Democrat army to battle against the historical adversary.[319] As detailed above, the tactic was straightforward: he would attract the PCI "mid-way through the ford" and, as Cossiga put it, proceed to "screw" them.[320] As the international situation evolved (with the geostrategic demise of the USSR), the PCI was expected to lose votes, return irreversibly to the opposition, and die a slow death. Which is exactly what came to pass.

In late 1977, as we saw, Berlinguer & Associates felt strong enough as to dictate to Moro & Friends the terms of a "deal," whose contents may be intuited only through guesswork. Berlinguer was pressed for time, and each faction mistrusted the other *completely*:[321] we may assume that under this "armed truce," *the two factions met to compose their mutually hostile programs into a peculiar arrangement, which the Christian-Democrats thought of scuttling at the first*

314 Satta, V. 2006. 29.

315 Limiti, S. 2009. 183; Flamigni, S. 2003, 190; Scarrano, M. and De Luca, M. 1985. 174.

316 S. Cacciapuoti.

317 Sechi, S. ed. 2009. 109, 164.

318 Imposimato, F. and Provvisionato, S. 2008. 234.

319 Gismondi, A. 1986. 62.

320 Farina, R. 2010. 117.

321 Chiara, V. 1997. 282; Colombo, A. 2008. 64–6.

suitable opportunity, and the Communists of using, instead, as a springboard into the upper level of government. In any case, *appearances had to be saved at all costs.* If politics is theatrics, why not turn the occasion into a "gigantic feat of dramatic display,"[322] the most memorable of the epoch?

Why not give the PCI three "technicians" in the new executive of March 1978? If that is all the Communists wanted to say "yes" to Andreotti's second government of National Solidarity, why not accede to such a trifling request? Why would Moro, allegedly the "friend" of the Left and the greatest of all mediators, veto it? *Could it be, then, that the whole abduction was to be a deception from the outset?* Could it be that it was engineered with the full-spectrum complicity of DC, PCI and the top hierarchy of the intelligence brethren with the objective of causing among the people so disorienting an impression as to distract them entirely from the macroscopic innovation of a Communist presence if not in the executive, at least in the majority? Ideally—like in Piazzesi's poli-sci-fi dime novel—the incident should have been "painless."[323] From the start, Berlinguer was aiming to obtain a handful of secondary ministries, though it would have been "stupid" on his part to insist on the request too strongly and too soon (after the abduction): he had to exercise caution not to be seen joining the majority by stepping over five warm bodies.[324] He was hoping he would have achieved that goal, one patient step at a time. It would thus appear that Andreotti double-crossed him immediately. The tug-of-war was on.

What of Moro? Could we possibly imagine that he, too, willingly lent himself to this horrifying mummery? That this "match" with Berlinguer signified so much that Moro would make himself the accessory to the murder of the five innocents deputized to protect him? That he had just been sitting in car, as it turned right on Via Fani, waiting knowingly and impassibly the carnage about to happen? It is unthinkable.

And yet one cannot help brooding over the utter disdain and indifference, with which men of power close to him greeted his suffering and death. It is disquieting on a variety of levels. It is not so much the case with his brothers-in-arms of the DC, or even with Berlinguer, who, when it was all over, confided to a collaborator that he found Moro's breakdown in the face of death a pathetic display of weakness: "when one assumes the responsibility of leading a great party, committing to the task before millions of people," he sentenced, "one should be ready for sacrifice, including that of one's life."[325] These were certainly not the words of a deferential confederate, let alone of a friend, and there is a tinge of resentment laced with contempt in that judgment which gives pause. More troubling than even these suggestions is an off-the-cuff comment that the then archbishop of Genoa, Cardinal Giuseppe Siri, made to a journalist not long after the event: "Moro got what he

322 Mosse, G. L. 1979. lxix.

323 Bernabei, E. and dell'Arti, G. 1999. 108.

324 Solé, R. 1979. 29.

325 Chiara, V. 1997. 289.

deserved," snapped Siri, "that is what you get by opening to the Communists."[326] Now, that is exactly the sort of (arch-conservative) view the leftist vulgate would expect a high prelate to express. Yet it came out too harshly; Siri himself felt it and tried to backtrack. Contempt, again, but why? What makes a leading personality of the Church, of all people, reflexively direct such obloquy at a revered Catholic statesman that had just been conferred the exaltation of State "martyrdom"[327]? Is differing political *opinion* sufficient warrant therefore? Something is out of joint here. We have retraced Moro's *démarche* in dealing with Berlinguer, and we have all read his somewhat inconclusive yet consistently and unambiguously *polemical* declarations on the spiritual valence of Communism and the eventual bi-party alternance with a reformed PCI.[328] We can safely affirm that neither his *cursus*, nor his overall demeanor versus the Communists, nor his speeches and writings, let alone the eerie and mysterious "letters from the people's prison"—which say everything and its opposite,[329] too little and too much[330]—form any strong evidence that he was "opening" to the party of Berlinguer. And a cardinal *papabile*, an experienced dignitary like Siri must have surely known this. So, again we ask, why the loathing? So, did Moro actually play with fire and suffer proper retribution? Had he got what he truly deserved?

Poring over the titles and leaders of the foreign press (especially French and German) at the time of the abduction, one cannot help noting the exceptional recurrence of the word "*trap*"—as in, "Moro fallen victim of his own trap"—and of the suggestion that the whole incident was to manifest benefit of the Communists.[331] On April 24, 1978 *Die Welt* wrote:

> To be something more than a simple episode of transformism the "historical compromise" needs to be *cemented* by a terrible or dramatic event, something upon which to construct its mythical ideal, a sort of human sacrifice. This is indeed the sense of Moro's martyrdom.[332]

But even if one dares to utter the ineffable, there remains in this outlandish landscape to account in some fashion for the epilogue, and even more so for the putative *mise-en-scène* of this incubus of Italy's First Republic. For if it was one giant deceit, what caused the abrupt turns, the sudden requests for a hostage

326 Valle, A. 2008. 35.

327 Silj, A. 1978. 186.

328 Moro, A. 1979. 269–76, 298, 320, 330–31, 365–9, 372, 384–91.

329 Di Nolfo, E. 1996. *La Repubblica delle speranze e degli inganni: l'Italia dalla caduta del fascismo al crollo della Democrazia Cristiana*. Firenze: Ponte delle Grazie. 495.

330 Pietra, I. 1983. 17.

331 Condorelli, N. B. 1982. La stampa francese, in *Cultura e politica nell'esperienza di Aldo Moro*, edited by P. Scaramozzino. Milano: Giuffré Editore. 201–76.

332 Brissa, E. 1982. La stampa tedesco-occidentalein *Cultura e politica nell'esperienza di Aldo Moro*, edited by P. Scaramozzino. Milano: Giuffré Editore. 289.

swap, the fake seventh communiqué, or the incomprehensible inflexibility of the regime in the face of the no less inflexibly irrational demands of the BR? What prompted Bettino Craxi's PSI to split unexpectedly from the front of intransigence and cast about for a "humanitarian" solution (i.e. an exchange of prisoners to save Moro)? Was this, too, a *coup de théâtre*, a contrivance within a contrivance, staged by the *registi occulti* to signal that the script had changed in the fourth Shakespearean act: that the "deal" with Berlinguer was off and that the PSI had been given the green light to erode the front of National Solidarity through this gambit of simulated compassion? It is possible: the Communists were literally enraged by it. Otherwise known for their mastery of self-restraint, this time they could not contain their wrath at the effrontery of this, they railed, perfectly "ignoble maneuver."[333] It could be that originally the plan was to free Moro after a few weeks in the course of a slam-bang, Swat-team-kaboom rescue operation, Mogadishu-style.[334] Such would have been indubitably a stipulation concerted for the greater benefit of the PCI. But then something must have changed, or, possibly, the double-cross had been contemplated from the beginning. Either way, the switch, which determined Craxi's "defection," decided the death of the hostage. By then, the game had become so contorted, and the tangles of complicity so liable to becoming unthreaded and exposed, that the circus macabre had to be wrapped up as expeditiously as possible. Barring a police rescue, if Moro had been released unharmed by the BR, the outcome would have been embarrassing for the DC, but *disastrous* for the PCI; with Moro dead, the DC earned sympathy and the PCI saved face (barely). For a brief spell, his death did indeed "cement" the compromise.[335]

In the end, Moro and the DC won the match. After nine months or so of a "National Solidarity" built on foundations as damned as these the PCI quit the majority in the wake of a polling and electoral drubbing. Berlinguer had not given up on the "compromise" just yet, but in actuality it was over. The USSR was in Afghanistan, and soon Gorbachev would come to pull the plug on the Soviet show. Not long after the end of National Solidarity, as he addressed his lieutenants in a moment of reflection dedicated to the *affaire* Moro, Berlinguer conceded that he and his "had been overly naïve." Naiveté: the politician's unforgivable sin.[336] From then on it would be a slow decline until Berlinguer's death in 1984 (he was 62)—at which time Red terrorism and the BR almost suddenly vanished. Just another freak correlation? In sum, what had happened was that for a parenthetical

333 Fava, N. 2008. *Aldo Moro, una tragedia aperta*. Roma: Adn Kronos.

334 On October 13, 1977, German Special Forces stormed in Mogadishu's airport a Lufthansa jet originally departed from Mallorca on October 13, 1977 (Flight 181), which had been hijacked by Palestinian terrorists in connection with the abduction of H. M. Schleyer (September 5–October 18, 1977) by the RAF; see, e.g., de Castro, R. and Campos, M. 1977. *Sabbia a Stammheim. Uno spettacolo terrorista*. Torino: Studio Forma Editrice.

335 Finetti, U. 2009. 110.

336 Mafai, M. 1996. 24.

excerpt of the 1970s, the USSR—and its Anglo-American supporters—thought it could buy more time by "social-democratizing" its European appendices—but, then, why have two Socialist parties when only one was "needed"?[337]

For all the glory of 1974–1977, Berlinguer is "distant"[338] these days—as is Moro, having both of them faded from memory like byproducts that only have meaning in the highly confined context of their drab epoch: the late era of the Cold Game. The victory of the DC (and of Craxi's PSI), however, would prove to be a 10-year long respite, until the post-Berlin winds of 1992 would splinter into pieces the tumbledown Palazzo of the First Republic.

> Time after time —I should say periodically— everyone assumes that the DC is scheduled to rendezvous the forces of Reaction with a view to engineering a political swerve, which, by clustering around Communism old and new alliances, would put Italy at the mercy of Communism; and by so doing, would warrant the resort to Fascist dictatorship in order to save Italy from Communist dictatorship. I can safely affirm [...] that this swerve has not happened, nor will it happen, ever. (Aldo Moro, October 24, 1959)[339]

It was not true, as they all said, that the death of Moro dramatically changed history's course. The BR would go on killing 17 more individuals after him—the power ratios had merely begun to budge. And, nested within tangles of conspiratorial threads, cock-and-bull stories kept circulating such as the one purporting that Moro's kidnap was the idea of three *commanditaires*: two parliamentarians and an official of the Vatican. In this setting, the assassins that sprayed that hail of bullets with professional precision in Via Fani were actually Carabinieri, who had to cut down the colleagues of the security detail for fear of being recognized. So the hit-men were cops; but the minds of the organization, those, instead, were to be found at the highest echelons of the magistrature. And here was the gem: the Deep Throat that had gone to DC leader Flaminio Piccoli to unbosom himself of such incandescent *mysteria* thereupon proposed to Piccoli that he feigned of being abducted by a commando a "trusted" *brigatisti*. Piccoli was to make a pretense of being kidnapped so that he could be spirited to the HQ of the BR, where he would have had the opportunity to unmask the three mysterious conjurors.[340]

337 Becker, J. J. 1981. *Le Parti Communiste veut-il prendre le pouvoir? La stratégie du PCF de 1930 à nos jours*. Paris: Seuil. 312; *International Herald Tribune*, April 28, 1979 quoted in Frank, A. G. 1980. 150.

338 Mafai, M. 1996. 89.

339 Moro, A. 1979. 237.

340 Story published by *L'Espresso* on February 17, 1979, in Flamigni, S. 2006. 401.

A Vulgate for Posterity

Ever since Moro died the way he did, and Berlinguer implicitly conceded defeat, it seems as though the regime settled on a version of the events that was to the satisfaction of the parties involved. This was to be the leftist vulgate: Berlinguer's version. By covering the truth with two inventions—Moro's leftism, and the PCI's victimization—and laying the whole blame for Italy's tribulations on "the CIA" (and lately, to a minor degree, on "the KGB"[341] or "the British"[342]), the Catholics kept the citadel while (the heirs of) the Communists continued to claim moral primacy.

And to Conclude, Carl Schmitt

Since the late 1980s, most terrorists have been "amnestied":[343] some have been reintegrated cum laude as sociology professors,[344] others as social workers, and others still have quietly withdrawn to a modest middle-class existence. And, to this day, only a fistful of *irriducibili* is languishing in prison. Piazzesi had seen far on this too: it was the Church that would oversee the process of pacification, and it began in the prisons.[345] Afterwards, it was understood that no one was ever to speak a word of all this (namely Curcio's "oath").[346]

Is this, then, a tale of the so-called "Dual State"?[347] Is the Moro *affaire*, in other words, a further illustration of the principle according to which the political machine of Liberalism is comprised of a legitimate façade—i.e. the institutions—and its illegal flip side? This theory claims that the illegal underground is managed on behalf of the elite by those sectors of the regime logistically contiguous to the liminal zone of criminal activity, namely, the police and the secret services. And this management, in point of fact, consists in recruiting assassins and saboteurs or strikebreakers[348] to muffle any kind of progressive yearning that might, by (mis)-chance, develop in the "legitimate," presentable half of society. This would imply that there is a villain on one side of the spiritual fence and a hero on the other, and that the villain, on average, always manages to crush the hero by turning against him, deceitfully, the violence of the underclass. The (Communist) vulgate is keen

341 Imposimato, F. and Provisionato, S. 2008. 193–244.

342 Cereghino, M. J. and Fasanella, G. 2010. *Il golpe inglese. Da Matteotti a Moro: Le prove della guerra segreta per il controllo del petrolio e dell'Italia*. Milano: Chiarelettere.

343 Pecorelli, M. cited in Flamigni, S. 2006. 295.

344 Namely Prospero Gallinari.

345 Valle, A. 2008. 208–9.

346 See note 115.

347 Cucchiarelli, P. 2009. 419.

348 Foucault, M. 1975. *Surveiller et punir, naissance de la prison*. Paris: Gallimard. 282.

to state that the Christian-Democrats were the henchmen, whereas the Catholics rejoin allusively, if sporadically, that they were the victims, instead. In Veblenian terms,[349] this is to say that whenever the modern agonistic space is disputed by two factions, each posits itself as the non-barbarous and enlightened elite, and by doing so perforce constructs the opponent as the evil, *inimical* mirror image of itself: i.e. as a counter-elite, equally tenacious yet *barbarous*. As such, one accuses the other—either a conservative incumbent or an iconoclastic challenger—of tapping the underworld (barbarous but non-tenacious) with sinister and hostile intent whenever the letter of the law does not reach far enough in this labor of conservative control or of revolutionary reconfiguration. One could proceed with this schema if a proper definition of "conservative" and "iconoclastic" could be had, but the endeavor might prove to be wholly futile considering that, in our case, the political fight took place between two fairly homogeneous groups of Italian bourgeois. Which fact then points to a higher, more encompassing level of allegiance: the supranational dimension.

Three factions were possibly at play here: the (Yankee) traditionalists, the Liberals and the Catholics. Unlike the Liberals of the Trilateral Commission, Nixon's traditionalists did not seem entirely hostile to the Vatican. The Communists merely figured as hirelings of the Trilateral at a time when the USSR, which owned them, was selling out to hold onto the half of the world it had earned at Stalingrad. To strengthen the empire, Nixon sought to weaken Europe economically while decompressing the game with Russia and opening to China so as to keep every player on its guard. Nixon was an imperial generation ahead of his time: what he foreshadowed was indeed something resembling the scheme of the Euro, by which Russia is kept at bay, and Europe is economically debilitated by the erasure of productive investment[350] and the wreckage of its manufactures by China's slave-driven export industry.[351]

Ultimately, the *affaire* Moro was a quite circumscribed expression of Cold War dynamics to the extent that the Liberals, having gained the upper hand over the traditionalists for a period of approximately three years (1974–1977), had attempted to challenge the Church by pitting the proxies of the DC versus the Communists. To that effect, as argued in this study, they appear to have also relied, as a matter of course, on fairly classic terroristic methods.

So this was not a story of "dual state" but, more simply, of "dual option," so to speak, in that both elites,[352] when they came to be split in the middle owing to higher

349 Thorstein, V. 1899. *The Theory of the Leisure Class: A Study of Economic Institutions*. New York: Macmillan. Chapter 9, 212–45.

350 Germany, Europe's only competitive zone, finances the trade deficits of the weaker partners, which are encouraged thereby to increase their level of indebtedness by selling IOUs not just to Germany but also to the rentiers most interested and vested in the scheme: the United States and the UK.

351 Cotta, A. 2010. *Sortir de l'euro ou mourir à petit feu*. Paris: Plon. 17–28.

352 Scarrano, M. and De Luca, M. 1985. 197.

political pressure, had standard recourse to the "lower depths" for fishing viler sub-species with which to fight their dirty (civil) war. In truth, swathes of enlightened individuals across the middle-class—that is, individuals that are entitled to call "others" "barbarous"—no longer seem to exist. In a postmodern world, what we imbibe, rather, is an undifferentiated mass-culture that has expanded in keeping with the geo-spiritual transformation of the earth as a consequence of Anglo-American domination. Such domination is a direct emanation of the islander's seafaring mindset, which does not reckon in terms of material boundaries, as the continental psyche does, but of unbounded water- and air-space.[353] Psychically, the deeper projection of the seafarer's imperial unconscious is a world in which all national divides are effaced, cultural variation annulled, religious worship abjured (and replaced with uniformed devoutness variously accented), and all languages Anglicized so as to make room for the onset of a permanent "global civil war." Such a metamorphosed battlefield allows Anglo-America to wage war in standardized fashion anywhere in the world, and even, if need be, by instigating populations against their own governments.[354] Accordingly, the martial style, too, has had to adapt to the shift: where nationhood has been obliterated, the deployment of conventional troops gives way to the regular use of *irregulars*: the "*partisans*"—i.e. sappers of the underbrush operating behind enemy lines. Originally conceived in occupied countries as guerrillas with a license to savagery, it was fitting that these partisans, rankless and faceless, would come to swarm the *undifferentiated* bellicose space of the global civil war. From defensive, the partisan has tuned into an aggressive force, which is gradually accumulated in proprietary form by international or supranational centrals. It was thus that these irregulars became the conventional effectives of techno-industrial armies, which the great powers needed to foment a series of "controlled wars." Given that the partisan is, essentially, a *terrorist*, the level of brutality and devastation characterizing such controlled disorder has greatly intensified.[355]

Carl Schmitt's pessimistic romance is a fair approximation of the environment in which the *affaire* Moro occurred. One discerns in it the transversal factions, the apodictic primacy of Anglo-America, and the USSR's standing as comprimario on account of its decidedly inferior "techno-industrial" apparatus. The relevance and importance of the partisan/terrorist is in this context obvious enough. Of course, it was no accident that the American centrals came into close contact and eventually into conflict with the Christian-Democrats, or rather, it was no accident that the

353 Schmitt, C. 1942. *Land und Meer. Eine weltgeschichtliche Betrachtung*. Stuttgart: Klett-Cotta.

354 Schmitt, C. 2007. *La guerre civile mondiale. Essais (1943–1978)*. Maisons-Alfort: Éditions èRe. 48. Think, in this connection, of the late mass uprisings, such as the "Arab Spring" (2011), which have been most disingenuously attributed by western propaganda to the allegedly spontaneous, democratic and coalescing powers of social media such as Facebook and Twitter.

355 Schmitt, C. 1962. *Teoria del partigiano*. Milano: Adelphi. 78, 104–5, 130.

DC would, after a war that had hollowed out the geo-spiritual notion of "Italy" of any residual substance, be the sole arbiter of the peninsula's political destiny: as stewards of the Church, the Christian-Democrats were the representatives of the only other boundless imperium of the West. One, indeed, without divisions, yet endowed with superior psychical might.

Chapter 11
Schmitt, Ergenekon and the Neocons

Len Bracken

A democracy can be militarist or pacifist, absolutist or liberal, centralized or decentralized, progressive or reactionary, and again different at different times without ceasing to be a democracy.

Carl Schmitt[1]

While Carl Schmitt was himself a different man at different times in his life, he consistently conceived of democracy as a political entity that had recourse to centralized, authoritarian power in a state of exception—an emergency unforeseen by the constitution requiring suspension of laws by the executive. This radical premise stems from the well-known Schmittian concept of "the political" that precedes political entities and is founded on a friend-or-foe dichotomy applicable to all political actors.[2] Schmitt was not averse to making exceptions to constitutional rule so long as these exceptions were in keeping with what he viewed as the national character. As can be gleaned from the epigraph, Schmitt held that a political system with the attributes of a dictatorship could still constitute a democracy.

Schmitt's personal history and evolution into a world historical figure should be viewed from several angles. He published his first books during World War I, when he traveled in German Expressionist art circles and then ardently performed his military service before working in the faculty of law of the University of Strasbourg. The chaotic debut of the Weimar Republic saw the publication of Schmitt's important works on dictatorship[3] and political theology[4] while he was at Strasbourg and then later in Greifswald. At the latter institution, one of the oldest in Europe, he was a professor of public law and "state theory," a term denoted in German as *Staatswissenschaft*. His *Crisis of Parliamentary Democracy* was published in 1923 as the new republic gained some stability and he was teaching law in Bonn. His *Theory of the Constitution* and *Concept of the Political* came out near the peak of this stable phase, in 1928, when Schmitt became a professor of law in Berlin and was widely recognized as an influential thinker. Publication of his

---

1 Schmitt, C. 1988. *The Crisis of Parliamentary Democracy*. Cambridge, MA: MIT Press. 25.

2 See Chapter 1, this volume.

3 Schmitt, C. 1994. *Die Diktatur*. Berlin: Dunker and Humbolt.

4 Schmitt, C. 1985. *Political Theology: Four Chapters on the Concept of Sovereignty*, trans. G. Schwab. Chicago: University of Chicago Press.

essay "Legality and Legitimacy" in 1932 coincided with events in which Schmitt played an active part that proved to be disastrous for the democratic republic.[5]

Legal scholars who have delved into the problems posed by Schmitt ask how a constitutional lawyer of his stature could entertain the idea that a coup d'état would save the constitution, and again how he could personally participate in such a project in the summer of 1932 and recommend the same solution in January 1933.[6] Schmitt was not one to remain a professor and theorist during such exceptional times, and in July 1933 he became a Nazi official who would go on to craft constitutional and international law policy positions for the regime. The Weimar Constitution remained in effect until 1945 despite the Enabling Act and Hitler's violations of even that law's constitutionally questionable provisions.

This chapter draws a line from Schmitt and the 1932 coup through to both Leo Strauss, a professor of political science at the University of Chicago from 1949 to 1969, and, ultimately, to U.S. neoconservative policymakers and their possible support for a coup plot in Turkey in 2003. The probability of this confidential or clandestine support for the coup plot is based on the logical implication of the intellectual inclination of the Schmittian worldview and the strategic situation created by the Iraq War. The primary arc of this line comprises three segments.

First, Schmitt was a key supporter of the 1932 coup d'état in Prussia and his subsequent writings expressed continued support for analogous exceptions that permit the subversion of constitutional democracy. Second, Schmitt and Strauss exerted reciprocal influence on each other as both based their thought on the Hobbesian principle that authority is derived primarily from power. Third, several of Strauss' students at the University of Chicago, chief among them Paul Wolfowitz, would later form the neoconservative network that successfully pushed for the 2003 Iraq War, but Wolfowitz's long-standing request to open a Turkish front in the conflict was denied—a request that predated the war by nearly two years.

Schmitt's support for the Prussian coup that paved the way for the Nazi regime is of interest in itself, especially given the lasting academic study of his political essays. This support for a putsch is of particular interest in light of a 2003 Turkish coup plan that was discovered later and foiled by the pro-Islamic prime minister, Recep Tayyip Erdogan of the Justice and Development Party (AKP), whose only close rival in the 2002 elections was Deniz Baykal of the Republican People's Party—a politician and party closely aligned with the Turkish, and, by extension, the U.S. military. The Turkish coup plan, code named Operation Sledgehammer, must be seen as a continuation of the much older Turkish Gladio and Ergenekon deep-state or shadow government movements that were organized by officers who favored the secular political orientation of the Turkish republic's founder,

---

5 Baume, S. 2008. *Carl Schmitt, Penseur de l'état.* Paris: Sciences Po. 280–286.

6 Beaud, O. 1997. *Les Derniers jours de Weimar: Carl Schmitt face á l'avènement du nazisme.* Paris: Descartes et Cie. 185.

Mustapha Kemal Atatürk.[7] Sledgehammer coincided with the beginning of the Iraq War that had been long sought by members of the U.S. neoconservative network who were uniformly pro-Israeli and disfavored the Islamic orientation of Erdogan and the AKP. Turkish public opinion was against the U.S. war with Iraq, and this opposition was reflected in a parliamentary vote disallowing the United States to use Turkey to open another front in the war. Connections and parallels between Schmitt, Strauss and the U.S. neoconservatives are made throughout the chapter based on three events: the successful Prussian coup, the foiled Turkish coup plan, and the denial of access to the United States by Turkey of another front in the war.

Schmitt and the 1932 Prussian Coup

> The fault lines of Weimar's failure are those of all contemporary liberal democracies, fissures traced and sometimes exacerbated by Carl Schmitt. (Ellen Kennedy)[8]

The highly contentious history of the Weimar Republic, when Nazi Party and Communist Party flags flew alternately from Berlin tenement windows, exemplifies what David Cumin, in *Carl Schmitt: Biographie politique et intellectuelle*, describes as the "triangular conflict" between liberalism, communism and fascism that existed from 1919 to 1945.[9] This is the context in which the German jurist sought to describe the essence of law and politics in the 20th century through his Manichean, friend-or-enemy concept of the "political."[10] The years from 1930 to 1936 comprised Schmitt's most crucial period, according to Cumin, when the legal theorist further developed his fundamental concepts while being personally and directly tied to the political situation.

As he approached this critical period, the conservative Schmitt was not immune to contradictions or the influence of his times. Virtually every field—from art and architecture to physics and philosophy—was radically transformed in the wake of the war. Europe underwent a cultural liberation in which past mores were either dead and buried or seen as irrelevant. The strongly Catholic jurist may have thought that the liberal Weimar Constitution was not up to the real-

7 See Chapter 8, this volume.

8 Kennedy, C. 2004. *Constitutional Failure: Carl Schmitt in Weimar*. Durham, NC: Duke University Press. 187.

9 Cumin, D. 2005. *Carl Schmitt: Biographie politique et intellectuelle*. Paris: Les Éditions du Cerf. 9.

10 Based on the research conducted for my Berlin novel *The East Is Black*, the triangle of conflict between liberalism, communism and fascism that Cumin says lasted until 1945 was at least a hexagon in 1989 that also included anti-colonialism, anarchism-autonomism and radical feminism. Bracken, L. 2006. *The East Is Black*. New York: iUniverse.

world challenges it faced, such as the economic crisis that eventually reached hyperinflationary proportions, and he no doubt deplored the decadence of the Berlin cabaret era. Yet from 1910 to 1920, Schmitt frequented avant-garde circles and was particularly close with the expressionist poet Theodor Däublers—a writer who was, in turn, friends with Berlin Dada artists George Grosz and Hans Richter and wrote the first critical appraisal of them in the journal *Die Aktion*.

Cumin notes that Schmitt claimed to be "100 percent a jurist and nothing else" but the jurist's substantial production of literary criticism reveals a writer who combined juridical logic with aesthetic appreciation.[11] This engagement with German expressionist circles was "highly significant" as Schmitt found in the movement an equivalent to Italian futurism's revolt against bourgeois decadence, thirst for moral renewal and apology for creative violence.[12] Schmitt exhibited early on his proximity with Italian fascist tendencies and shared with the expressionists an orientation toward "exceptions" as well as their intensity, directing his criticism along these lines against the Weimar Republic.[13]

According to Cumin, the jurist never overcame the aesthetic and existential origins of his theories while endeavoring to transform this avant-gardism into law and politics. This vanguard elitism is reminiscent of what Strauss and his followers saw as the need for an elite group of advisers who could sway a leader and the masses in favor of strong moral judgments about good and evil, as James Mann said of Wolfowitz and Strauss in *Rise of the Vulcans*.[14] Mann also stresses the denunciation of moral relativism by Strauss, who trained his students to reject the contention that all points of view are equal and thus none are worthy of a strong defense. Charges of elitism or anti-democratic tendencies are ignored by Straussians who argue for the superiority of a distinctive moral insight, which finds clear echoes in the extreme, although more benign, moral absolutism of some avant-garde artists.

The 2011 exhibit "German Expressionism: The Graphic Impulse" at the Museum of Modern Art, for example, grouped numerous Dada painters with the broader expressionist movement. The polemical tactics and extreme skepticism toward institutions, such as law, reflected the Dada tendency to take absolutist positions, even if this was for arch or artistic purposes. While some Dada participants viewed other German expressionist tendencies as being insufficiently radical, the Dada writer Hugo Ball was friends with Schmitt and reviewed the jurist's most noteworthy book *Concept of the Political*. It was after Strauss wrote a review of the same book that Schmitt initiated what would become a significant

11 Cumin, D. 2005. 27–8.

12 See Chapter 1, this volume.

13 Cumin, D. 2005. 27–32.

14 Mann, J. 2004. *Rise of the Vulcans: The History of Bush's War Cabinet*. New York: Penguin. 26.

correspondence with the professor of political science who shared the jurist's grievances with the Weimar Republic.[15]

The 1932 coup d'état against the Free State of Prussia, referred to as the *Preußenschlag* or "Prussian coup," is viewed by most historians as the lynchpin in undermining the Republic. In the event, President Paul von Hindenburg issued an emergency decree on July 20 dismissing the Cabinet of the Free State of Prussia following a deadly July 17 gun battle in Altona between Nazi and Communist party supporters. Since 1930 Hindenburg had ruled by presidential decree. This was called for under Article 48 of the constitution when a chancellor was unable to obtain a majority in the Reichstag, as was the case for a rapid succession of Hindenberg's chancellors. While the *Altonaer Blutsonntag* or "Altona Bloody Sunday" served to justify the July 20 decree, it also gave Chancellor Franz von Papen the title of commissar of the Reich for Prussia and relieved the Prussian minister-president, the interior minister and the chief of police of their functions.

This dismissal transferred two-thirds of the German police force to central government control. The Prussian ministers declared that they would not cede power until forced to, and Hindenberg was compelled to turn to the Reichswehr, the national army. The President declared a state of siege under Article 48(2) and gave power over the police to General Gerd von Rundstedt who used it to occupy ministry buildings.[16] The Left, which threatened to incite the population into a general strike, was not having much success, and the Reichstag did not demand the withdrawal of the siege using Article 48(3).

On July 21 the former Prussian Cabinet turned to the *Staatsgerichtshof* (the Constitutional Court or State Court, depending on the translation) with a complaint against the Reich based on Article 19 of the constitution—Section 1 of the constitution contains Articles 1–19 pertaining to the legal relationships between the Reich and the Länder or provinces. Article 19 grants jurisdiction to disputes between the Länder or between a single Land and the Reich to the *Staatsgerichtshof*, with invocation of this jurisdiction requiring a request from one party in a dispute. The former Prussian officials sought to have the appointment of a Commissar of the Reich for a Land declared illegal, with other Länder being supportive of the complaint, as they could suffer a similar fate. It was only shortly thereafter, in the July 31 elections, that the Nazi Party increased its number of seats in the Reichstag to 230 and became the single largest party. With Schmitt taking part in the defense of the Reich, the Court of Leipzig ruled on October 25 that Chancellor von Papen had the right to exercise power in place of the displaced ministers. The Court also ruled, however, that the Prussian ministers retained the right to represent Prussia in the Reichsrat, the upper house of Germany's bicameral legislature. Prussia effectively had two co-existing governments until November 8, when the president issued another degree that once again expelled the Prussian

15 Meier, H. 1995. *Carl Schmitt and Leo Strauss: The Hidden Dialogue*, trans. J. Harvey Lomax. Chicago: University of Chicago Press.

16 Cumin, D. 2005. 121.

government and reassigned to the Commissar of the Reich his previously held powers. With the help of von Papen and big business, Adolf Hitler would be named Chancellor in January, effectively putting an end to the "long political-juridical battle," as Cumin calls it, provoked by the July 20 coup d'état.[17]

Schmitt's defense of the Reich against the Prussian charges rested largely on his view that Article 48 vested the Reich president with the responsibility of guaranteeing public order. The jurist also noted that Hindenburg had participated in the Austro-Prussian War in 1866 as a Prussian officer seeking to defend Prussia against the German Confederation. The implied argument connoted by this statement, Cumin writes, is that the "Reich of today is in the situation of the Prussia of yesterday, fighting for the unity of Germany in the face of federalism."[18] Lutz Berthold contends on the basis of Schmitt's dairy that an important paper drafted by Horst Michael in mid-1932 titled "How can an Effective Presidential Government be Protected from an Incompetent and Obstructionist Reichstag, with the Goal of Defending the Constitution?" was written under Schmitt's influence and his constitutional advice. "This empirical evidence only demonstrates what careful reading of Schmitt's published work has long made obvious," Kennedy writes in confirming the jurist's role in the coup. She cites Schmitt's interpretation of Article 25 concerning parliamentary dissolution, Article 48 on presidential powers, and Article 76 dealing with constitutional reform as allowing constitutional reforms without the Reichstag. Strikingly, this type of appeal to the national character and Rousseauian general will was used by Turkish generals to justify their repeated coups, four of which have been successful over the past 50 years.

Following World War II, for reasons related to his provision of the Nazi legal foundations for oppressive domestic security policies and external wars of aggression, Schmitt was interned and interrogated at Nuremburg. He was not, however, tried. He died four years before the fall of the Berlin Wall, which ushered in a renaissance in his thought. In assessing Schmitt's legacy, Kennedy states in that he is the premier theorist of "interim regimes" and "transitional states."[19] The lifting of the Iron Curtain revived these Schmittian theories, designed now to lead from interim regimes to U.S.-friendly democracies. The neoconservatives bent on remaking the Middle East have doubtless kept Schmitt's ideas close at hand to help manage the transitional states formed by the Iraq War and, now, "the Arab Spring."

---

17 Cumin, D. 2005. 122.

18 Cumin, D. 2005. 126. Ellen Kennedy refers to Lutz Berthold as the premier authority on Schmitt's role in the emergency of summer and autumn of 1932. Kennedy, E. 2004. *Constitutional Failure: Carl Schmitt in Weimar*. Durham, NC: Duke University Press. 168.

19 Kennedy, E. 2004. 172.

Eregenekon and Operation Sledgehammer

> The fact that prosecutors are now touching senior generals is a turning point in the democratization process of Turkey … The military realizes it can no longer resist the democratization process and deceive the public. (Lale Kemal)[20]

Ergenekon is alternately described as a mythical place in the Altai Mountains and an actual village in Mongolia that, as the legend has it, was home to the mother wolf that gave birth to Turks or, alternatively, of the wolves that led the Turkish people out of Asia. Ergenekon is also the name now widely used to denote the Turkish "deep state" network that is the successor to the Gladio network set up across Europe by the North Atlantic Treaty Organization (NATO) after World War II that included secret, "stay-behind" armies. In the Turkish case, the network comprised adherents of Kemalism, the secular and nationalist ideology of the Turkish republic's founding father, the military leader turned politician Mustapha Kemal Atatürk.

Daniele Ganser documents in *NATO's Secret Armies: Operation Gladio and Terrorism in Western Europe* how the 1990 admission of Operation Gladio's existence by an Italian prime minister in parliament makes it perhaps the most notorious of the post-World War II stay-behind armies that were purportedly designed to wait for a Soviet invasion or institute military intelligence control of the population in the event of an emergency. An Italian judge was also able to elicit a confession from a false-flag car bomber that he received support from the state, and an Italian general famously testified in court to the use of the "strategy of tension" designed to shock the population into submission and discredit left-wing social movements.[21]

In what government investigators believe is an example of Ergenekon tactics, in November 2003 horrific bombings took place in Istanbul. The British Consulate, Turkish headquarters for the bank HSBC, and synagogues were bombed in four truck-bomb attacks killing 57 and wounding 700. The first set of attacks took place on November 15 and targeted two synagogues—27 people were killed, mostly Muslims, although six Jews died and 300 people were injured. The second set of attacks targeted HSBC and the British Consulate, leaving 30 dead and 400 wounded—again most of the victims were Muslims, although British Consul General Roger Short and other Brits were killed.

A group of Turkish Sunni Jihadis, the Great Eastern Islamic Raiders Front (Ilsamî Büyük Dogu Akincilar Cephesi), claimed responsibility and members

---

20 Quote taken from Butler, D. and Sezer, C. January 5, 2012. Turkish Court Remands Ex-army Chief Pending Anti-government Trial. *Reuters*.

21 Ganser, D. 2005. *NATO's Secret Armies: Operation Gladio and Terrorism in Western Europe*. London: Frank Cass; Willan, P. 1991. *Puppetmasters: The Political Use of Terrorism in Italy*. London: Constable; Brozzu-Gentile, J. F. 1994. *L'Affaire Gladio: Les reseaux secrets Americains au coeur du terrorisme en Europe*. Paris: Albin Michel.

of the group were arrested and tried. Government investigators, however, said the attacks were too sophisticated to have been the sole work of the Jihadis. The blasts were likely part of Operation Sledgehammer (*Balyoz* in Turkish), a coup plot hatched by senior military officials when Recep Tayyip Erdogan, head of the Justice and Development Party (AKP) won the 2002 election. The operation was advanced during a multi-day meeting from March 3–5, 2003 that was at the nexus of several events: parliament voted on March 1, 2003 not to allow U.S. troops access to a Turkish front, the prime minister took office on March 14, 2003, and the Iraq War invasion began on March 20, 2003.[22] According to investigators, the four car bomb attacks that took place eight months later were designed to destabilize Turkey and prompt a military overthrow of the government. The blasts are now regarded in Turkey as that country's 9/11 and they suspiciously coincided with a London visit by U.S. President George W. Bush for meetings with British Prime Minister Tony Blair.

The *Telegraph* states that in February 2010, prosecutors arrested 35 ex-military figures on suspicion of being part of the plot that also envisioned plans to provoke Greece into shooting down a Turkish fighter jet. "General Cetin Dogan, who has been described as the ringleader of the conspiracy as head of the First Army and then deputy chief of the military staff, faced questions over Istanbul bombings before he was remanded in custody on Sunday," the *Telegraph* said in its March 1, 2010 report. "General Ibrahim Firtina, the ex-Air Force chief, and Admiral Ozden Ornek, a former naval commander, also faced questions over the links to the Istanbul bombing."[23] The newspaper also reported that the British Foreign Office expressly said it was not asking for the investigations into the attacks to be reopened.

In order to evaluate the possible confidential or clandestine support from the United States to the Sledgehammer coup plotters, the history of prior coups and the context of the Gladio revelations are required. In a December 15, 2011 Resistance Radio interview, Ganser describes how in 1990 the European Union Parliament condemned the clandestine military structure and asked for an investigation into the chain of command—none was forthcoming. NATO initially issued a denial, then retracted the denial but refused to comment further, Ganser said, recounting how in several instances subordinates protected their superiors, with rare but notable exceptions, such as Italian intelligence officials testifying that the Central Intelligence Agency ordered the 1980 Bologna railway station bombing. The Turkish military rulers prohibited investigations into the matter when, also in 1990, two generals officially confirmed the existence of a Turkish Gladio.[24]

---

22 McElroy, D. March 1, 2010. Turkey Generals Accused of Links to 2003 Istanbul Bombing. *The Telegraph*; Bilgin, F. July 2010. Sledgehammer (Balyoz): How Turkey Averted a Coup in 2003. *The Washington Review of Turkish and Eurasian Affairs.*

23 McElroy, D. March 1, 2010.

24 Ganser, D. 2005. 241.

The Turkish stay-behind army was established by a right-wing extremist, Colonel Alpasan Türks—the contact person in Turkey for the Nazis during World War II.[25] "Convinced of the theories of racial superiority in general and the superiority of the Turks in particular, Colonel Türks in many of his speeches during his career quoted from Hitler's book *Mein Kampf*," Ganser writes. He added that the Turkish colonel made contact with the CIA in 1948 and allegedly set up a secret anti-communist stay-behind army in Turkey on orders from the agency.[26]

The secret army, then known as the Special Warfare Department, was actually housed in the same building in Ankara as the CIA in the early 1950s. In 1960 Colonel Türks, who was then a CIA liaison officer, participated in the May 27 military coup. Ganser holds that Turkey endured the most violence of any country victimized by a stay-behind army and highlights Turkish secret warfare expert Selhattin Celik's contention that the most important actions of the Special Warfare Department were three military coups between 1960 and 1980.[27] The military is also seen as having forced another government from power in 1997.[28]

Celik and other sources maintain that the United States was well informed about the 1960 coup and did nothing to stop it because the putschists were loyal to NATO. Early on Colonel Türks assumed a prominent role in the government that arrested politicians and judges. Later he ran the militant, right-wing youth organization of the National Action Party—the infamous Grey Wolves. The colonel would use his wolves to staff the stay-behind army operating under the name Counter-Guerrilla.[29] According to the Swiss newspaper *Neue Zürcher Zeitung*, the Counter-Guerrilla headquarters were located in the same building as the U.S. Defense Intelligence Agency.[30] General Talat Turhan, a whistleblower and researcher, published three books on the ghastly torture, assassinations, executions and massacres carried out by these so-called wolves, and Ganser further documents the CIA and NATO influence as well as the training of Counter-Guerrilla wolves at the School of the Americas in Ft. Benning, Georgia.[31]

When describing the use by wolves of the Pentagon's classified Field Manual 30-31 that includes instructions for false-flag terrorism, Ganser quotes Turhan as saying the instructions in the manual are incompatible with the constitution and laws, but the instructions were nonetheless implemented after the military coups of March 12, 1971 and September 12, 1980. The latter coup was conducted while NATO carried out a military exercise in Turkey, according to Ganser. He reproduces, moreover, several remarks, including one from President Jimmy Carter and another from National Security Adviser Zbigniev Brzezinski, attesting

25 Ganser, D. 2005. 226.
26 Ganser, D. 2005. 225–6.
27 Ganser, D. 2005. 227.
28 Butler, D. and Sezer, C. January 5, 2012.
29 Ganser, D. 2005. 228–9.
30 Ganser, D. 2005. 241.
31 Ganser, D. 2005. 234.

to tacit U.S. support for the coup.[32] Fevzi Belgin, an assistant professor of political science at St. Mary's College of Maryland, describes how the repeated beatings, bombings and murders in Turkey abruptly ended when the military took over in September 1980. "They [the military] had every opportunity to stop the violence before the full takeover but they did not," Belgin writes.

> Days after the coup, hundreds of thousands of people from every political inclination were rounded up and charged. Tens of thousands of people served in prison for years. More than ten thousand people were stripped of their citizenship ... Hundreds were hanged. All active politicians were arrested and banned from public service.[33]

Before leaving the subject of the 1980 coup, it is interesting to note the European Commission's commissioner for enlargement and European neighborhood policy has expressly stated that the 2010 deletion of the constitutional provision providing immunity "will provide Turkey with an opportunity to do justice for the tragic consequences of the 1980 coup." The commissioner mentioned in this regard the arrest of two former generals, Kenan Evren and Tahsin Sahinkaya, who were charged over the 1980 military coup. The EC's position is that the ongoing investigation into the "alleged criminal network Ergenekon and other alleged coup plans" provides an opportunity to strengthen the functioning of democratic institutions and the rule of law, but the EC is concerned about the transparency of the trail process and the lengthy detention of the defendants. "These concerns," the EC said, "if not addressed, might raise concerns in the public about the legitimacy of the cases."[34]

Wayne Madsen, a former Navy intelligence officer who worked with the National Security Agency and State Department and is now an investigative journalist, has twice traveled to Turkey to track the ongoing Ergenekon investigations. According to Madsen, Turkey stands alone among nations in setting a good example of how to handle its deep state networks by rooting them out and arresting the perpetrators. Turkish intelligence officials have provided Madsen with details on Ergenekon activities, including sensitive information about the roles played by the United States and Israel in the February 28, 1997 forced departure from office of then Prime Minister Necmettin Erbakan on charges of being pro-Islamist.

Erbakan's Welfare Party (*Rafah*) was declared illegal by the Turkish Constitutional Court, which would later also apply pressure on the government run by Erdogan and his AKP, seen as the successor to the Welfare Party. "Erbakan," Madsen writes, "like Erdogan today, attempted to diversify Turkey's foreign relations by establishing closer relations with Iran, Egypt, Pakistan, and other

32 Ganser, D. 2005. 239.

33 Bilgin, F. July 2010. Sledgehammer (Balyoz): How Turkey Averted a Coup in 2003. *The Washington Review of Turkish and Eurasian Affairs*.

34 An email transmitted to the author by a European Commission press officer.

Muslim nations and criticizing Israel for its treatment of the Palestinians."[35] In addition to information from his "sources connected to the Turkish government," Madsen was able to prove with other evidence the strong connection between Israel and the Turkish generals who deposed Erbakan, which is relevant to the 2003 Sledgehammer coup plot and the probable support of the U.S. neoconservative network.

Turkish Deputy Chief of Staff General Cevik Bir, who is considered to be the prime architect of the 1997 soft coup, wrote in 2002 that the army would not "sit by idly and watch Turkey turn toward Islam or allow Israeli-Turkish military relations to be jeopardized" in the fall issue of the *Middle East Quarterly*—a neoconservative publication whose president, Daniel Pipes, at least at one point accepted the neocon label. The article, "Formula for Stablity: Turkey plus Israel" by Bir and Michael Sherman, essentially exposed Bir's role in the coup.[36] Madsen also revealed in the same article an email message, reprinted in a June 24, 2009 article in *Radikal*, in which Bir had an alarming response regarding his plans if he were asked to retire: "I am planning to be the President." The People's Voice Party filed a criminal complaint on January 16, 2012 calling for the arrest of Bir and others involved in the 1997 coup.[37]

Madsen pointed out, moreover, that Bir was awarded the Secularism and Democracy Award of 1997 by the Atatürk Society of America in Washington and that in 1999 Bir received the first International Leader Award given by the Washington-based Jewish Institute for National Security for his "contributions to cooperation with Israel." It is important to note the close ties between the Turkish military and Turkish and Jewish groups in Washington because these connections involve the neoconservative officials in the Bush administration, and they expose the biases of the efforts by these groups to dismiss the overwhelming evidence accumulated by investigators related to Ergenekon.

Madsen's Turkish sources say the U.S. ambassador to Turkey at the time of the 1997 soft coup, who will be referred to as "Official X" in this chapter, is also a subject of the Ergenekon investigation. This individual is currently a high-ranking State Department official and was the unnamed subject of a January 6, 2008 article in the *Sunday Times* based on interviews conducted by journalist Joe Lauria with former Federal Bureau of Investigations translator Sibel Edmonds. Official X, who denied the claims, was allegedly heard on recordings taking bribes from Turkish agents as part of a network that, Edmonds says, included senior Pentagon officials and was involved in the sale of nuclear material or information to Turkish and Israeli intelligence operatives. "If you made public all the information that the

35 Turkey's investigation is Phase I, *Wayne Madsen Report*. May 11, 2010.

36 Bir, C. and Sherman, M. 2002. Formula for Stability: Turkey plus Israel. *Middle East Quarterly*, Fall 2002, IX/4, 23–33.

37 *Hürriyet Daily News*, January 17, 2012.

FBI have on this case, you will see very high-level people going through criminal trials," Edmonds told *The Times*.[38]

One of the people cited in the groundbreaking 2008 *Sunday Times* article containing the assertions by Edmonds is Lawrence Franklin—a Defense Department official charged with passing U.S. defense information to lobbyists working for the American-Israeli Political Action Committee. Franklin had, in 2006, pleaded guilty and was convicted of the charge. Edmonds painted a picture of close Israeli and Turkish cooperation on these operations, and she said Franklin was one of the top people providing information and packages containing nuclear secrets during 2000 and 2001.[39]

In 2002 and 2003, Franklin worked in the Defense Department's notorious Office of Special Plans, which was established by then Secretary of Defense Donald Rumsfeld and headed by Under Secretary of Defense for Policy Douglas Feith. In 1989, Feith had established International Advisers, Inc. that operated as a registered foreign agent for the government of Turkey. Richard Perle was the chairman of the firm's advisory board and had been a close associate of Wolfowitz for many years. Wolfowitz and Perle were the leading proponents in 2002 and 2003 of war with Iraq, according to James Mann.[40] After his 2001–2005 stint in the Pentagon, Feith's lobbying firm Feith & Zell represented Israeli and Turkish interests in Washington.

After Feith's resignation as the head of the Office of Special Plans, his successor would be none other than the U.S. ambassador to Turkey from June 2003 to July 2005, Eric Edelman. This was no coincidence. Prior to his ambassadorship, Edelman was the principle deputy assistant to the vice president for national security affairs from February 2001 to July 2003. Madsen's Turkish sources said that Edmonds had stumbled upon evidence revealing the existence of "deep states" in Turkey and the United States and that U.S. officials were doing all they could to prevent the exposure of U.S. and Israeli links to Ergenekon.

Part of this cover-up involved the disclosure by Bush administration officials—first among them Official X according to Edmonds—of Valerie Plame Wilson's use of the non-official CIA cover firm of Brewster Jennings and Associates during her anti-proliferation efforts.[41] Edmonds holds that long before the infamous 2003 *Washington Times* editorial by Robert Novak that focused on Joe Wilson but disclosed his wife's CIA affiliation, Official X tipped off his Turkish contact that the firm being used by Plame was a CIA cover operation and to be avoided. The information was in turn relayed to Pakistani intelligence agents in Washington and presumably passed on to the A. Q. Khan nuclear proliferation network.

---

38 Gourlay, C., Calvert, J. and Lauria, J. January 6, 2008. For Sale: West's Deadly Nuclear Secrets. *The Sunday Times*.

39 Gourlay, C., Calvert, J. and Lauria, J. January 6, 2008.

40 Mann, J. 2004. 36.

41 Giraldi, P. January 28, 2008. Found in Translation: FBI Whistleblower Sibel Edmonds Spills Her Secrets. *The American Conservative*.

Abdul Qadeer Khan, an engineer who began working for the Pakistani Atomic Energy Commission in the 1970s, roused proliferation suspicions in the 1990s while working on uranium enrichment projects and left his official post in March 2001. The network named after Khan would continue operating at least through 2003, and Khan confessed in 2004 to selling nuclear technology to Iran, Libya and North Korea. The chief of staff to the Vice President, Lewis "Scooter" Libby, who had studied under Wolfowitz, would be convicted of several felonies related to the Plame affair—perjury, making false statements to federal investigators, and obstruction of justice.

In his article on Edmonds and a subsequent interview, former CIA officer Philip Giraldi notes that the ex-FBI translator regards the American Turkish Council and the American-Israeli Political Action Committee (AIPAC) as "sister organizations" and draws connections between them and numerous other players. A pro-Israeli congressman, she said for example, would give classified documents to a staffer who worked directly for one of the advocacy groups and closely with Turkish spies, who in turn would sell information to the Pakistanis.[42] "Two sets of FBI files, but the AIPAC-related files and the Turkish files ended up converging in one," Edmonds said, noting that the original targets were intelligence officers at the Israeli and Turkish embassies but the targets spread out to the groups. "The FBI agents believed they were looking at the same operation."

Edmonds claims, moreover, that the American Turkish Council was used as a conduit for exchanging information and cash. The current chairman of the board of the American Turkish Council, as of January 2012, is Richard Armitage, who was deputy secretary of state from 2001 to 2005 and a strong advocate within the Bush administration for the Iraq War. Drawing on "senior Turkish government, media, and civil society officials," Madsen reports the Ergenekon network is linked to neoconservative think thanks in Washington that seek to paint Erdogan as a radical Islamist, and the investigative journalist names many organizations and individual Ergenekon supporters affiliated with these organizations.[43]

One of the reasons that St. Mary's College of Maryland assistant professor Bilgin was prompted to write his essay on how Turkey averted a coup in 2003 was his opposition to the public relations campaign being waged by Harvard University professor Dani Rodrik. This surprisingly successful media blitz by Rodrik sought to clear the name of his father-in-law, Cetin Dogan, who was arrested in 2010 with others in a roundup of Sledgehammer participants. The campaign, according to Bilgin, is "neither unbiased nor genuinely informational," and the research by Bilgin sets out to show the true details of the case. The evidence of the Sledgehammer plan allegedly drafted by Dogan in 2002 includes the slides for use in presentations that describe the operation plans in detail. These presentation

42 Giraldi, P. January 28, 2008; Edmonds, S. and Giraldi, P. November 1, 2009. Who's Afraid of Sibel Edmonds. *The American Conservative*.

43 Turkish Ergenekon "Deep State" Conspiracy Linked to Neocon Washington Think Tanks. *Wayne Madsen Report*, April 9, 2010.

slides were on compact discs traced to the Turkish military coup conspirators. Other evidentiary items were video recordings that include the voice recordings of military meetings in which the participants discuss a planned coup, a list of individuals to be detained during the coup, and a government action plan to be put into operation before and after the coup that included the bombing of eminent mosques during Friday prayers and the downing of a Turkish jet and blaming the act on Greece.

"The most important evidence of the plan is the voice recording of the meeting that took place on March 3–5, 2003, at a military headquarters in Istanbul under the leadership of Cetin Dogan," Bilgin writes, noting the discussions clearly refer to a plan that was prepared prior to the meeting—most likely right after the November 2002 Erdogan electoral victory. "The date of the meeting was ostensibly set to reflect the political commotion at the time thanks to the heated discussion of a proposal in Turkey's Parliament to allow U.S. troops to operate from Turkish territory in their campaign against Iraq (it was defeated by three votes)."

Implied Coup Support based on Inclination and Situation

> Everybody knows that it is easier to take something concrete than something vague. (Edward Luttwak)[44]

As stated at the outset, this chapter seeks to demonstrate the likely support for the Sledgehammer coup on the part of neoconservative U.S. policymakers based on the logical implication of their ideological inclination and the strategic considerations of the Iraq War. A Schmittian putschist could well have viewed a Turkish military coup as in keeping with the Kemalist national character and as necessary to maintain the republic's secular reforms, particularly given the country's tradition of military coups that Kemalists justified by various threats to the existing order—in this case the coming to power of the pro-Islam AKP and Prime Minister Erdogan who sought to restore certain Muslim rights. A contemporary Schmittian putschist who was an advocate of Israeli interests would also be inclined to depict Turkish Islamists in unfavorable terms normally reserved for the enemy and to oppose any deviation from a pro-Israel foreign policy by the Erdogan government. If the newly elected, pro-Islamist Turkish prime minister refused to make a constitutional exception to the parliamentary refusal to allow U.S. troops a Turkish front in the Iraq War, a Schmittian putschist would have a strategic rationale to confidentially or clandestinely back the coup plot with the expectation that a change in government would lead to a change in policy regardless of past parliamentary votes.

The record shows that Wolfowitz studied under the Straussian Plato scholar Allan Bloom at Cornell and continued on to Chicago where Strauss was still

44 Luttwak, E. 1968. *Coupe d'Etat: A Practical Handbook.* New York: Fawcett. 25.

teaching. The future Defense Department official took two classes with Strauss, one on Plato and another on Montesquieu, which prompts one to wonder whether senators should have asked at his confirmation hearing about the advisability of the Platonic concept of the noble lie and whether Wolfowitz considered himself to be a philosopher-king.[45] Although he disavowed being a Straussian or adhering to any other label, such a disavowal cannot be believed in connection with Strauss, who openly advanced the thesis that philosophers cannot say publicly what they mean lest they suffer fatal consequences—Strauss discusses this in the chapter "How Farabi Read Plato's *Laws*" in *What Is Political Philosophy?* and elsewhere.[46]

According to Mann—and this is hardly surprising given tutelage under Bloom—Wolfowitz thought Strauss was "a unique figure, an irreplaceable asset."[47] Mann also quotes Jean Kirkpatrick, the former U.S. ambassador to the United Nations, as saying in 2002, "Wolfowitz is still a leading Straussian."[48] Steven Smith states in *Reading Leo Strauss: Politics, Philosophy, Judaism*, that the question of whether or not one is a Straussian often has a "are you now or have you ever been" quality to it that customarily receives a less than forthright reply from Straussians.[49]

In passages that scarcely mask her scorn for Strauss' logic, Shadia Drury points out in *Leo Strauss and the American Right* the Platonic contention that democracy leads to tyranny was verified for Strauss in what he saw as Hitler's democratic ascension to power.[50] She adds that this argument—that Weimar set the stage for Hitler and the United States suffers the same ills as Weimar—was propagated first by Strauss then by Bloom in *Closing of the American Mind*.[51] Drury is quick to note, however, that it could readily be said that Hitler's rise was by means of the subversion of Weimar constitutional principles.[52]

The case can be made that for Platonists such as Bloom and Strauss, the tyrannical, or in more modern terms dictatorial or authoritarian, use of power loses its negative quality if exercised by a philosopher-king. This is especially so if it is done in accordance with what Rousseau called the general will. Two fundamental pillars of Bloom's thought were Plato and Rousseau, reflected in the fact that he

45 Mann, J. 2004. 28.

46 Strauss, L. 1959. *What Is Political Philosophy.* Chicago: University of Chicago Press. 134–54; Strauss, L. 1952. *Persecution and the Art of Writing*. Chicago: University of Chicago Press. 22–37.

47 Strauss, L. 1952. 26.

48 Strauss, L. 1952. 28.

49 Smith, S. 2006. *Reading Leo Strauss: Politics, Philosophy, Judaism*. Chicago: University of Chicago Press. 4.

50 Drury, S. 1997. *Leo Strauss and the American Right*. New York: St. Martin's Press. 5.

51 Drury, S. 1997. 6.

52 Drury, S. 1997. 7.

famously translated books by these philosophers.[53] With his intellectual pedigree stretching from Bloom to Strauss, and therefore indirectly to Schmitt as well as Alexandre Kojève and Hegel, did not Wolfowitz see himself as being more than a Defense Department official, as a philosopher-king with intuitive knowledge of the general will? Was he deep down, at least in part, a Schmittian?

Although Schmitt was fascinated with violence, his military service did not include combat in World War I because of a medical condition.[54] Schmitt's response to not facing combat while performing his military service finds evocative if inexact parallels in the U.S. neoconservative "chickenhawks" who sought Vietnam War deferments yet pushed to launch the Iraq War. Wolfowitz was deferred because of his matriculation at Cornell University in pursuit of a mathematics degree.[55] According to one biographer, Schmitt "overcompensated" for his noncombat status through an absolute devotion to military institutions, and as he rose through the ranks, he went so far as to write articles on the need for dictatorship in a time of war.[56]

After the war, Schmitt saw the Weimar Republic as erroneously attempting to prove its democratic credentials to the world when, to the contrary, it was in need of a strong executive power. He deeply resented the Treaty of Versailles having been written into the Weimar Constitution and this ultimately led him to question Germany's sovereignty. Schmitt likewise directed his disdain toward the League of Nations, in part through his support of the U.S. Monroe Doctrine, which from President Theodore Roosevelt on, was a de facto exception to international law whereby the United States asserted the right to prevent further European colonization of American continents and reserved for itself the unilateral privilege of intervening in any Latin American state guilty of "chronic wrong-doing." Schmitt saw in this "big stick" policy, which led to numerous U.S. interventions in Central America and the Caribbean in the first 20-odd years of the 20th century, as recognition of the reality that Hobbes placed in power relations throughout *Leviathan*.

Hobbes penned the first English-language translation of *The Peloponnesian War* by Thucydides and the two writers are seen as pillars, along with Machiavelli, of the Realist school of international relations, which has been the dominant school of the international relations discipline since World War I. Schmitt wrote a book on *Leviathan* and conducted a hidden correspondence with Hans Morgenthau, a founder of the Realist school. Morgenthau, incidentally, along with Strauss,

---

53 Bloom's translation of Rosseau, 1979. *Emile: Or, an Education*. New York: Basic Books.

54 Cumin, D. 2005. 37.

55 The closest Wolfowitz came to combat was the October 2003 bombing of the Hotel al-Rashid in Baghdad, where he was consulting with U.S. military commanders, that resulted in 15 deaths—Wolfowitz was unharmed.

56 Cumin, D. 2005. 38.

taught at the University of Chicago *and* both accused Schmitt of plagiarism.[57] In his *The City and Man*, Strauss devotes a third of the book to Thucydides, whom he regarded as a philosopher alongside Aristotle and Plato rather than strictly a historian.

Strauss hails Thucydides for identifying the reason Sparta and the other states went to war with Athens as the thirst for glory, the competitive spirit (*agon*), and the fear that Athens had risen too high and needed to be brought down—even though treaties establishing peace were still in place. In other words, the rules of international law only apply up to the point where they are useful. If the rules regarding aggression do not apply, then policymakers have a free hand to increase their use of military force to absurd levels.

Wolfowitz and his Straussian-influenced neoconservative cabal would in fact be accused by retired General Wesley Clark, a former Democratic presidential hopeful, of perpetrating a "policy coup" with regard to U.S. policy in the Middle East.[58] Clark publicly revealed the neoconservative game plan to destabilize the region in an extraordinary October 2007 speech given at the Commonwealth Club of California in San Francisco. The first person he named as being responsible for this coup was none other than Paul Wolfowitz.

Clark described a 1991 conversation he had with Wolfowitz, who was then undersecretary for defense policy when Dick Cheney was secretary of defense. Wolfowitz was upset that the Desert Storm campaign had not gone on to depose Saddam Heussein but granted that a lesson had been learnt. "We learned that we can use our military in the region, in the Middle East," Wolfowitz told Clark. "And we've got about five or ten years to clean up those old Soviet client regimes—Syria, Iran, Iraq—before the next great superpower comes in to challenge us."

Clark mentioned Wolfowitz, Vice President Dick Cheney and Secretary of Defense Donald Rumsfeld and "half a dozen other collaborators from the The Project for a New American Century" as taking over the United States in a policy coup aimed at reshaping the Middle East and putting it under U.S. control. The Project for the New American Century was a neoconservative think tank that advocated U.S. domination of the world through the waging of multiple simultaneous wars, and it famously sought a new Pearl Harbor to justify going on the offensive. Wolfowitz completed his dissertation at the University of Chicago under Albert Wohlstetter whose wife Roberta is the author of *Pearl Harbor: Warning and Decision*,[59] which Secretary of Defense Rumsfeld reportedly required his aides to read. Clark emphasized that there was no national dialogue on these Middle East policy objectives and no congressional consultation, so he was

57 Meier, H. 1995; Scheuerman, W. E. 1999. *Carl Schmitt: The End of Law*. New York: Rowman & Littlefield. 225–35.

58 Commonwealth Club of California website has an archive of the live recording of the October 3, 2007 speech by General Wesley Clark.

59 Wohlstetter, R. 1962. *Pearl Harbor: Warning and Decision*. Stanford: Stanford University Press.

astonished when an unnamed active duty officer pulled him aside in the Pentagon and told Clark of plans launched by Deputy Secretary of Defense Wolfowitz in the immediate wake of the 9/11 attacks in New York and Washington. The plans quite simply were to attack seven countries in the Middle East in five years.

Clark did not name all seven in this October 3, 2007 speech at the Commonwealth Club of California, but in a March 2, 2007 interview with Amy Goodman on her independent daily news program *Democracy Now!*, the retired general recounted much of the content of these same conversations he had in the Pentagon and, carefully reading from a paper, named the countries as: Iraq, Syria, Lebanon, Libya, Somalia, Sudan and Iran.[60]

Steve Pieczenik, a former high-level State Department official specializing in terrorism who served in the Ford, Carter, Reagan and George H. W. Bush Snr. administrations, said on May 3, 2011 on the *Alex Jones Show* that he is prepared to tell a federal grand jury the name of a top general on the Wolfowitz's staff who told him that 9/11 was essentially an inside job. "It was called a stand-down and false flag operation in order to mobilize the American public under the false pretense that we had been attacked by Al Qaeda and bin Laden which is an absolute unmitigated lie," Pieczenik said. "I was even told by a general on the staff of Wolfowitz—I will go in front of a federal committee and swear on perjury who that name was so we can break this open."[61]

There have been other 9/11 whistleblowers, but this claim is particularly interesting as it is associated with Wolfowitz and as it comes from Pieczenik who was a special envoy for Carter to Italy to assist in the search for Prime Minister Aldo Moro, whose eventual assassination has been attributed to the CIA as part of Operation Gladio by journalist Philip Willan.[62] Pieczenik's biography states that he is currently an adviser to the Department of Defense, and during the broadcast Pieczenik said that he and Rumsfeld actually discussed the Secretary of Defense's role in the 9/11 attacks. Rumsfeld said that if Pieczenik accused the Republican administration of creating 9/11 attacks, then Pieczenik must allow that President Roosevelt allowed Pearl Harbor to happen—which Pieczenik readily conceded. The former State Department official claims that he developed strategies and tactics that were implemented on several continents; on the radio broadcast, Pieczenik told Jones about his first-hand experience teaching stand-down operations at the National War College and that there was preoccupation with Pearl Harbor on the part of Wholstetter and his students at the University of Chicago.

---

60 *Democracy Now!* broadcast on March 2, 2007 is archived on YouTube.

61 For a useful discussion of the 9/11 attacks in relation to the Executive's declaration of "the state of exception," see Ganser, D. 2007. The "Strategy of Tension" in the Cold War Period, and Tunander, O. 2007. The War on Terror and the Pax Americana, in *9/11 and American Empire: Intellectuals Speak Out*, edited by D. R. Griffin and P. D. Scott. Northampton: Olive Branch Press. 79–99 and 146–67.

62 Willan, P. 1991. *Puppetmasters: The Political Use of Terrorism in Italy*. London. Constable. See Chapter 10, this volume.

The events around the attacks, Pieczenik said, followed a pattern of deception, denial, false-flag and stand down. "In this narrative, because Bush, Cheney, Wolfowitz and the rest of the neocons were not very bright in understanding psyops for war, they created two bad guys—Saddam Hussein and Osama bin Laden." Pieczenik said this was illogical because Hussein as a Baathist opposed bin Laden.

> When people in the intelligence community came back to Bush and said, "This is not true, we don't have weapons of mass destruction," the only fable out there to sustain this myth of the war, of why we were fighting terrorists that didn't exist—that we created under the Carter administration and the subsequent Bush administration—we had to have this phantom called Osama bin Laden.[63]

Schmittian exceptions par excellence were triggered by the attacks of 9/11, with the U.S. president three days later declaring a national state of emergency; the declaration has been renewed every year after it lapsed in 2003. The right of habeas corpus can be revoked in—and provisions in hundreds of laws are contingent on—a national state of emergency. As continuity of government (COG) plans formed under a Cold War-era executive order went into effect after the 9/11 attacks, even the mainstream *Washington Post* ran a front-page report on March 1, 2002 that a "shadow government" had been activated, but the story did not detail how this government had the ability to secretly assume new powers with little or no congressional oversight.[64]

Moreover, the enactment of the September 2001 U.S. law "Authorization to Use Military Force Against Terrorists," the USA PATRIOT Act in October of the same year, and the 2002 "Authorization to Use Military Force Against Iraq Resolution" all conferred extraordinary powers to the executive branch. Critics charged that the U.S. Constitution requires a formal declaration of war for the use of military force and note that both measures authorizing force waive the time limitation of the War Powers Resolution; others question the extra-constitutional surveillance powers granted to the executive in the euphemistically titled law that appeals to citizens' patriotism. The Department of Homeland Security—first proposed in the aftermath of the skyjackings and anthrax attacks and later enacted in November 2002 when President Bush signed the Homeland Security Act—will, according to critics, eventually leave citizens with absolutely no place to hide.[65]

---

63 Steve Pieczenik, interviewed on the *Alex Jones Show* by Alex Jones on May 3, 2011. The interview is archived on YouTube and numerous articles have been written about it, such as: Watson, P. J. May 4, 2011. Top Government Insider: Bin Laden Died in 2001, 9/11 False Flag Attack. Centre for Research on Globalization.

64 Helms, H. 2003. *Inside the Shadow Government: National Emergencies and the Cult of Secrecy*. Los Angeles: Feral House.

65 O'Harrow, R. 2005. *No Place to Hide*. New York: Free Press.

In a December 2011 essay[66] former CIA officer Philip Giraldi compared the Weimar Enabling Act with the USA PATRIOT Act (as enacted in 2001 and enhanced in 2006), the Military Commissions Act of 2006, and the National Defense Authorization Act of 2012. The declaration of the legality of torture by Justice Department Lawyers John Yoo and Jay Bybee, he writes, can be seen in the same light as Schmitt's arguments in favor of granting extra-constitutional powers to the executive in a time of crisis.[67] While readers are commended to read the essay's chilling details concerning the presidential authorization of assassinations of U.S. citizens overseas, Giraldi is even more relevant when interviewing Edmonds.

She holds that in mid 2001, before 9/11, Wolfowitz and others were already pressing the Turks for advance permission to have a "Turkish front" in a future war with Iraq. "The monitoring of the Turks picked up contacts with Feith, Wolfowitz, and Perle in the summer of 2001, four months before 9/11," Edmonds told Giraldi, of the monitoring by the FBI. "They were discussing with the Turkish ambassador in Washington an arrangement whereby the U.S. would invade Iraq and divide the country."[68] She also claims that U.S. officials proposed that the United Kingdom would take the south and the rest of the country would go to the United States. "They were negotiating what Turkey required in exchange for allowing an attack from Turkish soil," Edmonds said, but the Turks wanted their own occupation of the Kurdish region. The U.S. officials would not agree to this. She said that Brent Scowcroft, who was then chairman of the American Turkish Council, along with others, negotiated separately for a possible Turkish protectorate.[69]

The United States was weighing many ways to incite or provoke a war with Iraq, and this is documented repeatedly on the historycommons.org website, with its compendium of news articles grouped on a timeline running up to the 2003 U.S. invasion of Iraq. The December 2, 2001 London *Observer* article titled "Secret US Plan for Iraq War," for example, described a plan that called for U.S.-sponsored, stage-managed uprisings that would be supported by U.S. bombers. This news report of a secret U.S. plan would later be verified when it was revealed that the CIA was planning to create uprisings at this time. Efforts were made by senior administration officials to falsely link the 9/11 attacks to Saddam Hussein. Iran-Contra figures surfaced to fan the flames of war in what journalists called "Iran-Contra II."[70] Intelligence on Iraqi weapons of mass destruction was famously "sexed up," no-bid contracts were awarded to the likes of Halliburton to

---

66 Giraldi, P. December 29, 2011. A Tale of Two Cities: Weimar and Washington. *Antiwar Forum*.

67 Giraldi, P. December 29, 2011.

68 Edmonds, S. and Giraldi, P. November 1, 2009. Who's Afraid of Sibel Edmonds. *The American Conservative*.

69 Edmonds, S. and Giraldi, P. November 1, 2009.

70 Marshall, J. M., Rozen, L. and Glastris, P. September 2004. Iran-Contra II. *Washington Monthly*.

provide the Pentagon with support services in Iraq, and plans were drawn up for a postwar Iraq. Wolfowitz would go so far as to have the CIA investigate Hans Blix, chairman of the United Nations weapons inspection team, to make sure the search for Saddam's weapons of mass destruction was sufficiently aggressive.[71]

Wolfowitz openly stated his plans when he traveled to Ankara in December 2002 where he said: "Obviously, if we are going to have significant ground forces in the north, this is the country they have to come through."[72] Erdogan, however, was a well-known political foe of the alleged Operation Sledgehammer plotters in the Turkish military and by extension an enemy of the Schmittian U.S. neoconservatives in Washington.[73] Prior to winning the November 3, 2002 election, Erdogan had gone from being the mayor of Istanbul—having been elected in March 1994—to spending six months in prison for sedition. The charge stemmed from the reading of an Islamic poem at a rally in 1997 that began: "The mosques are our barracks; the minarets are our bayonets."

The Bush administration was reportedly prepared to offer Erdogan $5 billion for the "economic dislocation" that would be caused by a war with Iraq, but Turkish Foreign Minister Yasar Yakis stated publicly that deployment of more U.S. ground troops would not be politically feasible.[74] Wolfowitz argued that U.S. forces would play a stabilizing role, and he urged Turkish restraint with regard to the Kurdish regions of Iraq and participation in the war coalition. The fear on the part of Turks was that Kurds would seek independence from Baghdad or seize the oilfields near Kirkuk.[75]

---

71 Pincus, W. and Lynch, C. April 15, 2002. Wolfowitz Had CIA Probe UN Diplomat in Charge. *Washington Post*. In short, there would be no stopping the neoconservatives bent on war with Iraq.

72 Gordon, M. December 9, 2002. Threats and Responses: Turkey; Bush Will Meet a Leading Turk on Use of Bases. *New York Times*.

73 According to a translation of a February 17, 2004 column by Melih Asik titled "Wolfowitz the Middleman ...!" in the newspaper *Istanbul Milliyet*, the a member of the CHP opposition Republican People's Party, Parliamentary Deputy Mustafa Gazalci, lodged a question in Parliament for Erdogan concerning a possible November 4, 2002 letter from Erdogan to Wolfowitz. The letter, which was circulated in the Turkish press in early 2004, reportedly asked Wolfowitz to help arrange a private meeting with Turkish General Hilmi Ozkok, who then held the position of chief of the general staff. Bilgin writes in his article on Sledgehammer that according to the diaries of Turkish Navy Admiral Ozden Ornek, the Sledgehammer coup plotters were frustrated with Ozkok for not lending support to the plan.

74 Gordon, M. December 9, 2002.

75 Gordon, M. December 9, 2002. In my personal reporting as an international trade journalist in 2010 and 2011 for the Bureau of National Affairs in Washington, I can verify that the Kurdish authorities did sign independent contracts with western oil companies prior to the passage of a national resources law in the Iraqi Parliament. Bracken, L. May 5, 2011. Iraq Central Government in Negotiations With Kurdish Region on Oil Rights Deals. *International Trade Reporter*.

While the United States publicly stated that Erdogan was a moderate and sought to demonstrate openness to the Muslim world by supporting Turkey's candidacy for membership in the European Union, Wolfowitz may have revealed an ulterior motive in his December 2, 2002 speech to the International Institute of Strategic Studies in London. Speaking days before his trip to Ankara to meet with Erdogan, Wolfowitz quoted Mustapha Kemal Ataturk, who is worshiped as a hero by the Ergenekon movement, on the role of religion in the state:

> Modern Turkey demonstrates that a democratic system is indeed compatible with Islam, a Muslim understanding Ataturk once expressed when he said: "Islam means morals and values." And in upholding Islam's morals and values, there can be a separation of religion from state—a separation that is completely compatible with personal piety. As we understand in the UK and US, and as Ataturk captured it: "Religion is a matter between man and God."[76]

On March 1, 2003 the Turkish Grand National Assembly voted 264:251 on a measure that would have authorized 62,000 U.S. troops from the Fourth Infantry Division to stage an invasion on Iraq from Turkey. Parliamentary rules required a majority of members of parliament to vote in the affirmative for passage. There were 19 abstentions, so the legislation failed by three votes. Wolfowitz reportedly "lashed out" at the Turkish military after the vote, even though it reflected widespread public opposition to the war: "I think for whatever reason, they did not play the strong leadership role that we would have expected."[77] H. D. S. Greenway questioned whether the response by Wolfowitz meant that there should have been a military coup or whether the generals should have threatened parliament. "In the Turkish context, there is every reason to interpret the deputy secretary of defense's remarks in that way," Greenway said.

William Arkin provides some additional context for the situation leading up to the March 2003 denial for staging another front in the war with Iraq in *Code Names: Deciphering U.S. Military Plans, Programs, and Operations in the 9/11 World*. North Atlantic Treaty Organization (NATO) and alliance member Turkey have several long-standing agreements. The same is true for the United States and Turkey, with American nuclear weapons being stationed at Incirlik, the main U.S. base in Turkey. Arkin notes that while some facilities have been shut down, the United States operates "half a dozen" other facilities in the country, notably in Izmir and Diyarbakir, and has more than 1,000 military personnel assigned to other places in the country. In February 2003, he writes, the two sides signed a memorandum of understanding on the modernization of bases and ports in Turkey.

76 Wolfowitz, P. December 2, 2002. Building Coalitions of Common Values. *International Institute of Strategic Studies*.

77 Greenway, H. D. S. May 16, 2003. Democracy, Neocon Style. *Boston Globe*.

"The Turkish parliament voted in February 2003 to provide initial military support for the US in Iraq, but then decided on March 1 not to let the U.S. Army 4th Infantry Division stage from Turkey," Arkin wrote.

> [The] Incirlik air base (and other bases in eastern Turkey) continued to quietly support US special operations, intelligence, and combat search and rescue in northern Iraq, and Turkish bases later provided support for the rotation of American troops out of Iraq, but the decision was a blow to the US war plan at the time.[78]

In the run-up to the war, Deputy Secretary of Defense Paul Wolfowitz had long sought to use Turkey's southeast border with Iraq as a front in the war, but such authorization was not immediately granted even though the country was a member of the NATO and this authorization could therefore be expected by U.S. policymakers. While the department, via the embassy in Ankara, has issued a denial of involvement, the intellectual lineage of neoconservatives in the administration and the strategic situation at the time point to possible confidential—if not clandestine—support for the coup plan in Turkey. In short, the neoconservatives had the inclination and the incentive to support a coup in Turkey.

This U.S. neoconservative support for the Turkish Sledgehammer coup plan was understandably covert given the anti-constitutional nature of the plan—overt support would contradict the stated U.S. foreign policy in support of democracy. It is also worth recalling in this regard the characteristic use of intentional ambiguity and ambivalence by Schmitt in his writings, and the even more explicit call for the use of deception by Strauss. Given the revelations in James Bamford's *A Pretext for War: 9/11, Iraq, and the Abuse of America's Intelligence Agencies*, it is known that these U.S. policymakers who were trained at the university in the use of "noble lies," as Plato referred to them, called for freedom and democracy in Iraq when they had a globe-traversing invasion in mind. The nearly nine-year war was based on the erroneous and likely deceptive weapons-of-mass-destruction premise.[79]

If a coup was required in a neighboring democracy to help prosecute this war, the neoconservatives would have been able to at once distance themselves from it publicly and rationalize it among themselves privately or in the hidden meaning of their public remarks. When Strauss discusses the obvious and hidden meanings in Spinoza, whose early geometric expositions of Descartes led to his expulsion from the Jewish community, it is with the implication that too much was revealed.[80] Spinoza's posthumously published ethics would be based on a more cryptic Euclidian structure that to this day obscures even for experts the exact sense of

---

78 Arkin, W. 2005. *Code Names: Deciphering U.S. Military Plans, Programs, and Operations in the 9/11 World*. Hanover: Steerforth Press. 223.

79 Bamford, J. 2004. *A Pretext for War: 9/11, Iraq, and the Abuse of America's Intelligence Agencies*. New York: Doubleday.

80 Strauss, L. 1952. 142–201.

the author's words. In the 21st century such stratagems are uncalled for unless it is to mask support for false-flag terror, coups, and unjustified wars of aggression.

The 1932 Prussian coup and the Turkish Ergenekon coup plot exist on parallel planes that are unlikely to intersect any time soon in the minds of most political scientists even though in many respects they are on the same ethical plane. A Schmittian analysis, for example, could hold that a Turkish military coup can be democratic if it restores the secular essence of the country. The 2003 coup plot will exist on a separate plane from the well-analyzed coup that destroyed the Weimar Republic in part because Operation Sledgehammer was foiled but more because no matter how much evidence is uncovered, powerful efforts are being made at home and abroad to spread distrust of the Erdogan intelligence services and fan rumors that the Kemalist military officers are being framed.

The Turkish government's response to the failed coup is highly instructive in light of the fact that the successful 1932 coup is credited with ushering the National Socialist German Workers' Party to power. The justice system is setting an example for the world as many of the Turkish military coup planners have in fact been arrested and imprisoned while the democratically elected Erdogan remains in power. The neoconservative network in the United States, meanwhile, has barely even been tried in the court of public opinion. Members of this network continue to participate in the public debate on policy issues as if their deceptions have not been revealed, as if their masks are firmly in place and they have not themselves been exposed as coup plotters by an impeccable source in whom they confided their plans.

Chapter 12
The Spectacle and the Partisan

Jeff Kinkle

Following the attacks of September 11, 2001 the work of both Guy Debord and Carl Schmitt re-emerged in a variety of different contexts as critical prisms through which a wide variety of theorists—and in Schmitt's case Bush administration officials—considered the attacks and the subsequent "War on Terror." Schmitt was referenced by everyone from the Italian philosopher Giorgio Agamben to John Yoo of the U.S. Department of Justice during the Bush administration as his writings on sovereignty, the state of exception and the partisan were applied to the Bush reaction to the attacks and the legal standing of the "detainees" and "unlawful combatants."[1] During this same period, Debord was discussed primarily in relation to the so-called "image-war" being fought between radical Islamists and the West, between jihadists and the "coalition of the willing." What Debord dubbed "the society of the spectacle" was viewed as the general *mise-en-scène* of the global capitalist world order in which geopolitical actors engaged each other, with an emphasis on the ubiquity of the media and the importance of images and appearances in contemporary politics and warfare.[2] The goal of this chapter is to consider Schmitt's conception of the partisan in relation to some of the aspects of Debord's late theory of the "integrated spectacle"—essentially the global order that emerged throughout the 1970s and 1980s, solidifying itself with the end of the Cold War and the "Americanisation of the world"—that other commentators have neglected. Both theorists were writing from opposite ends of the political spectrum in periods they considered times of flux, where the figures of the revolutionary and the partisan were undergoing significant changes, and thinking the work of the two of them together in relation to the concept and field of parapolitics can

1 See Agamben, G. 2005. *State of Exception*, trans. Kevin Attell. Chicago: University of Chicago Press. Horton, S. January 23, 2008. Deconstructing John Yoo. *Harper's*. Available at: http://harpers.org/archive/2008/01/hbc-90002226 (accessed July 9, 2012). Agamben is particularly interesting in this respect because he has consistently framed his reflections as taking place within the society of the spectacle. For just one example of post-9/11 discussions of Schmitt see Rasch, W. ed. Spring 2005 World Orders: Confronting Carl Schmitt's The Nomos of the Earth. *South Atlantic Quarterly*, 104/2.

2 See, for example, Retort. 2005. *Afflicted Powers: Capital and Spectacle in a New Age of War*. New York: Verso; Giroux, H. 2006. *Beyond the Spectacle of Terrorism*. Boulder: Paradigm. Kellner, D. 2005 *Media Spectacle and the Crisis of Democracy*. Boulder: Paradigm; Compton, J. R. 2004. *The Integrated News Spectacle*. New York: Peter Lang.

be illuminating. This chapter seeks to explore two interrelated questions. Firstly, living under the "organised uncertainty" of the integrated spectacle, how is what Carl Schmitt considered to be the core of the political, the determining of the friend/enemy relation, possible? Secondly, what kind of partisan, what kind of politics, is possible under the integrated spectacle? Schmitt closed his *Theory of the Partisan* by reflecting on the emergence of the industrial partisan; this chapter will close with a consideration of the figure of the spectacular partisan.

While Schmitt's parapolitical relevance has been dealt with throughout this collection, a detailed discussion of the work of Guy Debord in a volume on parapolitics may seem out of place. Debord (1931–1994) is normally associated with his critique of the nascent "consumer society" of postwar France, primarily in relation to his position as the "prime mover" of the Situationist International (SI) and as the author of *The Society of the Spectacle* (1967). In the early 1950s he arrived on the French art scene as a member of the avant-garde group the Lettrists and then became a founding member of the splinter group the Lettrist International. In 1957, he co-founded the SI, which went on to become one of the most prominent of the postwar avant-gardes, introducing concepts like the *dérive* and *détournement* that are still crucial reference points for artists, activists and theorists throughout the world. The SI was involved in the build up to the events of May 1968, and *Society of the Spectacle*—an aggressive, engaged critique of consumer capitalism in the West and state socialism in the East—is occasionally considered the handbook of the students' movement. After the events of 1968 failed to overthrow the existing order, Debord is thought to have gone into exile, retiring from art and revolutionary politics only to re-emerge late in his life as a man of letters with the publication of his autobiographical *Panegyric* in 1989. Interest in Debord's work underwent a resurgence throughout the 1990s as he and the SI were characterized as early "culture-jammers" and precursors to Naomi Klein and *Adbusters*, with *Society of the Spectacle* considered a prescient critique of the rampant consumerism of the 1990s bubble. This discourse honed in on Situationist concepts like the colonization of everyday life and practices like *détournement* as being of particular relevance to theorists and activists in a period of triumphant capitalism. It focused on notions like alienation and commodity fetishism, and micropolitical strategies for understanding and resisting the forces that prevent one from living a fulfilling life in an age of abundance. Following the attacks of 9/11, references to Debord and discussions of his concepts have had a decidedly different emphasis. The subject of spectacle has gone from being hypnotized by images of commodities, celebrities and politicians to those of collapsing skyscrapers, hook-armed imams, "Shock and Awe" and the fear-mongering demagoguery of the 24-hour news channels.

What is missing from this consideration, utilization, and sometimes direct application, of Debord's work is any meaningful discussion of the works he published after the dissolution of the SI in 1972. Despite the way his oeuvre is normally framed, many of Debord's texts from the period following the SI's break up and extending to the end of his life can be usefully framed in relation to the study of parapolitics. Between the publishing of the *Society of the Spectacle* in 1967 and *Comments on the Society of the Spectacle* in 1988, Debord wrote, or was involved with the creation of, together with Gianfranco Sanguinetti, several minor works that dealt with phenomena like the Red Brigades, political terrorism, the assassination of Aldo Moro, and the strategy of tension in Italy. In all of these texts, including *Comments*, there are many obvious and significant overlaps between his interests and those of the burgeoning field of parapolitics. Many of his claims are echoed in the parapolitical literature, stretching from the manner in which the state manipulates, provokes or commits acts of terror to the centrality of the security services in contemporary politics and the importance of the mafia in the global economy. Debord was a theorist who over the course of his career grew to be more fascinated by the clandestine operations of the intelligence services than the vapid smiles of celebrity politicians and their campaigns, more interested in the spectacle's dark underbelly than its gleaming surface, more concerned with the deep state than the public state. Debord is valuable in this regard in that he adds a dimension never really addressed: he presents a novel way of thinking about the systemic relation between publicity and secrecy, consumer culture and the deep state, celebrities and secret agents. This stress on the importance of an approach that seeks to discover systemic and structural relationships between the public state and the deep state can also act as a corrective to certain drifts in parapolitical research that produce speculative theories of conspiracy that read like "a tedious series of lifeless, inconclusive crime novels."[3] Debord presents a vision of the state compatible with parapolitical research and also theorizes how the society of the spectacle generates epistemological challenges that constrain partisans and parapolitical researchers alike.

The Deep State Beneath the Spectacle

All of this needs to be contextualized in relation to the concept of the society of the spectacle, laid out in its greatest depth in Debord's 1967 book. In a letter dated December 14, 1971, Debord gives a succinct summary of the 221 theses that make up the book: "*this is capitalism today*."[4] *Society of the Spectacle* consists of 221 numbered paragraphs spread over nine chapters, covering topics like the workers' movement, the experience of time and history, ideology, alienation, commodity fetishism, urban planning and the world of art and culture. Influenced by the historical avant-garde and writers like Le Comte de Lautréamont, Debord's dialogue with Marx and Hegel, via Georg Lukács, Henri Lefebvre and Lucien Goldmann, attacks the contemporary capitalist society that Debord and the SI despised and had

3 Debord, G. 1998. *Comments on the Society of the Spectacle*, trans. Malcolm Imrie. London: Verso. 59.

4 [Emphasis by Debord] Debord, G. 2004. *Correspondence*, vol. 4. Paris: Librairie Arthème Fayard. 455.

been organizing to destroy *in its totality*. Their position amounted to a "systematic rejection of all forms of social and political organization in the West and the East, and of all the groups that are currently trying to change them," as a commentator in *Le Monde* laconically put it.[5] The concept of the spectacle was supposed to identify and attack everything wrong with the present organization of life. It was meant to illuminate the poverty underlying the age of abundance, the class antagonism that persists beneath the image of the affluent worker, the religiosity behind the modern secular state. In 1988 Debord defines the essence of the spectacle in perhaps the clearest terms in his oeuvre: "the autocratic reign of the market economy which had acceded to an irresponsible sovereignty, and the totality of new techniques of government which accompanied this reign."[6] Functionally, it is best thought of as a general term to describe a particular society that began in the United States and Europe in the mid-1920s and continues into the present, having spread to include most of the globe.[7] While Debord's 1967 book lays out the theory of the spectacle, the works he published over the rest of his career are by and large concerned with what he dubs in *Comments* the "practical consequences" of spectacular domination.

Most interesting are the counter-intuitive aspects of these practical consequences. Throughout Debord's first book on the subject, the sheer visibility of the spectacle is stressed: the spectacle marks the triumph of appearance and representation, it is "a negation of life that has *invented a visual form for itself*, it raises sight to the most important sense," and "*capital* accumulated to the point where it becomes image" is probably its most quoted definition.[8] The scientific name of the spectacle's model citizen is "Homo Spectator": a bipedal primate characterized by a propensity to look or watch.[9] What is surprising about Debord's later writings is that much of the focus is on precisely what cannot be seen: the invisible, the clandestine and the hidden. Rather than focusing on the impact of television on presidential campaigns or branding on happiness, Debord is obsessed with the intelligence services and their conspiracies. Beneath, behind, or beyond the political spectacle that everyone loves to decry, Debord identifies forces at play that are as sinister as they are obscure, and his late work allows one to understand the secrecy of power and the spectacle's pageantry as two sides of the same coin.

To over-generalize: if a book like 1967's *The Society of the Spectacle* is about the experience of late capitalism from the perspective of the street—"street" meant literally as the Situationist critique of urbanism and everyday life and "street" meant to denote the Debord that scrawled "Never work" on a Paris wall and felt

---

5 Quoted in Knabb, K. ed. 2006 *Situationist International Anthology*. Berkeley: Bureau of Public Secrets. 500.

6 Debord, G. 1998. 2.

7 This is not an unproblematic formulation, although it is one that I believe is in line with Debord's conception of the spectacle.

8 Debord, G. 1999. *Society of the Spectacle*, trans. Donald Nicholson-Smith. New York: Zone. para. 10, para. 18, para. 34.

9 Debord, G. 1999. 9.

more comfortable with alcoholics, dropouts and petty criminals than academics and artists—a critique of alienation, commodity fetishism and the banality of everyday life, exposing the falsity of the glimmering surface covering the rotten core of consumer capitalism in the West and the "workers' states" in the East, then we can say that a book like 1988's *Comments of the Society of the Spectacle* is about what goes on behind the scenes, the ways in which those in power stay there: the management of the spectacle and the consequences of its domination. There are personal reasons for this shift of perspective worth considering. The first is that after the dissolution of the SI, Debord moved to Florence and spent most of his time in Italy during the country's "Years of Lead," so dubbed because of the staggering level of political violence in the long decade that stretched from 1969 to 1980.[10] Two important texts for our consideration here came out of this period. While the exact authorial arrangement of the first of these texts is unclear, Debord was involved in the production of Gianfranco Sanguinetti's pamphlet *The Real Report on the Last Chance to Save Capitalism in Italy* (1975).[11] Written anonymously under the pseudonym 'Censor' from the perspective of a man in the upper echelons of the Italian state, Censor gives a blunt assessment of the threats to bourgeois class rule and advice on how to deal with the worker's movement. He hails the state's recourse to the creation of "the false card of artificial terrorism" in the Piazza Fontana bombing of December 12, 1969, and argues essentially that the state must "employ" the communists: that by bringing them into the management of Italian capitalism they'll be able to better repress the revolutionary movement (essentially a plan resembling Aldo Moro's "Historic Compromise").[12] The second text, "Preface to the Fourth Italian Edition of *The Society of the Spectacle*" (occasionally labeled "The State of the Spectacle"), was written by Debord after the kidnapping and murder of Moro in 1978. In this short text the historic compromise is depicted as a belief "in the capacity of the Stalinists to finally smash the movement of revolutionary workers" and Debord claims that Moro was essentially killed by those who would prefer to do without them: "there is no doubt a real Italian 'Censor' who played this card," as he puts it

10 While terrorism was highly visible throughout Europe and the world over this period, in Italy the sheer number of terrorist attacks is shocking: over 12,000 incidents of political violence, with 1,926 attacks in 1977 followed by 2,379 in 1978, perpetrated by both extremes of the political spectrum—at times with the assistance of elements within the state, especially the secret and intelligence services. Victims—356 dead and over 1,000 wounded in the two decades following 1969—not only included civilians but also judges, lawyers, bureaucrats, bankers, and even a prime minister in 1978. See Porta, D. D. 1995. *Social Movements, Political Violence, and the State: A Comparative Analysis of Italy and Germany*. Cambridge: Cambridge University Press. Willan, P. 2001. *Puppetmasters: The Political Use of Terrorism in Italy*. Lincoln: Authors Choice Press.

11 Sanguinetti co-founded the Italian section of the SI when he was only 20. The consensus amongst Debord's biographers is that Debord was definitely involved in writing the text but that it cannot be fully attributed to him.

12 See Chapter 10, this volume.

in his correspondence.[13] "Red Brigades" is written in quotation marks throughout and Debord claims that while some of the smaller acts of political violence may have been perpetuated by genuine left-wing and right-wing groups, the large attacks were perpetuated by elements of the state and that this is corroborated in "every detail of their style."[14]

It is also over this period that Debord developed a close relationship with his publisher/patron Gérard Lebovici, who mingled in the upper echelons of French and European cultural, economic and political circles and was found dead in a Parisian parking garage with four bullet wounds in the back of his head in 1984, a murder that remains unsolved. Debord wrote *Considerations on the Assassination of Gérald Lebovici* in 1985, which consists largely of citations from articles in the popular press on Debord and his possible role in the assassination mixed with commentary on these articles and society as a whole. Rather than offering a theory of the murder itself, Debord details the ridiculous surfeit of rumor, disinformation and lies published in the French press about him and the Lebovici affair, with the implication being this is just one case study and that this exercise could be repeated ad infinitum, revealing a constant barrage of daily lies about every conceivable realm of public and private life. When one considers Debord's proximity to these events and phenomena, it is not surprising that the focus of Debord's later work is no longer on the false consciousness of the population, hypnotized by commodities and celebrities and tricked into loving the spectacle, but about the cynical cunning, corruption and brutality of "those that run the spectacle." When Debord first coined the concept, the spectacle had been loved—or at least "it was convinced it was loved"; later, in 1988, it is feared. Concepts such as alienation, ideology, commodity fetishism and even the proletariat are rarely mentioned, if they are mentioned at all, and ideas of secrecy, conspiracy and disinformation are pushed to the fore.[15]

---

13 Guy Debord's Letters. September 18, 1978. Available at: www.notbored.org/debord-18September1978.html (accessed August 17, 2012). In his correspondence Debord writes, "This affair is evidently staged by the enemies of the 'Historic Compromise', not by revolutionary enemies [of the State]. The leftists are ordinarily very naive, even in Italy, where they gladly engage on these occasions in the completely *theological* discussions of the problems of revolutionary violence, like that chorus of children who, in their faded aestheticism of the 'anarchist assassin,' once believed that Oswald killed Kennedy."

14 Debord, G. 1978. Preface in *The Society of the Spectacle*, trans. Not Bored. Available at: www.notbored.org/debord-preface.html (accessed August 17, 2012).

15 See, for example, a letter from 1974 where Debord justifies his shift away from Hegel, Marx and Lautréamont: "The principle [*sic*] work that, it appears to me, one must engage in – as the complementary contrary to *The Society of the Spectacle,* which described frozen alienation (and the negation that is implicit in it) – is *the theory of historical action.* One must advance *strategic* theory in its moment, which has come. At this stage and to speak schematically, the basic theoreticians to retrieve and develop are no longer Hegel, Marx and Lautréamont, but Thucydides, Machiavelli and Clausewitz." Guy Debord's

In 1967, Debord identified two forms of the spectacle: the diffuse, which was dominant in the Western democracies, and the concentrated, which was dominant in totalitarian societies and those living under "really existing socialism." In his correspondence in 1978 he talks of the "contested spectacle" in Italy and in *Comments* in 1988 he identifies a new form—the integrated spectacle—which takes features from both previous forms and has spread to cover the entire globe.[16] Emerging in France and Italy, it is described as "simultaneously concentrated and diffuse," a rational combination of the spectacle's two previous competing varieties, and the result of the diffuse spectacle's general victory over the concentrated. Benefiting from this hybrid essence, the integrated spectacle is more powerful than either of its forbears. "When the spectacle was concentrated, the greater part of surrounding society escaped it; when diffuse a small part; today, no part. The spectacle has spread itself to the point where it now permeates all reality."[17] Everything has been polluted by this proliferation of spectacular power, even "the legacy of old books and old buildings" that preserved the only remaining trace of another world is being reclassified and absorbed into the spectacle. The integrated spectacle has also benefited "spectacular government," which "now possesses all the means necessary to falsify the whole of production and perception" allowing it to control and manipulate the historical record and with it people's understanding of the present and future. The societies that have reached the stage of the integrated spectacle share five principal features: incessant technological renewal, integration of state and economy, generalized secrecy, unanswerable lies, and an eternal present. These first two are said to be characteristics of the society

---

Letters. February 21, 1974. Available at: www.notbored.org/debord-21February1974.html (accessed August 17, 2012).

16 Guy Debord's Letters. September 18, 1978. Available at: www.notbored.org/debord-18September1978.html (accessed August 17, 2012). Debord is not the only theorist to use the term "integrated" to describe developments in capitalism around this time. Around the same time Debord was writing *Comments*, Felix Guattari was using the term integrated world capitalism (IWC) as a term synonymous with a post-industrial capitalism in which immaterial labor has become prominent. See Guattari, F. 2008. *The Three Ecologies*, trans. Ian Pindar and P. Sutton. London: Continuum. Guattari, F. and Negri, T. 1990. *Communists Like Us*. New York: Semiotext(e).

17 Debord, G. 1998. 9. It should be noted that the term "permeates" is perhaps somewhat misleading. The original French is, "*Le spectacle s'est mélange à toute réalité, en l'irradiant*," which the Not Bored collective, for example, translate literally as "The spectacle is mixed into all reality and irradiates it." Now Debord approved Malcolm Imrie's translation so we should perhaps give it the benefit of the doubt but "permeates" to me suggests something slightly more totalizing than "mixed into." This may seem like a slight difference of meaning but the consequences for how we think of the integrated spectacle based on this sentence are quite profound. For example, "permeates" seems to imply a Baudrillardian state where the spectacle has seeped into and polluted all reality while "mixed into" does not imply the same level of contamination.

of the spectacle since its origin, while the latter three are effects of the spectacle's domination in its integrated stage.

The society attacked by Debord in 1967 was in many ways dominated by a kinder, gentler spectacle. It denied life and reduced the population to an alienated existence full of pseudo-pleasures, but it at least tried to please or convince. By contrast, the integrated spectacle is much more menacing. The cynical and corrupt Manuel Noriega is this society's "modern prince."[18] Growing alongside the integrated spectacle is the Mafia ("the model of all advanced commercial enterprises"[19]), industrial food processing, shantytowns, the secret services and illiteracy.[20] It is no longer just men of state and criminals that have to worry about being assassinated but businessmen, bureaucrats, journalists and anyone in the wrong place at the wrong time. After the failed revolutionary moments of the late 1960s and 1970s, the society of the spectacle has concentrated on defending itself from these threats and occasionally launching counter-attacks.

This Machiavellian conception of the integrated spectacle as a society that prefers to be feared rather than loved comes directly from Debord's theorization of 1970s Italy. What Debord was witnessing in Italy over this decade was a shift from a spectacle that ruled via illusion, which projected a vision of happiness for its subjects, to a more nefarious spectacle that ruled via fear. Part of this is the state's "use" of terrorism. Sanguinetti wrote—in both *The Real Report* and his *On Terrorism and the State* (1978)—that fear of terrorism pushed the population to accept the status quo.[21] Debord takes this to be a general characteristic of the integrated spectacle in *Comments*. Spectacular democracy, he writes, wants

> *to be judged by its enemies rather than by its results*. The story of terrorism is written by the state and is therefore highly instructive. The spectators must certainly never know everything about terrorism, but they must always know enough to convince them that, compared with terrorism, everything else must be acceptable, or in any case more rational and democratic.[22]

The integrated spectacle no longer tries to convince the population that they are on the path to something great, but that all the other paths are fraught with even greater dangers or are simply dead ends. What this also means is that while the

18 Debord, G. 1998. 58.

19 Debord, G. 1998. 67.

20 Debord, G. 1998. 64.

21 Sanguinetti, G. 1982. *On Terrorism and the State*, trans. Lucy Forsyth and Michel Prigent. London: Aldgate Press. 97.

22 Debord, G. 1998. 24. Negri and Guattari in their *Communists Like Us* write about the role of terror and fear in what they dub Integrated World Capitalism. This fear is generated by the spectre of nuclear annihilation, economic crisis and the possibility of impoverishment, and the figure of the global industrial reserve army. Guattari, F. and Negri, T. 1990. 47–74.

diffuse spectacle at least ran on pure ideology, so to speak, the integrated spectacle needs a much stronger apparatus in order to rule. It must be careful since, following Machiavelli, it is necessary for it to be feared but not hated.[23]

Elaborating the practical consequences of spectacular domination, this totality of new techniques of government that accompany its reign is not merely an academic question for Debord. He claims that while the consequences of the spectacle have been demonstrated in practice, they have not yet been understood in theory.[24] In his later works Debord considers the effects of the spectacle for contemporary life and politics. The concept of the spectacle is taken not only as read, but its existence so obvious as to be unchallengeable. Even if the existence of the spectacle is completely obvious, and pointing out its existence completely banal, Debord argues that few have understood the *consequences* of this existence. The development and growth of the spectacle has altered society so profoundly that everything from the art of government and political activism to the production of cultural and political theory has to be completely rethought. This is not only true for the enemies of the spectacle, but also for its most gleeful proponents. Very few on either side have actually understood what the domination of the spectacle actually entails, and Debord suggests that this understanding will be a deciding factor in this struggle between the spectacle's defenders and those who seek to destroy it.

The Partisan in Transition

Carl Schmitt wrote his *Theory of the Partisan* (1963) cognizant of the fact that the figure of the partisan was in flux. The Cold War, nuclear proliferation, technological development and the very success of the partisan were in the process of creating a new *nomos* of the earth, a new international order emerging out of the period of *jus publicum Europaeum* and the Westphalian system. The partisan interested Schmitt not only as a figure that contributed to the fragmentation of the old *nomos*, but also as a figure who was keeping the political alive during a period of liberal and communist homogenization of the globe (and thus particularly relevant for the liberal democratic "end of history"). While it would not be accurate to say that Schmitt was a defender of the spectacle per se, he was certainly at odds with Debord politically. It should be kept in mind that the lectures that serve as the basis for *Theory of the Partisan* were delivered in Francoist Spain, a state Debord actively opposed and organized against. The vast subjective partisan gap between the two can be seen clearly in their varying perspectives on the Spanish Civil War: while midway through Schmitt claims that in the war "Spain defended itself against a war of national liberation sponsored by the international communist movement,"

23 Machiavelli, N. 2005. *The Prince*, trans. P. Bondanella. Oxford: Oxford University Press. Chapter XVII.

24 Debord, G. 1998. 85–7.

in a text from the same year Debord describes the war as a "civil war against local and international fascism."[25] This said, there is a tradition of Schmitt's writings being taken seriously by the left going back to figures like Walter Benjamin and Georg Lukács and continuing into the present, often related to his suspicions of liberal democracy.[26]

For Schmitt the partisan is defined by four primary characteristics: irregularity, mobility, intensity of political commitment, and a tellurian, or "earth-bound," character. The partisan's irregularity has to be understood in contrast to the regularity of the soldier. Schmitt argues that while guerrilla and irregular warfare existed throughout history, the irregularity of the partisan needs to be thought in opposition to the regularity of the state and army that first appeared on a grand scale following the French Revolution with Napoleon.[27] As such, it is the Spanish guerrilla war against Napoleon's armies from 1808 to 1813 that marks the historical origin of the partisan as considered by Schmitt. A regular fighter openly displays their uniform and weapon, their status as an active combatant in war; the partisan, on the other hand, wears no uniform and hides their weapon when they disappear amongst civilians.

> The partisan is still the one who refuses to carry weapons openly, who fights from ambush, and who uses the enemy's uniform, as well as true or false insignias and every type of civilian clothing as camouflage. Secrecy and darkness are his strongest weapons, which logically he cannot renounce without losing the space of irregularity, i.e. without ceasing to be a partisan.[28]

The partisan's mobility—their flexibility, speed and ability to quickly switch from attack to retreat—is connected to their ability to blend with the population and their smaller numbers. It is the partisan's intense political commitment that separates them from the criminal, thief or the pirate and is the etymological root of the word "party." This is related to the final characteristic of the partisan as

25 Debord, G. 1963. The Asturian Strike, available at: www.notbored.org/asturian-strike.html (accessed August 17, 2012). While one could argue there is a certain reactionary nostalgia in his late writings—a longing for a prelapisarian pre-spectacular society where tomatoes tasted like tomatoes and wine was cheap, plentiful and delicious—his politics remained drastically different from Schmitt's. Raoul Salan, the OAS terrorist, is also praised by Schmitt in *Theory of the Partisan*, whereas the liberation of Algeria was another cause Debord militantly supported.

26 See Müller, J. W. 2003. *A Dangerous Mind: Carl-Schmitt in Post-War European Thought*. New Haven: Yale University Press.

27 In could be fruitful to consider the board game, *Game of War*, Debord created with his wife Alice Becker-Ho in the late 1970s that was very much modeled on the battle between two regular armies conceived as a chivalric duel between gentlemen, to phrase it in Schmittian. See Becker-Ho, A. and Guy, D. 2008. *A Game of War*, trans. Donald Nicholson-Smith. London: Atlas Press. This edition comes with a board and counters for playing.

28 Schmitt, C. 2007. *Theory of the Partisan*, trans. G. L. Ulmen. New York: Telos. 37.

well: their tellurian character. The classical partisan defends their land from an intruder. The hostiles are limited and "spatially evident" as Schmitt puts it.[29] They are essentially defensive and victory is achieved when the intruder is expelled.

These four characteristics define what Schmitt calls the "defensive autochthonous defenders of the homeland." There is another classification of partisan, however, whose tellurian character is somewhat murkier: "globally aggressive revolutionary activists."[30] The first key figure of this partisan is Lenin. While this partisan may have a tellurian character to an extent, their (class) struggle is essentially global. "Lenin was the first to fully conceive of the partisan as a significant figure of national and international civil war, and he sought to transform the partisan into an effective instrument of the central Communist Party leadership."[31] It is this identification with the party and their role in bringing about the communist revolution that gives the communist partisan political legitimacy. This new global partisan also turns him into a key figure in world history, rather than just a factor in the science of war.[32] Yet, Schmitt argues, Lenin's theorization was still "abstractly intellectual,"[33] and while Stalin had been successful in linking the telluric defense of homeland with the aggressiveness of the worldwide communist revolution, it was Mao Tse-tung who became the century's greatest theorist and practitioner of partisan warfare.

Schmitt famously claimed in his *The Concept of the Political* that "the specific political distinction to which political actions and motives can be reduced is that between friend and enemy."[34] In thinking through the partisan, he identifies a shift from a contained and regulated enmity, or "real enmity," to what he calls "absolute enmity" (and thus a "real enemy" and "absolute enemy"). The real enmity of the telluric partisan is limited by their defensive disposition. The Spanish *guerrilleros* battling Napoleon's army wanted to expel the French from their nation but they did not necessarily want to annihilate the French. The partisan "defends a piece of land with which he has an autochthonous relation. His fundamental position remains defensive, despite the intensive mobility of his tactics … The real enemy will not be declared to be an absolute enemy, also not the last enemy of mankind."[35] This is not the case for Lenin, Schmitt writes: "Lenin, as a professional revolutionary of global civil war, went still further and turned the real enemy into an absolute enemy."[36] The absolute enemy for Lenin, Schmitt argues, was the class enemy, the bourgeoisie and the social order of

29 Schmitt, C. 2007. 20.

30 Schmitt, C. 2007. 30.

31 Schmitt, C. 2007. 49.

32 Schmitt, C. 2007. 77.

33 Schmitt, C. 2007. 61.

34 Schmitt, C. 1996. *The Concept of the Political*, trans. G. Schwab. Chicago: University of Chicago Press. 26.

35 Schmitt, C. 2007. 92.

36 Schmitt, C. 2007. 93.

all the countries in which the bourgeois capitalist was dominant. So while the traditional partisan just wanted to expel an invader to regain their independence, the communist partisan is embroiled in a global civil war and seeks the destruction of the entire structure of political and social order, and, as such, they cannot be victorious unless their enemy is annihilated. It is not difficult to see why Schmitt's work has been seen to be relevant for understanding the global jihadi.[37]

The tellurian character of the partisan is also challenged by what Schmitt calls a "technicistic ideology."[38] For Schmitt, techno-industrial progress has similar far-reaching effects on the development of the partisan as the Leninist "discovery" of absolute enmity. As he writes, long gone are the days of the old partisan peasant arming himself with a pitchfork; the contemporary partisan, the industrial partisan, fights with automatic weapons, plastic bombs, utilizes radar and advanced communication tools, and can potentially make use of tactical atomic weapons. The first effect of this modernization of warfare is that partisans becoming increasingly reliant on whoever can supply them with the latest weapons and technology. Schmitt writes:

> even the autochthonous partisan of agrarian background is being drawn into the force-field of irresistible, techno-industrial progress. His mobility is increased by his motorisation to such an extent that he is in danger of becoming completely disoriented. In the situations of the Cold War, he becomes a technician of the invisible struggle, a saboteur, and a spy.[39]

Therefore, when defending his or her homeland, the industrial partisan may be doing so by proxy. As Schmitt continues, "such a motorised partisan loses his telluric character and becomes only the transportable and exchangeable tool of a powerful central agency of world politics, which deploys him in overt or covert war, and deactivates him as the situation demands."[40] It is not difficult to think of examples from the past several decades where Schmitt's words ring true.

The interested third party, the partisan's techno-industrial sponsor, plays a double role for the partisan. On the one hand, the interested third party can turn the partisan into a mere tool. Afraid of a potentially devastating confrontation with another atomic power, two enemies can fight a proxy war: an "apparently harmless play of a precisely-controlled irregularity and an 'ideal disorder', ideal insofar as

---

37 See Kochi, T. November 2006. The Partisan: Carl Schmitt and Terrorism. *Law and Critique*, 17/3, 267–95. Scheuerman, W. E. March 2006. Carl Schmitt and the Road to Abu Ghraib. *Constellations*, 13/1, 108–24. Bülent, D. and Carsten Bagge, L. 2004. 7/11, 9/11, and Post-Politics. Published by the Department of Sociology Lancaster University. Available at: http://www.lancs.ac.uk/fass/sociology/papers/diken-laustsen-7-11-9-11-post-politics.pdf (accessed August 17, 2012).

38 Schmitt, C. 2007. 20.

39 Schmitt, C. 2007. 22.

40 Schmitt, C. 2007.

it could be manipulated by the world powers."[41] On the other hand, the interested third party provides the partisan with political legitimacy:

> the *interested third party* has an essential function in that he provides the relation to regularity that the irregularity of the partisan needs to remain in the political sphere. The core of the political is not enmity *per se*, but the distinction of friend and enemy, and the presupposition of friend *and* enemy.[42]

For example, in an interview in 1969, Schmitt gives an example of the contemporary partisan being "like a fish in water" in the techno-industrial society, which offers new opportunities for immersion and invisibility:

> I can imagine that here in Sauerland, where we are conducting our conversation, when the appropriate tactical-nuclear possibilities are given, a real partisan could, wearing the working-clothes of a pediatrician, take himself onto the next mountain and destroy the dam and the surrounding region – with the effect that the whole Ruhr valley would turn into a swamp.[43]

What would make this man a partisan and not an apocalyptic criminal terrorist would be his connection to a larger political struggle to an interested third party who would frame the attack politically.

The Spectacular Partisan

This notion of an interested third party standing behind the partisan provides a good point to bring the thinking of Schmitt and Debord together under the umbrella of the parapolitical. Debord ends the chapter in *Comments* in which he introduces the integrated stage of the spectacle with an intriguing assertion: the highest ambition of the integrated spectacle "is still to turn secret agents into revolutionaries and revolutionaries into secret agents."[44] (To this one could perhaps add: whether they know it or not.) Midway through *Comments*, Debord claims that the words fallacious, deceptive, impostrous, inveigling, insidious and captious "taken together constitute today a kind of palette of colours with which to paint a portrait of the society of the spectacle."[45] In the same paragraph he adds a second list of adjectives that is said to relate to the dangers to be faced by any group practicing subversion: misguided, provoked, infiltrated, manipulated, taken over, subverted.

41 Schmitt, C. 2007. 79.

42 Schmitt, C. 2007. 91.

43 Carl Schmitt interview in Schickel, J. 1993 *Gespräche mit Carl Schmitt*. Berlin: Merve Verlag. 16.

44 Debord, G. 1998. 11.

45 Debord, G. 1998. 43.

Debord described the integrated spectacle as "a world where there is no room for verification" where we "live and die at the confluence of innumerable mysteries," and as such one where the partisan faces enormous difficulties, but also perhaps new possibilities.[46]

One of the lessons Debord took from 1970s Italy during the period of the contested spectacle was the ambiguity of all political events. For the majority of citizens there was no way to know if a bombing was perpetrated by the left, the right in the guise of the left, or the state in the guise of the right impersonating the left. Members in radical groups could not be certain if their comrades were agents provocateurs or genuine radicals. One could not trust the courts to hand down a legitimate verdict, one could not trust investigative journalists, politicians or whistleblowers to undercover the truth. History was no longer decided, or even influenced, by the masses but by old white men meeting behind closed doors with the law of *omerta* binding elites in every segment of society. This position leads Debord into a difficulty, both epistemologically and strategically. As he writes, "it is no longer possible to believe anything about anyone that you have not learned from yourself, directly."[47] This may seem hyperbolic, but Debord has to be taken quite literally on this point. Peter Dale Scott cites the Church Committee's report from 1976 that revealed that the CIA was using several hundred American academics and that prior to 1967 they had published over 1,000 books (via subsidy, sponsorship or actual production). The same is true for journalists: "For example, a book written for an English-speaking audience by one CIA operative was reviewed favourably by another CIA agent in the *New York Times*."[48] Other studies have shown the effects the CIA had on movements and developments within art and culture following World War II.[49] The danger of course is that this position can become debilitating. There is relatively little that one can learn about the modern world "directly," whatever that even means, and it is unclear why one should necessarily trust one's own sensory experience or sense of judgment.

In *Comments*, Debord writes that rumor is "originally a sort of uncontrollable by-product of spectacular information," but that as the spectacle has become more developed rumors can be created, manipulated and spread consciously.[50] "Media/police rumours acquire instantly—or at worst after three or four repetitions—the indisputable status of age-old historical evidence."[51] Rumor is just one contributor to the seeming "eternity of noisy insignificance" that characterizes the integrated spectacle, a consequence of the fact that generalized secrecy is the integrated

46 Debord, G. 1998. 48.

47 Debord, G. 1998. 18–19.

48 Scott, P. D. 2007. *The Road to 9/11*. Berkeley: University of California Press. xix.

49 See Saunders, F. S. 1999. *Who Paid the Piper? The CIA and the Cultural War*. London. Granta Books; Guilbaut, S. 1983. *How New York Stole the Idea of Modern Art*, trans. A. Goldhammer. Chicago: University of Chicago Press.

50 Debord, G. 1998. 76–7.

51 Debord, G. 1998. 55.

spectacle's "most vital operation."[52] Like rumor, this is not just a consequence of the spectacle, but is actively organized. Debord writes:

> When almost every aspect of international political life and ever more important aspects of internal politics are conducted and displayed in the style of the secret services, with decoys, disinformation, and double explanations (one *may* conceal another, or may only seem to) the spectacle confines itself to revealing a wearisome world of necessary incomprehensibility. This tedious series of lifeless, inconclusive crime novels has all the dramatic interest of a realistically staged fight between blacks, at night, in a tunnel.[53]

Conspiracy has become generalized: "thousands of plots [*complots*] in favour of the established order tangle and clash almost everywhere,"[54] and like generalized secrecy, this muddled web of generalized conspiracy makes strategizing difficult for both partisans and their opponents.

What does this mean for the figure of the partisan struggling under the "organized uncertainty" of the integrated spectacle? In *Theory of the Partisan* Schmitt raises the possibility that the partisan could soon exit the historical stage:

> When the internal, immanent rationality and regularity of the thoroughly-organized technological world has been achieved in optimistic opinion, the partisan becomes perhaps nothing more than an irritant. Then, he disappears simply of his own accord in the smooth-running fulfillment of technical-functional forces, just as a dog disappears on the freeway. [55]

And just as the dog is hardly even a problem for the modern highway patrol, Schmitt continues, the partisan will cease to be a philosophical, moral or legal problem. In *The Concept of the Political*, Schmitt writes, "Political thought and political instinct prove themselves theoretically and practically in the ability to distinguish friend and enemy. The high points of politics are simultaneously the moments, in which the enemy is, in concrete clarity, recognized as the enemy."[56]

---

52 Debord, G. 1998. 12 and 15. For more on rumor in political struggles see Guha, R. 1999. *Elementary Aspects of Peasant Insurgency in Colonial India*. Durham, NC: Duke University Press. 251–77.

53 Debord, G. 1998. 59. Interestingly, this politically incorrect metaphor seems to have its origins in a 1882 monochrome, regarded as the first ever, by the poet Paul Bilhaud entitled *Combat de nègres dans une cave pendant la nuit*. See Danto, A. July 31, 2003. Paint It Black. *The Nation*. Available at: www.thenation.com/doc/20030818/danto (accessed July 9, 2012). Thanks to Alberto Toscano for the reference.

54 Debord, G. 1998. 82.

55 Schmitt, C. 2007. 77.

56 Schmitt, C. 1996. 67.

Let's start with a simple question: how does a partisan determine who their enemy is? For the autochthonous defenders of the homeland this is relatively straightforward. In the case of the Spanish *guerrilleros* battling Napoleon's army, the partisan was simply defending their homeland, their soil, their people and the enemy was the invader, the other. For the global revolutionary, the situation is a bit more complex, but Schmitt claims that it was Lenin's cognizance of the enemy and his ability to clearly articulate this that was the secret of his enormous effectiveness.[57] Not being able to determine friend from enemy is disastrous. It threatens the very concept of the political, which is not merely about martial conflict but the ability of a group to collectively identify their friends and enemies.

> The political does not reside in the battle itself, which possesses its own technical, psychological, and military laws, but in the mode of behaviour which is determined by this possibility, by clearly evaluating the concrete situation and thereby being able to distinguish correctly the real friend and the real enemy.[58]

This does not mean that any two groups can "objectively" be each other's enemy—"each participant is in a position to judge whether the adversary intends to negate his opponent's way of life and therefore must be repulsed or fought in order to preserve one's own form of existence"—but how can this be determined with anything approaching certainty under the integrated spectacle?[59]

As Debord claims in *Comments*, even the critique of the integrated spectacle must be cloaked in secrecy: it is both hidden and in hiding. There are two different senses in which this is argued to be the case. The first is the relatively standard Chomskian position that the corporate controlled media have a series of filters that remove positions and stories that are particularly unfavorable to their interests while simultaneously polluting civil society with diversionary bells and whistles.[60] The second is that because of the state's ability to infiltrate, manipulate and destabilize its opponents, and the proclivity of various secret services and security professionals to provoke in order to discredit groups and individuals taking hostile positions toward this society, genuine critique has to operate clandestinely in order to avoid being exposed. Revolutionaries and partisans are in a double bind as the death of the agora means that they are forced to spread their message through the mass media wing of the spectacle, so to speak, which will be neutralized and silenced by the powers that be. Simultaneously, any attempt to go public will leave them prone to surveillance, infiltration and manipulation.

This predicament is one of the main reasons why Debord claims he is forced in *Comments* to devise a new way of writing. It also raises pertinent questions

57 Schmitt, C. 2007. 52.

58 Schmitt, C. 1996. 37.

59 Schmitt, C. 1996. 27.

60 Chomsky, N. and Herman, E. S. 2002. *Manufacturing Consent: The Political Economy of the Mass Media*. New York: Pantheon Books.

about the strategy he and Sanguinetti were attempting to realize in their creation of "Censor." Right from his first published writings, his texts are filled with literary illusions, *détournements* and references to his personal history. Rarely easy or straightforward, they often require multiple readings for their richness to be appreciated. *Comments* is doubly awkward in that it presents a set of hermeneutic difficulties that arise from its self-professed ambiguity. The book can be read relatively quickly as the language no longer requires the reader to linger on every paragraph, trying to decipher what each sentence means (unlike the Marxist-"Hegelianese" of *Society of the Spectacle*). But this simplicity is superficial: a ruse hiding a text much more knotted and complex than it appears. The book begins with an epigram from Sun Tzu on the art of deception in warfare and the actual text starts by stating the context in which the book appears. In the book's first two paragraphs Debord claims that the book is sure to be welcomed by an interested elite of about 50 or 60 people: half of this elite will consist of people who seek to destroy the spectacle while the other half devote themselves to maintaining its rule.

In a sense, and as the quote from Sun Tzu indicates, the need to find new tactics and strategies to cope with infiltration and subversion is nothing new and has certainly been a concern for partisans for some time. Referencing Schmitt, Jan-Werner Müller has written:

> Partisans rely on confounding categories, and on blurring existing legal and political distinctions – part of what can make them successful is to throw their regular adversaries off track, to make states misapprehend their nature, and to have them react in ways that indirectly further the partisans' goals. The ideal-typical Schmittian partisan actively seeks to create confusion among his enemies; he tries to retain what one might call an *epistemological advantage* over regular, recognized political actors.[61]

Debord seems to suggest that gaining this epistemological advantage is more difficult than ever today, but also more important. After portraying a situation that seems as bleak as it is impassable, Debord closes *Comments* with an intriguing assertion: "To this list of the triumphs of power we should, however, add one result which has proved negative: once the running of a state involves a permanent and massive shortage of historical knowledge, that state can no longer be led strategically."[62] This notion, combined with the epistemological confusion created by generalized secrecy, unanswerable lies and disinformation, creates a situation where the ability to understand the new coordinates in which struggle takes place—the society of the spectacle—drastically influences the capabilities

61 Müller, J. W. March 2007. An Irregularity that Cannot be Regulated: Carl Schmitt's Theory of the Partisan and the "War on Terror." Available at: http://www.princeton.edu/~jmueller/Schmitt-WarTerror-JWMueller-March2007.pdf (accessed August 17, 2012). 16.

62 Debord, G. 1998. 20.

and effectiveness of the combatants. Since the study of history is at once about providing a timeline of important events and an understanding of the interrelations and consequences of various actions, it can allow one to both understand how the present has come about and to speculate and strategize about what might come next. The integrated spectacle is gradually creating a world in which the past is forgotten and thus the future is unimaginable, a world where de-politicization goes hand in hand with an increased fear of conflict and destruction. This new reality, Debord argues, has been either misunderstood or underappreciated by both the defenders of the status quo and its enemies, giving understanding the new coordinates and the new terrain of battle a huge significance in the cold and hot partisan clashes to come.

Chapter 13
Targeting Journalists and Media in the New World Order

Stig A. Nohrstedt and Rune Ottosen

Introduction and Theoretical Background

In November 2001 and again in April 2003 the U.S. Air Force bombed Al Jazeera's offices in Kabul and Baghdad, respectively. This is not the first or last time the media has been chosen as a military target; Serb television was bombed during the war against the former Yugoslavia in 1999.

What all these incidents had in common was that they ocurred in so-called "pre-emptive wars" lacking a UN mandate. As civilian targets, media outlets should have been protected by the Geneva Convention. Although there have been independent investigations of all the incidents by the Committee to Protect Journalists and the International Federation of Journalists, and there are no doubts over who were responsible, the attacks seemed to yield no legal or political consequenses.[1] This chapter will discuss the moral and legal basis for the attacks. Our thesis is that the concept of "humanitarian intervention" was a cornerstone in the pro-humanitarian propaganda both in 1999 and 2003. The idea to justify pre-emptive attacks with humanitarian rhetoric can be traced back to a policy document from the Carnegie Endowment in the beginning of the 1990s. Here we find influential contributers like former Secretary of State Madeleine Albright. Many of the arguments used to justify the Bush doctrine[2] can be traced back to this document.[3] This chapter will analyze the paradox of the Western media that, while so often expressing concern for "freedom of expression," has not protested more strongly against these attacks on media and journalists.

1 Ottosen, R. *Verdens Gang* March 17, 2007. *Den farlige journalisstikken* .

2 The Bush Doctrine was declared in the State of the Union address, January 2002, and included three main strands: (i) concept of "pre-emptive war"; (ii) regime change through military action; (iii) aggressive promotion of democracy, U.S.-style.

3 Gowan, P. 2001. *Krigen og dens følger*, in *Under evne. Media og Kosovo-konflikten*, edited by P. Hammon and E. Herman. Oslo: Idem forlag. 39.

The United States and the Geneva Conventions

The legal arguments in this chapter will mostly relate to the Geneva Conventions. The Conventions came to the fore of international law with the establishment of the normative legacy of the Nuremberg Trials which etsablished the principles that legalism and technicalities could not substitute for individual and moral choices and conscience. After World War II, the United States publicily defended these principles, including the humane treatment of all categories of prisoner taken in almost all manner of international conflicts. The United States was not just a signatory but also the custodian of the Geneva Conventions, the original signed copies residing in a vault in the State Department.[4] There are, however, many examples of the difference between speech and reality as a result of the numeorus U.S.-led interventions in other countries.[5] After being found against in a case concerning the use of military force against Nicaragua in 1986, Washington withdrew its approval of the International Court of Justice (ICJ).[6] Even though the first of our case studies, the bombing of Yugoslavia in 1999, occured during the Clinton administration, there is no doubt that the respect for international law fell dramatically during the presidency of George W. Bush Jnr. The lack of respect for the Conventions and international law was openly admitted by Vice President Dick Cheney talking at 'Meet the Press' the first Sunday after 9/11, when he frankly stated:

> We'll have to work sort of the dark side, if you will … We've got to spend time in the shadows in the intelligence world. A lot of what needs to be done here will have to be done quietly, without any discussion, using sources and methods that are available to our intelligence agencies—if we are going to be successful. That's the world these folks operate in. And, uh so it's going to be vital for us to use any means at our disposal basically, to achieve our objectives.[7]

The treatment of prisoners at Guantánamo and Abu Ghraib, the kidnapping of suspected terrorists and bringing them to other countries for torture and other examples are practices coming out of this rhetoric.[8] We will argue that the bombing of media outlets should be included in this list of shame.

---

4 Mayer, J. 2008. *The Dark Side. The Inside Story of How the War on Terror Turned into a War on Americn Ideals*. New York: Doubleday. 8.

5 Chomsky, N. 2004. *Hegemoni eller overlevelse: Amerikas søken etter global dominans*. Oslo: Oktober Forlag.

6 Eskeland, S. 2003. Krig og fredsbevarende operasjoner: Lovlig, ulovlig eller straffbart. *Norsk Militært Tidsskrift*, 12.

7 Mayer, J. 2008. 9–10.

8 Suskind, R. 2006. *The One Percent Doctrine. Deep Inside America's Pursuit of its Enemies Since 9/11*. New York: Simon & Schuster.

Media and Wars

All parties in a modern warfare acknowledge the media as an essential factor as a battlefield for propaganda and as a battleground to "win hearts and minds."[9] Although the CNN-effect as a phenomenon is debated and scholars argue to what extend the media has a direct or indirect effect on the decisions made by political and military leaders, nobody denies that the global media is a factor that all parties in a military conflict in one way or the other have to deal with.[10] The media themselves acknowledge their role as an arena of interest by the different parties, as this quote from the *Washington Post* indicates:

> Almost by definition ... a war waged on live television is a war in which political and public relations considerations become inextricably bound up with military tactics and strategy ... how victory is won is almost as important as victory itself.[11]

The fact that media to an increasingly degree play an import role in warfare puts on the agenda several issues of ethical and legal interest. The NATO attack on the television building in Belgrade in 1999 during the Kosovo War and the American attack on Al Jazeera in Kabul in 2001 and Baghdad in 2003 are examples of military interference in journalism which raises a lot of questions such as:

1. Were the media targeted because of the role they played in informing the global public about the warfare, including potential "collateral damage" such as civilian casualties?
2. If they were targeted because of their journalistic activity what was the rationale behind the decisions?
3. What potentially legal consequences could such acts have?
4. What will be the long-term effect for journalism if journalists and media are to be considered as legitimate targets in modern warfare?

The Impact of the Visual

The importance of visual images and pictures is essential in a modern warfare; thus the breakthrough of CNN during the Gulf War in 1991, with a de facto monopoly

---

9 Allan, S, and Zelzier, B. eds. 2004. *Reporting War. Journalism in War Time*. New York: Routledge; Andersen, R. 2006. *A Century of Media, A Century of War*. New York: Peter Lang.

10 Thune, H. 2009. *Beyond the CNN Effect. Towards a Constituive Understanding of Media Power in Internationa Politics*. PhD thesis. Department of Political Science. Faculty of Social Sciences. University of Oslo; Thussu, D. K. 2007. *Media on the Move. Global Flow and Contra-Flow*. Oxford: Routledge.

11 *Washington Post*, March 24, 2003.

of 24/7 broadcasting to a global audience, became a historical milestone.[12] The combination of effective management of the media and journalists through the international Press Centre in Riyahd, Saudi Arabia, and the new global television technology is the background to George Gerbner's statement that "The boiling point is reached when the power to create a crisis merges with the power to direct the movie about it."[13]

Jörg Becker has underlined the importance of iconic images in the collective memories of wars:

> Thus the perception of wars (Comparable only to top class sport competitions), especially of individual battles or victories, is almost always linked with a single image. An icon. This applies to D-Day in the Second World War, just as it does to a few photographs of the Vietnam War. It applies to the Spanish Civil War as it does to the USA American intervention in Somalia. In the latter case it was the image of a US American soldier dragged through the streets of Mogadishu and brutally killed by Somali civil war militias, to the cheers of the mob. War is always a war with images.[14]

We will argue that it is no coincidence that the three cases we will use in this study involve separate attacks on television facilities.

Theoretical Reasoning for the Hypothesis that the U.S. Military Forces Attack Journalists

The series of incidents discussed above have been interpreted as intentional crimes and violations of the Geneva Convention comitted by U.S. military forces. But we have also seen that clear and direct evidence is not easy to get. The research studies, reports and investigations that are available in many ways vindicate how difficult it is to substantiate beyond doubt that such crimes have been committed. We recognize this as characteristic and typical for suspicious cases of dual state activities. Therefore in such cases one must search for alternative strategies for analysis, and we make an attempt to make deductive conclusions starting from a theoretical and contextual analysis of warfare in the "the New World Order" (NWO). In the following paragraphs we will address four relevant points: the development of mediated war reporting, the importance of visual representations

12 Nohrstedt, S. A. and Ottosen, R. eds. 2001. *Journalism and the New World Order Gulf War, National News Discources and Globalisation*. Göteborg: Nordicom.

13 Gerbner, G. 1992, 244. Persian Gulf War: The Movie, in *Triumph of the Image. The Media's War in the Persian Gulf: A Global Perspective*, edited by H. Mowlana and G. Gerbner. Boulder: Westview Press.

14 Becker, J. 2004 Afghanistan, the War and the Media, in *U.S. and the Others. Global Media Images on The War on Terror*, edited by S. A. Nohrstedt and R. Ottosen. Gothenburg: Nordicom. 306–7.

in the new wars, the increased attention to civilian casualities (i.e. "the body count"), and professional strategies of integrity within the journalist profession. Exploring these aspects will make it possible to argue that U.S. military forces have developed a deliberate strategy of—in some special instances—shooting at journalists.

The Development of Mediated War Reporting and the New Western Way of Warfare

It is generally acknowledged today that media are strategically important in modern wars. Besides warfare on the ground, at sea and in the air, the media has become a battlefield.[15] This is partly explained by the dramatic development of the media sector, where ever more media, journalists and information providers compete for people's attention and opinions. In Martin Shaw's study, *The New Western Way of Warfare* (2005) he describes the changes as a "risk-transfer" kind of warfare. According to Shaw, modern wars are conducted under constant surveillance by international organizations, legal institutions, media and civil society. From this it follows that not only do wars actualize physical risks but also, increasingly, political risks. Military superiority is the traditional strategy to transfer the risks to the enemy forces. The new wars, however, are pursued in ways that in addition are aimed at placing the political risks at the opposite side of the conflict. This is evident for example when the UN Alliance in the Gulf War 1990–1991, NATO in the Kosovo conflict 1999 or the U.S. Alliance in Iraq 2003 at almost at any price tried to avoid its own military losses, choosing, for instance, air operations at high altitude, which simultanuously exposed the civil population to great risks due to reduced precision.[16] But this method of warfare was adequate for the prioritized aim of avoiding the political risks connected to rising numbers of casualties among American military personnel.

However, this kind of warfare created legitimacy risks, at least indirectly, since the effects were increasing numbers of civilian casualities as result of the Western warfare. Although Shaw is not entirely clear about the consequences on the casualty statistics—on the one hand he mentions the larger 20th-century trend of "overwhelmingly civilian casualties" but on the other hand he also speculates in whether this trend might be reversed[17]—he is very explicit when it comes to massacres of civilians as a "competely predictable consequence of …

15 Ottosen, R. 2009. *VG, Saddam og vi. Et kritisk blikk på nyhetsdekning av krig og konflikt*. Kristiansand IJ/Høyskoleforlaget.

16 Nohrstedt, S. A. and Ottosen, R. 2001; Nohrstedt, S. A. and Ottosen, R. 2004; Nohrstedt, S. A. and Ottosen, R. eds. 2005. *Global War – Local News. Media Images of the Iraq War*. Göteborg: Nordicom.

17 Shaw, M. 2005. *The New Western Way of Warfare*. Cambridge: Polity Press. 83.

the protection of Western military personnel."[18] And he further emphasizes how important it is in the new wars for the Western politicians to avoid public attention to "suffering and deaths" among civilians as *directly* caused by Western military forces. This could be avoided partly by defining these deaths as collateral and not intentional, and partly by media manipulation and "spin."[19]

In an analysis of the "risk economy" of the Iraq War 2003, Shaw elaborates on the relative importance of casualty figures for the general outcome of this war—"its military and political success has been the most problematic of all new Western wars."[20] In a comparison between the "casualty *rates*" of the Gulf War 1990–1991 and the Iraq War of 2003, which Shaw refers to and regards as credible, his conclusion is that costs in human lives "were actually higher in 2003."[21] Similar to the previous Gulf War in 1991, it was said by U.S. and UK politicians and militaries that civilian casualties should be avoided at all costs by conducting warfare with high-precision, "surgical" weapons. But mainly due to the goal of the invasion, i.e. to topple the Saddam Hussein regime, the ground operations were extensive which implied that reporters questioned the sanitized propaganda pictures: "It sounds surgical in theory. In practice, it still leaves a mess. Television pictures of weeping local residents suggested civilian casualties."[22] Body-counting has been the "holy grail of casualty information" in the risk economy of new Western wars, according to Shaw, because it tends to be the crucial argument for critics of the military conflict strategy and its ideology: "By showing that the outcome of war is more deaths than the ideology of 'precision weaponry' allows, body-counting can enter a countervailing entry in the bookkeeping of armed conflict."[23] This has happened very much because of the development of new media and particularly the Internet, which has opened up for "virtually real-time analysis" of casualties. This is why Shaw calls the wars from the Kosovo conflict and onwards "Internet wars."[24] However, some of the online sites for reports about the consequences of the warfare for human beings, not least civilians, are probably exaggerating the figures, and Shaw relies on Carl Conetta's analysis as a more sophisticated and conservative estimate. But even his assessments—although with lower casualty numbers—lead to the conclusion that "the portion of war fatalities that were civilian noncombatants may have been twice as great" in Operation Iraqi Freedom (2003) than in Desert Storm (1990–1991).[25]

18 Shaw, M. 2005. 86.

19 Shaw, M. 2005. 92ff.

20 Shaw, M. 2005. 99.

21 Shaw, M. 2005. 109 and 122.

22 Borger, J. and Millar, S. April 9, 2003. It Sounds Surgical in Theory. *Guardian*, quoted in Shaw, M. 2005. 110.

23 Shaw, M. 2005. 119.

24 Shaw, M. 2005. 120.

25 Conetta, C. 2003. *The Wages of War: Iraqi Combatant and Noncombatant Fatalities in the 2003 Conflict*. Cambridge, Project on Defence Alternatives. Available at:

Now, it is not completely decisive for the risk economy of wars—to continue with Shaw's terminology—as to whether the civilian casualty rates is higher or lower from one war to another. Shaw emphasizes that the major factor for failure or success for the war policy is how it affects the risk calculus for an intervening nation's *own* troops, personnel and citizens. The Iraq War became such a debacle for the U.S. and UK leaders because of the combined effects of a rationale for the intervention that was later revealed as flawed (the non-existent weapons of mass destruction) and the counter-productive consequences of the occupation for the terrorist threat, which increased rather than decreased after the war, together with the promise of a surgical war that was not at all the outcome "on the ground." Shaw contends that more important for the media agenda and the evaporating credibility of the Iraq War policy were the specific incidents of harm caused by the Fallujah assualt and the Abu Ghraib pictures of torture of Iraqi prisoners—both incidents breaking out in the media immediately after the most deadly month on record for U.S. soldiers in Iraq (April 2004). Shaw concludes: "it was *cruelty* rather than killing that in the end defined, in global media and politics, the violence of the occupation towards Iraqis."[26]

Mediatization of Modern Warfare

Even though Shaw emphasizes globalization within the media sector and that media monitoring today is not restricted by the issue of national borders that drives the need for the transfer of the political risks, he does not elaborate in more detail as to how the media through manipulations and staged events and spectacles has itself become part of the new warfare. This is, however, central for Simon Cottle's analysis of "mediatization" in connection with the 9/11 terrorist attacks on the United States as well as in the subsequent Global War on Terror (GWOT).[27] This is obvious in conjunction with the attacks on the United States which would not have had any purpose whatsoever unless they attracted the media's attention. To be completely clear: the special media-related conditions of Threat-Society[28] have never been more evident than in the case of the 9/11 terrorist attacks. With very modest manpower, economic and technical resources the terrorists managed to direct an onslaught which in terms of "mediatization" was generally targeted to get worldwide saturation and devastating global consequences. And as always when terror is involved the aim is to disseminate fear. But the War on Terror is also pursued dependent on the same media-related preconditions, and the Bush administration's new warfare has in many ways had the media as a centerpiece.

---

www.comw.org/pda/0310rm8.html, quoted in Shaw, M. 2005. 122.

26 Shaw, M. 2005. 124.

27 Shaw, M. 2005. 124.

28 Nohrstedt, S. A. 2011. Media and Threat-Society, in *Communicating Risks – Towards the Threat-Society?*, edited by S. A. Nohrstedt. Göteborg: Nordicom. 17–51.

Examples are legion: Colin Powell's accusations against Iraq in the UN Security Council on February 5, 2003 with all kinds of visual and audio communication techniques, the missile attacks on Baghdad with the purpose of causing "shock and awe" that started the war, the "rescue" operation to save Jessica Lynch, the toppling of the Saddam Hussein statue in Baghdad, the "embedded" war reporters and President Bush's "mission accomplished" speech on the *USS Abraham Lincoln* are all eminent examples of warfare in which the media are deeply involved. These spectacular events would not have happened without the media's presence—or at least not in the same way—because the combat role of the media is far more important than its function as conveyor or mediator of news.

Embedded within these media spectaculars are political-identity components that consequently polarize the conflict between a "We" and a "Them." Wheras the implicit We strive toward truth and justice, that weapons of mass destruction should not be in the possession of dictators, the bombardments that "We" conduct aim at minimizing the number of innocent victims and to shortening the war, that "Our" soldiers never leave a comrade behind, etc., "They," on the other hand, are marked by false promises, lies, injustice, the absence of the will to resist tyranny, as well as a power based upon coercion instead of democratic consent.

And in the case of President Bush's landing on the *Abraham Lincoln* and the speech to the troops on board, the spectacle reached an all time high by a scenography that clearly and intentionally aimed at establish connotations to the president role in the movie *Independence Day*, in which the "virtual" president mobilizes the peoples of the world against the inter-planetary invaders. In this "media-event" the military-entertainment complex elaborated by Robin Andersen in her analysis of media and war in the 20th century becomes extremely evident, alas almost parodical: "It was the choreographed final sequence of a narrative of invasion that turned battle into entertainment in real time, and took the representation of war to a new level – one of stagecraft on a grand scale."[29]

Some elements of the visualized mediatization may inspire, at least in retrospect, laughter rather than fear and terror. But there is a problem for the journalist profession that needs to be highlighted here, namely that visual reporting in news media might suffer from less reflexivity than textual reporting. In a study of how Swedish news media reported from Colin Powell's presentation of the accusations against Iraq before the Security Concil in February 2003, Stig Nohrstedt concludes that although the three studied newspapers—*Aftonbladet*, *Expressen* and *Dagens Nyheter*—treated the U.S. accusations critically in their written stories, in their visual material the representations presupposed that Powell's charges were accurate. For example, graphic illustrations showed maps where Iraqi missiles equipped with chemical warheads could reach the neighboring countries, and, in emphatic reports of Swedes living or visiting in these countries,

29 Andersen, R. 2006. 227. Mral, B. 2004. *We're A Peaceful Nation. War Rhetoric after September 11*. Stockholm. Swedish Emergency Management Agency. Special Feature 5. 60ff.

they reported that they were terrified of the prospect of being targeted by such weapons of mass destruction.[30] Other studies of the media coverage of the Iraq War confirm that in the African media it does seem to be the case that footage is less critically dealt with in the news rooms than the texts, and, therefore, visual war propaganda is probably more efficient than textual.[31] This can of course work either way—if the media were more receptive to the visual U.S. propaganda than to the textual representations, in other instances, e.g. the cases of Falluja and Abu Ghraib mentioned by Shaw, anti-war propaganda might have a major impact on the legitimacy and success of the war policy. Because of this, visual reports from the battlefield, and in particular from the effects of the warfare on civilians, tend to be extremely contested and controversial. Here we are approaching the key component of our analysis and deductive explanation as to why it has become increasingly dangerous for journalists to report from war theaters in the NWO. But before we sum up the argument we will address two other themes, firstly the issue of whether war journalism focuses more on civilian casualties in the most recent wars than in the previous ones, and secondly, how—if at all—journalists as professionals try to avoid becoming a propaganda tool for the belligerent parties in modern wars.

The Inter-Discursive Relations between the War Propaganda and the Discourse of Compassion

War propaganda is well-known for its polarized discourse when it comes to how the main actors, motives, warfare and truths are treated: the "enemy" is painted in black while the "own" side is white. This pattern has been empirically and historically verified again and again from the ancient to the modern wars. Not least has the war propaganda used images—written and visual—to depict innocent victims and civilian casualities in a polarized way. There are, to borrow the classical distinction from Edward Herman and Noam Chomsky (1988), "worthy" and "unworthy" victims, meaning that the innocent civilians killed by the enemy are "worthy" of all attention and empathy whereas the innocent civilians that are killed by our own forces are "unworthy" in the sense that they should preferably not be exposed and discussed in public too much. Only the enemy is guilty of intentionally bombing the civilian population in order to weaken resistance to its authoritarian will.

The media coverage of the Gulf War with its images of surgical warfare and "smart bombs" was probably quite extreme as a mediated war propaganda

30 Nohrstedt, S. A. 2005. Media Reflexivity in the War on Terror. Three Swedish Dailies and the Iraq War, in S. A. Nohrstedt and R. Ottosen.

31 Mucunguzi, J. 2005. Images of the Iraq War in Ugandan Newspapers; Kupe, T. and Hyde-Clarke, N. 2005. The South African Media and the War in Iraq, in S. A. Nohrstedt and R. Ottosen.

discourse in the Western countries. There are plenty of media studies confirming this and there is no need to repeat their findings here.[32] In one of our own studies, news editors of leading Swedish media were interviewed before Desert Storm started in January 1991 and were asked what they regarded as specially important to achieve in their reporting of the coming war events. Several of them responded that a major priority was to describe the "true face" or the "real face" of the war. This was important since it was expected that the belligerent parties would try to conceal how the civilians suffered during the military confrontations.[33] When some of the interviewees were contacted again after the war had ended and asked whether they thought that their coverage had been successful in reporting the "true face," they admitted that they had failed; furthermore, they expected this to be repeated in the future.

From the 1980s and onwards media reporting of distant sufferings, for example in connection to diseases, famine, genocide, etc., has grown and been heavily exposed in television coverage, from aid concerts to other celebrity media events. It seems that a discourse of compassion has reached the general audiences and triggered engagement for the innocent victims even at great distances and worldwide. Some theorists have taken that as an indication of globalization or cosmopolitanization of empathy and concern for fellow human beings.[34] Without elaborating on this topic in detail, we contend that this mediated discourse of compassion has a bearing on how victims are reported in war journalism. A study of media reporting from the Kosovo conflict in 1999 showed that the NATO propaganda-plan to once again televisually re-present a surgical war failed because journalists and media, approximately two weeks into the bombing justified as an effort to stop the ethnic cleansing in Kosovo by Serbian troops and paramilitaries, shifted from the one-sided coverage of the Kosovo-Albanian refugees as the "worthy" victims and widened the scope to include the Serbian civilan casualties. Hence there was no repetition of the clinical war image from the Gulf War of 1990–1991 reported in the studies of British, Norwegian and Swedish media.[35]

The 9/11 terrorist attacks on the United States initiated what in modern times must be the most emphatic and compassionate reporting in Western media. Never have the victims been exposed to such a degree. And never have the media on

---

32 See Andersen, R. 2006; Bennett, L. and Paletz, D. eds. 1994. *Taken by Storm. The Media, Public Opinion, and U.S. Foreign Policy in the Gulf War*. Chicago: The University of Chicago Press; Kellner, D. 1992. *The Persian Gulf TV War*. Boulder: Westview Press; Nohrstedt, S. A. and Ottosen, R. 2001.

33 Nohrstedt, S. A. 2009. New War Journalism. Trends and Challenges. *Nordicom Review*, 30/1, 98 note 1. Cf. Nohrstedt, S. A. 1992. 121. Ruling by Pooling, in *Triumph of the Image. The Media's War in the Persian Gulf: A Global Perspective*, edited by H. Mowlana and G. Gerbner. Boulder: Westview Press.

34 Beck, U. 2006. *Cosmopolitan Vision*. Cambridge: Polity Press; Chouliaraki, L. 2006. *The Spectatorship of Suffering*. London: Sage.

35 Nohrstedt, S. A., Höijer, B. and Ottosen, R. 2002. *Kosovokonflikten, medierna och medlidandet*. Stockholm Styrelsen för psykologiskt försvar Rapport. 190.

another continent identified so much with the shocked and mourning relatives and fellow countrymen. "Today we are all American" as the headlines announced in leading European press, constituting an unprecedented expression of an extensive and deeply felt sorrow with the "worthy" American victims.

When the Bush administration initiated the Global War on Terror shortly after 9/11 the prime target and battlefield was Aghanistan, which led to new reports about civilians being killed. Although the war leaders made attempts to control photographs of dead women and children, international media disseminated footage that showed the "true face" of the war. But nothing was equal to the images from the jet-powered onslaught on the WTC-buildings and the panic-stricken people rushing through Manhattan's streets. Al Jazeera as the single television channel allowed to work inside Afghanistan under the Taliban regime was the major supplier of visual representations of the Afghanistan War. This is definitely one important aspect of the U.S. attack on the channel's office in Kabul. Al Jazeera had become a main player on the international television market and that had consequences also for the subsequent phase of the GWOT, the invasion of Iraq in 2003.

When it comes to coverage of civilian casualties studies have shown that there is a trend from the Gulf War 1990–1991 until the Iraq War 2003 of increased media attention to the "true face." The available data do not indicate a very dramatic change, but nevertheless there is a gradual development of war journalism from a couple of percentage points of the total news material in the studied Swedish media in the Gulf War to 5–6 percent in the Iraq War.[36] The propaganda war about who are "worthy" victims had intensified probably because Arab media like Al Jazeera had begun competition with CNN and BBC World. But there might also be another explanation, namely that the journalistic task of revealing the "true face" of the wars had become a professional strategy, at least in the Swedish news media. It seems that the news editors interviewed in January 1991 indicated that this was an important aim but also regarded it a strategy for escaping the propaganda trap. By focusing on the civilians' fate in wars it would be possible to avoid the sanitized images and pictures that the U.S. press-officers were so happy to share with the media personnel that were gathered in the press center at the Hyatt Regency Hotel in Riyahd, Saudi Arabia, during the Gulf War.

The Dual State and Security Policy

The (Un)Legal Basis for the Attack on Former Yugoslavia

NATO decided to attack the former Yugoslavia on March 24, 1999 unilaterally. The UN Security Council did not authorize it. The political rationale given was that there was a humanitarian crisis going on with thousands of Kosovars in danger of being killed or ethnically cleansed if the international community did

36 Nohrstedt, S. A. 2009. 91.

not intervene against the Milosevic regime militarily. It is disputed how serious the situation was;[37] but even if the Kosovo Albanians were driven out in large numbers, it is not an acceptable explanation for an intervention that was not in accordance with international law. According to Ståle Eskeland, Norwegian professor of law, no NATO country could argue that they acted in self-defense since Milosevic had no plans to attack any of them.[38] The UN Security Council passed a a non-binding resolution formulated in a manner to avoid veto from Russia and China denouncing the actions on the ground as violations of the UN Charter and calling on Serbia to cease the fighting. One could argue like Michael Ignatieff who, in his book *Empire Lite: Nation-Building in Bosnia, Kosovo and Afghanistan*, asserted that the United States had a responsibility to create a "humanitarian empire" through nation-building and, if necessary, military force. We strongly disagree with this position but it is an argument that you can relate to and meet with counter-arguments. NATO instead went down the road of "new speak" and NATO "retro-actively" adopted (or "interpreted") the language, purpose and meaning of the non-binding resolution as a de facto authorization for international action to prevent a local breach of the UN Charter. We think it is highly unlikely that this move by NATO can be said to have a legal basis. And who had in the first place given NATO the mandate to start the bombing as a form of "executive decision"?

Former state secretary in the Norwegian Foreign Ministry, the lawyer Vidar Helgesen, wrote an unusually solid legal analysis of whether there was a basis in international law for the attack. He concluded:

> I have come to such a basis does not exist neither in the UN Charter or in customary international law. There is no basis for saying that the intervention has created the basis for new international law. (Author's translation)[39]

The Norwegian decision to join NATO's war against Yugoslavia was taken in a closed session in Stortinget (the Norwegian Parliament) without written communication between the cabinet and the Stortinget.[40]

What legal consequence could it be for Norway to take part in an illegal war? According to Eskeland, members of government can only be prosecuted for impeachment, where the Odelstinget, a chamber in Stortinget, is the prosecuting authority. It is beyond the political realities of the world to imagine that the

---

37 Chomsky, N. 1999. *The New Military Humanism. Lessons from Kosovo*. Monroe: Common Courage Press.

38 Eskeland, S. 2003. 12.

39 Helgesen, V. 1999. *Kosovo og Folkeretten*. Institutt for forsvarsstudier skriftserie 4/1999. 43.

40 Ottosen, R. 2001. *Patriotiske virveltrommer eller kritisk krigsjournalistikk. Norske nyhetsmediers dekning av Kosovokrigen i 1999*. Rapport til Rådet for anvendt medieforskning.

Odelstinget should have started an investigation and legal investigation to clarify whether there is a legal basis for an indictment against then Prime Minister Kjell Magne Bondevik and his former government colleagues. But should the ICJ decide that the intervention was in violation of international law, it would be difficult for the Odelstinget to continue to remain passive. Norway could potentially have been prosecuted for its military support for the illegal bombing, but this was not an issue in the political discourse of Norwegian politicians.[41] On the contrary, Prime Minister Bondevik insisted that the operation was a "humanitarian intervention" and not a war.

We will come back to what the implications of the use of humanitarian rhetoric to justify de facto violations of international law. To place this in a Scandinavian context we will emphasize that to misinform the public as part of a covert agenda is not a new phenomen as the following example from the Cold War in Sweden indicates.

Sweden and the Catalina Story

Journalists and media have particular difficulties when dealing with activities that can be characterized as dual state or deep politics. In Norway and Sweden both the Cold War and the wars after 1989 can illustrate this. In Sweden the so-called Catalina story is a case from the era of politically frozen relations between the Western countries and the Soviet Union in the begining of the 1950s, relations that also involved an officially non-aligned country such as Sweden in the shadows of secret intelligence operations for the West. Officially Sweden had stated after 1945 that it would continue its traditional foreign- and security policy with roots in the aftermath of the Napoleonic Wars and stay outside of military alliances. It was believed to be a position that would contribute to stability in Nordic region and avoid Soviet hostility and aggression. Strong national military defense forces should guarantee that Sweden was self-dependent and capable of protecting its territory without foreign assistance, which, for example, motivated investments in a national industry for production of military aircrafts and one of the strongest air forces in the world besides the major powers.

In reality the military links to the Western countries and the NATO alliance were many and important, although hidden from the general public and most MPs. The so-called Catalina case in 1952 was an event that threatened to draw away the curtain from the secret cooperation between the Swedish military and the NATO countries. Actually it was not one event, but two linked events which were about two airplanes that had been lost over the Baltic Sea. What was reported in the news was that first a DC-3 aircraft had disappeared without any explanation. A Catalina rescue plane that was sent out to search for the lost DC-3 was itself shot down by Soviet fighter aircrafts and the crew was killed. Many years later it was revealed

41 Eskeland, S. 2003. 12; Ottosen, R. 2009.

that the DC-3 was spying on behalf of the United States and that it was shot down over Soviet sea territory.

One well-known and successful reporter, Massi Svensson, at the leading quality newspaper in Sweden, *Dagens Nyheter*, had a remarkable chance to make a world-scoop when the widow of one of the DC-3 crew gave him her husband's personal diary in which he explicitly wrote about the secret spy operations and that the plane had been shot at by the Soviet forces before. But the journalist kept the diary without publishing anything about it until 20 years later when he tells the story in his memoirs. It is clear from his recollections that he never thought of releasing this news because it could have jeopardized Swedish national interests.[42] Hence the secret dual state activities by the United States led to the involvement of Swedish authorities in the same kind of operations, to the deception of the Swedish public and eventually to self-censorship by a leading journalist who resisted the temptation to make a world scoop. We will come back to the principal issues for journalism in relation to this type of activity in the concluding section.

Case Studies and Empirical Findings

Case 1: Bombing of Serb Television in 1999

On April 23, 1999, NATO planes bombed Radio Televizija Srbija (RTS) in Belgrade as part of the air war over Kosovo.[43] Sixteen media-related workers were killed and 16 others were wounded. It was officially acknowledged by NATO spokesmen that the station was a legitimate target at a press conference at Supreme Headquarters Allied Powers Europe (SHAPE) the day the bombing took place. Colonel Konrad Freytag, who spoke at the press conference, used the propagandistic nature of Serb television as a justification.[44] It was later admitted by personnel organizing NATO's information strategy that they used two different justifications for the bombing and that this was a tactical error. One justification was linked to the accusation of the alleged presence of military facilities in the television building and the other was the propagandistic nature of Serb television.[45]

Yugoslavia filed a lawsuit at the UN international tribunal in the ICJ against Belgium, Canada, France, Germany, Italy, Netherlands, Portugal and the UK,

42 Svensson, M. 1972. *Brännbart: Ur en kriminalreporters vardag. Forum; Guillou, Jan (2009) Ordets makt och vanmakt. Mitt skrivande liv*. Piratförlaget. 65.

43 Chomsky, N. 1999.

44 Gierhart, C. 2008. *Targeting Media: The Legal Restrictions on States Attacking Media in Times of War*. Unpublished manuscript summer 2008. 10.

45 The statement of two different line of arguments as a tactical error was made at a seminar attended by Rune Ottosen in Oslo in the autumn of 2000, when a NATO spokesman made the remark at the seminar organized by the Norwegian Atlantic Committee.

claiming that the attack on Yugoslavia was illegal, but the case was dismissed.[46] According to Cindy Gierhart the only way the bombing of RTS could have a legal basis would be if it could be justified under Article 79(2) of Protocol Additional to the Geneva Conventions of 1949, which gives journalists protection as civilians "provided that they take no action adversely affecting their status as civilians."[47] This means that journalists, apart from being employees of the belligerent state, had no part in hostilities; then they should be afforded protection by the Geneva Conventions as civilians. An example of the contrary was the case of three media workers who were brought before the International Criminal Tribunal for Rwanda (ICTR). One of them, Ferdinand Nahimana, was found guilty of inciting genocide for broadcasting on Radio Rwanda the contents of a fake document that led to the killing of hundreds of Tutsi civilians. Nahimana's case is extraordinary since he is also an academic and holds a Doctorate in History and is the author of many books. He was, however, a founder of the Radio Télévision Libre des Mille collines (RTLM) and was convicted for not having done anything to stop the inflammatory broadcasts of the RTLM after April 6, 1994, as he had, according to the judgment, operational control over the personnel of the radio station. The trial received attention since it was the first time since the Nuremberg Trials that "hate speech" had been prosecuted as a war crime. On December 3, 2003 Nahimana was sentenced to life imprisonment (reduced to 30 years after appeal) for the crimes of genocide, conspiracy to commit genocide, incitement, directly and publicly, to commit genocide, complicity in genocide and crimes against humanity. In his defense Nahimana claimed that he had no formal responsibility at the station when the massacre started. According to his French lawyer Jean-Marie Biju-Duval, the conviction, "marks the end of a certain right of evidence before international justice"; "There was the idea that there was a right of evidence inherited from Common law (legal system mainly used before international courts) the protection barriers have been removed one after another," said Biju Duval.[48] We will not go into the issue of whether the evidence against Nahimana was good enough to rule a sentence of 30 years in prison, but rather see the discussion in light of the bombing of RTS in 1999.

The sentence against Nahimana was welcomed by human rights activists all over the world. Even though the ruling can be said to legitimize the right to intervene in the "free flow of information" an organization like Reporters Without Borders welcomed the ruling since the stopping of the massacre in Rwanda in the short term was more important than protecting the freedom of expression of those responsible for the genocide in the long term. In the statement the following argument was used: "Even if no country is today in a situation comparable to Rwanda's at the time of the genocide, these sentences should serve as a call to

46 Eskeland, S. 2003. 12.

47 Gierhart, C. 2008. 6.

48 *World News*, April 28, 2004. Available at: www.africannewsanalysis.blogspot.com/ (accessed February 28, 2011).

order to all the publications that constantly flout the most elementary rules of professional ethics and conduct."[49] Could the same arguments have been used to bomb RTS? In our view this is not the case.

Since the 16 media workers killed in the RTS building had no known involvement in any hostilities and were not accused by anybody to have taken up arms or any other hostilities, they clearly should have enjoyed protection as civilians. They had done nothing other than show up for work. The Final Report of the Committee Established to Review the NATO Bombing Campaign Against the federal Republic of Yugoslavia came to the conclusion that: "NATO intentionally bombed the Radio and TV station and the persons killed or injured were civilians."[50] There is no doubt that the RTS broadcasts were highly propagandistic. But even though one could question Milosevic's views on journalism, it is not regarded as an international crime and cannot, according to the Geneva Convention, be used to justify the use of military power. A historical precedent was made during the Nuremberg Trials; Hans Fritzsche was found not guilty even though he was head of the Radio Division of the Propaganda Ministry and Plenipotentiary for the Political Organization of the Greater German Radio. The reason given was that he was not in a high enough position to formulate the propagandistic and anti-Semitic broadcast, he simply carried it out. The legal issue here is that propagandistic statements alone have historically not constituted criminal activity.[51] When the prosecutors for the International Criminal Tribunal for the former Yugoslavia decided not to bring charges against NATO countries for bombing the RTS, it was because they believed that the military rationale for the bombing was the main reason for the attack. Gierhart, who has analysed the legal aspects of the bombing, holds that this decision cannot be legally justified:

> While this author agrees that military command and control centres are legitimate military objectives, it does not seem the committee's report went far enough to prove that RTS served as a command and control centre for Milosevic. The report proved that NATO believed, or at least claimed, that I targeted RTS for this reason. But the report did not prove that RTS really served that function. While this author cannot prove that RTS did *not* serve as part of the command, control, and communications centre for Yugoslavia, there is absolutely nothing to suggest that it did serve that purpose. And here we must remind that, when "in case of doubt whether an object which is normally dedicated to civilian purposes (…) is being used to make an effective contribution to military action, it shall be presumed not be so used (Article 52(3) of Protocol 1)."[52]

---

49 Reporters Without Borders 2003. December 3, 2003. Available at: http://en.rsf.org/rwanda-two-sentenced-to-life-imprisonment-03-12-2003,08709.html (accessed July 22, 2011).

50 Gierhart, C. 2008. 12.

51 Gierhart, C. 2008. 15.

52 Gierhart, C. 2008. 16.

If one accepts Gierhart's legal arguments one possible conclusion is that NATO countries were not brought to court because it could be problematic to justify the whole bombing as a "humanitarian intervention" which was the core argument in NATO's propaganda to start the illegal war in the first place.[53]

Case 2: The Bombing of Al Jazeera in Kabul 2001

Al Jazeera was established in Qatar in 1996 and represented an ideological alternative to Western channels by offering Arab perspectives on global events. It was established as an independent channel financed by the Qatari government through a $150 million loan. Though controversial for broadcasting detailed images of civilian casualties and dead American soldiers, it has established itself as a respected news organization. Not only did Al Jazeera provide a platform for the criticism of Western policy, but, for the first time Arab journalists publicly criticized Arab governments and Arab regimes. As a result governments from Morocco to Iraq closed down Al Jazeera offices and expelled reporters.[54] Al Jazeera was the only news organization to remain in Kabul in 2001 after the Taliban expelled all other foreign reporters, and through this Kabul office—which was bombed twice during the Afghanistan invasion—it had access to Taliban leaders and Osama bin Laden. Al Jazeera was condemned by the U.S. administration for giving voice to terrorist leaders, and even though attempts were made to put pressure on the government in Qatar, the Western monopoly over global news broadcasts was broken for ever.[55] Al Jazeera was attacked on November 13, the same day Kabul fell to the Northern Alliance. Al Jazeera reporters were out in the streets covering the city's fall when their office was hit. "The office has been known by everybody, the American airplanes know the location of the office," said Al Jazeera's managing director Mohammed Jamin al-Ali.[56]

The respected BBC reporter Nik Gowing made his own investigation and concluded that it was the responsibility of the Americans although he could not establish that the television station was deliberately targeted.[57] When Gowing interviewed a high-ranking U.S. officer and asked whether the electronic signals were the reason for the attack according to Pentagon, the officer answered that it

53 Eskeland, S. 2003. 12.

54 Berenger, R. 2006, 68. Media in the Middle East and North Africa, in *Global Communication: Theories, Stakeholders and Trends*, edited by T. L. McPhail. 2nd edn. Boston: Blackwell.

55 Figenschou, T. U. 2004. *Courting, Criticism, Censorship and Bombs: A Study of the Relationship between the Al Jazeera Channel and the US Administration during the War in Iraq 2003*. Hovedoppgave i journalistikk IMK-UIO /Avd. JBI HIO 2004.

56 Suskind, R. 2006. 138.

57 Ottosen, R. 2009.

was not the responsibility of the U.S. military to determine whether the signals from a news office are regular news broadcasts or espionage or the like.[58]

Ron Suskind in his book *The One Percent Doctrine* analyzes the event and, based on conversation with high-ranking officials in the CIA and the White House, he concludes that "there was satisfaction that a message had been sent to Al Jazeera."[59] Evidently his sources clearly saw this as a deliberate attack.

Case 3: The Bombing of Al Jazeera in Baghdad 2003

On April 8 during the invasion of Iraq, the Al Jazeera office in Baghdad was bombed and television journalist Tarek Ayyoub was killed. Abu Dhabi TV was hit almost at the same time. Abu Dhabi TV is based in the United Arab Emirates and is operated by the government. Before the Iraq War, Abu Dhabi TV was an entertainment channel rather than a news channel, but started to broadcast news around the clock when the war broke out. As Al Jazeera and Abu Dhabi were the only two international media to have their own office in Baghdad, Gierhart concludes that these attacks most likely were deliberate.[60] At that time, the head of Al Jazeera had offered the American government detailed information about the location of their office, and the leadership of Al Jazeera asked ironically whether by doing so they had offered the Pentagon the necessary information to put them out of business.[61] After an independent investigation, the U.S.-based Committee to Protect Journalists found no evidence that the bombing of Al Jazeera was a deliberate hit, but nonetheless held the U.S. government accountable since media companies should be protected as civilians under the Geneva Convention.[62] In a leaked memo, which appeared in the British newspaper the *Daily Mirror* in November 2005, Bush allegedly told Tony Blair that he wanted to bomb Al Jazeera's headquarters in Qatar as well, but, according to the leak, Blair talked him out of it. An indication that the story was based on fact came when a British Cabinet Office civil servant was charged under the UK's Official Secrets Act for leaking the document. Former British Home Secretary David Blunkett wrote in his diary, later sold at auction, that Bush had urged Blair to bomb Al Jazeera headquarters. Clearly Blunkett obviously did not realize that targeting media in order to stop it from broadcasting is illegal.[63] Although U.S. officials have never admitted it, all indications point in the direction that Al Jazeera and Abu Dhabi were targeted because they were broadcasting outside the control of the United States and the "Coalition of the Willing."

58 Gowing, N. 2003. Journalists and War: The Troubling New Tensions Post 9/11, in *War and the Media*, edited by D. K. Thussu and D. Freedman. London: Sage. 234.

59 Suskind, R. 2006. 138.

60 Gierhart, C. 2008.

61 Figenschou, T. U. 2004.

62 Gierhart, C. 2008.

63 Gierhart, C. 2008. 24.

Case 4: Attacks on Journalists

We have now gone through three cases where four different television buildings were most likely to have been targeted by NATO and U.S. forces for being just that—television facilities. If we go into the issue of attacks on individual journalists, the picture becomes even grimmer.

On April 8, 2003, the Palestine Hotel came under attack the same time that Abu Dhabi and Al Jazeera offices were bombed, and television journalist Tarek Ayyoub was killed when he was on the roof of the building about to broadcast. That day around 100 other journalists in Baghdad were operating out of the Palestine Hotel as well, when a U.S. tank opened fire. Reuters cameraman Taras Protsyuk and Spanish cameraman José Couso of Telecinco were killed. The day before an Al Jazeera staff member was stopped at a U.S. Marines checkpoint. His car was shot at after he had been stopped and given his ID as a journalist. He was not hurt but his car was badly damaged. The Al Jazeera staff also read this as a message. Although the United States admitted these episodes, the official story was that they were all accidental. It has been established that the Palestine Hotel was on a list for possible target prior to the invasion.[64] An independent investigation for the Committee to Protect Journalists (CPJ) concluded that the shelling might have been accidental, but the military had the responsibility for the killings since information about the journalists staying there was not distributed to the ground forces.[65]

When we look at the statistics, some facts indicate that journalists might be targets in recent wars. According to the International Federation of Journalists (IFJ) more than 1,100 journalists and media employees were killed on duty between 1995 and 2007. Even though this chapter has concentrated on journalists killed by the United States/NATO, it must be underlined that in Iraq the vast majority of the journalists were killed by militants and insurgents. For the year 2004 statistics showed that 65 percent of all killed journalists were killed by Iraqi militants or their foreign supporters; 95 percent of the journalists killed were Iraqis.[66]

The number of journalists killed worldwide rose to 244 percent between 2002 and 2007. Statistically, journalists were 10 times more likely to be killed in Iraq than the 250,000 American and British soldiers deployed. Iraq has been the most dangerous place to work as a journalist in recent years.[67] Of the 129 journalists who were killed in Iraq, only seven were embedded, the others were non-embedded.[68]

The embedded journalists were protected physically by being in military units and, perhaps even more important, their presence was regarded as legitimate by the military. The question is whether non-embedded journalists and media

64 Gierhart, C. 2008.

65 Ottosen, R. 2009.

66 Ottosen, R. *Verdens Gang*, March 17, 2007. Den farlige journalisstikken.

67 Gierhart, C. 2008. 1.

68 Gierhart, C. 2008. 20.

facilities in all practical terms are regarded as illegitimate. And the concern is whether their independence from the United States/NATO is one of the reasons they lack protection. This has a legal and an ethical side to it.

Deductive-Theoretical Conclusion

The Legal Issue of the Protection of Journalists

The United States has admitted bombing of the RTS station in Yugoslavia in 1999, but has not admitted purposefully targeting media in Afghanistan or Iraq.[69] If the attacks have been deliberate they would have been violations of international humanitarian law. The most essential law in this respect is the Protocol 1 Additional to the Geneva Conventions, which states that non-embedded journalists are civilian unless they jeopardize that status by taking part in hostilities. Principally this article is a solid legal framework for protecting journalists against attacks. Because the United States has never ratified Protocol 1, we must rely on the customary nature of the protocol.[70] In formal legal terms this means that all states are bound by the protocol, whether they have signed it or not, if the rules are considered to be fundamental and/or widespread. To become customary international law two criteria must be fulfilled:

1. It must be present in state practice.
2. There must be proof that states follow this rule because they believe it is the law (the legal term for this is *opinio iurus*).

The International Committee of the Red Cross (ICRC) in 2005 published a book containing all the rules of humanitarian law it considered to be customary. Article 79 regarding journalists was among the rules mentioned in the book. Even though United States has not ratified the protocol it has resigned itself to be bound by the same wording of Article 79 reproduced in Security Resolution 1738 of December 23, 2006. It reads: "journalists, media professionals and associated personnel engaged in dangerous professional missions in areas of armed conflict shall be considered as civilians and shall be respected and protected as such, provided that they take no action adversely affecting their status as civilians." In legal terms this means that Article 79 of Protocol 1 binds the United States even though they never ratified it.[71]

69 Hammon, P. and Herman, E. S. eds. 2000. *Degraded Capability: The Media and the Kosovo Crisis*. London: Pluto Press.

70 Gierhart, C. 2008. 8.

71 Gierhart, C. 2008. 9.

Finally there is the ethical aspect of bombing television stations you dislike.[72] Is it acceptable to send a military unit across the globe and bomb it just because you disapprove of its content? Or to put it more polemically, what would the reaction be if the Taliban decided to send a mission to Atlanta to blow up CNN because of its perceived anti-Muslim character?

Althought it is not possible to draw any absolute conclusion in cases of dual state activities because of their intrinsically covert character, it is plausible to conclude that the sequence of military attacks from the U.S. troops on media personnel from the Kosovo conflict in 1999 to the Kabul incident in 2001 and the simultaneous attacks on international media in Baghdad on April 8, 2003 are all elements in a media management strategy. The purpose, as Phillip Knightley has said, being to issue a serious warning:

> The Pentagon is determined that there will be no more reporting from the enemy side, and that a few deaths among correspondents who do so will deter others. To that end I believe that the occasional shots fired at "media sites" are not accidental and that war correspondents may now be targets, some more than others.[73]

Available evidences do not support the alternative explanation, i.e. that these are all collateral damage in violent and dramatic situations. The motives are there, documented by explicit statements of members of the Bush administration, such as Condoleezza Rice. From the U.S. military and propaganda perspective it would have a certain rationality to emphasize the risks and dangers for un-embedded journalists to visit the war theater. As a dual state strategy it is by definition something that would not be officially admitted and hence the denials from the U.S. side have no relevance for testing the hypothesis that we have discussed here. But what are the responses from the international community? Are there signs of the international legal institutions having drawn the same conclusion as we have argued for? We argue that Security Council Resolution 1738 protecting journalists indicate that the United Nations as the highest body for interpretation of customary law has already concluded that it is plausible that the cases we have discussed are examples of deliberate, strategic killings of journalists. If that is not the implicit conclusion, it would not be necessary to issue the resolution.

The use of humanitarian rhetoric was a part of the NATO propaganda to justify the war.[74] Only years later, after he had left office, would Bondevik admit that Norway took part in a war.[75] To have an open and frank debate over whether

---

72 Amnesty International (AI). 2004. *USA: Amnesty International Calls for a Commission of Inquiry into "War on Terror" Detentions*, AMR 51/087/2004.

73 Knightley, P. 2004. History or Bunkum?, in *Tell Me Lies. Propaganda and Media Distortion in the Attack on Iraq*, edited by D. Miller. London: Pluto Press. 104.

74 Chomsky, N. 1999; Hammon, P. and Herman, E. S. 2000.

75 Ottosen, R. 2009. 28.

Norway was about to break international law before the attack took place was in the area of what Pierre Bourdieu classifies as doxa (the not mentionable).[76] In reality all major decisions in military and security policy matters are decided according to Norway's membership in NATO and the alliance with United States.[77] For Sweden the present policy to send troops to Afghanistan and the NATO/ISAF operation is apparently a new policy since Sweden is formally a non-allied country. In a dual state perspective, however, this is the logical and inevitable consequence of a clandestine pro-U.S. policy that can be traced back to the aftermath of World War II and the resultant Cold War. Like the Catalina case from 1952 the situation in Afghanistan illustrates the consequences also for officially non-aligned countries of dual state-activities pursued by the United States as the remaining superpower.

76 von der Lippe, B. 1991. Kirurgisk krigføring eller kirurgisk medie- dekning, in *Mediekrigen–Søkelys På Massemdienes Dekning av Golfkrigen*, edited by Jan Johnsen and Thomas Mathiesen. Oslo: Cappelen Forlag. 145–67.

77 Linneberg, A. 2001. *Tretten triste essays om krig og litteratur*. Oslo: Gyldendal.

Afterword: Dual Schmitt, Deep Schmitt

William Rasch

In this volume (Chapter 5), David N. Gibbs critically addresses the methodological claim that qualitative (not just quantitative) research in the social sciences should be replicable, that is, that researchers using the same data (texts, ethnographic observations and interviews, etc.) as prior researchers should be expected to arrive at the same results. To someone trained and working in the humanities (as I am), this methodological demand seems incomprehensible. The virtue of multiple perspectives on the "same data" (whether creative or conceptual, written or spoken, visual or musical) is precisely the *difference* of outcomes; which is to say that the virtue of qualitative research in general is the *quality* of the research, what its reasoned modes of presentation and judicious use of evidence (textual or other) add to previous research on a given topic. And what new research "adds" is not countable. Good research opens up new avenues of thought with the aim of disabusing us of our habituated and casually careless thinking. Far from being tested for its ability to be replicated, good qualitative research ought to be catalytic, ought to provoke argument, contradiction and further inquiry. It seems to me that what holds true for the humanities holds true for qualitative research in the social sciences as well.

Nevertheless, in a body of work, certain commonalities must be presumed. In this volume, commonality is marked by terms like "parapolitics," "dual state," "deep state," and is expressed in a series of theoretical investigations and case studies. It is assumed that the visible political state (generally considered now to be liberal-democratic) is shadowed by political, legal and economic operatives, agencies and institutions that at least in certain situations (primarily concerning military/security matters and global commerce and finance) actually exercise the decisive influence on policy. The core purpose of the volume, in other words, is to explore and substantiate the claim that the liberal-legal and supposedly democratically-governed state secretly cedes its sovereignty to an invisible and unacknowledged *deep state*. Theoretical elaborations of this claim are provided by Wilson, Reifer and Ahmed. Sometimes fascinating historically documented case histories along with more speculative accounts are provided by Tunander (Sweden), MacGregor (Canada), Preparata (Italy), Bracken (Turkey) and Carisch (Congo/Zaire). In some cases these histories focus on the security state, in others, most notably in the splendid piece by Carisch, the spotlight is on the "civilizing" process as a collusion of public humanitarian rhetoric and corporate/banking interest. Special topics are addressed, such as the geopolitics of oil (Ganser), the targeting of journalists in the new wars of the 21st century (Nohrstedt and Ottosen), the theory and seemingly decreasing viability of the partisan in our funhouse society of the spectacle (Kinkle), and the prospects for a beneficent post-state world order (Findlay). If you have been a determined, cover-to-cover reader of this volume, you will no doubt have noticed these rough groupings. You will also have noticed a singular thread that runs explicitly or implicitly through virtually every contribution, a thread that goes by the name of Carl Schmitt. Finally you will have noticed that there are two Carl Schmitts in play, one who is in some way held accountable (along with co-conspirators like Leo Strauss and even Plato) for the prominence of the dual state on the world scene, and the other who offers diagnostic tools for the scholar in search of the workings of the *deep state*'s mechanism. These two Schmitts are often merged or only faintly distinguished. With one breath Schmitt's definition of sovereignty, the state of exception, or the distinction between legitimacy and legality are looked upon askance and with the fear that Schmitt's conceptual language itself let loose the hounds against whom this book's wrath is aimed. At the same time, however, these very concepts turn out to be the lens with which one can clearly see how the dual state functions or even how it might be combatted. The very first sentence of Eric Wilson's opening paragraph neatly encapsulates the problem. "If Carl Schmitt (1888–1985) did not exist, it would have been necessary for the parapolitical scholar to have invented him." We are provoked to ask why. Because Schmitt's work is seen in some way as responsible for the problem that the parapolitical scholar attacks? Or because without Schmitt, the parapolitical scholar's toolkit would be insufficient for the task? That the posing of each question has its plausibility would seem to affirm that qualitative research is not and perhaps ought not to be replicable; for having to settle only for Schmitt the sinner or Schmitt the saint would be an impoverishment.

Having said that, I will make the case for Saint Carl, by which wry hyperbole I mean to say only that I will highlight some aspects of Schmitt's usefulness.

How could we not start with: "Sovereign is he who decides on the exception."[1] With this definition from 1922, Schmitt entered an early 20th-century debate on the state, more specifically, on whether the state (and state sovereignty) had in fact now been replaced by the rule of law, as argued by Duguit in France (supported by Laski in the Anglophone world), Krabbe in Holland and Kelsen in Germany. Schmitt found the equation of the state with the legal system, and the legitimacy of the legal system with a transcendentally deduced *Grundnorm* or basic norm (Kelsen), to be not only unpersuasive but dangerous on two counts. On the one hand, he asserted, law that is legitimated merely normatively cannot defend itself.

1 Though it does not have the same snap as the commonly accepted translation, it could be rendered more accurately and in a less gender-compromised manner as: "Sovereign is whoever decides on the exception."

It is a technique and a bureaucracy that can be manipulated equally well by those who oppose the norms upon which it rests (as the Nazis demonstrated in 1933) as by those who are devoted to those norms. For this reason—and this is the second point—law (like morality and economy) serves ultimately only as a screen behind which real power operates. It is not law that decides on the exception (for law, especially on Kelsen's view, knows no exception and can therefore never recognize an exception when it presents itself); it is not law but the sovereign power behind the law that decides. This power can be openly proclaimed or it can deceptively hide in the shadows. That is, the true sovereign reveals itself not during the normal operations of governmental (or legal) administration, but in those moments when foundational decisions are made. Schmitt's definition, therefore, can be seen as a kind of Geiger counter or metal detector attempting to locate the source of the "sovereign exception."

In the Germany of 1922, it is reasonable to assume that Schmitt located the sovereign in the *Reichspräsident*, the figure who represented for him the public unity of the German people, not its party-political division into private interests (as in the parliament). It was, therefore, the president who decided on the exception, which in fact was the case. Article 48 of the Weimar Constitution gave the president emergency powers (within limits) to suspend the normal workings of government in exceptional circumstances. Those circumstances, alas, were more the rule than the exception in the early years of the new Republic, as civil war (e.g. the leftist Spartikist uprising of January 1919, the right-wing Kapp Putsch of 1920, and other crises), border wars (in the fluid east), Allied occupation (the Rhineland) and the Franco-Belgian invasion of the Ruhr caused existential, political and economic tensions beyond the normal capacity of the government to deal with. The "legitimacy" that lay behind the president's powers rested ultimately with the *demos*, "the people" as a collective singular, as Schmitt articulates it in his 1928 *Verfassungslehre* (*Constitutional Theory*).[2] In laying this out (however briefly) I do not wish to minimize the dangers in giving a single "sovereign" entity the power to suspend the law in self-declared emergencies. The potential for cynical abuse is abundantly clear. But occasionally in the pages of this volume there seems to be an overly quick assumption that "sovereignty," "legitimacy," and especially "emergency powers" are essentially and irremediably ominous and somehow automatically lead to a generalized "state of exception." For instance, Ahmed, in his lucid articulation of a "political economy" of the dual state, makes the following statement:

> Anti-Western terrorist attacks such as 9/11 prompt state-level emergency responses which, justified by the perception of unprecedented threat, lead to adoption of extraordinary military and police responses. Yet these responses do not merely suspend constitutional laws in the face of emergency—they establish

2 Schmitt, Carl. 2008. *Constitutional Theory*, trans. Jeffrey Seitzer. Durham, NC and London: Duke University Press.

> permanence precisely through exploiting the declared state of emergency to legitimize the *institutionalization of exceptional measures within the body politic*, thus purporting to permanently transform the constitutional order.

If one thinks of the U.S. situation, I believe Ahmed is correct to talk of the "institutionalization of exceptional measures within the body politic"; but the problem is worse than he thinks precisely because this condition did *not* come about through the suspension of constitutional laws. The "declared state of emergency" was predominantly a *psychological* state of emergency designed to induce fear in the electorate so that politically it would accept legally sanctioned presidential actions and constitutionally mandated legislative decisions that it might not otherwise have been willing to support. The Patriot Act was passed by Congress; torture was sanctioned by legal memos stating that "enhanced interrogation techniques" did not violate American law; the violation of the Geneva Convention on treatment of prisoners of war was precisely that, a *violation* of international law, not a suspension (to the extent that it ever can be maintained that a powerful country like the United States "violates" international law instead of merely ignoring what cannot be enforced anyway); and almost all the supposedly "exceptional" provisions that sprang up after September, 2001, have been upheld in the courts. If there has been an institutionalization of putatively exceptional measures, it was unfortunately *not* brought about in an exceptional way. Rather, the American people have done this to themselves in a purely "legal" and liberally democratic way. We have not been the victims of a "Schmittian" president; we are the victimizers even as we suffer the consequences of our (in)actions.

It would seem, then, that if there is something like a the dual state in the United States and other countries with nominally democratic institutions, then it has emerged gradually and in unexceptional ways as a result of actions that have been implicitly approved by the majority of the citizens. Yet even as we mutely sanction the existence of a *deep state* behind or below the political state, this duality remains largely unperceived; which is to say that when actions which are undertaken at the behest of the deep state become visible, they seldom if ever disturb the political machinery at the surface—precisely because they are seen as abnormal and not the new norm. Here, then, is where the Schmittian metal detector may come in handy, as Ola Tunander recognizes: "This hidden deep state defines when a 'state of emergency' will emerge. This is what Carl Schmitt called the sovereign, and during the Cold War it was linked to the protecting power: the U.S. with its Western security apparatus. Thus, the Schmittian sovereign is here rather the parallel hierarchy of informal Western structures with their military/intelligence centre in the U.S." Tunander writes about Sweden, the structural link between the U.S. deep state and its Swedish counterpart during the Cold War, especially in the 1980s, when Olaf Palme was assassinated; and because it is all now safely in the past, those involved are candid about their past actions, allowing Tunander to piece together a narrative. Preparata can do the same for the Italy of roughly the same time. If, as the Swedish author Stig Dagerman, once wrote,

"Journalism is the art of coming too late as early as possible,"[3] then the historian limps even further behind. This observation is not meant as a criticism of the journalist or the historian, but leads to the question: what can be done in the here and now?

To the extent that one believes there are any options at all, there seem to be two. Findlay imagines a post-state world much in the same way as Schmitt's early 20th-century interlocutors did, as a world ruled by law supplemented by compassion, empathy and a spirit of selfless cooperation. I wish I were that young at heart again, but I believe that Reifer and especially Carisch show us what such a world would (will?) ultimately look like. Behind the façade of law and pacific commerce would lurk the agents of power guiding the scramble for natural resources, not just minerals and rare earth but soon water itself. The noblest of sentiments will become the ideological weapons of choice. Reflecting on the original "scramble," the scramble for Africa, Carisch writes: "True to the pattern set by their British moralist predecessors—who in part acted for the interests of the New Imperialists—today's campaigns are driven by idealism and humanitarian concerns but end up acting as attack dogs and diversions for anyone who stands in the way of the policies of highly industrialized and resource dependent states, the World Bank or the OECD, and the most influential Western mineral mining and trading companies."[4] Therefore the second option, the one that is usually vilified, remains pertinent, namely the state, or at least some sort of political entity of whatever necessary size that enjoys "sovereignty," that is, a certain quantum of power that allows for a minimum of autonomy. That such a "state" ought to be democratic is part and parcel of modern dogma, so the "he/she" who decides on the exception ought in some way to be "the people." How all this is to be organized in the modern capitalist world in which power is diffuse and privatized, and in which the people as a collective singular ferociously guarding its autonomy has also been privatized, splintered into consumers and voters, remains thoroughly unknown. I will leave you therefore with a mere parable.

In the 1950s, Schmitt, aping Hobbes' *Behemoth*, wrote a dialogue on power.[5] One of the problems addressed is the issue of who has access to the holder of power, who lines the corridor of power. There is an antiquated air about the discussion, as if we were talking of courtiers vying for the favor of an absolute monarch, but clearly aides and political operatives, governmental officials,

3 Quoted from a letter in the Introduction to Dagerman, Stig. 1988. *German Autumn*. London and New York: Quartet Books. 1. The autumn in question is 1946. The book, originally published in Sweden in 1947, is an account of life in occupied Germany at the time.

4 Carisch too seems to use Schmitt as a kind of guide or signpost, as his use of the famous passage from Schmitt's *The Concept of the Political* at the very start of his chapter would indicate. It is the passage which, evoking Proudhon, ends: "whoever invokes humanity wants to cheat."

5 Schmitt, Carl. 1994 [1954]. *Gespräch über die Macht und den Zugang zum Machthaber: Gespräch über den Neuen Raum*. Berlin: Akademie Verlag.

lawyers, military and intelligence officers, and above all lobbyists, fill the roll of courtiers nicely in the modern world. The issue for Schmitt in the 1950s, as it was in the 1920s, was one of indirect influence and, in the final analysis, divided sovereignty. In the context of this volume, we could say the issue becomes the problem of the dual state. Where precisely does power lie? More importantly, is publicly displayed power the actual power? What for Hobbes was the contest of the monarch versus the Catholic Church and the Protestant conscience, becomes now the contest between democratic institutions and what Reifer wants to call the National Security State Corporate Complex. Schmitt wants the sovereign to be clearly recognizable. Power exists, power cannot be avoided; therefore in a democracy, where the ruler is said to represent the ruled, the sovereign must display its power openly. So here is the fable:

In a land ruled by what is conventionally called a democratically-elected leader, those with access to the corridors of power have begun to monopolize the organs of governmental decision and do so without the leader's consent or even full knowledge. The leader enjoys general state-wide popularity and commands loyalty from some of the highest military officers as well as regional militias. In a moment of crisis she steps out onto the balcony (i.e. in front of TV cameras) to address "the people" and says:

> I think the society must take every means at its disposal to defend itself against the emergence of a parallel power which defies the elected power in this country and I think that goes to any distance. So long as there is a power in here which is challenging the elected representative of the people I think that power must be stopped and I think it's only, I repeat, weak-kneed bleeding hearts who are afraid to take these measures.[6]

She also declares a state of emergency, suspends normal governmental operations, and sets up investigative committees to identify and root out the executors of the "parallel power" that threatens the sovereignty of the duly elected, political state. In short, she cleans house and restores public order, meaning she restores complete power to the political state, restricts the military to carrying out the wishes of elected officials who make publicly known what those wishes are, and she imposes necessary limitations on the political influence of commercial and financial institutions. Ninety days after her initial proclamation, political institutions (parliament, the higher courts, etc.) are restored to their constitutional power. The crisis is declared to be over, the "parallel power" crushed.

This fable has a fairy-tale ending. No matter the ending, however, such a fable frightens us. It seems wrong. Law should always prevail. Such willful wielding

6 Those of you who have read Chapter 9 on Canada will recognize the author of these words, namely Pierre Trudeau (as quoted by MacGregor). I make no claim to knowing what "parallel power" Trudeau was talking about and therefore remind the reader that these words are embedded in a "parable."

of "naked" power seems uncontrolled and uncontrollable. The unintended consequences—economically, morally, legally—are not calculable. Yet, if we complain about the existence and machination of a deep state, is there another way for it to be purged? Can an existing state of exception, especially one that has gradually and in a seemingly legal way attached itself to the political state like barnacles on a ship, be destroyed only by way of another state of exception? If, in the society of the spectacle, the partisan no longer has a hold on our imagination or on its own objectives and situation, and if revolution seems more remote today than ever before, can we think of any other alternative?

I do not know the answer to these questions. Certainly, however, the old enlightenment solution of casting light and reason on the situation is not enough, not in an age like ours. So, instead of the power of reason I leave you with a passage from Schmitt that delineates the reason for power:

> According to democratic principles, equality in private law is dominant only in the sense that the same private law statutes are valid for everyone, not, on the contrary, in the sense of *economic* equality of private wealth, property, or income. In its consequences and applications, democracy as an essentially political concept involves, to begin with, only the public law. However, the superiority of the public over the private results unconditionally from democracy's essentially political character. As soon as political equality is destroyed or endangered by economic inequalities or by the social power of private property, it can become politically necessary to eliminate, by statute or measure, that type of disturbance or threat. In regard to this necessity, appealing to the sanctity of private property would be undemocratic.[7]

7 Schmitt, Carl. 2008. 283.

Index

Page numbers followed by 'n' refer to a footnote at the bottom of the page.

FSC
www.fsc.org
MIX
Papier | Fördert gute Waldnutzung
FSC® C083411

Kolibri 360 GmbH
Ferdinand-Jühlke-Straße 7
99095 Erfurt, Deutschland
produktsicherheit@kolibri360.de